CANADIAN MULTIMODAL TRANSPORT
POLICY AND GOVERNANCE

Canadian Multimodal Transport Policy And Governance

G. BRUCE DOERN, JOHN COLEMAN,
AND BARRY E. PRENTICE

McGill-Queen's University Press
Montreal & Kingston • London • Chicago

ISBN 978-0-7735-5668-3 (cloth)
ISBN 978-0-7735-5669-0 (paper)
ISBN 978-0-7735-5778-9 (ePDF)
ISBN 978-0-7735-5779-6 (ePUB)

Legal deposit second quarter 2019
Bibliothèque nationale du Québec

Printed in Canada on acid-free paper that is 100% ancient forest free
(100% post-consumer recycled), processed chlorine free

This book has been published with the help of a grant from the Canadian
Federation for the Humanities and Social Sciences, through the Awards
to Scholarly Publications Program, using funds provided by the Social
Sciences and Humanities Research Council of Canada.

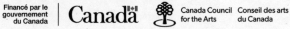

We acknowledge the support of the Canada Council for the Arts, which
last year invested $153 million to bring the arts to Canadians throughout
the country.

Nous remercions le Conseil des arts du Canada de son soutien. L'an dernier,
le Conseil a investi 153 millions de dollars pour mettre de l'art dans la vie
des Canadiennes et des Canadiens de tout le pays.

Library and Archives Canada Cataloguing in Publication

Doern, G. Bruce, author
    Canadian multimodal transport policy and governance/G. Bruce Doern,
John Coleman, and Barry E. Prentice.

Includes bibliographical references and index.
Issued in print and electronic formats.
ISBN 978-0-7735-5668-3 (cloth). – ISBN 978-0-7735-5669-0 (paper). –
ISBN 978-0-7735-5778-9 (ePDF). – ISBN 978-0-7735-5779-6 (ePUB)

1. Transportation and state – Canada – History – 20th century.
2. Transportation and state – Canada – History – 21st century. I. Coleman,
John, 1948–, author II. Prentice, Barry E., author III. Title.

HE215.A2D64 2019   388.097109'045   C2018-906660-1
                                                   C2018-906661-X

This book was typeset by Marquis Interscript in 10.5/13 Sabon.

Contents

Figures and Tables

FIGURES

TABLES

Abbreviations

AC	Air Canada
AIT	Agreement on Internal Trade
ANAC	Aboriginal and Northern Affairs Canada
ANS	Air Navigation System
ANSP	Air Navigation System Provider
APEC	Asia Pacific Economic Cooperation
AV	autonomous vehicles
BCF	Building Canada Fund
BIF	Border Infrastructure Fund
BTAP	Beyond the Border Action Plan
CAAS	Canadian Airport Authorities
CAC	Canadian Airlines Council
CAIL	Canadian Airlines International Ltd.
CANUTEC	Canadian Transport Emergency Center
CAPP	Canadian Association of Petroleum Producers
CARAC	Canadian Aviation Regulation Advisory Council
CATSA	Canadian Air Transport Security Authority
CAVCOE	Canadian Automated Vehicle Centre of Excellence
CBBA	Canadian Business Aviation Association
CCC	Canadian Chamber of Commerce
CCE	Council of Chief Executives
CCO	common carrier obligation (US)
CDRM	Cabinet Directive on Regulatory Management
CDSR	Cabinet Directive on Streamlining Regulation
CEO	chief executive officer
CEPA	Canadian Environmental Protection Act

CESD	Commissioner of Environment and Sustainable Development
CETA	Canada–EU Trade Agreement
CFA	Canadian Fuels Association
CMSCC	Canadian Maritime and Supply Chain Coalition
CNR	Canadian National Railway
COA	Certificate of Authorization or Waiver
COP21	Conference of Parties (Paris 2015)
CP Air	Canadian Pacific Airlines
CPR	Canadian Pacific Railway
CSIF	Canada Strategic Infrastructure Fund
CTA	Canadian Transportation Agency
CTC	Canadian Transportation Commission
CUSFTA	Canada–United States Free Trade Agreement
CURCC	Canada–United States Regulatory Cooperation Council
CWB	Canadian Wheat Board
DG	dangerous goods
DOT	Department of Transportation (US)
EC	Environment Canada
ECCC	Environment and Climate Change Canada
EMR	Energy, Mines and Resources
ERAPS	Emergency Response Assistance Plans
eTV	ecoTechnology for Vehicles
EU	European Union
FAA	Federal Aviation Administration (US)
FCM	Federation of Canadian Municipalities
FGTF	Federal Gas Tax Fund
FMRA	FAA Modernization and Reform Act of 2012 (US)
FRA	Federal Rail Administration (US)
GATT	General Agreement on Tariffs and Trade
GDP	Gross Domestic Product
GHG	Greenhouse Gases
GHTS	Grain Handling and Transportation System
GLSLS	Great Lakes St Lawrence Seaway Study
GNP	Gross National Product
GST	Goods and Services Tax
GTA	Greater Toronto Area
GTAA	Greater Toronto Airport Authority
HASMAT	hazardous materials
IATA	International Air Transport Association

ICAO	International Civil Aviation Organization
ICS	International Chamber of Shippers
IFFA	International Freight Forwarders Association
IGOPP	Institute for Governance of Private and Public Organization
IJC	International Joint Commission
IMO	International Maritime Organization
INAC	Indigenous and Northern Affairs Canada
IR	international relations
IRTU	International Road Transport Union
ISEDC	Innovation, Science and Economic Development Canada
ISF	International Shipping Federation
ISTC	Industry, Science and Technology Canada
ITF	International Transport Forum
IUR	International Union of Railways
LAAS	Local Airport Authorities
LOS	legitimate objectives
LOS	level of service
MC	Memoranda to Cabinet
MMA	Montreal, Marine and Atlantic Railway
MOU	memorandum of understanding
MRE	Maximum Revenue Entitlement
NACC	National Airlines Council of Canada
NAFTA	North American Free Trade Agreement
NAS	National Airports System
NAP	National Airport Policy
NBCF	New Building Canada Fund
NEB	National Energy Board
NEP	National Energy Program
NGO	Non-governmental Organization
NHTSA	National Highway Traffic Safety Administration (US)
NIMBY	"Not in My Backyard"
NPM	New Public Management
NRC	National Research Council Canada
NRCan	Natural Resources Canada
NSERC	Natural Sciences and Engineering Research Council of Canada
NTA	National Transportation Agency
OAG	Office of the Auditor General

OECD   Organization for Economic Cooperation and
            Development
OEMS   Original Equipment Manufacturers
OTA   Office of Technology Assessment (US)
PCO   Privy Council Office
PHMA   Pipelines and Hazardous Materials Administration (US)
PMO   Prime Minister's Office
PRAC   Prairie Rail Action Committee
PTB   Passenger Transportation Board (British Columbia)
P3S   Public–Private Partnerships
PTPS   private transportation providers
RAC   Railway Association of Canada
SeMS   Security Management System
SCC   Supreme Court of Canada
SD   Sustainable Development
SFT   Speech from the Throne
SIU   Seafarers International Union
SLSDC   St Lawrence Seaway Development Corporation (US)
SLSMC   St Lawrence Seaway Management Corporation
SMES   Small and Medium-Sized Enterprises
SMS   safety management system
SOLAS   Safety of Life at Sea
SPS   sanitary and phytosanitary
SPTP   Shore Power Technology for Ports
TBS   Treasury Board Secretariat
TBT   Technical Barriers to Trade
TCA   Trans-Canada Airlines
TDG   Transportation of Dangerous Goods Directorate
TDGGPAC   Transport of Dangerous Goods General Policy
            Advisory Council
TPP   Trans-Pacific Partnership
TRB   Transport Research Board (US)
TSB   Transportation Safety Board of Canada
TSEP   Tanker Safety Expert Panel
UAS   unmanned air systems
UAVS   unmanned air vehicles
UK   United Kingdom
US   United States
USC   Unmanned Systems Canada
USDA   United States Department of Agriculture

VIA Rail	VIA Rail Canada
WDBA	Windsor–Detroit Bridge Authority
WGTA	Western Grain Transportation Act
WTO	World Trade Organization

Preface

This book is the product of the authors' work on transportation policy in Canada and internationally over the last five decades. During this extensive period of teaching, reading, discussion, research, and interviews, we owe numerous debts of thanks, gratitude, and learning to many individuals and to many agencies and institutions involved directly and indirectly with the story of Canadian transportation policy, governance, and democracy.

We are also grateful to many transportation policy academics and practitioners from across Canada and internationally. We have drawn on their scholarly research, which we cite and debate throughout the book. In particular, we would like to thank colleagues whose research, ideas, or comments on drafts of the manuscript chapters have informed this book. We are especially grateful to the two McGill-Queen's University Press peer reviewers for their very probing and insightful in-depth comments on an earlier draft. As a result of their advice, the final book has been strengthened in valuable and needed ways. The same is true for the excellent detailed editing by McGill-Queen's editors and copy editors Jacqueline Mason, Kathleen Fraser, and Shelagh Plunkett.

A continuing intellectual and personal set of thanks are owed to colleagues and staff at our home academic and research institutions, the School of Public Policy and Administration at Carleton University, the National Research Council (NRC), the Department of Supply Chain Management, Asper School of Business at the University of Manitoba, and the Politics Department, University of Exeter in the UK.

G. Bruce Doern, John Coleman, and Barry E. Prentice
January 2019

CANADIAN MULTIMODAL TRANSPORT POLICY AND GOVERNANCE

Introduction and Analytical Framework

This book provides an extensive and in-depth academic account and explanation of Canadian multimodal transportation policy and governance. This kind of pan-Canadian story is long overdue. Most Canadian academic transport policy books are either quite dated or tend to focus on only one transport mode or on one policy aspect, such as transport deregulation. We draw on existing analyses in chapter 1, where we outline the book's conceptual foundations, but, in subsequent chapters, the authors then offer greater breadth and depth with an analysis of seven transport policy and governance domains covering a fifty-year period, 1968 to 2018, across the five federal prime ministerial eras from Pierre Trudeau, Brian Mulroney, the Chrétien–Martin era, Stephen Harper and Justin Trudeau and through an examination of twenty policy and governance histories and related future policy challenges. While the book has a federal focus and starting point, the analysis and coverage also extends to complementary provincial and city/urban transport policies and governance to a much greater extent than in any existing transport policy book and in doing so captures and draws on literature dealing with Canada's spatial and geographic/place imperatives and related changing dynamics. This crucial feature covers developments from 1968 to 2018 but also, necessarily, periods and decades prior to 1968.

We look closely at Transport Canada as the lead federal transport policy department but we don't stop there because it is not the only federal department that makes federal transport policy or influences it structurally. Indeed, to tell the Transport Canada story, the book has to examine the department *per se* but also at least fifteen other arm's length entities that emerge across the seven transport policy domains studied, including the massive shared-governance realm involving Canada's dozens of airports. Our comparative coverage of current provincial transport ministries also shows their mandates and designations as combined transport and infrastructure entities and their multistatute responsibilities, anchored in highways legislation. (See chapter 1.) All of this is set in the context of Canada–US and related international transport institutions, forces and imperatives, the intricate realms of public and private governance, and political, economic, and social power and agenda setting.

In this introduction, it is also essential to emphasize the practical transportation and analytical notion that transport policy is about dealing with motion, mobility, and the movement of goods and people. Seen as the dynamics of "getting from here to there" it evokes a temporal/structural journey showing how Canadian transport policy has evolved from a 150-year early rail-centred, nation building past to 1930s and 1940s interregional nation building and to the present where transport in cities is the needed complementary focus because that is where most Canadians live. Transport policy, as such, is analysed variously through the academic analytical disciplines of policy, politics, and governance; economics and public and private business; and engineering and technological transport logistics, the rapidly changing information and digital economy and society which the authors jointly seek to bring to bear in as coherent and useful a way as possible.

This book also addresses a set of medium- to longer-term challenges that are partly known but in many ways are also uncertain. The notions of getting from "here to there" are numerous and, in many ways, everyday in nature, for Canadians and their families, and for journeys involving both goods and people. Getting from "here to there" in its broadest sense evokes notions of travelling and visualizing Canada from coast to coast to coast, including its many "norths" and even the thought of Canada's "snowbird" families getting to Florida or other warmer climes to escape Canada's winters or simply taking holidays at lakeside cottages or in other parts of Canada or the world. As an overwhelmingly urban society, "here to there" in transport terms involves logistical dynamics of commuting to work and transporting children to and from school, on time, at reasonable cost, while fighting traffic and congestion.

The book is mainly for academics and students interested in the developments, strengths, and weaknesses of Canadian transportation policy and its related governance and democracy. We have also kept in mind governmental, business, labour, and professional transport readers who follow transport policy issues on a regular basis and those citizens and interest-group participants who benefit from, or may be disadvantaged or in some cases harmed by, transport policy and governance developments, delays, and shortfalls.

Three principal questions are addressed in this book: 1) How and to what extent has Canadian transport policy and its related governance changed in the last fifty years; 2) Where has transport policy resided in federal policy agendas in the last fifty years; and 3) Is Canada developing the needed policies, institutions, and capacities to enable it to have a viable socioeconomic and technologically advanced transportation system that is fit-for-purpose for the challenges of the next twenty-year and longer-term period?

FIVE KEY DEFINITIONS

"Transportation policy" refers to formal statements of transportation policy goals and values expressed in laws; in throne speeches and budget speeches as primary agenda-setting processes and events; in government reports and studies; in regulations, guidelines, codes, and standards; in tax and spending measures; in speeches that are a form of political exhortation; and in departmental websites with language and discourse that, in the internet and social media age, are often easily and quickly embellished for partisan and political communication purposes.

"Multimodal" refers to the existence in complex transportation systems of interactions between, and competition among, different modes of transportation such as rail, air, trucking, road, shipping, canals and waterways, cycling, walking, buses and trams, pipelines, and city and intercity transit.

"Governance" is a concept that emerged in the practice and literature on politics, policy, and public administration over the past thirty years (Aucoin 1997, 2008). It can be expressed simply as an effort to recognize more explicitly that governing involves more than government, more than the state, and more than public policy as pronounced and implemented by the state and its bureaucracies. It implies the state fostering more explicit public–private efforts to improve the content, quality, and implementation of policy and the delivery of services. But it also is a test of the continued need, in many instances, for strong state-led capacities (Bell and Hindmoor 2009). In Canada the broad manifestations of governance have also been present in varied forms at the level of provincial governments and policy systems involving urban and local government (Atkinson et al. 2013) and internationally. Provincial governments most certainly form a key reality of transportation policy and its multimodal features and content both directly and in relation to cities and municipalities. Governance also refers to the deployment of a varied array of policy instruments (Hood 1986). They include the traditional tools of spending, taxation, and regulation but also softer, more exhortative instruments of governing through guidelines and codes of behaviour designed to influence and change the behaviour of all sorts of organizations and their clients and beneficiaries (Jordana and Levi-Faure 2004; Schultz and Alexandroff 1985; Doern, Prince, and Schultz 2014).

"Markets" are systems of voluntary commercial exchange between business (and other suppliers and sellers of products and services), consumers (including businesses as consumers), and labour. Such exchange is based on the features, performance, price, quality, and reliability of such products and services and the terms on which the exchange takes place. Markets involve extremely fluid commodities and services and they defy easy characterization. In a field such as transportation policy (and in other policy fields as well), the notion of consumers is usually not the simple one of a hypothesized "average" consumer (Doern 2006). For example, all "shippers" in the railway industry are also "business consumers" of rail carrier services and they in turn deal with their own other consumers of diverse kinds. All markets, including transportation markets, are governed by varied and complex economic and social laws, rules, and norms ranging from property rights, corporate law, contract and insurance law, bankruptcy law, competition law, consumer safety and environmental laws and practices, and international free trade and internal trade policies and agreements. In most important ways markets could not exist or function at a basic level without the state.

"Democracy" we define broadly to include all the main values, criteria, and arenas at play in the Canadian political system. These include elected, representative, cabinet-based parliamentary democracy; federalism, provincial, and urban democracy; interest group pluralism; civil society; and the tools and practices of direct democracy including internet-based social networks (Pal 2014; Bickerton and Gagnon 2009; Williams 2009; Rainie and Wellman 2012). The roles of and impacts on labour, unions, and employees also loom large but are embedded in systems of policy communities and networks (Pal 2014; Jackson and Baldwin 2007) as will be shown in all of the domain accounts dealing with freight rail, airports, airline company employees, dangerous goods, safety and security regulatory bodies, and several analyses of disruptive technology-enabled transport. All of these involve various types of engagement and consultation, but they also can involve exclusion by political and policy design or neglect.

ANALYTICAL FRAMEWORK

Our analytical framework involves two components: a) Transport policy "domains" defined as interacting systems of ideas, policies, and institutions that both contain and cut across modes and supply chains; and b) Three policy and governance "elements" deployed analytically in each domain as ways of studying and understanding change and examples of inertia, as well as future policy needs and challenges. These elements are ideas, discourses, and agendas; economic and social power; and technology and temporal realities and conflicts. (See figure I.1.) These are analyzed partly through the twenty policy and governance histories across the seven domains (see more below) but they also emerge in chapters 1, 2 and 3. This kind of overall framework builds on similar, previous approaches used in other recent books on major Canadian policy and governance fields such as science and technology policy, environmental policy, regulatory policy, budgetary policy, and biotechnology policy (Doern, Castle, and Phillips 2016; Doern, Auld, and Stoney 2015; Doern, Prince, and Schultz 2014; Doern, Maslove, and Prince 2013; Doern and Prince 2012).

The book investigates transformations and changes and examples of inertia and thus resistance to change that have occurred in Canadian transportation policy and governance. We want to understand whether, and to what extent, various concerns raised about transport policy, either recent/current or embedded and long standing, are capable of being changed and reformed in the upcoming twenty-year and longer-term period.

Transport policy vastly precedes the modern post-World War II social welfare state, but it has had intrinsic socioeconomic values from the outset. National railway policy was nation building in its core values, as the CPR brought immigrant families to the vast Canadian prairies dominated by food production and agriculture as

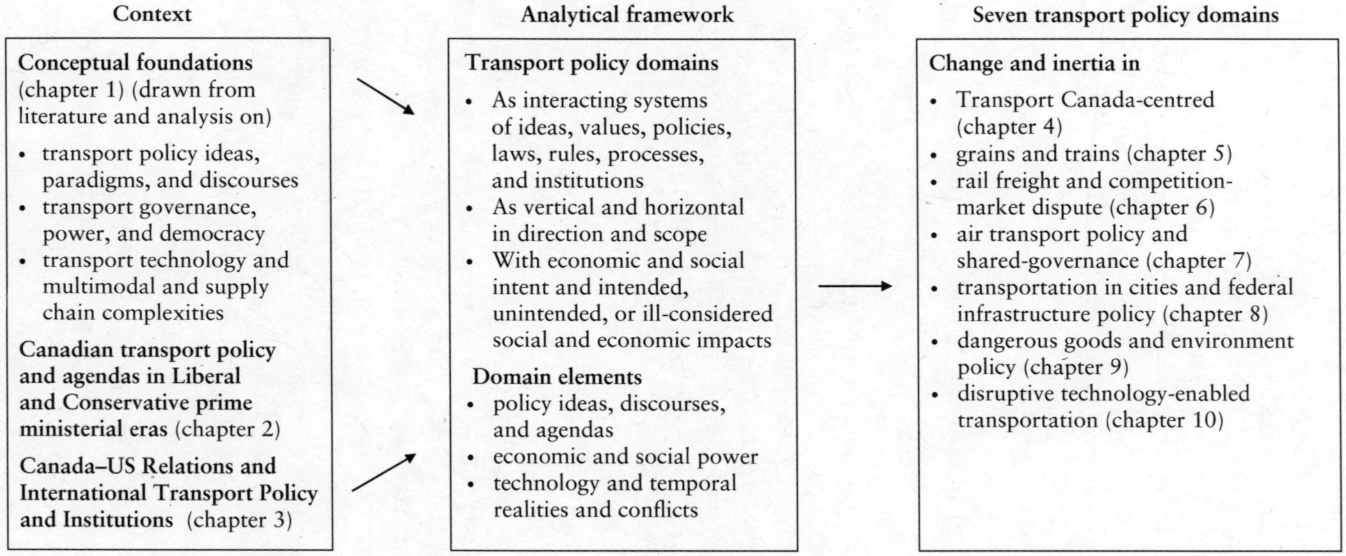

Context

Conceptual foundations (chapter 1) (drawn from literature and analysis on)

- transport policy ideas, paradigms, and discourses
- transport governance, power, and democracy
- transport technology and multimodal and supply chain complexities

Canadian transport policy and agendas in Liberal and Conservative prime ministerial eras (chapter 2)

Canada–US Relations and International Transport Policy and Institutions (chapter 3)

Analytical framework

Transport policy domains

- As interacting systems of ideas, values, policies, laws, rules, processes, and institutions
- As vertical and horizontal in direction and scope
- With economic and social intent and intended, unintended, or ill-considered social and economic impacts

Domain elements

- policy ideas, discourses, and agendas
- economic and social power
- technology and temporal realities and conflicts

Seven transport policy domains

Change and inertia in

- Transport Canada-centred (chapter 4)
- grains and trains (chapter 5)
- rail freight and competition-market dispute (chapter 6)
- air transport policy and shared-governance (chapter 7)
- transportation in cities and federal infrastructure policy (chapter 8)
- dangerous goods and environment policy (chapter 9)
- disruptive technology-enabled transportation (chapter 10)

Figure I.1 Analyzing Canadian transportation policy

Canada's staple export industry. (See further conceptual discussion in chapter 1 and in chapter 5 on the grains and trains domain.) The development of CNR as a public enterprise was also an expression of Canada's changing and growing political sovereignty in the interwar years (Perl 1994; Stevenson 1981). The railways were subject historically, in Canada and the US, to statutory policies such as "common carrier" principles and obligations. Principles of constrained commercial power are part of this socioeconomic policy, but that concept has undergone considerable change over the years (Gwyn 2011; Murray 2011; Heaver 2009; Doern 2015; Eby 2008).

Multimodal transport as noted above refers to the existence in complex transportation systems of interactions between and competition among different modes of transportation such as rail, air, automobile, truck, bus, bicycle, walking, transit, pipelines, and marine, and through airports, ports, gateways, and border facilities. Each mode functions via one or more changing technology. Each is, as well, an industry with technological change sometimes occurring on an incremental basis and sometimes via disruptive technologies. Current examples of the latter, such as in chapter 10, include automated vehicles, Uber ride-sourcing and related digital practices impacting in major ways traditional regulated taxi industries and also urban transit systems (International Transport Forum 2015; Rayle et al. 2016; Flemming 2016). But other examples of disruptive technology are also examined in chapters 4, 7, and 9.

Transport policy is intricately linked to other neighbouring and conjoined policy fields such as energy, environment, safety, security, trade, finance, northern, indigenous, and regional–urban–rural policy. Governance issues also involve key differences between Canada and the US regarding which departments or agencies regulate the transport of oil via pipelines. In the US most oil pipelines are regulated by the US Department of Transportation whereas in Canada, overall jurisdiction lies mainly with Natural Resources Canada (NRCan) and the National Energy Board (NEB). These conjoined policy fields should be no surprise. Policy theory and practice in Canada and elsewhere increasingly shows as a key principle and feature that few if any policy fields operate in isolation within governments, in the economy, or in society (Pal 2014; Doern, Prince, and Schultz 2014; Howlett 2011). There are always boundary issues between intersecting policy fields, and players, as the domain analyses in this book will show.

We also see these conjoined policy fields in Transport Canada's annual state of transportation review reports (Transport Canada 2014), where the discussion of each separate transport mode begins with the economic marketplace for that mode, then links it to infrastructure as a policy field. These annual reports then link transportation to three other policy realms: environment, safety, and security. Moreover, they include an assessment of gateways, corridors, and related multimodal transportation and spatial phenomena. And separately we know that supply chains are a crucial form of policy and economic reality paired increasingly and necessarily with the field and profession of logistics (Christopher 2016; Handfield and Nichols 2002). All these boundary realities and conceptual features also ultimately relate to economists' concepts of externalities (positive and negative impacts on third parties) and also concepts of public goods, private goods, and common property resources (Stopher and Stanley 2014; Borck 2007; Le Grand, 2003; Coase 1960). In diverse ways, transport policy functions within and is affected and changed by a complex transport system itself functioning within and also colliding with city planning and land development policy imperatives and with mobility, congestion, and concepts of time and the value of time (Litman 2017; Giuliano and Hanson 2017; Rodrigue, Comtois, and Slack 2016; Coleman 2015; Van Wee, Annema, and Banister 2013).

Policy and Governance Domains

Policy and governance "domains" are the first feature of our analytical framework. Domains are complex, integrated realms of policy ideas, institutions, interests, instruments, and rules (Doern, Maslove, and Prince 2013). The seven transport policy domains mapped and examined empirically are listed above in figure 1.

The notion of a domain is often used interchangeably with terms such as "jurisdiction," for example in the federal, provincial, urban or international constitutional jurisdiction, or as a "regime," such as in analyses of risk regimes or of individual policy areas such as the food safety or the drug approval system (Hood, Rothstein, and Baldwin 2001; Harris and Milkis 1989). We map and examine domains within transportation as relatively complex policy and governance spheres, levels, and temporal periods where different policy, taxation, spending, regulation making, and compliance challenges are faced, debated, reframed, or ignored.

Wherever there is political–economic debate, academic discourse, and institutional politics there are bound to be agreements and disagreements about the precise boundaries of what we refer to as domains. Indeed, boundary issues and overlaps are often a key feature driving the analysis of domain challenges, debates, and outcomes. Some of the domains we discuss in this book have been present and recognized in academic analysis of transport for long periods (for example the Transport Canada-centred policy domain; the rail freight and competition-market dispute domain; and the trains and grains domain) but others, such as the transport in cities and federal infrastructure policy domain and the dangerous goods and environment domain, are a more recent focus (but certainly not brand new). Numerous pressures, ideas, technologies, logistics, and changing institutional forms are present in the overall domain structure and mix. We refer to these developments in our literature review in chapter 1 and elsewhere in the domain chapters.

Policy Domain Elements

"Elements" are the second needed feature of our analytical framework. They refer to basic important features that help us understand and explain some of the basic causes of both transportation policy change and inertia, as well as providing insights into the overall socioeconomic content of this policy field. The three main elements we discuss and then analyse summarily at the end of each domain chapter are

- policy ideas, discourses, and agendas
- economic and social power
- technology and temporal realities and conflicts

The above three elements that we map and deploy in the seven domain chapters are essential features for understanding domain change and inertia. But each of the three elements poses different challenges about qualitative and quantitative evidence and the time periods being covered.

The mixes of dominant and contending policy ideas, discourses, and agendas are found in the historical and current advocacy and adoption of policy. They show up in the changing content of laws, speeches from the throne, budget speeches, and ministerial speeches and talking points. Ideas and preferred discourse are also revealed in opposition political party, interest group, think tank, and academic papers and sound-bite discourse developed by the electronic digital media, internet bloggers, and social networks.

Our seven domains deal with entrenched and shifting systems of economic and social power. Within the state, power can grow, ebb, or wane based on minority versus majority government situations and on the styles and performance of ministers and prime ministers. Firms and industry associations largely project private economic power. Both Canadian and foreign transport businesses are important in this field, including in the automotive and aerospace sectors. Labour and worker/employee interests are also important in both an economic and social context. For the most part, private economic power works in tandem with Transport Canada (and provincial transport ministries). But economic power also works with the federal Department of Finance and Industry Canada (recently renamed as Innovation, Science and Economic Development Canada, ISEDC) as well as with certain line ministries such as Agriculture and Agri-Food Canada or special operating agencies with industry-specific mandates and capacity. Consumer and environmental interests exercise social power and influence, albeit usually not on as sustained a basis as business, often crucially focused on safety and security and conceptions of the public interest. All of these actors are networked with each other, whether consciously or intentionally or not.

Varied and changing kinds of technology and temporal realities and conflicts underpin the structure and dynamics of the different domains. Transport technologies have been previewed above regarding modes and across modes. Time and temporal realities interact or collide with technologies and related policy advocacy. These realities range from temporal decision processes, cycles, and realities including intermittent or frequent crises or disasters; annual or multiyear business, political, or electoral cycles; and long-term, structural, life-cycle, generational, or intergenerational demographic changes.

THE EMPIRICAL ANALYSIS OF POLICY
AND GOVERNANCE HISTORIES

Across the full seven domain analyses we examine twenty policy and governance histories, some related in different ways as well as to longer-term future policy challenges (see table I.1). We draw empirically on reports and studies of Canadian and international transport policy and regulation by academics, think tanks, and government, complemented by our own transport and related research in the disciplines of policy, politics and governance, engineering and logistics, and economics and business. This work is supported by a large number of interviews conducted by the authors with transport policy officials and players across the seven domains.

The historical content of the empirical chapters as a whole mainly covers a fifty-year period but some goes back even further, such as in the grains and trains domain. We proceed sometimes in chronological order but often we necessarily move back and forth among the five federal prime ministerial eras and in our coverage of provincial–urban transport policies in an effort to show the complex interplay of ideas, power and technology, and temporal realities and conflict.

The contextual discussion in chapter 3, of six Canada–US and international transport policy developments, forces, and institutions, adds to the conceptual and empirical coverage and depth of our analysis overall. These contextual discussions include transport policy and related developments such as a) Canada–US transport economic deregulation and privatization dynamics triggered in the late 1970s and extending into the 1980s and to the present day but always also tied to the imperatives of transport safety; b) trade liberalization, agreements, and transport impacts that emerged especially in the 1980s and 1990s but which also face new volatile challenges at present; c) core characteristics and developments in 2001 regarding post-9/11 and later transport security and terrorism policy and governance regarding air, borders, bridges, and trade; d) *cabotage* as a transport concept involving the transport of goods from one point to another within a country but also rules specifying that the transport of goods or people within a country be carried out by a domestic carrier and its workers rather than a foreign carrier; e) St Lawrence Seaway and Great Lakes management through linked authorities involving the US and Canada; and f) key features of relations with international transport modal and intermodal agencies are sampled, including the International Maritime Organization (IMO), the International Civil Aviation Organization (ICAO), and the International Transport Forum (ITF) affiliated with the Organization for Economic Cooperation and Development (OECD).

These contextual analyses are linked here and as well in chapter 2 to the approaches and agendas of prime ministerial and political party eras at the federal level from 1968 to 2018 as revealed by, or obscured

Table I.1
Transport Policy and Governance Histories in the Seven Domains

Transport policy domains	Policy and governance histories
Transport Canada-centred domain (chapter 4)	From "Ministry" of Transport to Department of Transport with "portfolio": Levels of control versus independence (late 1960s to late 1980s)
	Transport Canada regulatory policy, processes, volumes, and forward plans (2006 to present)
	Safety policy, regulation, and the Transportation Safety Board of Canada (1990 to present)
	Expressed transport policy mandates and macro reform agendas and priorities (2001 to present)
Grains and trains transport policy domain (chapter 5)	The globalization of grain (1897 to present)
	Deregulating Western grain (1970s to present)
Rail freight and competition-market dispute domain (chapter 6)	In search of optimization: Federal policy and the freight railways' business models (mid-1960s to present)
	Policy and governance of competition and settling marketplace disputes (mid-1990s to present)
Air transport policy and shared-governance domain (chapter 7)	Air Canada, managed competition, and regional airline policy (1970s to present)
	Airports policy and shared-governance authorities (1992 to present)
	NAV Canada as navigation service provider and air safety regulator (1996 to present)
	Security policy and the Canadian air transport security authority (2001 to present)
Transportation in cities and federal infrastructure policy domain (chapter 8)	The elusive quest for urban mobility (1960s to present)
	Follow the money: The dodgy evolution of federal financing of urban transportation infrastructure (mid-1980s to present)
Transportation, dangerous goods, and environmental policy domain (chapter 9)	Dangerous goods policy and regulation (1992 to present)
	Dangerous goods policy and oil transport via pipelines versus rail (2010 to present)
	Transport policy and environment policy (1995 to present)
Disruptive technology-enabled transportation domain (chapter 10)	Uber ride-sourcing technology and related taxi and urban transport market governance (2005 to present)
	Autonomous vehicles transport technology and related emerging policy and guidance (2010 to present)
	Unmanned air vehicles (drone) technology and policy and governance (2005 to present)

in, speeches from the throne (SFTs) and budget speeches. Some initial glimpses are also supplied in chapters 2 and 3 of how federal approaches and agendas have worked compared to those in the US and internationally over the same period.

MAIN ARGUMENTS

We advance seven main arguments that contribute to answering the book's three research questions as brought together in our conclusions in chapter 11.

1 Transportation policy in Canada is, to an ever greater extent, provincial–urban policy and governance-centered, with ongoing, more traditional federal-led nation building therefore becoming less present and noticeable.

2 Transportation policy has shifted across regulatory eras, deregulatory phases, and coregulation and regulatory capitalism phases, but all forms of regulation are still in place and are still contested.

3 Transportation policy encompasses a world of increasingly complex supply chains, but they also interact with governance networks that often and, not surprisingly, do not have the same institutional boundaries as supply chains. That sets up jurisdictional conflicts and dysfunctionalities that so far have proven difficult to resolve.

4 Transportation policy has, overall, not been a high priority federal policy sphere compared to others on the agendas of Canada's federal prime ministerial eras in the last fifty years, as revealed in throne speeches and budgets as key agenda-setting occasions and processes. The same is true in measured public opinion.

5 Canadian transportation policy is, has been, and will increasingly be a policy challenge of linked/overlapping policy fields including economic deregulation, regulatory safety and security, infrastructure, borders, bridges, energy pipelines, environment and dangerous goods, northern and regional–urban–rural trade, and transport science, technology and innovation policy.

6 Transport policy needs major reforms to deal with transport infrastructure as a socioeconomic capital asset currently subjected to funding and budgeting limitations and concepts, and

the growing presence of retail politics in infrastructure policy in general.

7 Such infrastructure, and who shares in paying for and benefiting from it, includes shippers and customers within and across modes, and taxpayers within and across political jurisdictions within Canada.

8 Transportation policy as it evolved over the past five decades has an uneven record of keeping Canada competitive with the world in this vital field and, despite periodic bursts of progress, by and large the country too often has been resting on its laurels.

Part I of the book examines Canadian transport policy conceptually and in an historical context. Chapter 1 examines key parts of the foundational literature. Chapter 2 analyses key prime ministerial eras and maps the changing interests and power structures that underpin transport policy and governance agenda setting. Key Canada–US and other international policies, developments, institutions, and pressures are also identified and mapped in chapter 3. Part two provides an extensive empirical analysis of the seven key transport policy and governance domains, including their basic historical features and the manner in which the three domain elements of our analytical framework help us to understand change and inertia. Our conclusions and main final arguments follow in chapter 11.

PART ONE

Conceptual Foundations
and Historical Context

1

Conceptual Foundations

INTRODUCTION

This chapter examines the conceptual foundations, which, along with our empirical research, led to the development of the book's analytical framework as set out in the introduction. The present chapter draws on a range of academic, governmental, and other studies on transportation policy and governance and other closely related policy fields. The literature on which we draw is historical and contemporary as well as Canadian and comparative. It emerges from a variety of social science and natural science disciplines and fields, including political science, economics, engineering, logistics, business, risk management, public policy, science and technology studies, urban policy, sociology, geography, governance, and public administration.

This literature reveals an ever-broadening level of complexity in the nature of transport policy and governance in Canada as it seeks to influence, interpret, benefit from, and, at times, partly resist or reshape domestic and international pressures. Chapters 2 and 3 and the transport domain analysis in part two of the book draw on an additional subset of transport and related policy and governance-relevant literature.

Our perspective on the foundational theoretical and applied literature on transport policy is organized into three central streams: ideas, paradigms, and discourses; governance, power, and democracy; and technology and multimodal supply chain and logistics complexities and constraints. We explore each stream, highlighting key literature and authors, and commenting on ways in which they are linked and overlap as well as how they can be used both in our analytical framework and the discussion of our central themes throughout the book.

IDEAS, PARADIGMS, AND DISCOURSES

Our survey of ideas, paradigms, and discourses looks first at major transport policy ideas *per se* such as common carrier; competition; supply chain; logistics; congestion; mobility; and transportation safety, security, and carriage of dangerous goods. Second, we examine broader socioeconomic *statements* of transport policy ideas and purposes, first at the federal level and then at the provincial and city, municipal, and local levels of jurisdiction and policy expression. Table 1.1, later in this chapter, profiles the basic provincial transport policies and governance structures, which we will refer to in this and the next section of the chapter. Our third brief section on ideas, paradigms, and discourses complements these larger first two sections with a particular look at public policy and governance theory and in particular at a useful sample of a growing range of ideas about policy paths, path dependence, and subsystem dynamics used as a further aid to some parts of the detailed analysis in other chapters including the domain chapters.

Major Transport Policy Ideas

The *common carrier* public policy idea is historically pivotal in Canada and the US (Transportation Research Board 2015, Heaver 2009; Crawford 2009). In the US, "common carriage" as a concept and provision had its roots in two different sources of law: the law of bailment "under which carriers were responsible for goods that they carried," and the law of franchise and monopoly, "under which companies allowed by the state to provide general transport (and later communications networks) were required not to discriminate and to serve each customer equally" (Crawford 2009, 878). Canadian and US concepts and features of common carriage initially involved national carriers rather than foreign ones. This was the case in the building and initial operation of the CPR and CNR. It was also true in later periods. Cramer's historical account of North American freight rail is of particular interest here (Cramer 2007). He shows how railways "were crucial to the integration of national territories from the mid-1850s through the 1920s" and how common carrier policy was forged to deal with early abuses by railways, of which there were many. He then traces how a dramatic shift began in the 1970s "as three prongs of economic liberalization were implemented: deregulation of the industry, privatization of state-owned firms, and liberalization of controls in foreign investment" (Cramer, 1), albeit in different ways in the US, Canada, and Mexico (the three NAFTA countries).

In his review of Canadian railway services, Heaver (2009, 1) stresses that,

> The common carrier obligations of the railways have meant that their actions and inactions related to their service offerings have always been matters of public scrutiny. The railways have been required to provide reasonable facilities for the receiving, loading, unloading and delivering shippers' traffic without delay and to accept and carry traffic offered by shippers without delay. Regulations have flowed from these obligations such as the general interswitching order of the Board of Railway Commissioners in 1908.

Heaver also notes that the MacPherson Commission on Transportation, which reported in 1961, related common carrier issues to competition among modes but did so with a focus on rates rather than on rules of carriage or levels of service (see also Gratwick 2001). The latter became the determining issue in the early 2000s and remain so today.

While the common carrier concept was forged in the railway age, it also acquired relevance in other transport modes. Before railways, canals had to be governed, and then came airlines, automobiles and trucking, and extended marine services and ports. Each mode had its own particular characteristics, including the levels and types of competition and of public utility infrastructure. Consider the analogy of Robert Bothwell's history of Eldorado Limited as Canada's national uranium company. It shipped raw uranium ore on the Mackenzie River, but "until the late 1930s, common carriers on the Mackenzie had been responsible to no one" (Bothwell 1984, 361–2). It was not until C.D. Howe, as the then minister of transport who got the Board of Transport Commissioners to introduce the licensing of common carriers on the Mackenzie and elsewhere, that this changed.

The current Canada Transportation Act (CTA) does not refer to the common carrier concept *per se* but instead refers in Section 113 to obligations about "level of services" (Doern 2015). Despite the omission, many or most accounts of the evolution of transport and rail policy in the last thirty years consider those service obligations as tantamount to a common-carrier provision under the law, and yet they recognize that the key obligations have been changed in major ways. We take up this analytical story in our analysis in chapters 2 and 6 where service levels and vestiges of common carrier discourse are part of the emerging story.

Cabotage as a transportation idea and practice refers "both to the transport of goods from one point to another within a country and to the requirement that the transport of goods or people from one point to another within a country be carried out by a domestic carrier" (Blank and Prentice 2012, 1). The failure to eliminate cabotage policies and practices and produce free trade or full deregulation in transportation is seen as a seriously unfinished agenda by some, but to others it is not necessarily a problem, given the need for a national transportation system that to some continuing extent supports Canadian transportation industries, individual firms, and workers and employees. Cabotage policy shows up in any number of policy fields and arenas including customs and border measures, tax policy, immigration, and jobs and employment in the transport sector and system, and in concepts of national defence and security. The more recent focal point for major policy change is aimed at limiting such practices in the EU. Indeed, the EU, first when it was a much smaller set of member countries and now as a twenty-eight (and soon twenty-seven) member-country entity, was compelled to institute such cabotage-limiting policies if it was to have any chance of becoming a vast internal market.

Competition as a general and transport policy idea has been present in many forms linked initially to the common carrier concept, which was originally centred on concerns about business monopoly power and abuse and later extended to multimodal and intermodal competition. In this context the Canada–US situation is also pivotal. Canada–US differences in policy are related mainly to competition policy and to the regulation of transport competition policy by competition regulators (not just transport regulators). The stated aims of US freight railroad regulatory policy include "to prohibit predatory pricing and practice, to avoid undue concentrations of market power, and to prohibit unlawful discrimination" (Transportation Research Board 2015, 27). This is interpreted in US law as applying to regulation at a macro, economy-wide level – not to case-by-case determinations by transport regulators, as is the situation in Canada. The difference is very important.

The most attention-getting issues about competition policy center on merger reviews and the approval or rejection of mergers. For example, if CN and CP sought or planned to merge, or if one took over the other, it almost certainly would be strenuously opposed by the commissioner of competition and the Competition Bureau. Mergers decisions are centered on *prospective or hypothesized future behaviour* that may arise after firms have merged. The merger issue is not itself something that flows directly from the common carrier concept, except that common carrier principles over the years were themselves partly, and at times primarily, a response to raw monopoly power. In the US this was cast historically as grounds for strong anti-trust policy.

Competition policy ideas seek to promote rivalry among firms, buyers, and sellers. They do this by restricting anticompetitive activities such as mergers, cartels, conspiracies in restraint-of-trade, misleading advertising, and other criminal and economic offences (see Doern, Prince, and Schultz 2014, 210–18; Competition Bureau 2015a; Doern and Wilks 1996). Most areas of competition law deal with offences or behaviour that has already occurred or are alleged to have occurred. The Competition Bureau's stated view is that competition

- makes the economy work more efficiently;
- strengthens businesses' ability to adapt and compete in global markets;
- provides consumers with competitive prices, product choices, and the information they need to make informed purchasing decisions;
- balances the interests of consumers and producers, wholesalers and retailers, dominant players and minor players, the public interest and the private interest. (Competition Bureau 2015a)

The Competition Bureau itemizes the many types of anticompetitive activities it investigates. Of interest to our discussion is "abuse of dominant position, when a dominant firm engages in anticompetitive practices that substantially lessen competition in a market or are likely to do so" (ibid., 2). The latter calls for a determination of what the relevant market is, as a basis for analysis and the triggering of enforcement. In transportation policy, this could (and should) concern questions of whether there is more than one mode of transport available to the shipper.

The commissioner of competition's annual report for 2013 emphasized what he described as the "beginnings of a shift toward greater transparency and more frequent use of strategic regulatory interventions to encourage fair and competitive practices" (Commissioner of Competition 2013, 4). For example, the Competition Bureau intervened in a case in which Air Canada and United Continental Holdings Inc (United Continental) "announced plans for a joint venture that would effectively merge their flight operations on high-demand Canada–United States routes" (ibid., 6). The commissioner announced that the bureau had reached a consent agreement with the airlines, ensuring that they "will not use their joint venture or any existing agreements to coordinate prices, price-specific seat quantities, pool revenues or costs, or share commercially sensitive information related to 14 key passenger routes – all of which would be detrimental to consumers. The agreement will remain in force as long as the joint venture or any of the airlines' coordination agreements are active, [and will be] overseen by an independent monitor appointed by the Bureau" (ibid., 6). The commission has also published a white paper on the Canadian taxi industry, mainly in light of the rapid growth of the tech firm Uber as a global supplier of ride-hailing services in hundreds of cities internationally, including Canadian ones (Competition Bureau 2015b), which we discuss later in this chapter.

Free trade, neoliberalism, and the regulation of international trade as general and transport impact ideas are important conceptually but also in relation to deregulation and regulation debates and intertwined realities. Not surprisingly, free trade involves reduced intervention by government to gain sustained access to foreign and regional markets (Cameron 1988; Doern and Tomlin 1991; Mendoza, Low, and Kotschwar 1999; Cameron and Tomlin 2000). This also involves neoliberalism and globalization as free trade and related ideas were advocated, acted upon, and opposed within and among countries. But from the outset Canadian trade authorities and agencies also knew they had to deal with the regulation of international trade (Trebilcock and House 1995, 1999; Trebilcock, et al. 2013). These included trade authorities involved with GATT/WTO, NAFTA, and the European Union. These trade authorities had to deal with rule making regarding dispute settlement, exchange rates and balance of payments, tariffs and the Most Favoured Nation Principle (MFN); health and safety regulation and standards; antidumping; subsidies and countervailing duties; safeguard regimes; trade in agriculture; trade in services; trade-related intellectual property (TRIPS); trade and investment; trade and environment; trade and labour rights; trade and competition policy;

and the international movement of people. Within Canada the issues of opening up the internal trade system emerged leading to an initial Canadian Agreement on Internal Trade cast as free-trade federalism (Doern and MacDonald 1999) and revised and reformed in different, often slow, ways. Trade within Canada was also bound up in the diverse features and policy fields functioning in and across Canada's system of multilevel governance (Doern and Johnson 2006). It should be no surprise that we provide further discussion of free trade and its regulation in chapter 2 where prime ministerial era agendas are examined via a close look at throne speech and budget speech content and in chapter 3 when we map key features of Canada–US transport relations, including in the current Trump era and its aggressive "America first" trade agenda and also border issue politics and aggressiveness.

The *supply chain* concept emerged in the early 1980s and was certainly linked to free-trade liberalized markets. We discuss it in the third section of this chapter in institutional terms and in subsequent chapters as well. It captures the idea of a system of companies, organizations, logistics, information, and expertise involved in moving and transforming resources, products, and services and delivering them to end-customers and users domestically and internationally, in the context of liberalized trade and trade agreements (Baldwin 2012; Council of Supply Chain Management Professionals, 2015; Wieland and Handfield 2013; Jacoby 2009; Phillips and Nolan 2007; Nagumey 2006; Hadfield and Nichols 2002). It is a key feature of contemporary business school education focused on supply chain management, unfortunately in most cases without much coverage of the transportation side of "delivery."

Even the definitions of the idea of supply chains are complex, and in practical situations the supply chain is also a de facto "demand and supply" chain in market terms. The notion of a chain, however, is metaphorically too linear sounding when examined from even a short distance back from the coal face, given that it is closer to what in other policy and governance spheres would also be cast as a network. Nonetheless, "supply chain" ideas have grown in importance and have driven transport and regulatory policy, for example in national and international food regulation, seen increasingly as having to deal with intricate supply chains that go in complex and often circuitous ways from "farm gate to plate" (Doern and Prince 2012).

Logistics, already referred to above, is combined conceptually with supply chains. Christopher's pivotal book on *Logistics and Supply*

Chain Management (Christopher 2016) contains a fifteen-chapter analysis, but none of those (nor their ten or so chapter subsection headings) mentions transportation at all (although transportation is discussed in the text). Transport Canada's discussion of the emergence of strategic gateways and trade corridors (Transport Canada 2011) easily could have spoken about both logistics and supply chains but it used other concepts instead. Industry Canada (now Innovation, Science and Economic Development Canada) conducted an analysis of the logistics and supply chain management industries and defined them as a "sector" whose "establishments engaged primarily in transporting and warehousing goods as well as providing logistics services. It includes the four transport modes (trucking, rail, air, and marine) as well as postal services, couriers and messengers, and warehousing and storage" (Industry Canada 2015).

A recent analysis in *The Economist* (2018b) critiques "global logistics" and relates it to more complex supply chains and growing digitization. It refers initially to the highly computerized Munich Maersk entering the transport marine shipping market in 2017 and that "sailing her 214,000 tonnes from port to port takes a crew of just 28. Loading and unloading the 20,000 containers she carries only needs the supervision of one crew member" (ibid., 18). The analysis then goes on in some detail to show how many other merchants, transport networks and supply chains are slowed by their inherent business strategies and experience all built around the value of complexity, which leaves them "adrift in a sea of paper" (ibid.). The analysis also cites data on "cascading costs" by sector, including infrastructure, execution in road, rail, sea, and air transport but also postal delivery and courier, express and parcel, and services and advisory regarding forwarding and contract logistics (ibid., 19).

Academic literature in the field comes from journals that usually contain the words "supply chain" or "logistics" in their names, but, not surprisingly, even when they have different titles there is overlapping content. In a 2005 edition of the *Journal of Business Logistics*, an article on supply chain management focused on "the pursuit of a consensus definition" about the field (Gibson, Mentzer, and Cook 2005). The authors showed that this is a "widely discussed but unresolved challenge" among logistics professionals (ibid., 17). This dilemma is not surprising nor is it found only in this particular field. Other policy and governance fields and their professions have similar dilemmas and in fact are features of complexity discussed briefly in the final section of this chapter.

In the institutional and professional context, the Logistics Institute emerged in Canada in 1990. The institute defines logistics as

> the art and science of managing and controlling the flow of goods, energy, information, and other resources from the source of production to the marketplace. More than 750,000 Canadian workers are employed in the logistics field, making it the second to third largest employment sector in Canada. Many logisticians work in supply management, executive management, consulting, transportation, traffic, customs, distribution, manufacturing, purchasing, and warehousing. They work in small, medium and large companies. (Logistics Institute 2016, 1)

"Almost overnight," the institute writes, "the responsibility of logistics grew from simply getting the product out the door to the science of controlling the optimal flow of goods, energy, and information through purchasing, planning and transportation management" (ibid.).

Congestion and its costs are an analytical idea and concept, and as a transport condition to be dealt with, is an engineering, logistics, and economic idea involving relationships among mobility, time, and space. It takes on complex social meanings and impacts, particularly in large cities, where most Canadians live and work (see chapter 8). Congestion costs relate to "delay and increased risk due to interference between road users" (Victoria Transport Policy Institute 2013). Journeys are slowed and take longer, and traffic jams and frustrations can cause social impacts including road rage and the simple inability of individuals to get to work or to other destinations important to them and their families. Road tolls are a policy lever that has often been advocated by economists to put a price on the cause of congestion in order to reduce it. The social implications relate to questions of public versus private transportation and to the location of jobs and where lower-income workers can afford to live and travel (Litman 2017; Stopher and Stanley 2014; Dijst, Rietveld, and Steg, 2013). Recent analyses and commentary on choked roads referred to intracity and intercity transport as being on the "verge of carmageddon" (Monbiot 2016).

Coleman's analysis of congestion in rail and intermodal transport sees congestion most directly in relation to transport infrastructure capacity (Coleman 2015), with capacity in engineering terms being difficult to determine precisely despite being related to traffic peaks. He stresses that when an artery is close to its theoretical maximum capacity, "almost any kind of perturbation will trigger the onset of serious congestion" (ibid., 48) and argues, for example, that,

> It is not just corridors on railways that matter. At the end of every corridor is an intersection – a classification yard, an intermodal terminal, a port facility, or a connection to another railway. The behavior inside the intersections is partly random, meaning that there is statistical variation in their performance. And every intersection is connected to at least one other corridor, often another mode, like marine or trucking. (Ibid., 48)

As a result, highly nonlinear and complex features exist in transport and congestion systems and in their diagnosis and possible cure (or partial cure), and even in how they can be expressed in policy terms as ideas and meaningful discourse. We see this in more detail in chapters 6 and 8 where the complex degrees of difficulty both rhetorically and practically on the demand and supply sides of the policy/political equation are featured.

Mobility as a transport idea is explicit or implied in transport literature especially regarding cities and transport policy. Stopher and Stanley (2014, 119) define mobility as "the ease with which a person moves around" and then examine it in relation to a discussion of social exclusion (ibid., 116–30) as well as in relation to how "mobility can be ascertained simply by determining access to vehicles (both freight and passenger) and the level of performance of the network on which the available vehicles can be operated" (ibid., 185). Authors such as Annema (2013) treat mobility much more indirectly by examining "transport resistance factors" including "time, money and effort" (ibid., 101–24). In chapter 8 we will see that urban mobility in terms of optimization theory is an increasingly "elusive quest" in Canadian cities because maximizing the mobility of people or goods individually, which is what nearly everyone wants, will reduce mobility for everyone as a whole. But we also take note of other analysis that focuses on city planning and land development policy as crucial also to mobility solutions in a larger context (Litman 2017; Cervero, Guerra, and Al 2017; Giuliano and Hanson 2017; Rodrique, Comptois, and Slack 2016).

Transport *safety, security, and dangerous goods* as core policy ideas are also pivotal in Canadian and international transport policy (Doern, Prince, and Schultz 2014). Historically transportation *safety* has of course been a crucial focus in transport regulation across all modes. In 1990 the Transportation Safety Board of Canada (TSB) was established partly to replace earlier institutional forms of safety regulation (see chapter 4). It investigates transportation incidents and accidents in the marine, pipeline, rail, and air modes of transportation. It works with other federal departments and regulators, but its jurisdiction is strongly protected. When the TSB investigates an accident (such as the 2013 Lac-Mégantic rail disaster) no other federal department except National Defence and the RCMP "may investigate for the purpose of making findings as to the causes and contributing factors of the accident" (Transportation Safety Board of Canada 2013). But if change in safety policy is required, then Transport Canada has the lead jurisdictional role most of the time. The Lac-Mégantic disaster is examined in detail in chapters 4 and 9.

For the last fifteen years in particular, safety issues have been joined by concurrent needs to provide transportation *security*. Indeed, in Canada these security-risk concerns began not just with post-9/11 terrorism prevention concerns in 2001 but even earlier with the 1985 Air India crash, which was caused by terrorism. Indeed, the combination of safety and security issues with regulatory and management needs led to the production of Transport Canada's 2007 *Moving Forward* policy document, whose subtitle stressed the imperative of "changing the safety and security culture" (Transport Canada 2007).

Differences in the regulatory nature of safety versus security were in need of emphasis in Transport Canada as a multimodal and intermodal regulator. As its former deputy minister, Louis Ranger, stressed, "transport safety and security programs are fundamentally different in that they focus on very different types of risks. 'Safety risks' originate from unintended failures, errors or misfortunes whereas 'security risks' originate from deliberate or malicious attempts to disrupt, disable or destroy" (Ranger 2010, 12). Quigley (2014) has examined differences in the security risk profiles and regulatory strategies in major modal regimes in Canada.

Interwoven into these ideas are others tied to concerns about the transport of dangerous goods or hazardous materials ("hazmat" is the term used in the US). Abel (2011, 973) points out in a US context that, as a result "of the operation of the common carrier doctrine and the modal strengths of freight transportation via rail, railroads are prohibited from refusing shipment of dangerous cargo." Remarkably, this prohibition against refusing to carry dangerous goods is unique to railroads. Truckers and ship owners are free to refuse such goods if they wish.

In 2014, following the Lac-Mégantic rail disaster, the Canadian Transportation Agency reviewed the safety and liability issues surrounding the transport by rail of dangerous goods (Krugel 2014). In February 2015, Transport Minister Lisa Raitt announced new legislation to ensure that any railway or company that transports crude oil will share accountability for the costs of cleanup and compensation in the event of an accident. Her new legislation also provided for imposing mandatory minimum insurance levels on railways in amounts that depend on the type and volume of dangerous goods being transported.

Of considerable conceptual and practical importance is recent research published in the US focused on *Designing Safety Regulation for High-Hazard Industries* (National Academies of Sciences, Engineering and Medicine 2017; Coglianese and Menzies 2017). The study focused on the "salient design features that follow from the macro–micro and means–ends distinctions" ... that "suggest four basic regulatory design types; micro-means; micro-ends, macro-means and macro ends" (Coglianese and Menzies 2017, 3). The essence of the problem of choice is that,

> Often contrasted with "prescriptive" or micro-means regulations, and sometimes mislabeled as "performance-based," management regulations are more aptly described as having a *macro-means* design. They require firms to address overall risk – that is, at a macro-level by using a specified *means* of a management system. (Ibid., 3)

Notably, these management regulations do not require firms to achieve specific ends, or performance outcomes such as a demonstrable reduction in the risk of major incidents. Such an outcome would be particularly difficult to demonstrate when regulations are intended to prevent catastrophic failures, given their complexity and rare occurrence. The core problem is that "unfortunately, for many years regulatory professionals have placed too much emphasis on ambiguous and often misleading labels such as 'performance-based' and 'prescriptive' and they have gravitated toward simplistic lists of generic advantages and disadvantages of regulatory design types" (ibid., 4). This kind of analysis is highly relevant both here and in earlier works in which safety regulation and transportation regulation have been expressed but also glossed over.

These issues and choices are of particular interest because the full empirical work examined in the National Academies of Sciences, Engineering and Medicine 2017 report involves regulatory studies/topics of four countries governing two high-hazard industries. But all of them as indicated in the full report have transportation content and focus with transportation hyphenated with expressed links to energy, freight transportation, marine transportation, motor carriers, pipelines, safety and human factors, terminals and facilities, and vehicles and equipment.

Nation building and *province building* as changing and variously expressed and grouped ideas have been pivotal in the transportation policy field. Common carrier ideas were tied to such aspirations and discourse, but core values were not limited to statutory–regulatory policy alone. They often were combined with federal spending and subsidies linked to natural resource development, especially in Western Canada. Prime Minister Sir John A. Macdonald saw the building of the Canadian Pacific Railway (CPR) as the physical linchpin in forging Canada as a nation. A related later version of sovereignty and nation building was forged under the first Mackenzie King government including the reorganization of the Canadian National Railways (CN) (Murray 2011; Gwyn 2011; Perl 1994; Stevenson 1981). Nation building linked to Western Canada was also part of the policy package that became the Crow's Nest Pass Agreement in the 1890s, which combined federal subsidies to CPR with freight rate guarantees to meet the needs and concerns of farmers and settlers who, in an era of strong Prairie populism (Laycock 1990; Cruikshank 1991; Darling 1980), were angry about the CPR's power and assymetrical pricing practices (see chapter 5). And the battle over the ending of such favoured rates for grain transportation involved intricate politics by the Pierre Trudeau Liberal Party in the early 1980s as it pursued a western diversification strategy (Kroeger 2009; Doern 1982). It also extended into the Mulroney era, when the free trade debate and the agreements that arose from it drew in related issues as to what constituted a subsidy – and this even as the Crow's Nest policy package was being wound down.

In the context of province building, each province's history is centered on the building of transport links within its territorial boundaries, including trails, roads, river systems, canals, and, as new modes developed, air transport and airports. These often included north–south connections, small remote airfields, and airports. Yet even today, as table 1.1 shows, most provinces show the Highways Act as their focal point for transportation policy. Even so, provincial transport ministries are now usually cast as transport and infrastructure ministries (about whose significance we will say more later in this chapter). While province building is an appropriate further element, actions are rarely provincial only. Thus Prentice 2015a, 2015b shows the dynamics and issues extending federally in the rail transport sector and with regard to airports and also northern development in transport to failure and struggle in ports such as Churchill Manitoba. Recently, after a long series of failures and adverse consequences Churchill now has a new set of corporate rail ownership linked closely to local/regional area resident involvement in detailed ways (CBC News 2018).

Broad Socio-Economic Statements of Transport Policy Ideas and Purposes

Federal transport mandate ideas and discourse can be found in the overarching Canada Transportation Act, especially in section 5 where both economic and social values intermingle as follows.

> It is declared that a competitive, economic and efficient
> national transportation system that meets the highest practicable
> safety and security standards and contributes to a sustainable
> environment and makes the best use of all modes of transportation
> at the lowest total cost is essential to serve the needs of its users,
> advance the well-being of Canadians and enable competitiveness
> and economic growth in both urban and rural areas throughout
> Canada. Those objectives are most likely to be achieved when:
> a competition and market forces, both within and among the
>   various modes of transportation, are the prime agents in
>   providing viable and effective transportation services;
> b regulation and strategic public intervention are used to achieve
>   economic, safety, security, environmental or social outcomes
>   that cannot be achieved satisfactorily by competition and

market forces and do not unduly favour, or reduce the inherent advantages of, any particular mode of transportation;
c rates and conditions do not constitute an undue obstacle to
the movement of traffic within Canada or to export goods
from Canada;
d the transportation system is accessible without undue obstacle to
the mobility of persons, including persons with disabilities; and
e governments and the private sector work together for an integrated transportation system." (Canada Transportation Act, 5)

This excerpt from the act comes from its preamble but, amazingly, the
individual features do not all appear in the body of the statute. Section
b) of the preamble implies that some of its social outcomes can be
achieved by "competition and market forces" but with the apparent
standard being as in b) above: to achieve them to a "satisfactory" level
(whatever that is). This lack of precision has led to contentiousness
and dysfunction in the administration of transportation policy, as we
will show in several chapters.

In earlier transportation policy reviews such as the one that led
to the report of the Canada Transportation Act review panel (2001),
there was a discussion of previous multivalue socioeconomic policy
expressions and purposes (chapter 20, 305–15). But the panel's report
was titled *Vision and Balance*, and its scope was arguably even
broader than that. A research report for the panel (Gratwick 2001)
was very critical of the tone (and narrow breadth) of previous federal
policy goals and ideas, and of the earlier Royal Commissions that
had shaped national policy and the way in which that policy was
expressed. But the range of transport policy values and ideas is now,
if anything (and appropriately), far greater than it used to be in
political terms as revealed by papers and materials fed into the recent
2014–15 review panel's work, including by the chair of the 2001
review (Flemming 2012, 2014).

The most recent federal government statement on transportation
policy and governance is centred on ministerial announcements regarding the Transportation Modernization Act (Bill C-49) and its values
and content as it has been proceeding in the Justin Trudeau era in
2017 and 2018 in both the House of Commons and the Senate. As
introduced by Transport Minister Marc Garneau, the new legislation,
preceded by a year of consultation with key multimodal transportation

interests, will "provide a better experience for travellers and a fair, efficient and safer freight rail system to facilitate trade and economic growth ..." key measures would include:

- establishing new air passenger rights;
- liberalizing international ownership restrictions for Canadian air carriers to provide travellers with more choice through increased competition;
- improving access, transparency, efficiency, and sustainable long-term investment in the freight rail sector; and
- increasing the safety of transportation in Canada by requiring railways to install voice and video recorders in locomotives. (Transport Canada 2017c)

The backgrounder elaborating "travellers initiatives" highlighted air passenger rights via new legislation in the Transportation Modernization Act that would "mandate the Canadian Transportation Agency to make new regulations to strengthen Canada's air passenger rights" in relation to issues such as denied boarding, lost or damaged baggage, tarmac delays over a certain period of time, seating children near a parent or guardian at no extra charge (Transport Canada 2017d). Also included under the traveller's initiatives were changes to liberalize international ownership restrictions regarding Canadian air carriers; new provisions for joint ventures between two or more air carriers; and provisions for CATSA to provide new or additional screening services on a cost-recovery basis.

The backgrounder on "growing Canada's economy with modernized rail transportation" highlighted key measures including

- new data reporting requirements for railways on rates, service and performance to enhance system efficiency;
- a new mechanism, Long Haul Interswitching, to provide captive shippers across all sectors and regions of Canada with access to a competing railway, to ensure they have options;
- a definition of "adequate and suitable" rail service that confirms railways should provide shippers with the highest level of service that can reasonably be provided in the circumstances;
- the ability for shippers to seek reciprocal financial penalties through their service agreements with railways to enhance accountability; and

- more accessible and timely remedies for shippers on both rates and service, to support fair negotiations. (Transport Canada 2017e)

We analyze and comment further on these statements and reforms in several of the domain chapters.

Provincial transport mandate ideas and discourse show some common normative policy features but also some differences. Eight of the ten provinces have "infrastructure" combined with "transportation" in their ministry titles. Infrastructure is itself therefore a mandate policy idea, but this raises the question of how the ideas and priorities might be brought forward and judged, given that in most such ministries the infrastructure elements relate to the government's entire infrastructure purview and not just to transport infrastructure! It seems as if the concept of "transportation" is being equated with (i.e., reduced to) that of static infrastructure – like bridges and gazebos – a diminution that ignores the intelligence and strategies with which freight and passenger traffic is actually moved and that, arguably, have at least as much influence on the evolution, performance, and efficiency of transportation as the physical infrastructure does.

In more specific mandate terms, British Columbia, as indicated in table 1.1, currently sees transport and infrastructure policy as promoting "economic growth and diversification in support of ... creating jobs to secure a strong tomorrow for communities across the province; and to invest in transit, cycling and walking infrastructure." Saskatchewan says its transport vision is "connecting Saskatchewan to the world" and "increasing transport safety and enhancing the quality of life." Ontario leads off the discussion of its mandate by saying it "strives to be a world leader in moving people and goods safely, efficiently and sustainably to support a globally competitive economy and a high quality of life." And Nova Scotia aims to deliver "quality public infrastructure for Nova Scotia" and "to provide a transportation network for the safe and efficient movement of people and goods." If the focus of these descriptions seems rather blunt or disjointed, that's probably because it is.

While these and other provincial mandate statements are important, they are by no means the only policy ideas at play in each province. Each province also has about ten transport-related laws that also embody statutory goals and ideas. They are typically anchored first

and foremost in various highway acts but they also extend to dangerous goods, safety, persons with disabilities, and also floodways.

Cities and Multilevel Governance Ideas and Discourse

There is a growing policy, political, and governance literature on
Canadian cities and urban places and spheres. Transportation is not
necessarily a major focus in this literature because the urban space is
where multiple policy fields and ideas are shaped by city agencies and
fall under different academic disciplines (Horak and Young 2012;
Bradford and Bramwell 2014; Graham and Andrew 2014; Filion et
al. 2015; Andrew and Morrison 2001).

The above kinds of literature are also often centred on multilevel
governance as an idea *per se*, in part because cities and municipal
governments are the constitutional creations of the provinces that
include ideas about limited revenue raising powers and capacities
focusing mainly on property taxes (Atkinson, et a.l 2013; Bird, Slack,
and Tasronyi 2012; Bird and Slack 1993). Multilevel features of
city governance also emerged because of occasional bursts of federal government interest in urban affairs in the 1970s and 1980s
(Cameron 1974; Doern and Phidd 1992) but even more obviously
when federal deficit periods in the 1980s and 1990s ended and the
federal government in the Chrétien–Martin era made cities an explicit
part of its agenda in both spending and multigovernance terms
(Doern, Maslove, and Prince 2013). Transportation policy ideas have
been briefly explored in some of the literature both in general (Fowler
and Layton 2001) and with regard to infrastructure (Andrew and
Morrison 2001) and federal infrastructure funding (Champagne
2014) as well as in relation to innovation in urban economics
(Bradford and Bramwell 2014). These inform and underpin the basics
in city governance and politics and multilevel governance in our
analysis in chapter 8.

Also relevant here is the lobbying role in Ottawa of the ideas
and priorities of the Canadian Federation of Municipalities (CFM)
(2016) and within it the Big City Mayors' Caucus composed of
twenty-two of Canada's biggest cities. CFM membership includes
1,976 municipalities and associations representing 80 to 100 per cent
of municipal populations in most provinces and territories. The CFM
membership captures both small and medium sized municipal governments but within is largely driven by the more powerful Big City

Mayors Caucus (ibid.). The latter's advocacy theme is "nation-building through city-building" (ibid.). Its priorities in lobbying the feds are climate change, transit, partnerships, and housing. Regarding city transit, the caucus calls for funding and action for "reducing gridlock and cutting commutes" (ibid.).

Social ideas in transport and related policy fields have a long trajectory of changing and overlapping discourse including the public interest in the context of social regulation, ideas and aspirations about the social license, and corporate social responsibility. Safety goals have been a part of this larger story and indeed in many ways were given renewed emphasis in the 1960s. Concepts of "the public interest" and those of "social regulation" were then (and still are) closely entwined. Public interest as a concept and process has been of major relevance for decades (Pal and Maxwell 2003). It involves the role of values and interests beyond private market interests and, moreover, even beyond the interests of the state as represented by elected governments. The notion that governments, their officials, and private firms have to act in the public interest emerged most sharply in democratic societies when the concept of social regulation emerged.

Social regulation has long been differentiated from economic regulation (Prince 1999). The latter refers to rules governing entry into, and exit from, markets, and it covers competition law and policy and corporate law, which center on how companies are born and incorporated as limited-liability entities as well as how they die or disappear under bankruptcy law and policy (Doern, Prince, and Schultz 2014, chapter 7). Social regulation was born at the same time as the formal emergence of the consumer movement and under the strong influence of the labour movement and unions. It was primarily concerned with notions of consumer safety, consumer protection, and the fairness of markets (Schultz 2000; Sparrow 2000). Only later did environmental issues come under the ambit of social regulation, for example as with the requirement for formal environmental assessment of projects proposed or planned by private interests and government (Doern, Auld, and Stoney 2015).

Some authors argue that the term "social licence to operate" emerged in the last two decades starting with the domestic and global mining industry (Bursey 2015; Bice 2014; Prno and Slocombe 2012; Gunningham, Kagan, and Thornton 2004). For example, Bice's analysis of social licence in the Australian mining industry argues that such a "licence" is "now widely recognized by companies as vital to successful operations" (Bice 2014, 63) and that it has arisen "at the same time that corporate social responsibility (CSR) practices have been embraced by major corporations internationally" (ibid., 63). Bice is careful to stress, however, that,

> While social license is intended as a metaphor to encapsulate values, activities and ideals which companies must espouse within society to ensure successful operation – and not a literal licensing arrangement – even metaphors require clear boundaries to make them meaningful. Research suggests that certain "minimum standards," such as upholding basic human rights, avoiding bribery and corruption, and working to minimize harm to the environment, denote fundamental "licensing requirements" for a social license to operate ... but the criteria defining these metaphorical licences remain relatively murky. (Bice 2014, 63)

He explains how business reporting on sustainable development helps to show the degree to which Australian mining companies understand their social licence to operate. Social licence is often seen as "the level of acceptance or approval continually granted to an organization's operations or project by the local community or by other stakeholders" It has also been described as a "perception of legitimacy – does the company go about its business in a proper way?" (Black and Bice 2015, 1).

In the Canadian context, Eisler argues that the concept of a social licence has taken strong root in debates over natural resource development. He says that, "to some, social licence is considered a new test, an additional hurdle to overcome. But history and experience tell us that it is not new. The label might be [new], but the need for it is not" (Eisler 2014, 1). He argues that today "industry faces a triple licensing hurdle: a commercial licence, a policy/regulatory licence and a social licence ... [T]he expectation is that each must be addressed separately" (ibid., 2).

Policy research bodies such as the Public Policy Forum, in its study of the Canadian nuclear industry and nuclear policy, use the term "social licence" in a broad way to refer to permissions to build nuclear reactors in particular and more generally to values and obligations about safety, due process, and the environment as well as health in relation to nuclear medicines (Public Policy Forum 2014, 6). That makes it rather tangible. But other authors such as Bursey (2015) argue that social licence is still a concept in search of a definition and boundaries.

Public Policy and Related Analysis
of Paths and Subsystem Dynamics

The study of public policy and related governance consists of a massive volume of books and articles by authors analyzing the subject in various countries and others looking at one or more policy field and writing about events and dynamics covering different time periods over the last several decades. These have included analyses of macrorational policy stages set in the context of incrementalism and intragovernment imperatives in government structures that are by definition complex. Not surprisingly there are also conceptual insights by authors focusing on other complementary real and emerging paths and subsystem dynamics. We draw on several of these as previewed very briefly here but referred to as needed in later chapters and indeed in this chapter as well.

The insights of Jones and Baumgartner (2012) on "punctuated equilibrium" is of analytical value in our discussion in chapter 2 of agenda-setting dynamics in political and policy life, including in our analysis of the rhythms of agendas functioning around speeches from the throne and budget speeches and their transport content presence or absence. It focuses on patterns of periodic stability broken by short, sharp, punctuated change. But related linked theories are also discussed regarding the attention spans of governments, political parties, the media, and voters.

Les Pal (2014) offers a valuable focus on policy development dynamics where crisis management and turbulence are fast moving imperatives. Pal's book is titled *Beyond Policy Analysis* and addresses "public issue management in turbulent times." Fast moving and often major crises are not abnormal because turbulent times are not abnormal and for this and other reasons, the political and communication skills on policy and options are ever more important. These kinds of policy and decision paths and sudden speeds are of import when we examine the dynamics of the Lac-Mégantic disaster of 2014 in chapter 4 as a transport safety accident issue but also in chapter 9 as a transport of dangerous goods problem.

The insights of Michel Foucault (1991) are centred on what he labels "governmentality." Broadly speaking, governmentality refers to thinking about the state and different mentalities of government but is also centered on ideas of how the state rationalizes its exercise of power. Foucault wrote on a wide variety of subjects and areas of policy and society but his concept of governmentality referred initially to aspects of the art of government and even more broadly to the state and its practices and the different mentalities that underpin these practices in directing human behaviour. In this key sense "govern-mentality is far from a theory of power, authority, or even of gover-nance" (Rose, O'Malley, and Valerde 2009, 3). It is appropriate not only in parts of the current chapter where governance is discussed but also in key parts of chapter 4 on the entities centred on, but also extending from, Transport Canada as the lead transport department. And it is valuable as an aid to understanding the "shared-governance" system examined in chapter 7's analysis of airports.

The approach suggested by Howlett and Rayner (2013) on "policy patching versus packaging" is of analytical use as an indicator of policy drift and complexity in some respects but also of the frequent need to merge and defend in public combined policy areas or linked problems. They conclude after their review of policy portfolios and design literature that "adding the notion of policy 'patching' to con-siderations of intelligent design ... better connects design consider-ations to practice than do many earlier discussions firmly centred in the 'planning' orientation" (ibid., 176). These kinds of needed tactics and practices are of use in understanding the analysis in chapter 6 of the freight rail and competition-market dispute domain and also in chapter 7 of the air transport and shared-governance domain.

In a similar manner but with different starting and end points, the approach of Agranoff (2007) provides useful analytical relevance for the analysis of the dynamics of "managing within networks." Agranoff links these network policy and governance imperatives, as have others, as a key feature of the internet age both in its early formation and, of course, now in its social media complexity. Again, we see some of this in this chapter, in chapter 2 on Canada–US transport policy relations, in chapter 7 on air transport and shared-governance domain, and in chapter 10 on the need to deal with major gaps in responding to the diverse and disruptive technology-enabled transport incursions of Uber ride-hailing services, driverless vehicles, and drones.

The dynamics of complex "regulatory breakdown" (Coglianese 2012) and regulatory "unruliness" (Doern, Prince, and Schultz 2014) is drawn on to show how deregulation has been halted and, in fact, rule making increased in complex and even chaotic ways. The Coglianese volume focused on the US through an analysis of ten different regulatory realms over the previous two decades with "regulatory breakdown" having occurred because "US regulation clearly suffers from a crisis of confidence. Government has become less trusted and politics more polarized, with debates over regulatory policy readily devolving into highly charged ideological disputes" (ibid., vii).

The Doern, Prince, and Schultz analysis defines "unruliness" as "inabilities to effectively develop regulatory policy and enforce rules (in parent laws, delegated laws, guidelines and codes) because of any number of policy and mandate conflicts, democratic gaps and governance challenges" (ibid., 46). Three types of unruliness are mapped and analyzed: regulatory agency-related unruliness, regulatory regime complexity-related unruliness, and agenda-setting related unruliness (ibid., 47). We relate the "regulatory breakdown" and "unruliness" features in the discussion below and in chapters 4, 6, 9, and 10, where regulatory matters are paramount.

GOVERNANCE, POWER, AND DEMOCRACY

Federal Prime Ministerial Power in Cabinet Government and Parliament

Policy governance and power as exercised over all policies, including transportation policy, is centred in Canada in the prime minister, cabinet, and Parliament, with Canada's transport minister being but one voice in a cabinet presently of thirty ministers, and but one MP in a 338-member House of Commons.

The structure of cabinet power resides under increasing amounts and forms of prime ministerial oversight and control. This has been true for some time but especially since the late 1990s under the Chrétien–Martin and, from 2006 to 2015, Harper governments (Savoie 2010, 2013; Doern, Prince, and Maslove 2013). In significant ways, prime ministers act as de facto transport policy ministers, through various actions that support, discourage, or sideline considerations of transportation in national and international agendas. Closely aligned in this portfolio and power equation is the minister of finance, who exerts varying degrees of control vis-à-vis macroeconomic fiscal, economic, and budgetary policy. Indeed, some tax measures affect transport firms and activities either directly or indirectly, even when transport is not the main focus of the tax measure itself (Prentice 2015). In the 1980s and early 1990s, the cabinet decision structure was centred on an overall Cabinet Committee on Priorities and Planning, which had pivotal control of the spending of new money. The transport minister was on this committee but was then removed from it, a fate shared by some other ministers as well, thus signalling the ups and downs of where ministers fit in the pecking order and in the eyes of the prime minister (Doern and Phidd 1992, 141, 174–7).

While executive governance is our primary focus, the House of Commons as the elected house of representative democracy, is also a part of the story (Aucoin, Jarvis, and Turnbull 2011; Fletcher and Blais 2012; Malloy 2004). Opposition parties and their transport agendas (or lack thereof) will be examined in later chapters, as will the roles of Parliamentary committees and Parliamentary watchdog agencies. At present those committees include the Standing Committee on Transport, Infrastructure and Communities, and other subject matter committees where transport issues bubble up, for example in energy pertaining to oil and gas pipelines, and even some social and social policy contexts and fields such as those concerned with disabilities and access to transportation. Also showing up here are accountability reports by Parliament's auditor general of Canada and also the commissioner of the Environment and Sustainable Development (2011), who conducted and published one of the few major reviews of policy and practice on the transportation of dangerous goods – and a very critical one it was, too, about failures in their implementation (see chapter 9).

Transport Canada, Transport Ministers, and Inter-Ministerial Coordination and Power

Transport Canada is Canada's lead federal department and ministry (see chapter 4 for the domain analysis of its core mandate). A transport department was first established in 1936 replacing a department previously headed by a minister of Railways and Canals, which had been established in 1896. Since 1936 there have been thirty-one nominal transport ministers, who have each served an average of only 2.5 years in office – itself an important tenure dynamic as prime ministers move ministers into and out of different portfolios. But de facto transport policy was (and still is) made by departments of Agriculture (now Agriculture and Agri-food Canada), which were first formed in 1867 when the Canadian Pacific Railway and the settlement of Western Canada were underpinning the very formation of Canada. Transport policy as it relates to oil and gas pipeline transport has been made by energy and natural resource ministries in their various incarnations, such as with Energy, Mines and Resources (EMR, created in 1966) and then the current Natural Resources Canada (Doern and Gattinger 2003). Since the formation of Environment Canada in 1971, environment ministers have also had transport policy impacts and crossovers, in particular over the dynamics of environmental assessment law and practice affecting projects, including current aspects of the St Lawrence Seaway Authority and other vital transport waterways (Doern, Auld, and Stoney 2015).

The dynamics of interministerial jurisdictional and political power are to be expected in cabinet government, given that few issues are ever confined to a single minister's scope of interest or authority. And they are in turn impacted by dictates and interventions from prime ministers and finance ministers as well as other cabinet executive central agencies (Pal 2014; Savoie 2015; Doern and Phidd 1992). The dynamics can often play out behind the scenes and occur via bilateral and multilateral meetings, discussions, and ministerial leaks to the media, and include political threats and counter threats.

One interesting development in interministerial dynamics under the Justin Trudeau Liberal government, elected in October 2015, is the publication of ministerial mandate letters from the prime minister to each minister. These are expected to be operational for the four-year life of the government (Tang 2015). In addition to expectations for the minister of Transport about his own department, the letter says that he will, "work with the Minister of Infrastructure and Communities, who will have the lead, and in consultation with provincial and territorial governments, as well as municipalities, to develop and implement an Infrastructure Strategy which will see significant investments made to improve public transit infrastructure and green infrastructure" (Prime Minister of Canada 2015, 2). Another clause says that the minister will work with the minister of Infrastructure and Communities "who will have the lead, on the delivery of newly focused *Building Canada Fund* which will make greater investments in Canada's roads, bridges, transportation corridors, ports, and border gateways, helping Canada's manufacturers get their goods to market" (ibid.). The transport minister will also "lead, with the support of the Minister of Agriculture and Agri-food, and in the context of responding to the review of the *Canada Transportation Act*, a full review of the Canadian grain transportation system" (ibid.).

Some of the threads and dynamics of interministerial cabinet government are important, for good and for ill – historically as well as at present – and they emerge in the part two domain chapters of this book, such as those on freight rail, transport infrastructure, grains and trains, and dangerous goods and environment policy.

The Provinces and Transport Governance:
From Transport Ministries to Infrastructure
"and" Transport Ministries

Regarding the provinces' role in transport governance, unfortunately there is no fully comparative study on which to draw or build, and hence we refer the reader again to table 1.1 at the end of this section. All of the provinces have had transportation ministries from the time of their entry into Confederation. This was even before the first nominal federal "transportation" ministry was formed in 1936. At the turn of the millennium, seventeen years ago, most transport departments bore the "transport" nomenclature. But now, as table 1.1 shows, the vast majority are called transport and infrastructure ministries, either in that order or even the reverse. Infrastructure nomenclature and mandates reflected the overall emergence of infrastructure as its own policy field both federally and provincially and, perhaps especially, in patterns and sources of federal–provincial and federal–urban funding, as we discuss further below and later in chapter 8.

Provincial transport governance, combined as it now is with transport–infrastructure governance, must therefore find its own ministerial and interministerial bargains and balances, precisely because it has political duties for all infrastructure across the government and not just for transport interests and projects *per se*. In funding terms, they function like minitreasury boards or budget offices. Provincial transport governance also involves periodic reviews and review processes. Table 1.1 shows how British Columbia's B.C. On the Move, a ten-year transportation plan, emerged from a broadly inclusive engagement process in 2014–15 involving major modal interests (e.g. road, rail, and marine) as well as cities and smaller communities, many in remote areas. Newfoundland and Labrador's transportation department functions in part with a Minister's Advisory Committee on Labrador Transportation whose purview extended (recently) to marine services.

But ultimately, infrastructure and its governance in concert with transportation is a challenge and a puzzle because it is a conjoined and complex part of the federal-provincial-cities-communities governance space. Moreover, as mentioned earlier, the intermixing of the two (transportation and infrastructure) implies that policy making does not differentiate between static infrastructure and infrastructure that consists of the movement of aircraft, vehicles, and ships, and – especially – the intelligence and strategies by which these movements are choreographed and executed to provide services for individual Canadians and the economy. We see that as a serious policy problem and will discuss it in later chapters.

The Canada Transportation Act's final report refers to the need for "strategic infrastructure" (Canada Transportation Act Review 2014, 12). This is not particularly well defined, but the report correctly argues that, "Canada has no unifying policy framework from which national priorities can be established across transportation modes" (ibid.). It points out that there was a significant increase in public investment in transport infrastructure over the past decade but that it peaked between 2009 and 2011. Since 2006 about $4.8 billion of federal money has been invested in infrastructure generally and $4.7 billion for public transit in particular (ibid., 12). The paper puts its finger on the inherent conflict – even inconsistency – in the fact that "while the National Transportation Policy is [ostensibly] neutral regarding what mode should carry a product/person on a trip, the majority of federal transportation infrastructure funding contributes to new highway capacity" (ibid., 13).

Brian Flemming's analysis for the review refers to the need to relate infrastructure to reforms of road pricing policy and to a paradigm in which "the ownership of roads might be devolved to a new 'network institution' that could be given the responsibility of maintaining and improving the network and charging users for this purpose" (Flemming 2012, 2). The idea of infrastructure banks, publicly or privately funded (or joint public and privately funded), is also starting to gain some currency, and indeed the Justin Trudeau government has announced the creation of just such a bank (see chapter 8). The Conference Board of Canada's research centre that focuses on transportation policy and infrastructure stresses that the "most immediate challenge is to determine the best ways of financing transportation infrastructure

Table 1.1
Provincial transport policy and governance: A comparative look

Province	Ministry	Policy mandate ideas	Core laws	Process issues and events
BRITISH COLUMBIA	Ministry of Transport and Infrastructure (therefore dual overall mandate) Minister responsible for seven Crown corporations	Promotes economic growth and diversification in support of the government's priority of creating jobs to secure a strong tomorrow for communities across the province; invests in transit, cycling, and walking infrastructure Actions prioritized in B.C. On the Move will grow the economy, improve safety, maintain and replace aging infrastructure, and support BC's expanding resource sectors	Transportation Act Several related acts and regulations, as well as federal–provincial funding programs	B.C. On the Move, BC's ten-year Transportation plan (following extensive 2014–15 engagement process Priorities in order include rehabilitating highways, bridges, and side roads; improving highway safety; improving highway capacity and reliability; investing in transit; investing in cycling; investing in airports
ALBERTA	Ministry of Transport includes Department of Transport and Alberta Transportation Safety Board	Provides a safe, innovative, and sustainable multimodal transportation system that supports a strong economy, a high quality of life, and a healthy environment for Albertans Support for society includes options to connect Albertans to their friends, family, work, schools, health care, recreation, and communities	Traffic Safety Act Railway (Alberta) Act Dangerous Goods, Transportation, and Handling Act	2014 second phase of consultation to enable online opportunity for commenting on a draft long-term (fifty-year) multimodal strategy Consultations and focus groups also used, as well as consultation with other Alberta government departments

SASKATCHEWAN	Ministry of Highways and Infrastructure	Vision: Transportation – Connecting Saskatchewan to the World Goals: Supporting trade and investment; increasing transportation safety; enhancing quality of life; efficiently managing the transport system Mission statement: To optimize the role of transportation as it relates to the economic and social development of Saskatchewan	Highways and Transportation Act Railway Act Provincial Railway Guides (more than 2,000 km of railways under provincial jurisdiction, which include shortline railways moving grain, oil, and wood products Traffic Safety Court of Saskatchewan Act	Ministry supports the government's "Steady Growth" agenda and the goals of the Saskatchewan Plan for Growth – Vision 2020 and Beyond Strategy and key actions include improving road conditions, including replacement of twenty-five bridges, and support for community airports
MANITOBA	Manitoba Infrastructure and Transportation (MIT) responsible for more than $11 billion in infrastructure assets Multiple overall mandates including 19,000 km of roads, water control, twenty-two northern remote airports, and the Emergency Measures Organization	Vision: A unified department proactively leading the delivery of excellent and sustainable public infrastructure and services for Manitoba Mission: To enable economic prosperity and social well being for Manitobans through partnership and integrated stewardship of safe, reliable, and efficient infrastructure, transportation, and logistics services Integrate sustainable development principles and guidelines into all aspects of department's programs and activities	Highways and Transportation Act Highways Protection Act Highway Traffic Act Provincial Railways Act Red River Floodway Act Sustainable Development Act Crown Lands Act (plus twenty other acts).	Restoration of 2011 flood-damaged infrastructure including flood-damaged water control infrastructure Implementation of recommendations from the Independent Flood Review Task Force report Support trade activities and development along the midcontinent trade corridor and the Manitoba international gateway strategy, linked to global supply-chain-based commerce

Table 1.1
Provincial transport policy and governance: A comparative look (*continued*)

Province	Ministry	Policy mandate ideas	Core laws	Process issues and events
ONTARIO	Ministry of Transportation Affiliated with a number of agencies, which are independent bodies and not a part of the ministry, including Metrolinx, created to improve the coordination and integration of all modes of transport in the Greater Toronto and Hamilton areas, and the Ontario Highway Transport Board	Strives to be a world leader in moving people and goods safely, efficiently, and sustainably to support a globally competitive economy and a high quality of life Premier's mandate letter to the minister leads off by saying that the minister "will support *Moving Ontario Forward*, our 10-year transit and transportation strategy." Specific priorities include "building the next generation of transit and transportation infrastructure," "developing a transportation framework," and "strengthening road safety"	Highway Traffic Act Ontario Highway Transportation Board Act Dangerous Goods Transportation Act Metrolinx Act Shortline Railways Act Ontarians with Disabilities Act Motorized Snow Vehicles Act Ambulance Act	Strong links via Moving Ontario Forward process led by the minister of Economic Development, Employment, and Infrastructure Infrastructure consultation in 2015 for regions outside the Greater Toronto and Hamilton areas
QUEBEC	Transports Québec (Ministry of Transport of Québec) Includes Société de l'assurance automobile (SAAQ)	Ministry's most recent strategic plan focuses on transport infrastructure including investment in several designated routes in the 2015–17 period; planning more integrated transport, including contributing more to the accessibility and vitality of communities; electrification and climate change; and transport security	Transport Act Automobile Insurance Act Highway Safety Code Act respecting the Société de l'assurance automobile Act Respecting Owners, Operators, and Drivers of Heavy Vehicles	New action plan on electrification of transport 2015–20 2015 initiative on industries for transport by taxi and for research on innovation solutions

Jurisdiction	Department / Agency	Mandate / Mission	Legislation	New processes or initiatives
QUEBEC (*continued*)		Continuing mandate responsibility for provincial highways, maintenance of roads and bridges, and driver licensing	Act Respecting Transportation Services by Taxi; Environmental Quality Act	
NOVA SCOTIA	Transportation and Infrastructure Renewal (TIR) (dual mandate)	Mission: Deliver quality public infrastructure for Nova Scotia; Mandate: Provide a transportation network for the safe and efficient movement of people and goods; serve the building needs of government departments and agencies; Strategic outcome goals include enhanced value and safety of the transportation system in support of provincial economic growth, and effective and efficient construction of government buildings and other public works infrastructure	Public Highways Act; Railways Act; Off-highways Vehicles Act; Motor Carrier Act; Motor Vehicles Act	Support for three new sustainable transportation projects in Halifax Regional Municipality that help connect residents and visitors to community hubs and promote active living
NEW BRUNSWICK	Department of Transportation and Infrastructure (DTI); Responsible for The New Brunswick Highway Corporation (crown corporation)	Mission: To build and maintain safe and sustainable building and transportation infrastructure for the people of New Brunswick; Operates and maintains 18,785 km of highway, connected to 3,212 bridges and ten ferries	Highway Act; Motor Carrier Act; Public Landings Act; Public Works Act; Shortline Railways Act	No new processes or initiatives evident

Province	Ministry	Policy mandate ideas	Core laws	Process issues and events
NEW BRUNSWICK (*continued*)	DTI was created in 2012 as a result of a merger between the former Department of Transport and a portion of the Department of Supply and Services	Responsible for 355 provincial government-owned buildings		
PRINCE EDWARD ISLAND	Department of Transportation, Infrastructure and Energy (energy added recently; before that it was Department of Transportation and Infrastructure Renewal) (multiple mandates)	Vision: Leading in the delivery of safe and efficient infrastructure and services Mission: To serve the public and government by providing professional services to develop, deliver, operate, and maintain public infrastructure in a manner that emphasizes quality, safety, cost-effectiveness, and environmental responsibility 2012–15 Strategic Plan and related framework has six guiding principles that have led to focus on six strategic goals including enhance safety, promote environmental stewardship, and adapt to changing demographics	Highway Traffic Act Public Work's Act Dangerous Goods (Transportation) Act Off-Highway Vehicle Act Roads Act Land Survey Act Oil and Natural Gas Act Mineral Resources Act Renewable Energy Act Expropriation Act	Energy part of the mandate not yet fully reflected in values, plans, and strategies

| NEWFOUNDLAND AND LABRADOR | Department of Transportation and Works (dual – in fact, multiple – mandates) | Vision: A safe, reliable, and sustainable transportation and public works infrastructure, and services demonstrating the department's commitment to service excellence in supporting the social and economic needs of Newfoundland and Labrador

Mission: As per 2014–17 Strategic Plan, with greater emphasis on service delivery and service excellence

Responsible for transportation; transportation infrastructure re. provincial roads; marine passenger, vehicle, and freight services; and provincial airstrips, air ambulance, and forest fire suppression services and other air services | Transportation and Works Act*
Executive Council Act
Highway Traffic Act*
Expropriation Act
Local Road Boards Act
Motor Carrier Act*
Rail Service Act

*shared with Government Services | Minister's Advisory Committee on Labrador Transportation (e.g., 2015 consultations and report on Marine Services)

Shared commitments and related consultations with other government departments and communities on infrastructure renewal in fields of health care and also schools, climate change, and energy efficiency |

requirements – in particular, how to attract private funding for infrastructure projects" (Conference Board of Canada 2015, 1). It (the centre) says the second most immediate challenge is how to prioritize infrastructure projects (ibid.).

Any such challenges, including those for the current Trudeau Liberal government, ultimately have to deal with the persistent retail politics of infrastructure budgets and their allocation, both in general and among competing transport modes and multiple federal-provincial-city geographies and regions (Doern, Auld, and Stoney 2015). There are also several dimensions tied to public budgeting of a temporal kind (Doern, Maslove, and Prince 2013, 214–17). The first is that public sector budgeting does not make useful accounting distinctions between capital and operational spending the way private companies do. Assets and related capital items are neither costed nor shown with annual depreciation allowances over their useful life. Instead, they are typically shown as a once-only disbursement. As a result, governments fail to remind themselves through their financial accounting practices of the need to set aside money every year to eventually recapitalize the infrastructure they have already built. In other words, the political attractiveness of building new infrastructure is allowed to trump the humble practical reality of keeping the existing stock in decent repair.

Clearly there are difficulties in assigning monetary value to public assets and in assigning depreciation and replacement capital costs. And there can be little doubt that the basic method of financial accounting in current use significantly distorts not only the way in which deficits and surpluses are reported and debated politically and economically but also the way in which basic decisions are made in government and are understood by Canadian citizens, voters, and taxpayers. Many kinds of decisions and forms of spending simply do not get treated or analyzed as if they were investment decisions, even though they absolutely should be, because they clearly involve capital assets. Instead, they are accounted for as if they were consumption-based or what financial managers would call "current" expenditures.

It would not be hard to identify physical/capital assets for transportation with an expected stream of long-term benefits and utility, such as ports, bridges, highways, railways, and airports (Gaudreault and Lemire 2003). Other assets like hospitals, sporting and cultural facilities, and university research assets qualify, too. But despite their indisputable character in this regard, they are being treated less and less like it. Large publicly funded infrastructure initiatives have become more commonplace in recent years. Infrastructure Canada was established to give tangible expression to supporting the capital asset needs of Canadian cities and communities (Infrastructure Canada 2015). But such funding is treated like normal government "spending." The spending tempo grew during the (2008–14) recession with the then Harper government's economic stimulus program and its parade of "shovel ready" projects.

Notions of capital, the discourse of "investments," and concepts of long asset-based time periods in budgetary politics extend well beyond the idea of physical capital. They also encompass ideas of human, social, and natural or environmental capital. The lifecycle of these assets is usually measured in human generations. In each realm of these extended conceptions of "capital," there is legitimacy for the underlying ideas in the use of public funds, but there are serious ambiguities of definition and problems of measurement. And it is often hard to detect whether valid needs (as opposed to less valid ones) materialize in concrete spending and tax decisions or program innovation and structure. For example, are "shovel ready" projects the most valuable ones when it comes to allocating money to new infrastructure? No one knows. In other words, the analysis behind the expenditures is anything but transparent. That does not help support the disciplined improvement of the socioeconomic basis of infrastructure as long-term assets. On the contrary, it tends to subvert it.

As mentioned in this book's introduction, Transport Canada's annual reports make a link between each transport mode's "economic marketplace" and the infrastructure it uses. But what "infrastructure" actually is, is highly varied and surprisingly ill defined. Each mode gets its infrastructure funding from a variety of federal budgets and programs but it is not clear to anyone to what extent the federal funds constitute investments in a genuine capital-asset sense or simply represent "government spending," in the retail-politics sense of that phrase. Public policy is not well served by the opacity.

Infrastructure Canada's reports of its priorities and plans (Infrastructure Canada 2015) reveal the complexity and the inherent distributive politics of its spending. That makes for a world in which the transport sector has to manoeuver and hopefully "scheme virtuously" if it is to access much or any of the money. In chapter 8 we demonstrate the flexibility afforded to municipalities in trolling for federal dollars. Infrastructure Canada's funding is broken down into six programs. They are not unreasonably defined but they are highly arbitrary. The groupings are provincial–territorial priorities, permanent and flexible infrastructure funding, investments in national infrastructure priorities, large-scale infrastructure investments, infrastructure investments in small communities and rural areas, and a new bridge for the St Lawrence Corridor Project. The last of these – and the only one in which transport is given any emphasis – was of particular interest to the then Harper Conservative government minister in charge of Infrastructure Canada. All the other programs were the products of lobbying and advocacy, and subject to exercises in superficial categorization and relabeling. In short, it is not just ministers who practice the arts of infrastructure politics as short-term "spending" versus long-term asset "investment" policy but also the constituents and interest groups whose projects receive the money – or who would like to. So both the dispensers and recipients of the funds have a shared interest in obfuscating the grounds on which the financial transfers are actually made.

Cities and Urban Government Structure and the Presence of Transport Organization

Earlier we drew attention to cities in relation to *ideas* about multi-level governance within which transportation may or may not be conceptually related. In this section, we need to look briefly at city and urban government structure *per se*. How are city governments actually organized and what might this tell us about transportation? There is very little comparative analysis at this level, and so our sources here involve a brief and only illustrative look at two midsized cities, Winnipeg and Halifax, via their websites to see how they describe their structure of government departments and, within that structure, how transport is presented, either directly as "transportation" or in other ways or perhaps not at all. Both cities refer to the roles of the elected mayor and the elected city council, but here we focus on government structure departmentally and organizationally. Our range of cities examined increases in the domain analyses in chapters 7, 8, 9, and 10 and includes Canada's largest cities such as Toronto, Vancouver, and Montreal but also major cities such as Edmonton and Ottawa.

The City of Winnipeg (2016) directs its citizens and voters to a set of fourteen "departments." These include water and waste, residential assessment, libraries, and permits and licenses. There is no department of transportation, but there are separate departments for "parking" and for "major projects" and reference is also made to "public works," which covers information and programs such as snow hauling and disposal, lane closures, and parks and open spaces. Traffic control information is also featured. The Public Works Department receives considerable attention and more detailed information about things like current major projects, past projects, construction studies, and capital projects. The city also lists forty-three boards and commissions over which City Council has delegated management responsibilities. These include the Taxicab Board of Manitoba and the Winnipeg Airports Authority Board.

Transport aspects can be found, but city transportation policy does not leap out as a central departmental feature. Still, the city has published a Transportation Master Plan (TMP) (Winnipeg 2011). It is "intended to set out a strategic vision for transportation in Winnipeg over the next two decades (to 2031). It will ensure that future transportation needs for an integrated network of highways, roads, rapid and conventional transit, cycling and pedestrian facilities can be planned and budgeted for" (ibid., 3). The TMP's strategic goals are a transportation system that is "dynamically integrated with land use; supports active, accessible, and healthy lifestyle options; a safe, efficient and equitable transportation system for people, goods, and services; transportation infrastructure that is well maintained; and a transportation system that is financially sustainable" (ibid.). That doesn't leave much out.

Halifax Regional Municipality is an amalgamated regional city government (Halifax Municipal Government 2016a). Its "government" listing is highly administrative in nature because it is under two other lists. Various government programs and services are highlighted, including a "residents" list and a "business" list. The sixteen programs/functions for residents include culture and heritage; police, fire and emergency; and garbage and recycling; and what seem to be "transport" terms like programs for "getting around," construction projects, streets, sidewalks, and parking (ibid., 2). Under the "business" list, there are programs and services such as building and construction permits; business permits and licenses; and "planning and development." (ibid., 3). Curiously, a transport-related section of its website is not called Transport but rather "streets, sidewalks & municipal infrastructure" (City of Halifax 2016b), and its lead statement is that "every day tens of thousands of residents and visitors travel on streets and sidewalks across the Halifax region. It is up to the municipality to ensure that infrastructure is safe and responsive to the needs of all users" (ibid., 1). If that means "mobility" – an overriding purpose of transportation – it is well disguised.

Like the Winnipeg example, the Halifax story also shows a more explicit reference to transportation *per se* in a separate planning document. In the Halifax case, however, it is one that is focused on Making Connections: 2014–19 Halifax Active Transportation Planning Priorities Plan (City of Halifax 2014). The plan states that the "municipality will take (measures) to increase walking and bicycling trips" and "to increase the number of residents who travel by sustainable transportation modes" (ibid.), hence the "active" designation in the plan's title.

Shared-Governance Organizations

Transport Canada draws attention to a further key part of the transport governance structure, namely the forty-two shared-governance organizations under Canada Port Authorities and Canadian Airport Authorities (Transport Canada 2015). These organizations manage and make policy for airports and ports as well as other assets that are vital parts of transport corridors like the St Lawrence Seaway (see chapter 3). They are also tied into transport gateway initiatives highlighted separately in Transport Canada's annual state-of-transport reports. This is a shared-governance system that clearly flows from the embedded socioeconomic values of transportation policy and governance, particularly as it is reflected in the not-for-profit nature of the organizations. Their mandates and the expertise they need in order to function in the public interest, as well as to discharge their duties as public assets, go well beyond commercial imperatives, even though they function in markets, supply chain, and gateway contexts. The intermixing makes for some interesting bedfellows.

It is fair to say that there has been no systematic assessment of this forty-two-entity shared-governance realm. The collection was established gradually, starting in the 1990s and expanded with continuing federal ownership of the entities. It was created using a model designed to make the collection much less government-run. When the 2001 CTA review panel looked at the forty-two-entity collection, it titled the chapter of its report as the governance of "newly commercialized infrastructure providers" (Canada Transportation Act Review Panel 2001, 149). There were certainly commercialization instincts and goals implied in their DNA, but the chapter toned down the implications of that by stressing that these new providers were "non-share corporations that cannot raise equity capital and must rely on fees and debt to finance their activities" (ibid., 149) and that "the government has attempted to give these new entities the means to achieve financial self-sufficiency and to give interested parties, including users and community groups, opportunities for input on their decisions" (ibid., 149–50).

The authors of this book have, for this conceptual foundations chapter, sampled some of the reports of some of these authorities. One example is the Greater Toronto Airports Authority (GTAA) 2014. Although anchored around the *operational functioning* of Pearson airport, the GTAA has a broad socioeconomic mandate as well. It was incorporated in 1993 as a nonshare capital corporation, but in 2014 it was "transitioned to the *Canada Not for Profit Corporations Act*" (ibid., 25). It functions without share capital and has "[m]embers rather than shareholders or other equity holders" (ibid.). It reports publicly and engages regularly with groups and local governments impacted and shaped by airports (and other related transport modes) in the area. Some bodies such as the Canadian Airports Council (2015) have some general knowledge of the workings of many airport authorities, but this forty-two-entity realm is only beginning to be examined in more depth, as we see in chapter 7 on the air transport and shared-governance domain.

Business and Corporate Power

Claims about democratic governance in any policy field, including transportation policy, have to contend with at least five arenas and kinds of democracy and various notions of democratic deficits, imperfections, and power (Lenard and Simeon 2013; Doern and Prince 2012; Dryzek and Dunleavy 2009; Pal 2014). They are defined briefly in our book's introduction: 1) representative democracy, 2) federalized democracy, 3) interest group pluralism, 4) civil society democracy, and 5) direct democracy.

Business and corporate power is invested partly in interest-group pluralism. But it is typically discussed in terms of the more privileged advantages of corporations in Canadian and international capitalist economic systems. Transport lobbies and power systems concentrate their attention on federal and provincial transport ministries, but they also have good access to other ministries and centres of cabinet power – the prime minister, and ministers of finance, industry, agriculture, natural resources, and, increasingly of course, of infrastructure.

To the best of our knowledge there is no systematic or complete analytical literature on Canadian transport business and corporate power as exercised by individual transport corporations or transport interest groups and associations. There are accounts of corporate power and influence of individual firms such as CPR and CN in rail transport. The former was pivotal in nation building terms under Prime Minister Sir John A. Macdonald and the latter when CN was formed as a public enterprise (Stevenson 1981) and then later in a very different way when CN was privatized in the 1990s (Gwyn 2011; Murray 2011; Doern and Phidd 1992). And of course CP and CN continue to have privileged access as oligopoly or duopoly firms in the freight rail industry. Even so, the extent of their political power in specific situations is difficult to gauge. Shipper lobbies, and in particular the Western grain lobbies, are also wielders of power as later chapters will show.

The same corporate power structure is evident with firms in the airline industry and air transport equipment manufacturing. Air Canada (Pigott 2014; Milton 2004; Langford 1981), Pacific Western Airlines (Tupper 1981), and now Westjet and also Porter are influential carriers, most of them regional. Bombardier as a multimodal economic and technological player in rail and aircraft manufacturing is also pivotal (Hadkel 2004; MacDonald 2001). The auto manufacturing sector also has power but not so much with transport ministries as with trade and economic ministries. This extends back in time to the Auto Pact with the US, the Canada–US free trade agreement, and the recent auto bailout during the 2008–12 recession (Doern and Tomlin 1990; Waddell 2010).

With regard to transport interest groups and associations in the role of lobbyists and players, probably the best sense of their number and diversity emerges during the periodic public consultation processes by Canada Transport Act review panels. Various groups submit briefs and reports to the panel, including unions and organized labour, and employee associations. These are made public. In the recent 2014–15 review panel process, there were all manner of submissions from across-the-board business associations such as the Business Council of Canada (formerly the Council of Chief Executives) and the Canadian Chamber of Commerce, and from modal associations such as the Railway Association of Canada, the Air Transport Association, the Association of Canadian Port Authorities, the Canadian Trucking Alliance, the Canadian Shipowners Association, and the Freight Management Association. More than 200 submissions reached the review panel, with most submitted by far from organized transport interest groups at all levels – federal, provincial, and urban/local (Canada 2015).

In addition there are associations, firms, and entities involved in more particular transport product markets including Bombardier Recreational Products (2016), the Canadian Recreational Vehicle Association (2016), and the National Recreational Boating Advisory Council (2016). Spanning virtually all transport modes are Canada's tourism industries (Industry Canada 2015) and the Tourism Industry Association of Canada (2015), which has broad concerns about travel, pricing, safety, and security and how Canada's tourism markets are faring, competing, and changing in relation to international and Canada–US tourism routes and destinations.

Of course, we cannot analyse all of these entities, but some are discussed in our later domain chapters including the varied positions and roles of labour and employees. What can be said at this stage is that this interest-group structure is complex and multilevel in nature, and even this brief inventory still does not specifically include the forty-two shared-governance authorities mentioned earlier, which both lobby actively themselves and are the object of lobbying and engagement by numerous other players.

Network governance has received growing analytical attention in the study of economic and social institutions, and thus it holds considerable importance for understanding contemporary debates on transport policy content, consequences, and governance. We take note of them briefly here, but they also emerge in discussion in the third stream of conceptual foundations, the one tied to technology, multimodal dynamics, and supply chain and logistics imperatives.

In political and policy analysis, some authors cast networks as a particular feature of broader arrays in a world of "policy communities" (Coleman and Skogstad 1990). They were conceived as an analytical category that went beyond traditional interest or lobby groups to embrace broader nongovernmental organizations (NGOs). Later analyses broadened the concept of networks to encompass various kinds of scientific expertise and the roles of universities (Howlett and Ramesh 2003; Montpetit 2009). In economic and related fields, however, networks are being analysed in a much broader context, often by contrasting them with markets and hierarchies as basic modes of social and economic organization (Agranoff 2007; Thompson et al. 1991).

Hierarchies are associated with bureaucracy, especially traditional Weberian state bureaucracy. They are systems of top-down, superior–subordinate political and administrative relations accompanied by formal rules, with many forms of civil service bureaucracies whose role is to support representative cabinet–parliamentary and other systems of democratic government (Aucoin 1997). Markets are organized on the basis of "voluntary" means of exchange involving money, commerce, and the making of profits but with the state providing and enforcing key rules and protections for property rights and transactions. Networks differ from both of the above: they are forms of organization characterized by nonhierarchical and voluntary relations based on trust, and commonality of shared interests and values, where profit is not necessarily a defining characteristic (Agranoff 2007; Thompson et al. 1991). Hierarchies, markets, and networks are being increasingly combined by the players in them in very complex and creative ways.

Some attributes of networks as an institutional concept are expressed in terms of constructing partnerships. These include transportation partnerships. They can be truly voluntary in nature, but more often they take on the form of policy-induced or policy-required and contractual (or quasi-contractual) partnerships between or among public- and private-sector entities and interest groups. In this context, networks are similar to, or criss-cross with, supply chains and logistic functions. They also often acquire some of the characteristics inherent in markets or hierarchies (Kinder 2010), and they are a key part of theories of regulatory capitalism and regulatory breakdown where coregulation is the norm. We discuss this further below.

Regulatory Governance: Deregulation, Regulatory Capitalism, and Rules and Unruliness

We have already entered this analytical realm in our brief initial discussion about free trade and the regulation of international trade agreements. Here we draw out transportation issues but also other areas where regulation of various kinds has been reduced, increased, and changed. Beginning with the National Transportation Act of 1967 and then further advanced by the 1985 Freedom to Move framework

(Canada 1985), the rail sector was significantly deregulated in economic terms and the regulatory burden on railways significantly declined as a result. Revisions to the law in 1988 and 1996 continued this trend (Hill 1999; Waters and Stanbury 1999; Heaver 1990). Significant deregulation was also occurring over the same period in telecommunications and energy. During the 1960s, 70s, and 80s the railways lost significant market share to other modes, primarily trucking, but certain types of cargo did not (and could not) shift in that direction, and so the railways continue to carry it. This means that much existing rail traffic is inherently "rail-based," and shippers of those products have few if any affordable transportation alternatives. But not all of it is. The railways have built a significant amount of business transporting intermodal containers that usually carry high-value manufactured goods (Canada 2011). Some of this could go by truck. The customers, often large retailers, tend to be more satisfied than other customer groups with their rail carriers in terms of both price and service. The same is true of passenger automobiles. Carmakers ship most of their newly manufactured vehicles to market by rail, even though many of them could go by truck.

One possible reason for this greater satisfaction is the presence of competition in these markets and the railways' response to it. Railways are efficient at moving goods over long distances from A to B but much less so in servicing locally – when they are actually *at* A or B. This means that most service problems seen by shippers are "first-mile/last-mile" in nature. For example, railways work 24/7 on their main lines but not on branch lines or switching leads where pick-ups and deliveries occur. The service problems seen by shippers are sometimes not network-based but local servicing (Canada 2011). Thus deregulation worked for some players but not for others, and not all the time.

It may be tempting to argue that the era of economic deregulation continues in the Canadian economy but, strictly speaking, this has not been true for the past twenty years in Canada or in many other countries either. Some scholars have cast this era, quite accurately in our opinion, as one with a strong element of what has become known as regulatory capitalism. The concept emerged both conceptually and empirically (Braithwaite 2008, 2005; Levi-Faur 2005). It involves large numbers of companies in setting and enforcing rules over the behaviour of their respective industry sectors and the players in them. Enforcement usually consists of applying marketplace tools. Granting or withholding influential certifications is one of many examples. It reflects the fact that regulation is growing markedly, but not so much by rules and their enforcement by governments alone but increasingly as a system of coregulation that involves governments and businesses, and nongovernment interests and networks as well (Grabosky 2012). The distributed (and often unruly) nature of this coregulation does not mean it is any less authoritative than government rule making and enforcement alone. And it provides a wider range of tools for dealing with complex situations, including those which governments acting alone as regulators often have difficulty discovering or using. In short, the marketplace can often be more creative and nimble at this sort of thing than governments can be when enacting statutes and standards that normally have to pass a broader range of tests and hurdles than those which accompany business-to-business deal-ings. But the previously cited research published in the US focused on *Designing Safety Regulation for High-Hazard Industries* (National Academies of Sciences, Engineering and Medicine 2017; Coglianese and Menzies 2017) is relevant here. As we have seen, the study focused on the "salient design features that follow from the macro–micro and means–ends distinctions" that suggest "four basic regulatory design types; micro-means; micro-ends, macro-means and macro-ends" (Coglianese and Menzies 2017, 3).

A review of fifty years of Canadian regulation by Doern, Prince, and Schultz (2014) demonstrated that recent history can be character-ized by the growth of rules and unruliness. Research by Coglianese (2012) is centred on the US system in terms of growing "regulatory breakdown." When it comes to systems of governance, unruliness consists of a growing inability on the part of governments in concert with businesses and other social interests and partners to make effec-tive rules and to enforce them. Regulation also extends well beyond statutes and delegated law. It also includes codes, guidelines, and standards, both domestic and international.

Transport Royal Commissions and Review Panels on the Canadian Transportation Act

The role and dynamics of Royal Commissions and review panels on transportation have been mentioned earlier, but we refer to them now in two additional ways: as arm's length policy engagement vehicles and as research and study processes that draw in various interests and communities. The Royal Commission on Transportation (the MacPherson Commission) (1961, 1962) conducted its work and hearings over a three-year period. It was appointed by the Diefenbaker Conservative government in 1959 and led to the passage, under the later Pearson Liberals, of the National Transportation Act in 1967, Canada's first overarching transportation policy. Among its products was the creation of a new, multimodal Canadian Transportation Commission (Heaver 2009; McGuire 2004; Gratwick 2001; Currie 1967). As it took stock of transport in the context of a changing Canadian economy, the MacPherson Commission shifted the focus way from regulating railways in isolation and toward issues of competition among modes, especially trucking (Madar, 2000). It also supported the need for railways to be able to abandon uneconomic rural rail lines in a considerably less protracted process than before.

There had been other forays in a similar vein. The Royal Commission on Canada's Economic Prospects (the Gordon Commission) (1956) had a separate chapter on transportation, which expressed similar kinds of ideas, but they were not given legislative effect. And much later, in 1985, the Royal Commission on Economic Union and Canada's Development Prospects (1985) (the MacDonald Commission) – probably best known for the impetus it provided on the eventual Canada–US free trade agreement – also advocated measures for internal free trade. And later, the 1994 Agreement on Internal Trade (AIT) had a chapter on transportation that called for the greater opening of interprovincial transport markets by reducing existing rules and providing for dispute settlement measures (Doern and MacDonald 1999). Such broadly based Royal Commissions were augmented by more focused reviews such as the 1998 grain handling and transportation review headed by Willard Estey (1998).

The Canada Transportation Act review panels are the result of statutory requirements for periodic policy review, a relatively rare institutional concept. Most other statutory reviews are associated with the Bank Act. Much like Royal Commissions, but functioning at a faster pace, the transport reviews are ostensibly about the Canada Transportation Act alone, but in fact they are much broader than that. Like earlier Royal Commissions, they seek to put transportation policy in new and different contexts, and they suggest policies and ways of dealing with them over the coming decade or so. The Canada Transportation Act review panel (2001) report, *Vision and Balance*, saw the context for its review (and for national policy) as residing in several "pressures and challenges" including globalization and North

American economic integration, weak commodity prices, tighter controls on public spending, the internet and e-business; environmental concerns, and urbanization (ibid., 9–12). These were factored into a model for decision-making based on a "modal perspective" that involved rail, road, air, water, and urban transportation.

The Canada Transportation Act review (2015) received and considered 230 briefs and submissions from all kinds of transport interests and players, and it commissioned thirty-six research papers. Titled *Pathways: Connecting Canada's Transportation System to the World*, its report stressed that "it looks at the kind of global environment in which Canada will find itself 30 years from now. It aims to provide both a navigational beacon for enlightened development of the transportation system and critical actions required now to give Canadians the best possible shot at success" (ibid., 4). It stressed that it has "concentrated primarily on economic concerns. The Review has not examined security and safety on a systematic basis" (ibid.). Its central theme is that,

> in a world of massive and complex webs of interconnectedness, the quality of transportation and logistics systems may be the single greatest contributor to a country's economic performance. With rapid, often dramatic change as a modern constant, transportation investment is more complex and regulatory time frames longer and more demanding than ever. Ten or twenty years from inception to operational conclusion is increasingly the norm for major infrastructure projects or major framework changes.
> (Ibid., 4–5)

Indeed, the report's central premise and, as we see in chapter 4, its key macrogovernance reform recommendations stressed that the transportation system could no longer wait fifteen years for another review, and in effect new governance reforms ought to make this review the last one Canada should or would need (ibid., 5). We examine and critique some of the review's themes and recommendations in several domain chapters.

Transportation Policy Agenda Setting

Among the most complex and interesting elements of policy and governance dynamics is that of transportation policy agenda setting.

It needs to be seen in the context of broader conceptual theories of agenda setting. They are built around the complex interactions between politicians and policy makers, the media, and the public. They arise from the issue–attention cycle by which all the different players – voters, citizens, the mass media, and even governments themselves –engage in framing and reframing problems and opportunities (Eisler, Russell, and Jones 2014; Wolfe, Jones, and Baumgartner 2013; Howlett 1998; Kingdon 1993). But the dynamic nature of the system and the collective inability of people to sustain focus and interest on most (or perhaps any) issues leads to "punctuated equilibria," a phenomenon in which most policy stays stable for long periods, while, in a punctuated fashion, some policies change quickly and dramatically (Baumgartner and Jones 1993; Jones and Baumgartner 2005, 2012).

Public opinion research adds to the picture of transportation agenda setting. Environics polling has repeatedly asked a sample of Canadians what, in their opinion, was the most important problem facing Canada. The responses show some interesting results for the period from 1987 to 2011. They are captured in twenty-five polls spanning the last half of the Mulroney era and all of the Chrétien–Martin and Harper years until 2011 (Canadian Opinion Research Archive 2013). In them, transportation policy is rarely even mentioned in response to this question. It is not even offered as a possible concern in a list of twenty to thirty possible or likely expected issues used as prompts by the pollsters. The economy and jobs are floated as possible responses. So are health care and national unity. Those tend to garner the highest responses, varying in magnitude only by year. The environment and even the B S E/mad cow crisis made appearances. But not transportation.

A different type of question was asked: "Do you think Canada is spending too much, just the right amount, or should be spending more on 'transportation services'?" This question was asked every year from 1987 to 2010. The "too much" response hovered around the 12 to 16 per cent range over the period. The "just right" response in both the Mulroney and Chrétien–Martin years ranged in the 50 to 60 per cent area until 2000, but declined in the 2003 to 2010 period to the mid-30 per cent range. The "should spend more" response rose to the 60 per cent range in the mainly Harper years from 2004 to 2010 (Canadian Opinion Research Archive 2015).

These kinds of polling data suggest a very oddly mixed picture. And they raise some concerns about the type of questions posed or even not posed. It is by no means clear that Canadians would have any way of actually knowing whether spending was too much, too little, or just right. The reported opinions could easily be more a reflection of whether or not a government was "handling transport appropriately." In other words, public perception – and the agenda setting it partly drives – is probably not based on anything that reflects the actual performance of the transportation system in an economic (or any other quantitative) respect. To a lot of people in a world of growing disregard for reality, if it feels right it must be right. We address these kinds of agenda-setting dynamics and puzzles in chapter 2, in our discussion of prime ministerial eras, and their throne speech and budget speech content and dynamics.

TECHNOLOGY, INNOVATION, DISRUPTION, AND MULTIMODAL SUPPLY CHAIN AND LOGISTICS COMPLEXITIES, RESPONSES, AND CONSTRAINTS

This is the third stream in which we explore the foundational literature. It is based on technology-driven and technology and innovation-enabled developments examined in the diverse literature such as (Doern, Castle, and Phillips 2016; Christensen, Raynor, and McDonald 2015; Nagy, Schuuessier, and Dubinisky 2016: Phillips 2007). These and other analyses discussed below bring out developments and discourse such as disruptive innovation, disruptive technology, innovation, and innovation systems and transformative technology, and innovation that arises quickly and with fast moving impacts and slower uncertain or very experimental policy, regulatory and governance impacts within and among national multilevel governance systems and vis-à-vis other countries.

The analysis by Nagy, Schuuessier, and Dubinisky (2016) in important but more particular ways asks key questions about disruptive innovation not sufficiently addressed by the competing approaches. It asks more explicitly questions such as "First what is a disruptive innovation? Second how can a disruptive innovation be disruptive to some and yet sustaining to others? and third how can disruptive innovations be identified before a disruption has occurred in an organization." Our final domain analysis in chapter 10 accurately has "disruptive" in its title but other domain chapters have components of innovation, technology, and disruption and related speed and regulatory and other response dilemmas including after transport accidents such as the Lac-Mégantic crash examined in chapter 9, earlier airline accidents in chapter 4, airport safety and security as new aircraft types emerge in chapter 7, mobility technology needs and developments and delays in chapter 8, and transport policy and governance responses in the face of new environmental impacts in chapter 9 on dangerous goods regulation. We are interested in how these developments play out in single and cross-modal transportation contexts. We are also interested in the constraints and complexities of supply chains and logistics, and whether policy makers and regulators have the capacities to assess and act with the needed kinds of technical and market expertise which can be mobilized and used in practical situations and with varied claims to democratic and governance competence as well.

As mentioned in the book's introduction, all transport modes are, first and foremost, the embodiment and expression of technologies – indeed, multiple and changing technologies, technology platforms, and technology packages. The propensity of technology to change is a major source of complexity in transportation policy because policy is often left struggling to catch up. And the technology is often not at the core of what is normally considered "transportation." In some cases, the most influential technology is not easily distinguishable from other kinds of science- and knowledge-based innovation operating at the periphery of transportation, like the internet and modern social media. Hall (1999, 1–2), for example, argues that,

> Transportation can be defined as a science discipline that transcends transportation technology and methods. Whether by car, truck, airplane – or by a mode of transport that has not yet been conceived ... transportation obeys fundamental properties. The science of transportation defines these properties and demonstrates how our knowledge of a mode of transportation can be used to explain the behaviour of another.

There is some validity to this argument, but the effect of science on transportation probably is less than that of transport policy and governance – especially in light of the complexity of intermodal dependencies and supply-chain dynamics. There is not a lot of agreement on this subject in the literature. It seems to depend on the academic disciplines through whose eyes each author perceives things and what he or she chooses to include, emphasize, or leave out. For example, in a work that both analyzes and favours urban bicycling – which is the embodiment of a certain technology – Fentus (2012) examines the concept of "effective speed" and argues that cycling is actually faster than the alternatives. Furth (2012) argues for the importance of bicycle infrastructure to encourage mass cycling. Authors who focus on sustainable transportation (e.g., Schiller, Bruun, and Kenworthy 2010) show historically how cities can be compared and characterized as walking cities, transit cities, and automobile cities, and also how some have gone from walking to wheels and back to walking. These represent the waxing and waning of various individual technology platforms.

Technology Assessment and Transformative and Disruptive Technologies

To be of much ultimate value, case studies, including the ones above, need to be related to broader principles and issues, often found in the literature. We turn now to the evolving discipline of technology assessment and the evaluation of transformative and disruptive technologies and innovation. Formal calls for better technology-assessment institutions and processes emerged after World War II, when the accelerating pace of technology development suggested that society and politics needed to assess them and their benefits and their potential adverse impacts *before* they emerged in the form of new products and production processes (Nordman 2004). Several high profile cases arose in the late 1960s and early 1970s, including in transportation, for example, over the benefits and disbenefits of supersonic passenger aircraft. The United States established the Congressional Office of Technology Assessment (OTA) in 1972. It published numerous technology assessments but was abolished in 1995 in the wake of a Republican victory in the midterm elections in 1994 (Mooney 2005; Nye 2006). Its demise was due less to its usefulness and relevance from a public policy standpoint, than it was to sharp partisan politics by a (conservative-dominated) Congress which was portrayed as "anti-science" as well as being opposed to government intervention of the kind implied in technology-assessment processes initiated and sponsored by government.

Canada has never had as formal an effort to undertake prospective technological assessments as a matter of public policy; nevertheless, it tried in its own way to build capacity, for example via the establishment of the Science Council of Canada, although, as in the US, that capacity has subsequently been atrophied. Technology assessment institutions and issues continue to be examined through international bodies, for instance the International Association for Technology Assessment and Forecast Institutions and various university institutes. Academic and think tank literature and journals remain active, but it is not clear what net effect the assessments actually have had by way of influencing public policy in transportation.

Transformative and disruptive technologies tend to define those periods of time and development in which economies and societies are remade by changes in foundational technology. This idea is closely linked to Schumpeter's powerful concept of "creative destruction" (Schumpeter 1954, 1934). The concept of disruptive technologies has found its way into analytical use, including by describing and characterizing intertwined technologies like digital technology, nanotechnology, and the neurosciences, and even smaller kinds of disruption that create new industries and products based on information and data (Zussman 2014). The latter are embodied in online businesses that can grow with astonishing speed (such as the Uber example examined in chapter 10) and quickly become an existential threat to established players in the industry (*Economist* 2014a). Industry Canada has described disruptive technologies as a key presence in the Canadian economy in both a positive and negative sense – and an unavoidable one at that (Industry Canada 2014).

In light of these technologies' profound effect, both positive and negative, a debate began about the need to reengage in a formal technology-foresight process to help guide future developments. Amazingly far-reaching technologies recently have emerged and are combining in unexpected and powerful ways. They find expression in applications that generate both intended and unanticipated consequences for economic affairs, social interactions, and even notions of human identity. They include the internet, information and communications technology, biotechnology, and nanotechnologies, all of which have links to other sectoral technologies, products, and processes in a wide range of industries and social realms (Mazzucato 2013). Many or most such analyses look not just to the future but also to historical developments in terms of strategies of social resistance and how they change the technologies' trajectories and shapes (Bauer 2015).

Phillips (2007) stresses the inherent complexity, multistakeholder-shared relations, and competing nature of the models of governance of contemporary transformative technology. He shows the highly linked stages of innovation. Phillips also cautions against assumptions of unbridled technology determinism. Not surprisingly, these have involved wide-ranging debates about particular products and processes, or at the level of individuals and groups which are actually or potentially harmed by such technologically centred and fast changing features (O'Doherty and Einsiedel 2013). The upshot of all this is that the development of frameworks and practices in technology assessment for public–policy applications is struggling to keep up with the accelerating pace and unruly nature of technological innovation. This includes technologies that are impacting transportation in all kinds of ways.

The Internet and Theories of Complexity

The internet is a defining, dominating, and enabling "technology platform" whose infrastructure has become a crucial engine of, and site for, massive social and economic network formation. It has enabled the design and building of systems of e-commerce and e-governance, and fast-forming kinds of social media such as Google, Facebook, and Twitter. It is the heart of "big data," where data is accumulating at unbelievable rates. An estimated 90 per cent of the world's data and information have been captured in the last five years (Haldane 2013, Etzioni 2013). The internet and its presence via the World Wide Web is transformational in the most utterly profound ways. It is both an infrastructure and a repository of new theories and practices, positive and negative alike, and covers almost all human information and knowledge including scientific data and theory (Naughton 2012; Floridi 2012; Coleman and Blumler 2009).

For all kinds of public and private interests, including transportation carriers, shippers, consumers, labour, and public interest and business lobby groups, the internet has greatly reduced the costs of communication and joint action. It has also opened new avenues for direct democracy by individual citizens, including via social networks (Rainie and Wellman 2012; Borins and Brown 2008). This makes it easier to transact business and influence transportation policy. But it also has multiplied the size and complexity of networks and embedded them with transaction costs and layers of bureaucracy. This is not so much bureaucracy of the hierarchical kind but of a more horizontal, transactional, and vertical kind (Flinders 2008; Doern and Kinder 2007).

Theories of complexity *per se* have been developed and used within the natural sciences and engineering for decades. Some of this has crossed over into work to characterize systems of society and social innovation, where it has become a part of public policy theory in the twenty-first century. Authors like Geyer and Rihani (2012) and Morcol (2012) advocate more use of complexity theory based on their view that too many policy makers and policy scholars treat policy and governance systems as being orderly, predictable, and controllable when in reality they are anything but. Complexity notions have also been needed, as Pal (2014) argues, in matters of policy and decision making because of the need to model chaos in the face of accidents, floods, terrorism, crises, and infrastructure protection. Norberg and Cumming (2012) also use the idea of complexity to analyze sustainable development in a variety of policy fields, and Walby (2007) uses it to examine the nature of what she describes in social policy terms as "multiple intersecting social inequalities."

Indeed, concepts of complexity are a part of the literature on public policy and governance even when complexity theory is not centrally or overtly used. In his analysis of the internet, Naughton (2012) describes complexity as the "new reality," arguing that it is not easy to unpack complexity and hence it is hard to understand or predict (162–3). He also points out that the challenging "architecture" of complexity was initially raised by Nobel economist Herbert Simon (1962) well before the rise of the internet. This extends to innovation policy (economic and social) and the behaviour of network-based clusters, including transportation systems, which embody or display most or all of the features of networks, clusters, and issues surrounding innovation policy. They are thus complex whether anyone has a theory of complexity about them or not.

There are striking parallels between transportation networks and the internet. Both have been overlaid with notions of "common carriage" – with transportation, in terms of moving people and freight without discriminating against one passenger or shipper in favour of another, and with the internet in terms of "transporting" information under what has come to be known as "Internet neutrality." The internet can be traced to the 1966 to 1972 period, when the US Department of Defense developed the ARPANET network. That took more specific shape in 1973 as part of the "internetworking" project led by Vinton Cerf and Robert Kahn, both engineers who had worked on ARPANET before. They advocated two principles that became pivotal for the internet: no central control and internet neutrality. The latter is a premise that the network should not be optimized for any particular application (Leiner, Cerf et al. 2014). The internet (later in combination with the web) is a communications technology that fosters innovation without the need for permission by authorities. Indeed, the internet and the web were themselves created without any government authority's explicit permission.

By design and intent, this kind of unguided structure is chronically disruptive because benign and subversive interactions alike can destabilize markets and society, often by intent. Social movements and NGOs have connected with each other in ways that challenge industry, governments, and societies everywhere. Social media involves massive forms of social production by citizens, groups, and communities at the national, international, and local levels. And the absence of gatekeepers has enabled people with malevolent goals to introduce malware, viruses, and spam and to engage in cybercrime, cyberwarfare, and cyberterrorism (Schneier 2015). This echoes past, and even recent, efforts to sabotage transportation arteries.

There is another parallel with transportation. Concerns about competition policy have emerged in the European Union over the alleged anticompetitive actions of information giants like Google, just as they have over transportation monopolies and oligopolies beginning in the 1800s and continuing to the present.

Transportation and transport policy will continue to be affected by technology tied to internet and digital dynamics. Google is at the forefront of autonomous car development as mentioned earlier. Uber has moved swiftly as a seemingly permissionless disruptive innovation manifesting itself as a business. Other such impacts and dynamics are a part of our domain analysis in part two of the book.

CONCLUSIONS

Drawn from three broad but crucially relevant strands of literature, but also subsets within them and across them, we have set out the conceptual foundations underpinning our analysis of transportation policy, governance, and democracy in Canada. Such conceptual scope is needed all the more so because policy and political governance institutions have been changing rapidly and such scope is needed when one seeks to look at and understand change and inertia in any single policy field such as multi modal transportation across a fifty to sixty-year period and occasionally at even longer ingrained historical periods.

These foundations, Canadian and comparative in nature, and drawing on diverse research disciplines and sources, have informed the development of our analytical framework set out in the book's introduction, and we draw upon them again in our seven domain chapters along with other literature sources more specifically relevant to each domain. Transportation policy and governance is one that consists of complex multimodal content, influenced by and embedded in several linked policy fields and ideas and therefore different political arenas of expression, advocacy both within the federal government and increasingly extending to provincial and especially city/urban governments where most Canadians now live.

2

Canadian Transportation Policy and Agendas In Liberal and Conservative Prime Ministerial Eras

INTRODUCTION

This chapter surveys the major federal transportation policies and expressed agendas and agenda dynamics in the prime ministerial eras of Pierre Trudeau, Brian Mulroney, Jean Chrétien and Paul Martin, Stephen Harper, and now Justin Trudeau. The analysis includes, where appropriate, important features of the governing political party platforms and agendas. These party dimensions show both continuities and key differences across Liberal and Conservative governments and prime ministerial eras. The nature of federalism and federal–provincial agendas and urban policy and agendas are also a part of the story and will be noted as the analysis proceeds.

We examine the Pierre Trudeau Liberals from 1968 to 1984, the Mulroney Conservatives in the 1984 to 1993 period, the Chrétien and then Martin Liberals in the 1993 to 2006 period, the Harper Conservatives from 2006 to 2015, and finally the Justin Trudeau Liberals elected in October 2015. This involves a three-stage task in each main section of the chapter. First, we sum up the core political and policy agenda of each era, within which transportation seeks a vision or goals to serve, along with recognition, support, and the funding needed to achieve it. Second, we examine the place and content of transport policy issues and challenges, if any, in the PM era agendas as they are revealed in the periodic speeches from the throne (SFTS). Third, we analyze the place and content of transportation policy as revealed in annual budget speeches. In our presentation of the SFTS and budget speeches, we focus on the extent to which and the way in which transport policy is ranked, expressed, and mentioned on these occasions. The chapter's conclusions suggest some findings across these prime ministerial eras and cycles of agenda and agenda-setting content.

SFTS are the quintessential agenda-setting expression of priorities and values by the federal government as developed by prime ministers as political party leaders. They do not appear annually but rather at approximately eighteen-month intervals on average, as new sessions of Parliament begin. SFTS tend to be thematic narratives centred on new or changed laws and ways of expressing agendas and priorities.

Budget speeches are also pivotal. They are presented annually, typically in February or March. They usually feature a wide variety of individual policy themes, sometimes including transportation, but their primary role is to shape and guide the country's macroeconomy and macrofiscal policy; to that end they always include numerous specific tax and expenditure measures, whether new, altered, or cancelled (Doern 2009). As we will see, these measures can be large, medium, or small in size, not to mention gesture-like, and applicable for a wide range of time periods extending from small amounts of money for a couple of years, to very large sums with time commitments of seven to ten years (and thus likely well beyond the incumbent government's tenure in office) and everything in between.

Both SFTS and budget speeches are bound up in the inherent nature and dynamics of agenda setting and issue management in Canada (Pal 2013; Soroka 2002; Doern and Phidd 1992) and in the continuously changing art of "patching and packaging" complex ends and means in policy formation and political communication (Howlett and Rayner 2013). We are interested in how transportation policy gets presented (if at all) in SFTS and budget speeches, in the changing discourse used, and in how it ranks (or seems to rank) in federal government priorities expressed on these occasions. Transportation policy overall may be a small or larger component of an SFT or budget speech, or may simply be subsumed in a section dealing with another policy field or agenda item. Also of interest is when and why transportation policy gets ignored in these agenda-setting occasions.

The chapter's account of these events and processes needs to be seen in the context of the broader conceptual theories of agenda setting as previewed in chapter 1, including the Jones and Baumgartner (2012) concept of "punctuated equilibrium." There are several reasons why. First, it is important to keep in mind the long and variable times between action on transport policy and the evolution of technologies that affect transport as previewed in chapter 1. These dynamics complicate the framing of policy and may not fit easily in the context of planning for speeches from the throne or annual budgets, or the formation of government election campaign mandates. Second, this context helps account for two observed phenomena in agenda theory. In such policy spaces we are more likely to see "punctuated equilibria" where overall policy remains stable for long periods before, in a disrupting fashion, certain policy elements change quickly and dramatically in response to a pressing threat or opportunity (Jones and Baumgartner 2012, 2005). The long, variable, and uncertain timing of change along these lines also reflects the attention spans of different players, including citizens and especially voters, as well as the mass media and government communication efforts which seek to frame and reframe issues (Eisler, Russell, and Jones 2014; Wolfe, Jones, and Baumgartner 2013). Governments, not surprisingly, often see themselves as functioning in a sea of critics and thus these pivotal agenda-setting events are even more important to parties in power.

Here we summarize and comment on references to transportation policy in the thirty-four federal SFTs and forty-eight budget speeches from 1968 to 2016. The economic and social agendas are also revealed in policy and reform agenda strategies related to overall macroeconomic policy, embodied in measures relating to taxation, regulation, and public spending and also in political exhortations. The realities and complexities of these policy instruments are a necessary part of our historical account of each prime ministerial era both here and in later chapters. These instruments range widely across systems of hard rules, soft guidance, tax systems involving deductions, credits, and tax expenditures, and spending attached to levered rules and provisions, diverse forms of exhortation and nudging, and diverse complex agreements and contracting among a huge range of participants in the industrial and governmental sectors of Canadian society (Doern, Maslove, and Prince 2013; Howlett 2011).

Not all aspects of transportation policy, priorities, and agendas show up in SFTs and budget speeches. For example, major transport and other accidents occur periodically and often lead to quick responses and policy changes without being captured in either the periodic rhythms of SFTs or the annual rhythms of budget speeches. But even these regular rhythms of agendas are lodged in larger agenda content, including major crises and macro political–economic

imperatives as seen through the periods in office in each prime ministerial and political party era.

PRIME MINISTERIAL AND POLITICAL PARTY ERAS: TRANSPORTATION POLICIES, IDEAS, AND REFORMS

The Pierre Trudeau Liberals

CORE POLITICAL AND POLICY AGENDA IN BRIEF

The Pierre Trudeau Liberals were in power through majority governments in 1968–72, 1974–79, and 1980–84 and in a minority-
government interregnum from 1972–74. Under its initial "Just Society"
and rational decision-making ethos, Trudeau focused on distancing
his government from the seemingly chaotic decision making of the
previous Pearson Liberal minority government by pushing reforms
calling for greater public participation (Doern and Phidd 1983).

The Trudeau government inherited a significantly revised transportation governance regime based on passage by Parliament of the
National Transportation Act in 1967. That was the first in a series
of significant promarket steps for some parts of the transportation
sector, especially railways. As a result, the Trudeau Liberals presided
over a national transportation system without a long list of unad-
dressed problems. On the contrary, it was just beginning to adapt to
important changes made only fifteen months before and this no doubt
had an effect on the degree of priority transportation occupied in
the new government's agenda. For example, while the railways
focused more and more on rail freight opportunities, problems arose
regarding passenger rail services. The Trudeau government in 1977
arranged for the formation of VIA Rail Canada Inc. as a subsidiary
of CN and a year later VIA became an independent Crown Corporation
responsible for operating all passenger services formerly operated
by CN and CP.

As further recent analysis shows, VIA Rail got a sluggish federal
response mainly because of CN and CP's ownership and maintenance
of the track VIA Rail would have to use (Dupuis 2015; VIA Rail
Canada 2018). This led to repeated efforts by VIA Rail to have a
dedicated passenger track built and funded, an objective still not
reached. VIA's ridership increased over the years, but it could never
reach its full potential. We see also later in this chapter how different

governments reduced the subsidies they provided for VIA Rail both initially and in later periods of severe fiscal deficits.

In the early and mid-1970s the Pierre Trudeau Liberals were forced into a policy agenda centred on wage and price controls as Canada (and the global economy) faced high and rising inflation that was not responsive to normal central bank monetary or intentionally counter-cyclical fiscal policy. Following its defeat and the very brief interregnum of the Clark Conservative minority government in 1979–80, the Pierre Trudeau Liberals returned to power with a government agenda that was both broadly aggressive and interventionist. It aggressively launched initiatives that ranged from repatriation of the constitution and the creation of a Canadian Charter of Rights and Freedoms and, on the economic front, the introduction of a National Energy Program as a partial response to a global energy crisis in the wake of a tripling of oil prices and a resource-centred megaprojects industrial strategy (Doern and Toner 1985). The latter sought to revive the economy with an array of planned natural-resource megaprojects that had been queuing up for investment and construction in all regions of Canada. Some of these included transport infrastructure for railways and highways. This broad initiative was not dissimilar to the infrastructure projects for resource and energy–pipeline transport that were promoted in the 2008–15 period under the Harper Conservatives (see below).

SPEECHES FROM THE THRONE

In the thirteen Pierre Trudeau era SFTS, transportation policy issues were raised in five and received no mention in any of the other eight. The first explicit mention of transportation did not come until 1973 (five years into the Trudeau government's tenure in power). Prior to that, the Liberal SFTS had often mentioned the grain industry in Western Canada, expressing concern about getting products to markets but without explicit mention of transportation as an inherent feature of this problem. In the 1 April 1973 SFT, brief mention was made of "a possible joint study for improvement in the total transportation system" as part of an "agenda for western development" (SFT 1973, 10–11). The 30 October 1974 SFT expressed similar views in a concerted but longer way (SFT 1974, 9 and 10). It said that "transportation is vital to Canada ... it is at the heart of our ability to function as a national economy and as a trading nation" (ibid., 9). Notwithstanding the promarket changes in governance introduced by the National Transportation Act in 1967, it stressed that "the principles of the current transportation system are inadequate" (ibid., 10). In the 18 October 1978 SFT, the Liberals indicated that several measures would be "presented to improve the national transportation system" (SFT 1978, 6). These included "new ports legislation ... to enhance local autonomy" (ibid., 6).

By the time of its final two SFTs, in 1980 and 1983, the Trudeau Liberal government had changed its transportation policy discourse. In the 14 April 1980 SFT, it cast transportation policy as a "vital part of industrial strategy" (SFT 1980, 14), linking it to "prairie grain as a national priority" (ibid., 14). In the 2 July 1983 SFT, transportation policy was discussed as one feature of "developing regional strength" (SFT 1983, 6). The specific measures planned or mentioned in this context included a review of domestic air transportation "with the objective of reducing fares (ibid., 9) and the creation of "a new independent Aviation Safety Board" which would assume Transport Canada's responsibility for investigating accidents (ibid., 9). The latter arose at least in part from a perceived need to remove Transport Canada from a conflict-of-interest position that came from operating airports and investigating accidents, some of which occurred at those airports.

BUDGET SPEECHES

In the Pierre Trudeau era's seventeen budget speeches, seven contained transportation policy content and mentions, and ten did not. Similar to the SFT story above, there were no references to transportation policy until the Liberal budget speech of 18 November 1974 – the government's eighth budget. In a section near the end of that budget speech, on "measures to sustain capital investment," the transportation industry is referred to as a "vital part of the infrastructure with which our economy must operate. But it is being exposed to cost pressures which are both weakening its vitality and forcing it to translate these cost pressures into price increases. These increases pyramid in turn into cost increases throughout the economy" (Budget Speech 1974, 20). In response, the minister of finance proposed to eliminate the federal sales tax on transportation equipment effective immediately.

In the budget speech of 23 June 1975, which stressed concern about world inflation and a national recession, the only transport policy mention was that Transport Canada would be among those departments whose capital budgets would be cut (Budget Speech 1975, 15). In three subsequent budget speeches in the late 1970s, certain aspects of transportation policy emerge. In the 25 May 1976 budget speech, provisions are included to extend the Air Transportation Tax "to 2.3 million travellers using Canadian airports annually, who do not now pay the tax because they purchase their tickets outside the country" (Budget Speech 1976, 28). In the 16 November 1978 budget speech, the Air Transportation Tax was increased to 15 per cent of the airfare because the costs of airport services "have been increasing rapidly" (Budget Speech 1978, 11). This reflects a policy to shift costs from the general taxpayer to those who use the airports – in other words, a move in the ideological direction of user pay. The 10 April 1978 budget in between these two budget items gives some focus on "railway investment" (Budget Speech 1978, 8–9), with increases announced in capital cost allowance for railway assets. This was premised in part on the key role of railways for "long hauls and heavy commodities" (ibid., 9). But the rationale for these changes in government tax policy, and hence of the government's involvement in the economics of the transportation marketplace, was not mentioned.

In the early 1980s, Liberal budgets committed the government to provide "sufficient funds to finance major expansion of our activities in ... the improvement of transportation" (Budget Speech 1980, 5). This included a $4 billion Western Development Fund with funds directed at "the modernization of the western grain handling and transportation system" (ibid., 5). The fund and its focus were expressly linked to the Trudeau Liberals' lack of any Liberal MPs from Western Canada. The second last Pierre Trudeau-era budget, that of 19 April 1983, featured transportation in two major ways. Transportation was listed first as a feature of the initiative on "Special Recovery Capital Projects" (Budget Speech 1983, 9) and second as a recognition of "the critical importance of the government's Western Transportation initiative for national recovery" (ibid., 10). The latter had been proposed by the minister of transport and included $3.7 billion of funding over the next four years, separate from the Special Recovery Capital Projects Program (ibid., 10).

It seems likely that the allocation of money to transportation was a by-product of the government's perceived need to spend its way out of an economic downturn and to improve its fortunes in the waning years of the Pierre Trudeau era, with the Mulroney Conservatives knocking vigorously on the door. In other words, transportation policy was woven into a complex means–ends set of choices and ways of expressing them and presenting them politically.

The Mulroney Conservatives

CORE POLITICAL AND POLICY AGENDA IN BRIEF

For its entire period in office, from 1984 to 1993, the Mulroney Conservatives had to deal with large fiscal deficits, the largest in Canadian history. This meant that funds for new initiatives, on transportation or anything else, were scarce for most of this nine-year period. In addition, this was the period when postwar macroeconomic stabilization, through demand management as the prime macrofiscal policy approach, came to an end. The shift during the Thatcher–Reagan era towards a microeconomic policy of growth, economic deregulation, privatization, and supply-side structural fundamentalism, which swept up Canadian policy making as well, was pivotal in this regard (Doern, Maslove, and Prince 2013). Transportation policy was affected accordingly.

The Mulroney government's policy battles in its first term revolved around energy and trade. New energy accords replaced the interventionist National Energy Program (NEP) introduced by the Liberals and much reviled in Western Canada. Free trade, through the Canada–US Free Trade Agreement (CUSFTA), absorbed the rest of the Mulroney government's energies and provided the platform for the 1988 election, which ultimately was a de facto referendum on free trade itself (Doern and Tomlin 1991). Later came the North American Free Trade Agreement (NAFTA), which extended the scope of CUSFTA and added Mexico into the deal (Trebilcock 2011; Cameron and Tomlin 2000).

The second-term Mulroney agenda centred on restructuring the Canadian economy. This was done through tax reform, by the introduction of the Goods and Services Tax (GST), and by further economic deregulation of various sectors including telecommunications, airlines, and railways. The Mulroney agenda was also ultimately caught up in constitutional wrangling. This energy-sapping work led to the Meech Lake and Charlottetown accords initiated during its first term, which ended in abject failure and led to a crushing defeat for the Conservatives in the 1993 general election. Given these major preoccupations, it is hardly surprising that transportation *per se* only infrequently gained the attention of the government over its nine years in office – but one of them was the pivotal Freedom to Move promarket transport policy in 1985 (see more below and in chapter 3).

Another that garnered much less attention and follow-up was the government's decision to create a Royal Commission on national passenger transportation. Its final report (Royal Commission on National Passenger Transportation 1992) simply titled *Directions*, assembled data and research on estimates of intercity travel overall in relation to rail versus other modes, rail infrastructure issues including running rights and joint track usage, the environmental effects of intercity passenger transportation, and developments affecting people with transportation-relevant disabilities. Despite the impetus of a Royal Commission, running rights and joint track usage could still not move the CN–CP power regarding their own priority track usage. As we see later in this chapter, the Mulroney government's budgetary transport expenditures were reduced by $75 million and $200 million and the operations of VIA Rail in the Windsor to Quebec City corridor were moved toward full cost recovery.

SPEECHES FROM THE THRONE
In the five Mulroney era SFTs, transport policy featured to some extent in three SFTs and received no mention in the other two. The 11 May 1984 SFT stressed that the then new government contained representation from all regions of the country. It set out plans to review all government programs and it promised an economic renewal plan to reduce the deficit. It also said that the government would seek "to ensure our critical transportation and communication links better serve the national purpose" (SFT 1984, 23). The 30 September 1986 SFT, which followed sixteen months later, included a promise that the government "will again be placing before Parliament measures to give Canadians a more efficient, competitive, and safe transportation system by reducing the burden of unnecessary regulations on the transport sector" (SFT 1986, 11). This was described as part of greater efforts to diversify the economic base of Western Canada (ibid., 12). By then the Mulroney government's pivotal Freedom to Move transport policy had been announced (Mazankowski 1985). As Hill points out, this policy white paper by the transport minister, Don Mazankowski, "never mentioned deregulation *per se*, but its direction was clear" (Hill 1999, 68), and as a result a new promarket impetus, significantly expanding on the National Transportation Act of 1967, was put firmly in place. The effect of Freedom to Move on the development of Canada's transportation system was an element of the government's agenda in its own right – rather than a subsidiary

issue, which for transport policy is far more common. Its impact on the national economy was still important but only on a selected and often delayed basis for some jurisdictions – for example, within cities (see chapter 8) – and for some transport modes that were affected by other transport policy issues as they emerged (see below and also in chapter 3).

The Freedom to Move initiative had its own executive-centred Mulroney Progressive Conservative 1984 election proposal based on advocacy research and analysis by officials and others, and it involved different kinds of interest group and citizen engagement (Hill 1999). Mulroney also cast his reforms in support of the entrepreneurial zeal and capacities of Canadians from coast to coast, partly as a strong reaction against the Pierre Trudeau 1980–84 government's highly interventionist National Energy Program (NEP). Doern and Tomlin (1991, 52–7) also show how in the 1985–87 period following the Freedom To Move policy, the early work and logic of the Royal Commission on the Economic Union (the MacDonald Royal Commission) had impacts. Some of its research studies and personnel were finding its way in the 1985–87 period into a receptive Mulroney government in the PMO, PCO and finance department and into the work of Parliamentary committees. The MacDonald Commission, forged as an inquiry initially into the internal market, was gradually becoming a supporter of what became the Canada–US Free trade Agreement. Mulroney became a strong free trade supporter and in 1988 won what was de facto the free trade election (ibid., 226–42).

There were no transportation references in the 12 December 1988 preelection SFT nor in the first postelection 3 April 1989 SFT. Transportation was mentioned in the final SFT of the Mulroney era, on 13 May 1991, where it was included in a package of measures to foster greater access for "disabled Canadians" in a variety of public and private settings (SFT 1991, 10).

BUDGET SPEECHES

In the Mulroney era, there were nine budget speeches, six with transportation policy content and three in which there was no reference to transport issues at all. The government's first budget speech, on 23 May 1985, stressed that there would be "tough measures to reduce the deficit," but it was linked with efforts to "free-up the entrepreneurial spirit of our citizens" (Budget Speech 1985, 4). The transport content was limited to budget cuts. Transport expenditures would be "reduced by $75 million this year and $200 million next year" (ibid., 11) and the operations of VIA Rail in the Windsor to Quebec City Corridor "will move toward full cost recovery" (ibid., 11).

The next budget speech, of 26 February 1986, made some reference to transportation. The first was through pride expressed in both the transport regulatory reforms already achieved and the reduction of subsidies to VIA Rail (Budget Speech 1986, 5). The only new transport policy content was related strictly to northern travel in an announcement of a "new $50 ceiling on the air transport tax on domestic flights, offset by a one percentage point increase in rates" (ibid., 21).

The 18 February 1987 budget speech found room for only one transportation item, namely an increase in the "air transport tax by $4 per ticket" for tickets purchased in Canada and abroad (Budget Speech 1987, 9). This was done at the request of the minister of transport and was described as a necessary measure "in order to recover a greater proportion of these costs from those who benefit from the services and to help provide enhanced levels of security at airports" (ibid., 9). The brief preelection budget speech of 10 February 1988 once again expressed pride and satisfaction with the way in which the government had "deregulated the energy and transport sectors" (Budget Speech 1988, 2), but in the main it focused on touting past achievements such as modernizing competition policy and the free trade agreement with the United States.

In the Mulroney government's second-term budget speeches, transportation items found their way in but without much fanfare. For example, the 27 April 1989 speech drew attention to the fact that VIA Rail's subsidy had grown and not fallen, and that VIA must henceforth report publicly on options for substantial subsidy reductions. These options could include the "closure, sale, or transfer of substantial parts of the system" but that "assistance to provide service to remote communities will continue" (Budget Speech 1989, 7–8). The 25 February 1992 speech, with Don Mazankowski, formerly a transport minister now in the role of finance minister, took note of three transport measures already underway: working with the private sector to develop airport infrastructure, pursuing a fixed link (i.e., bridge) from the mainland to Prince Edward Island, and discussions with the provinces to explore ways in which the national highway system might be upgraded (Budget Speech 1992, 12). There were no transport matters discussed or advocated in the final Mulroney budget of 26 March 1993. Electoral defeat followed about six months later.

The Chrétien and Martin Liberals

CORE POLITICAL AND POLICY AGENDA IN BRIEF

The three Liberal majority governments of Jean Chrétien from 1991–2004 (with Paul Martin as minister of finance) and the Paul Martin minority government from 2004–06 offered an expansive "innovation economy" agenda that was first unveiled in its 1993 election campaign Red Book agenda (Liberal Party of Canada 1993). Some of these promises resulted in the creation of the Canada Investment Fund to help leading-edge technology firms secure long-term capital. It also led to technology partnerships among universities, research institutions, and the private sector. In addition, a Canadian strategy for the information highway was unveiled.

But these agenda plans were buffeted by the spectre of a now fifteen-year-old, federal fiscal deficit and large accumulated debt (Pal 1998; Swimmer 1996; Hale 2000, 2001). Major expenditure cuts flowing from the Liberals' program review included reductions in joint federal–provincial social welfare programs and in science funding and staff reductions ranging from 20 to 30 per cent in key federal science-based departments (Swimmer 1996; Kinder 2010). That did not augur well for supporting the "innovation economy" espoused in the Red Book.

Following reelection in June 1997, the Chrétien–Martin government's agenda focused on its promise to balance the budget by 1998–99 and to do so particularly in the context of fostering an innovation and knowledge-based economy as well as by fostering regulatory reform through strategies for smart regulation (Doern, Maslove, and Prince 2013). By the time of its 27 November 2000 reelection victory, the Chrétien Liberals were basking in an era of fiscal surpluses and economic growth (Pal 2000).

Paul Martin became leader of the Liberal Party and prime minister in 2003 after a bitter battle with Jean Chrétien. His initial agenda offered parliamentary reform, measures to rebuild trust in the wake of the Chrétien government's sponsorship scandal, a new deal for cities and communities, and a renewed focus on Aboriginal issues.

SPEECHES FROM THE THRONE (SFTS)

In the Chrétien–Martin era there were eight SFTS, five containing transport policy references and three with no transport content of any kind. The first three (17 January 1994, 27 February 1996, and

22 September 1997) were silent on transportation issues, although each of them contained some emphasis on a new federal focus on the "information highway" and hence on the emerging internet – metaphorically cast as the highway for the transport of information but not the transportation of people or goods.

The 12 October 1999 SFT stressed the need for a "dynamic economy for the coming 21st century" (SFT 1999, 4), including steps to "ensure that Canada has modern infrastructure" (ibid., 4) and thus a "capacity to move people and goods safely and efficiently" (ibid., 6). Transportation was listed first among the examples of infrastructure areas to be supported (ibid., 7).

In the SFT of 29 January 2001, in a section on "strong and safe communities," the government promised that it would "cooperate with provincial and municipal partners to help improve public transit infrastructure" (SFT 2001, 7). No mention was made of the government's intended response to a report due to be submitted in June that year from the panel conducting a statutory review of the Canada Transportation Act, even though it had the potential to bring about fundamental changes in the economic deregulation of transportation in Canada.

The following year's SFT, on 2 January 2002, continued these themes but recast them under the rubric of "competitive cities and healthy communities" (SFT 2002, 6). The government promised a "ten-year program for infrastructure" and said that within this framework it would "introduce a new strategy for a safe, efficient and environmentally responsible transportation system that will help reduce congestion in our cities and bottlenecks in our trade corridors" (ibid., 6). This was one of the few times when transportation *per se* was identified explicitly for its role in Canadian society and the economy rather than as a byproduct of pursuing some other item on the government's agenda. The higher profile did not last long. The next SFT, on 2 February 2004, with the Chrétien government having been reelected, promised "a new deal for communities" that "targets the new infrastructure needed" and a deal that "delivers reliable, predictable and long-term funding" (SFT 2004, 6). The $7 billion funding over the next decade would be for "real and ongoing investments in urban transit, affordable housing, clean water, and good roads" (ibid., 7). Transportation was present in both the urban transit and roads context but obviously community infrastructure involved other areas of activity as well. In other words, transportation was to be a recipient of infrastructure spending but was at best only partly the reason for it.

In Paul Martin's first and only s FT, after he succeeded Chrétien as Liberal prime minister, the discourse had morphed somewhat again, with infrastructure centred on "the New Deal for Canada's Cities and Communities" (s FT 2004a, 6). The funds devoted to this would enable "municipalities to make long-term financial commitments needed to help contain urban sprawl and to invest in new sustainable infrastructure projects in areas like transit, roads, clean water and sewers" (ibid., 6).

BUDGET SPEECHES
There were eleven budget speeches in the Chrétien–Martin era, four with transport policy content and seven without. The first, on 22 February 1994, had no transportation policy content, but the second, on 27 February 1995, had significant transport implications because of the overall deficit reduction plans now fully underway. From a financial standpoint the implications for transportation were mainly negative given the budget cuts, but there were also some newer funding moves paired with them as well. The cuts included "$1.4 billion reductions at Transport Canada", the second highest listed cut among the departments mentioned (Budget Speech 1995, 8). Transport subsidies, the budget stated, "are being eliminated or substantially reduced" (ibid., 11) and subsidies under the Western Grain Transportation Act were subjected to a reduction "resulting in savings of $2.6 billion over the next five years" that was described as allowing Canada to "develop a more efficient and effective transportation system while also being consistent with our international trade obligations" (ibid., 11). Atlantic freight subsidy elimination would total $500 million, but a new five-year, $326 million "transport adjustment program would be created for Atlantic Canada, focusing on highway system modernization (ibid., 11–12), Budget cuts for the National Research Council, at a little over $110 million per year, resulted in the termination of funding for the NRC's only institute devoted to transportation R&D and turned it into a full cost recovery operation. Last, but certainly not least, the budget speech also announced that the minister of transport would "initiate steps to sell CN" (though these steps had been underway as early as 1992) and the government will also "commercialize the Air Navigation System" (ibid., 14).

Following these major transport policy changes, there were no transport mentions in any of the next four Chrétien–Martin era budgets of 1997, 1998, 1999, and 2000. But then, in the budget speech of 10 December 2001, three short months after the 9/11 terrorist attacks on the US, a major focus appeared on transport security and keeping an open Canada–US border. The budget speech stressed that, "tourism, airlines and aerospace had been particularly effected" (Budget Speech 2001, 5). It announced that Transport Canada "will set rigorous new national standards for security at airports and on board flights origi-nating in Canada" (ibid., 8) and "will create a new air security author-ity." These security changes would cost "$2.2 billion over the next 5 years [including] a new security charge to be paid by air travellers" (ibid., 8). Also announced was a $600 million open-border program consisting of "first-class road access, new truck processing centres, and intelligent transport systems that pre-clear vehicles" (ibid., 10).

There were two budget speeches under Paul Martin as Liberal prime minister. The first was on 23 March 2004. One transportation item drew early mention when the government announced it was "forgoing VIA Rail capital expansion" plans (Budget Speech 2004, 5). Later in the speech the government drew positive attention to the $7 billion planned for community infrastructure over the next ten years that centred on "improved roads and better transit" (ibid., 14). The final Martin-era budget speech of 23 February 2005, had no transport content – but not surprisingly started with a defence of its "sound financial management," including having achieved its eighth balanced budget and "the longest unbroken string of surpluses since Confederation" (Budget Speech 2005, 5).

The Harper Conservatives

CORE POLITICAL AND POLICY AGENDA IN BRIEF

The two Harper minority governments from 2006 to 2011, and its majority government from May 2011 to October 2015, centred their agenda on dealing with the recession and fiscal deficits and, especially after 2011, on energy and natural resources and related oil sands and pipeline development. These resided at the centre of the Conservatives' Alberta and western Canadian political–economic base. The minority government agenda that began in 2006 was anchored in a five-point program of accountability (as a direct response to the scandals that had plagued the Liberals) (Doern 2006). The government also promised reductions of the Goods and Services Tax (GST), and it stressed the need to tackle crime and to deliver benefits and good government for "hard working Canadian families." The GST reductions were enabled by the Harper government having inherited a $13 billion annual surplus from the Chrétien–Martin Liberals (Doern, Maslove, and Prince 2013; Hale 2006). The Harper agenda also made clear that it would practice what it called "open federalism" which largely meant that it would respect provincial jurisdiction and focus (almost) exclusively on areas of federal jurisdiction – notwithstanding the blurry (and often disputed) line separating the two, especially insofar as responsibility for paying for things was concerned.

The surplus was gone, however, and by the time of the Harper government's second minority government the global banking and economic crisis of 2008 had begun and was growing. The Harper government's agenda shifted focus to the fast-growing fiscal deficit and the development of its economic stimulus program, marketed under the banner of the Conservative's Economic Action Plan (Maslove 2009). This agenda shift sought to increase and then maintain economic growth, deal with the recession, and tackle specific issues such as an Ontario auto industry bailout (Waddell 2010) as well as regulatory streamlining by means of red tape reduction initiatives.

The stimulus measures of the Conservative's Economic Action Plan continued to be a central part of its agenda as time went on. They included plans to return to budgetary balance through future expenditure cuts that would eventually impact, in ways unknown, federal budgets and staffing, largely because Harper committed *not* to cut, in any major way, federal spending or transfers to the provinces as the previous Liberal government had done in its mid-1990s deficit-reduction strategy.

In its majority government period from 2011 to 2015 Harper's personal controlling one-man government instincts and habits loomed ever larger, although they were starting to be described as a key feature of his time in power going back to the outset (Savoie 2013; Martin 2010). A further continuous major thread in the Harper majority agenda and its action plans was its continued emphasis on infrastructure investment and funding plans, including a focus on cities and communities (Doern and Stoney 2014; Dutil and Park 2012; Pal 2011). Some of that included transportation aspects.

SPEECHES FROM THE THRONE (SFTS)

In the Harper era, there were seven SFTS, five with some transport policy content and two that were completely silent on the subject. There was none in its first SFT, of 3 April 2006 as it kicked off its initial minority government agenda. The second Harper SFT, on 16 October 2007, mentioned transport near the end when it promised that "through our new infrastructure plan, our Government will promote a cleaner environment by investing in public transport and water treatment and by cleaning up contaminated sites" (SFT 2007, 7). Transport clearly had a secondary role in the scheme of things. But it emerged again in the post-election 18 November 2008 SFT. Midway through, in the "securing jobs" section, it said that the "Canadian manufacturing sector, particularly the automotive and aerospace industries, has been under increasing strain. Our Government will provide further support for these industries" (SFT 2008, 4). In the "expanding investment and trade" section of the SFT, the government worked in transport content more directly by promising to "continue to invest in expanding gateways on our Atlantic and Pacific coasts, and in vital border corridors such as the Detroit River International Crossing, to ensure that Canadian goods and services can reach markets in Europe, Asia and the United States" (ibid., 5).

In the (extremely brief) SFT of 26 January 2009, as the global recession and banking crisis were taking hold, there was no transport content at all (SFT 2009). The Harper government's next SFT, on 3 March 2010, gave top billing to Canada's Economic Action Plan (SFT 2010, 2) and drew attention to almost 16,000 projects underway from coast to coast, that ranged "from roads and bridges to colleges and universities, from social housing to our cultural and heritage institutions" (ibid., 2). Thus transportation got subsumed, as it often had before, as an object of public spending.

Following the Harper government's reelection in 2011 as a majority government, the 2 June 2011 SFT contained only one explicit transportation item, this time relating to Canada's north. The government committed to work "to complete the Dempster Highway by linking Inuvik to Tuktoyaktuk thereby realizing Conservative Prime Minister John Diefenbaker's "vision of connecting Canada by road from sea, to sea, to sea" (SFT 2011 5).

In the Harper government's final SFT, of 16 October 2013, transportation policy issues were more numerous and varied and were mentioned under different policy headings. They included under resource development reintroducing the "*Safeguarding Canada's Seas and Skies Act* to protect our oceans and coasts" (SFT 2013, 3) and to "act on advice from the Expert Panel on Tanker Safety, to create a world class tanker safety system in Canada" (ibid., 3). Under the section on infrastructure, the government promised investment over the coming decade of $70 billion on "projects such as building subways in the Greater Toronto Area (GTA), replacing Montréal's Champlain Bridge, and building a new Windsor–Detroit crossing" (ibid.). Under the "safeguarding families and communities" section, in a subfocus on Canada's railways, the government referred to an amended Railway Safety Act in the wake of the huge Lac-Mégantic railway accident, as well as creating a clean-up and rebuilding fund for the town of Lac-Mégantic itself. It also said that the government "will take targeted action to increase the safety of the transportation of dangerous goods" (ibid., 5).

BUDGET SPEECHES

There were eleven budget speeches in the Harper era, with eight having explicit transportation content and three without. In its first budget speech, of 6 May 2006 – the first of ten for Finance Minister Jim Flaherty – there was explicit transportation content under the rubric of a "$16.5 billion investment program over 4 years" (Budget Speech 2006, 11). In it were five designated funds, including one for highways and border infrastructure and another for a public transit capital trust fund, which was partly linked to "transit and the environment," and there were related concerns expressed about traffic congestion (ibid., 12). A borders-and-security theme was also mentioned, including a "$133 million commitment over 2 years for the Canadian Air Transport Security Authority" (ibid., 14).

The second Harper-era budget speech, on 19 March 2007, asked early on, "what is fiscal balance?" and answered its own question with a lead-off example saying "it's about better roads and renewed public transit" (Budget Speech 2007, 4). The budget also contained a commitment of $16 billion for investments in "national growth-oriented projects like the Asia-Pacific Gateway (ibid., 7). Flaherty was expansive about these kinds of transport and infrastructure endeavours. He explicitly linked them to Sir John A. Macdonald's national railway, Louis St Laurent's Saint Lawrence Seaway, and John Diefenbaker's vision of the North, achievements which "have connected our great country, united us, shaped who we are" (ibid., 18).

Midway through the next budget speech, delivered on 26 February 2008, the government committed itself to "creating a seamless, safe and secure transport system for the benefit of all Canadians" (Budget Speech 2008, 11), illustrating what it meant with several new specific public transit projects including "the Evergreen Light Rapid Transit System in Vancouver, re-establishment of the rail link between the City of Peterborough and Toronto's Union Station following an existing right of way, and new equipment and upgrades to the dedicated rapid transit for the Aéroports de Montréal" (ibid., 11).

In the next budget speech, on 27 January 2009, the budget early on emphasized a major building infrastructure commitment, with the lead-off items on the list mentioning the "construction of roads, bridges, public transit" (Budget Speech 2009, 5) and drawing attention, later in the speech, to the way in which projects "from coast to coast to coast" were involved – two of them in total, most in transportation" (ibid., 19). The next budget speech, on 4 March 2010, reminded its readers that the government was "building better roads, bridges, border crossings, and public transit" (Budget Speech 2010, 5) and was still doing this at the halfway point of "the largest federal investment in infrastructure in over 60 years" (ibid., 6). These transport-related investments were reiterated in the budget speech of 22 March 2011 (Budget Speech 2011, 2) but nothing new was added.

Following its reelection as a majority government in 2011, the Harper government's first two budget speeches, of 6 June 2011 and 29 March 2012, contained no transport content of any kind. Transport references reappeared in the 21 March 2013 budget speech under what were now described as initiatives for "Long-Term Infrastructure Funding for Long Term Prosperity." It started with bridges (including a new bridge for the St Lawrence Seaway – in other words, a replacement for the Champlain Bridge, which was mentioned in the SFT seven months later) and went on to stress that coverage would include "roads and runways, community centers and commuter rail" (Budget Speech 2013, 12).

The next budget speech, on 11 February 2014, mentioned new support for the Windsor–Detroit crossing and the provision of funds "for review of projects like the Energy East Pipeline" and hence pan-Canadian energy transport (Budget Speech 2014, 7). The final Harper-era budget was delivered on 21 April 2015 by Joe Oliver, who had become finance minister following the death of Jim Flaherty. It was very much a preelection budget. Among its proposals was the establishment of a new Public Transit Fund, whose financing would increase to $1 billion per year by 2019 (Budget Speech 2015, 15).

The Justin Trudeau Liberals

Elected with a strong majority on 19 October 2015, the Justin Trudeau Liberal government's overall agenda as expressed in its first (and at time of writing only) Speech from the Throne of 3 December 2015 developed priorities and themes that built on its election campaign platform. The relatively brief SFT expressed the government's planned agenda in terms of five realms of change: "growth for the middle class" (including tax cuts and a new child benefit), "open and transparent government" (centered partly on planned electoral reform), a "clean environment and a strong economy" (closely linked to climate change and carbon pricing), "diversity is Canada's strength" (with initiatives tied to strengthened relations with Indigenous peoples), and with the welcoming of 25,000 "new Canadians from Syria," and "security and opportunity" (including renewed support for defence and for UN peacekeeping) (SFT 2015, 2–5). There was no room for transportation in this very short inaugural SFT. There will undoubtedly be a further SFT in 2018 or 2019 before the 2019 federal election.

The government's first budget speech on 22 March 2016 (Budget Plan 2016) reiterated the theme of support for the middle class, expressed with emphasis on "long term growth for the middle class" and economic growth via "new investments in infrastructure from coast to coast to coast" (Budget 2016, 4). Here, as in other recent federal budget speeches, traced above, transportation is immediately stressed with reference to investments in "new roads and bridges," the way "traffic jams ... slow the movement of people, goods and services" (ibid.). The need to focus also on "investment in mass transit" is given emphasis both because "it boosts the economy ... [and] it helps the environment" today and for "years and decades into the future" (ibid.). The big deficit budget plans are anchored on $11.9 billion on infrastructure over five years but also $120 billion over the next decade (ibid., 4–5).

In the Trudeau Liberals Budget Plan 2017, transport features in a chapter 2 subsection on "building strong communities with public transit" that includes expansion support on 132 transit systems (ibid., 115) and a new Public Transit Infrastructure Fund (ibid., 119). There is also a subsection on "delivering better transportation to support trade" (ibid., 138), which includes a "National Trade Corridors Fund" (ibid., 139) and "Connecting Communities by Rail and Water" with provisions such as $867.3 million to support VIA Rail operations and capital requirements (ibid., 140). A year later, Budget Plan 2018, contained no explicit transport content sections or subsections.

Of some interest in the early Trudeau era is the previously mentioned new agenda device deployed by Prime Minister Trudeau via his "mandate letters" made public when his new cabinet was announced. His letter for his new minister of transport, Marc Garneau, (Prime Minister of Canada 2016) states that "as Minister of Transport, your overarching goal will be to ensure that Canada's transportation system supports our ambitious economic growth and job creation agenda. Canadians require a transportation system that is safe, reliable and facilitates trade and the movement of people and goods" (ibid., 3). The letter also identifies a number of instructions as the minister either "works with" other named ministers or "leads" other named ministers on given initiatives. The former "works with" instruction includes the minister of Infrastructure and Communities on developing an infrastructure strategy and the latter lead role is with the support of the minister of Agriculture and Agri-food on "a full review of the Canadian grain transportation system" (ibid., 7). Meanwhile, as these processes and implied priorities are underway, Marc Garneau as minister has stated that, "rail safety is my top priority" and announced in October 2016 the "new Rail Safety Improvement Program with over 55 million in funding" (Transport Canada 2016q). It is targeted "at reducing incidents and accidents on rail lines" by expanding "the list of eligible recipients and broadens the scope of projects that could be funded to enhance rail safety" (ibid., 1). In 2018 when several new ministers were appointed to an enlarged Trudeau cabinet in preparation for a 2019 federal election, a further set of mandate letters was announced.

In November 2016 a much more ambitious Transportation 2030 strategy was announced by Garneau (Transport Canada 2016r) following a lengthy consultation process. It made a government commitment "to create a safe, secure, green, innovative and integrated transportation system that supports trade and economic growth, a cleaner environment and the well-being of Canadians and their families" (ibid., 1–2). The strategy "groups areas of work under five themes" that enabled the government to take a "whole system" view and "each theme has its own specific goal to guide our actions today and over the longer term" (ibid., 2). The themes in order of presentation are "The Traveler" (support greater choice, better service, lower costs, and new rights for travelers), "Safer Transportation" (build a safer, more secure transportation system that Canadians can trust), "Green and Innovative Transportation" (reduce air pollution and embrace new technologies to improve Canadians' lives), "Waterways, Coasts and the North" (build world-leading marine corridors that are competitive, safe and environmentally sustainable, and enhance northern transportation infrastructure), and "Trade Corridors to Global Markets" (improve the performance and reliability of our transportation system to get products to markets to grow Canada's economy). There was a small sampling of items under each "theme" (with more to come later) but by far the biggest financial commitment came under the trade corridors theme to invest "$10.1 billion for transportation infrastructure to help eliminate bottlenecks and building more robust trade corridors" (ibid., 2–3). Somewhat differently, we now have under the Trudeau Liberals a transportation strategy that awkwardly consists of "themes" that have "one specific goal" and that is "whole system" in nature but with each theme having complex policy socioeconomic values.

After this 2016 announcement, the transport minister introduced in 2017 the key provisions of Bill C-49, the Transportation Modernization Act, whose key provisions we have already set out in chapter 1. It had some similar themes regarding "travellers initiatives" and "growing Canada's economy with modernized rail transportation."

In terms of agenda-setting theories, the overall analytical picture in some ways shows the value of concepts such as "punctuated equilibrium" where most policy stays stable for long periods, while, in a punctuated fashion, some policies change quickly and dramatically (Baumgartner and Jones 1993; Jones and Baumgartner 2012, 2005). The closest transport example of this dynamic is the post-911 transport and border security burst of punctuated major change. But equally, this could just as easily be seen as an example as in Pal (2014) of responding to crises and major turbulence. And overall, as one sifts through SFTs and budget speeches, but also prime ministerial eras (of varying lengths in power) one sees at play complex issue–attention and management cycles where governments, but also players such as the media (including social media), voters, citizens and interest group players, engage in framing and reframing problems and opportunities, including buying time (Eisler, Russell, and Jones 2014, Howlett 1998; Kingdon 1993).

CONCLUSIONS

The chapter has examined federal transportation policy agendas and evolution in the main federal prime ministerial and governing political party and partisan eras, the Pierre Trudeau Liberals from 1968 to 1984, the Mulroney Conservatives in the 1984 to 1993 period, the Chrétien and then Martin Liberals from 1993 to 2006, the Harper Conservatives from 2006 to 2015, and the Justin Trudeau Liberals starting in 2015.

The main thrust of the chapter has been to tell the agenda story chronologically through the sequence of SFTs and budget speeches as formal apex agenda events but each set in the context of a needed brief account of the core socioeconomic agendas in each prime ministerial era. We have presented them in the ways in which the different governments themselves expressed them.

Table 2.1 offers a concluding look across the five eras, both with respect to SFTs and budget speeches and the extent to which transportation content is present in them. We then comment briefly on the transport content *per se* and its discourse.

In the combined evidence of both SFTs and budget speeches, the degree of mention and presence is lowest in the Pierre Trudeau era and highest in the Stephen Harper era. At the time of writing, the Justin Trudeau era is too early to judge. However, as stressed from the outset, these raw figures say nothing about where transport (when it is mentioned) is situated and ranked in the structure of the agenda narrative of each SFT and budget speech. Most transport references, when they do occur, are not in the early pages and paragraphs but rather in the latter half or near the end. One exception was in the wake of the 2001 9/11 terrorist crisis where transport, security, and open borders were emphasized from the outset of the next immediately following budget speech. And of course, as we have indicated earlier, not all transport policy priorities/changes are announced on these occasions, an example being responses to transport accidents, which always occur without prior notice and catch governments off guard, but even the pivotal Freedom to Move policy of 1985, a consciously planned initiative of the government of the day, was not announced in a budget speech or SFT but rather was announced separately.

Table 2.1
Transportation content in thirty-four SFTs and fifty-one budget speeches
over five prime ministerial eras (1968–2018)

Prime minister	SFTs (Total#) (Transport# and %)	Budget speeches (Total#) (Transport# and %)
Pierre Elliot Trudeau 1968–83	(13) (5 Transport = 38%)	(17) (7 Transport = 41%)
Brian Mulroney 1984–92	(5) (3 Transport = 60%)	(9) (6 Transport = 67%)
Jean Chrétien– Paul Martin 1993–2005	(8) (5 Transport = 62%)	(11) (4 Transport = 36%)
Stephen Harper 2006–15	(7) (5 Transport = 71%)	(11) (8 Transport = 73%)
Justin Trudeau 2015–18	(1) (Transport = 0%)	(3) (2 Transport = 67%)

The SFT and budget speech narratives in which transport is mentioned reveal both the changing ways in which it is expressed and grouped with other policy fields, and are seen to be aspects of it in these related fields. This comes in the form of stated priorities or simply as individual, stand-alone transport modal or issue items (such as air transport fares and charges, ports, subsidies for VIA Rail, and accessibility for disabled Canadians). The Pierre Trudeau era had several expressions of transport policy (old and new) related to Western Canada including links to the grain trade and to energy and resource projects. The Mulroney era certainly linked transport to promarket regulatory reform overall and to eliminating what it considered unnecessary or excessive regulation. The Chrétien–Martin era began the more expressed linkage of transportation to infrastructure policy and funding overall, and especially in relation to communities and cities – hence its references to dealing with public transit, congestion, and good roads. Often these were also expressed in relation to environmental sustainability. The early Chrétien–Martin era was not shy about identifying and emphasizing cuts in Transport Canada's budgets and subsidies to VIA Rail. It also privatized CN and commercialized the Air Navigation System. The Harper government had the highest percentage of transport mentions in its SFTs and budget speeches overall, typically in an infrastructure and cities/communities narrative, and in a longer-term funding focus but also in the context of stimulus spending during the 2008–12 global recession. There were also some references to initiatives for gateways and ports, and Canada–US cross border bridges as well as to some requirements in the North such as the Dempster Highway. The Justin Trudeau government has led off with no transportation features in its only SFT to date but with stronger mentions in its first and second budget plans centred on infrastructure investment and cities transit support but not much in its 2018 budget plan.

Overall in this chapter's transport in the federal agenda story, railways (freight and passenger) were mentioned occasionally but the broader modal and intermodal trajectory was a focus on urban transit, better roads, and ports/gateways and hence explicitly within provincial and local government jurisdiction – despite, for example, the Harper government's ostensible focus on "open federalism" and on staying within areas of exclusive federal jurisdiction. Federal government interest in such infrastructure realms were a product of weaker (and arguably "weak" in the absolute sense) budgetary capacities in cities and communities, plus a strong direct lobby on the federal government by cities and their related advocacy groups. Increasingly, and overwhelming, federal prime ministers were responding to the fast growing imperative that most federal and provincial voters lived in cities.

Transportation policies and agendas increasingly also come from sources and developments outside Canada. We now turn in chapter 3 to a discussion of some of the key international determinants of Canadian transportation policies and agendas in the past fifty years. In our later domain chapters we also comment on the extent to which transport policy can focus on the overall movement of goods and people as a single defined policy field as opposed to one linked inexorably to other aspects of transport in numerous policy areas, as mentioned already in chapter 1 and as we see further in the international account in chapter 3.

3

Canada–US Relations and International Transportation Policy and Institutions

INTRODUCTION

The changing nature of international transportation policy, and Canada's role in shaping it and responding to it, forms an essential context for understanding Canadian transport policy and for selected aspects of the empirical analysis of the seven transport policy domains in part two of this book. We have already described some of the impacts of these international dimensions in chapters 1 and 2, including "common carrier" ideas in Canada and US railway regulation and nation-building policy and the different degrees of scope and intensity between the two countries of competition policy as applied to transportation. We also need, however, an appreciation of the basic contours of the evolution of international transportation policy and institutions, particularly during the past five decades. Our focus is on the policy and institutional story but is necessarily linked to the nature of international relations and power, globalization, neoliberalism, free trade, and to the more specific governance structures that changed transportation, as well as those that were produced by it.

The subject is necessarily complex. The analysis of international transportation policy deals with all kinds of conceptual and theoretical lenses and vantage points about international institutions and political–economic power (Baylis et al. 2014; Dryzek 2013; Wijen et al. 2013; Volger 2013; Elliott 2004; Held et al. 1999). All these lenses are different and overlap with each other. For example, with international relations (IR) theory the focus is on power and on interpreting the international system through the lens of realism or "realpolitik," which applies to transportation policy as much as any other field of policy, and globalization theory increasingly contends that all policy is influenced by strong and complex forces that need to be seen through the lenses of economic liberalism, free trade, and transformative technologies, global public interest, and the forces of civil society. Canada's international story in this chapter involves both its relationship with the US and an array of engagements and memberships in international transport agencies. The United States functions in this and other policy fields as a neighbour, Canada's main trading partner, an investor, and a global superpower. The global power structure has also been reshaped in multipolar ways by the EU, China, Russia, India, Brazil, and East Asian countries. The emergence of multiple new points of power and influence is symbolized by the decline of the G-8 and the rise to prominence of the G-20 bloc of relatively wealthy and large economies. These twenty countries determine most of the world's trade patterns and therefore impact transportation in complex ways, although there are informed arguments that digital technology is pivotal and therefore changing future trade patterns within and among developing and developed countries and also supply chains (Lund and Tyson 2018).

Hoberg (2002) proposes a framework for understanding Canadian–American relations that is useful in this chapter and in the domain analysis in part two of the book. His framework is anchored on six mechanisms of American influence on Canada–US relations: the physical environment, US policies and actions through emulation, diplomacy, trade agreements, economic integration and harmonization pressures, and cross-border lobbying (Hoberg 2002, 170–3).

All go through more complex processes for Canada because of the nature of the US political system and the sharp separation of powers in Washington, including the independent power of Congress, the frequent use of litigation through the courts, and the effect of very short electoral cycles – as little as two years for the House of Representatives. There is rarely one-stop shopping for any lobby in any democratic political system, but in the US federal system this is further compounded by sheer numbers: there are fifty state governments to contend with. Fourteen of them share the 3,000-mile border with Canada, and there is a dizzying array of transport, environmental, trade, and regulatory concerns associated with the movement of people and goods that show up in diverse ways. Agenda setting regarding how to recognize, address, regulate, fund, research, and hopefully solve problems and reach agreements are almost never easy to arrange in ways that suit both countries or interests in both countries regarding both content and timing.

We start the analysis in this chapter with six policy and governance examples and related lenses in the evolution of an increasingly complex international transport policy and institutional system. There are several core features of Canada–US transport policy relations, and they span the decades of interest. We look at them in rough chronological order, and, of course, all the issues and challenges overlap with each other.

The first lens is Canada–US transport economic deregulation and privatization dynamics from the late 1960s to the present day. We emphasize economic deregulation initially, but the dynamics and outcomes vary greatly by transport mode. Transport safety, moreover, is never far from the surface, and, when it arises, it almost always trumps economic considerations and new or extended regulation emerges. The second lens is centered on the example of trade liberalization and free-trade agreements that emerged in the 1980s and 1990s and their impact on transportation. Third, we look at developments that arose after 9/11. From a transportation viewpoint, their common characteristic was security and antiterrorism policies applied to borders and the goods being traded. Fourth, we examine cabotage, a transport-centred concept that involves the transport of goods from one point to another within a country, and the rules specifying that the transport of goods or people within a country be carried out by a domestic carrier. We sample this as an entrenched transport feature in the trucking, marine, and air transport modes and also draw out the ways in which they become Canada–US and international policy challenges and irritants that make it difficult to find the right kinds of agenda arenas, timing, and favourable circumstances to produce solutions to the transport puzzles at hand. Our fifth and sixth examples and lenses are centred on international transportation institutions, first a mainly Canada–US one in the form of the St Lawrence Seaway and Great Lakes management and its bilateral governance through two linked mirror image authorities and related forms of coordination and conflict, and the last a broader fully international example centred on three international transport agencies, namely the International Maritime Organization (IMO), the International Civil Aviation Organization (ICAO), and the International Transport Forum (ITF), the latter affiliated with the Organization for Economic Cooperation and Development (OECD). To end this chapter we draw conclusions from our six examples and the lenses they provide.

CANADA–US RELATIONS AND TRANSPORT ECONOMIC DEGREGULATION, SAFETY, AND PRIVATIZATION POLICY

A key first contextual feature of Canada–US transport relations centres on the combined and interacting policy realms of economic deregulation, safety, and privatization with the core story usually seen as covering the period from the late 1970s to the late 1980s. As we see in this account, none of the developments (and their remaining legacies) can be understood without dealing with core geographic and constitutional imperatives of the US versus Canada. The geographic imperative for the US is that its large population is distributed so that it has dense and multiple north–south and east–west patterns for transport to develop. For Canada, it is still the case that its population is mainly strung out across an east–west pattern with most Canadians (80 per cent) living within 200 miles of the US border, and of course in both countries, growing and ever higher percentages of the population live in cities (Winston 2010; Madar 2000; Oum, Stanbury, and Trethaway 1991).

The constitutional imperative for the US is that there is strong federal jurisdiction for interstate commerce, as a primary base for transport policy and also policy fields such as competition or antitrust policy. In Canada, interprovincial trade has not had an easy federal entry point, depending instead on more elusive aspects of constitutional provisions regarding "peace, order, and good government" or the federal spending power (Doern and MacDonald 1999). In a US research report by a broad coalition group called Transportation for America (2011), the group opens with the interesting statement that "our nation's transportation network is based on a policy that has not been significantly updated since the 1950s" (ibid, 3). This is a startling assertion given the major US economic deregulation policies, especially late-1970s airline deregulation (see more below), but it is less startling when one sees that the research report examines mainly the long established US federal role (a regulatory and spending role) in the interstate highway system and also in urban transit. These programs were also the product of political involvement at the federal level by both individual city mayors and lobby groups of mayors. These features had indeed begun in the 1950s. In Canada no equivalent federal presence of mayors and municipal lobbies occurred until the mid to late 1990s (Stoney and Graham 2009). The federal government did fund the trans-Canada highway construction and system in the 1950s, but that was an aberration until the late 1990s when cities, as we have seen in chapters 1 and 2, emerged as part of an explicit infrastructure agenda overall and with increasing transportation content (see also chapter 8).

When one shifts to the well-known economic deregulation agenda as a Canada–US policy dynamic, the story is different regarding transport modes, and their partly separate political–economic dynamics and paces of announcement, law making, implementation, and funding. The air transport deregulation occurred in the US in a sudden way in the 1978 to 1980 period. Based explicitly on economics research and the views of the economists who headed the main air transport regulatory bodies, the US saw a system emerge within months when a small set of dominant, incumbent airlines were challenged by literally dozens of new airlines which were allowed immediate entry into the market, subject to safety certification.

Assessments of airline deregulation in the US were positive in many ways. Looking at it over a thirty-year period, Goetz and Vowles (2009) conclude that some of the good results "from the industry and consumer perspective, include higher passenger volumes, more service to the most popular destinations, and lower fares on average" (ibid., 251). Goetz and Vowles went on to argue that the "bad results include financial and employment instability, diminution in the quality of airline service overall, and fewer flights and higher fares to smaller places" (ibid.). Winston (2010) reached similar kinds of conclusions though based on a look at other transport modes as well.

The Canadian airline industry had no such similar sharp market economic deregulatory change. There were aspirations to that effect, but airline politics and policy centred on the role of Air Canada as a federally owned airline and then as a private company but always bound up in intricate east–west regional dispute in Canada (see chapter 7) among newer, but much fewer, airlines (Pigott 2014; Langford and Huffman 1988; Oum, Stanbury, and Trethaway 1991).

The cross-border deregulation story was different for different transport modes (Doern, Prince, and Schultz 2014). Madar (2000), whose analysis is on trucking, drew attention to the fact that railway deregulation occurred earlier in Canada than in the US. Thus, changes in 1967 to the National Transportation Act contained promarket measures and even served partially, at least, as an applied learning factor for the Americans in the later 1980 US Staggers Act, which contained major rail deregulation and reform measures (Madar 2000, 5).

Thus, deregulation overall involves analytical judgement about precisely how an old set of rules is changed and in what precise ways. The 1978 US air transport policy declaration allowed massive new market entrants, arguably the most radical notion of what economic deregulation could, and for some should, mean. Stevenson (1988) had earlier noted about the Canadian rail changes of 1967 that, "although popularly described as 'deregulation' what took place is more accurately described as the imposition of a new and different regulatory framework on Canadian railways" (ibid., 74). For various key constitutional and political–legislative reasons, Madar's extensive account of Canada–US trucking deregulation shows vastly different speeds of achievement. The US deregulated trucking in 1980 and thus caught the larger wave of change spearheaded by airline deregulation. Canada, on the other hand, did not achieve some deregulation or federal regulatory reform of trucking until 1987 when a federal Motor Vehicle Transport Act was passed following extensive negotiations with the provinces and with a trucking industry used to dealing only or mainly with the provinces (Madar 2000; Kaplan 1989; Schultz 1995).

It is important to pause in this diverse multimodal Canada–US deregulation policy account and give emphasis to the fact that throughout these events and dynamics the issue of transport safety was always preeminent. Particularly in the air transport sector, as we see below in our discussion of international transport institutions, the continuously expressed highest priority by national and international transport departments and modal institutions was on safety. Key interests knew that these were coterminous with any ability to profit economically or to grow the transport industry.

It is important to see this also in the context of the release in 1985 of the previously discussed federal Freedom to Move policy paper (Transport Canada 1985). The "freedom" part was cast not as some form of unfettered deregulation but rather as freedom from the burden of excessive economic regulation (Hill 1999). Safety was not seen as economic regulation. It was and is social or public interest regulation. It was also different in many ways from transport security regulation as discussed later in this chapter (see also chapters 4 and 7). Security implied and involved increased regulation of particular kinds aimed not at unintended accidents but at persons and behaviour intended to injure and kill transport employees and users and to destroy transport infrastructure (Doern 2010).

Last but not least in this overall period of Canada–US transportation (and related policy) was the related issue of privatization policy. The US Reagan and British Thatcher era was cast as the era of privatization and deregulation, but in transportation policy in the US privatization in the sense of selling off government enterprises was not an issue in air or rail, since private firms were already the norm. In Canada, Crown corporations such as Air Canada and CN were a part of the story, and this fact alone slowed the process of deregulation and privatization (Langford and Huffman 1988; Stevenson 1988).

Air Canada was not privatized until 1988–89 by the Mulroney Conservative government, and CN followed later in 1995 under the Chrétien Liberals. CN immediately acted to reduce its staff and rid itself of considerable track. And within a decade it had also acquired several transport companies, including some in the US. Analysis of the CN privatization by Boardman et al. (2013) concluded that "CN performed substantially better following privatization both from an operational perspective and from a broader social welfare perspective" (ibid., 19). The privatization of Air Canada did not produce similar types of results in part due to its continuing struggle over profitability and also due to the fact that related areas of the air transit system, such as airports, were not privatized but rather, as discussed in chapter 1, operated by socio-economic corporate not-for-profit entities (see also Standing Senate Committee on Transport and Communications 2012).

Also woven into the realities and agendas of Canada–US transport policy were the imperatives of economic recessions in the early 1980s, the mid-1990s, and the 2008–12 period. These impacted on transport firms including, in the US, the bankruptcy of some airlines and, in Canada, some tough times for trucking firms. In the US during the most recent recession, informed transport authorities argued that there was unprecedented retrenchment in federal, state, and city transport funding (Kellogg 2012). As we have seen in chapter 2's account of Canadian federal budgets, transport funding was also struggling, except for the relatively recent growth in infrastructure funding, most of which is aimed at cities and transit infrastructure rather than federal government transport areas *per se* (see chapter 8).

TRADE LIBERALIZATION AGENDAS AND AGREEMENTS, AND THEIR IMPACTS ON TRANSPORTATION

Transport policy and governance has long been part of, and influenced by, liberalized markets and the construction of international and regional free-trade agreements. These market liberalizations and trade agreements, as chapter 1 has shown, always have a direct effect on the businesses in Canada that use transportation services. They also have a direct and indirect effect on the transportation carriers themselves.

The post-Second World War trade reform agenda got rolling with the General Agreement on Tariffs and Trade (GATT) that took effect in 1948 and morphed into the World Trade Organization (WTO) that came into force in 1995. There was a multitude of regional agreements, too, such as the Canada–US Free Trade Agreement (CUSFTA) and then the North American Free Trade Agreement (NAFTA) signed in 1994 by Canada, the United States, and Mexico. These agreements interacted and overlapped with all kinds of deregulation and privatization dynamics described above. That has been a boon and a bane to Canada's industrial, technology, and innovation policies because the agreements in some ways restrain and in other ways support national measures.

The central reality of trade agreements is that they seek to liberalize trade by controlling and restraining governmental behaviour. An early GATT focus was on tariffs (essentially a tax on imports at the border) and their gradual reduction through several rounds of GATT negotiations (Trebilcock 2011). High tariffs had been a key instrument used to protect firms and industries in Canada (and other countries) and a basis for national industrial and technology policy. Historically they were paired with the building and operating of Canada's railway system. The match was good because railways provided a means of distributing domestically produced goods as an alternative to importing them from just across the Canada–US border. As tariffs came down in the twentieth century, the focus shifted to controlling other governmental measures that were understood to distort production and trade.

Domestic and export subsidies were the next obvious target for trade liberalization. Countries have used subsidies in all kinds of creative and clever ways in the name of industrial, transport, agricultural, defence, and regional policies. Such subsidies had both good and adverse effects, as well as intended and unintended impacts, on international and internal trade and on particular industries. We traced this in chapter 1 with respect to the Crows Nest Pass freight rate subsidies. The eventual ending of such subsidies also had been criticized for other domestic political–economic reasons (Langford 1982).

As the global production system has become more interconnected, the concept of national "borders" has become fuzzier and more complex. International trade policy used to concentrate on dealing with trade *at* the border, where the policy instruments found expression in tariffs, quantitative limits, and entry rules. But it has now come to include trade *over* the border, and that often manifests itself in requiring that governments give "national treatment" to foreign investments and foreign-owned businesses *within* their sovereign territory. That means trade policy now affects virtually all policy fields that used to be considered exclusively "domestic," including transportation.

Every trade agreement in one way or another allows some residual limitations on the liberalization values. These include rules for what are referred to as "legitimate objectives" (LOS): for example health, safety, environment, and moral concerns, ostensibly backed by scientific or some other form of evidence about their validity. In the international trade realm, LOS are defined as policy rights that states may use legitimately to pursue national sovereignty and the public interest. But the qualifier in trade agreements is that when LOS are pursued, they must be carried out in the least trade-distorting manner possible by adhering to rules and processes dealing with sanitary and phyto-sanitary (SPS) rules and provisions that apply to technical barriers to trade (TBT). In a perfect world, everybody would agree on what these processes consist of, but in reality they generate disputes because of differences of opinion over the role and applicability of science, evidence, and knowledge in decision making. And the clarity of their meaning is compromised by the concept of "precaution," as a result of inevitable uncertainties in the fields of health, safety, and the environment (Trebilcock, House, and Eliason 2013; Heydon 2012; Coglianese 2012). Human nature being what it is, governments (and private firms and industries) sometimes look for ambiguity to find ways around the rules. That includes transportation. Concerns about transport security, in all its ambiguity, have led to new rules, agencies, and exceptions that can often look suspiciously like nontariff barriers to trade. In other words, countries sometimes use transportation policy as a means of effecting trade policy, for example if the latter is being scrutinized a little too closely for comfort. We will say more about that in the next section of the chapter, on security, and in later domain chapters as well, such as chapter 7.

Meanwhile, despite vigorous opposition from groups worldwide who object to outsourcing, offshoring, the state of working conditions in third-world countries that produce goods for first-world markets, and so on, the impetus for trade liberalization is strong, but the impact of Brexit in the UK and the Donald Trump election as president in the US has produced new uncertainties and dynamics (Doern and Stoney 2016).

Some of the Trump era "America First" trade policy dynamics need to be highlighted, albeit briefly, with the aid of some current analytical work (Donnan 2018; Georges 2017; Swanson 2018; *Economist* 2018). President Trump's America First rhetoric was intended to invoke the notion that Americans had been unfairly treated in various trade agreements and resulting in job losses, but there was also a sense in Trump's discourse that one could not have mutual winners from trade. Trump's target was NAFTA, and so he launched a process of negotiating and renegotiating NAFTA with Canada and Mexico that he backed with the threat of ending the agreement.

The Trump belligerence against Mexico also made the purely trade issues difficult for Canada and Mexico. Different parts of the transport industry also became a part of the tactical politics and economics, especially the car industry regarding changing its "rules of origin" features (*Economist* 2018) and jet aircraft manufacturer, Bombardier. On the car industry, a key US demand was to rewrite NAFTA's rules about cars and especially about NAFTA's rules of origin, where any changes would redefine what counts as a North American car. The Bombardier element of the Trump era dynamics involved the US Commerce Department imposing a steep 300 per cent duty on imported Canadian jets. Boeing had sought the trade penalty regarding Bombardier's new CSeries aircraft. But in January 2018 another US agency, the United States International Trade Commission, unanimously struck down the 300 per cent duty (Swanson 2018). Meanwhile, the Trudeau government was also adopting the strategy of visiting and lobbying in several US states where there had been demonstrable success in mutual trade and job gains (Georges 2017).

More and more countries, however, had been signing regional or bilateral trade agreements. That included Canada. Canada now has bilateral trade and investment agreements with more than fifty other countries. Virtually all of the agreements have implications for transportation in one form or another. And more agreements emerged – for example, the Canada–EU Trade Agreement (CETA) signed in 2014 was eventually approved by EU member states. The Trans-Pacific Partnership Free Trade Agreement (TPP) was opposed by the US Trump Administration and is now still proceeding. If nothing else, every new agreement will alter trade patterns – which will *always* affect (a) supply and demand for transportation, (b) the pattern of trade routes by which goods move from producer to consumer, (c) competition among nations to attract those trade routes into their countries because of the prosperity it tends to bring, and (d) competition among marine, air, and land carriers to haul the goods, which in turn usually dictates the kind of infrastructure (for example, depth of harbours and throughput capacity of container ports) that a country must offer or the carriers will go elsewhere and serve other markets, taking the vigorous trade routes with them.

A larger "trade and" agenda has also emerged as a prominent feature of the expanding liberalized trade regime. This refers to the broadening content of agreements, which usually include "trade and" services, procurement, investment, intellectual property, and so on. Trade and transport has joined this club of linked policy fields. The US "open skies" initiatives followed the deregulation of air transport and the formation of international alliances among airlines (like the Star Alliance of which Air Canada is a member) to serve and develop new markets including the growing travel and tourism industry (US Department of Transport 1999, 2000). In other words, important new *business* opportunities for US carriers were the impetus for an American national policy to negotiate an international *transportation*-related agreement in furtherance of its own interests.

These "trade and" agreements have tested (and often stirred) the policy and regulatory waters in such realms as competition policy, too. These issues were partly resolved in the overall Uruguay Round WTO agreement through separate related agreements on these subjects, with links to WTO institutions. Many of these changes arguably were the product of US power and aggressive unilateralism – or, in short, raw hegemonic American political and economic power (Ostry 1997; Sell 1998). Transportation was swept along with the current.

Trade (and therefore transportation) is also being transformed by digital technology (Lund and Tyson 2018) in at least three ways. Lund and Tyson highlight three transformational changes already well underway. They show that "the movement of data is already surpassing traditional physical trade as the connective tissue in the global economy" (ibid., 132). Second, they show the imperatives of the "rise of the rest" (ibid., 133) by which they mean China but also how the geography of globalization is changing "within" the developing world in that "more than half of all international trade in goods involves at least one developing country and the trade in goods between developing countries – so-called south–south trade – grew from 7 per cent of the global total in 2000 to 18 per cent in 2016" (ibid., 134). This has implications for the nature of supply chains and augurs further "the coming disruption" (ibid., 135) that impact dynamics related to immigration and migrants and changing rules of competition, including those around patents, as well as concerns about cybersecurity and decisions about where companies decide to locate their factories in this larger north–south, and south–south context and set of choices. (ibid., 136–7).

POST-9/11 AND LATER BORDER, BRIDGES, AND TRANSPORT SECURITY POLICY

Our third international and Canada–US realm is concerned with transportation security policy in the aftermath of the 9/11 terrorist events in the US in 2001. Canada–US relations and, fully in step, Canadian *internal* policy priorities as well, shifted massively and immediately to national security concerns. This included national defence, transport, and border security measures. All were driven by trade and by keeping the Canada–US trade corridors secure and therefore open (Gattinger and Hale 2010; Whitaker 2003; Doern 2002; Hart and Tomlin 2002). The purpose was both to support the US as a neighbour, ally, and global power and to protect Canadian access to its largest trade market. Gattinger and Hale's analysis, *Borders and Bridges*, describes an array of Canadian measures in trade policy, with "bridges" used both literally and metaphorically to refer to transport and border infrastructure that enables both countries to trade with each other. That is a double meaning of which we make use in this section.

All of these developments hit the freshly reelected Chrétien Liberal government without warning. The most prominent measures taken by the government in this regard were antiterrorism legislation, which featured new (and remarkably draconian) powers; changes to immigration law; and new financial and personnel resources for the Department of National Defence, csis, and national police and border control; enhanced capacity at Health Canada to deal with anthrax infection and other forms of bioterrorism; and measures to deal with airport safety and security. Almost forgotten by now in the hubbub of those days were further measures taken to deal with the precarious state of Canada's airline industry, including the demands of Air Canada for bailout funds. All of this had a powerful effect on domestic transportation – yet it was driven from abroad. Also established within the government was a Cabinet Committee on Public Security and Antiterrorism. Within days of the 9/11 attack, the US was demanding that Canada join in the construction of a North American security perimeter (Molot 2002).

New antiterrorism legislation was introduced on 22 November 2001 by the transport minister, David Collinette. Called the Public Safety Act, it changed nineteen existing laws and greatly strengthened antiterrorism measures. The federal government was empowered to collect air passenger data from airlines and reservation systems and share it with foreign governments. These and other provisions in the law were criticized by opposition parties and privacy advocates for their (the provisions') intrusiveness into the personal details of people using the transportation system. In other words, international security issues found their way, via transportation policy, directly into the lives of individual Canadians (see chapter 7).

Security measures were also a part of a comprehensive border agreement with the US. It included joint border policing, expanded international security teams, and coordinated immigration measures. All of these features came to a sharp point wherever people and goods were being transported across borders. Some of the pressure from the US was a result of the growing view there that Canada's borders were porous, even though it was conclusively shown that none of the 9/11 terrorists had entered the US via Canada.

The primary US legislative response to the 9/11 events was the Patriot Act and the establishment of the Department of Homeland

Security. American insistence on a perimeter security arrangement raised questions about whether this was a Canada–US perimeter or a North American perimeter. One immediate response came in Canada when four major national business groups formed the Coalition for Secure and Trade-Efficient Borders that went on to lobby for what was, in effect, transportation policy aimed at preserving the crucial gains in liberalized trade that had flowed from NAFTA and the WTO, while minimizing the costs to business of the new US measures (Whitaker 2003). The concept of "smart borders" also quickly emerged as a way of using technology to raise confidence in security measures, mostly on the part of the US in respect to Canada, and thereby preventing delay in the transport of Canadian goods to American customers.

That mattered because according to Globerman and Storer (2006) the new security measures were "producing significantly higher ship-ping costs and shipment delays" (ibid., 1) and "both US exports to and imports from Canada were lower than they would otherwise have been in the post-9/11 period, given traditional determinants of bilateral trade" (ibid., 1). The effects of the measures were anything but homogeneous, either geographically or by mode of transportation. Globerman and Storer report that "trade shortfalls are not uniform across land ports at the Canada–US border … in part because of dif-ferences in the mix of transport modes serving the ports" (ibid., 2) and that "ports that are more intensive users of rail as a transport mode are more likely to evidence a persistent import shortfall" (ibid., 2). The study also emphasized that, "bilateral trade is concen-trated in a relatively small number of ports. Specifically, of the esti-mated 75 land ports along the Canada–US border, just three account for the bulk of bilateral trade" (ibid., 3) (see more below on the Detroit–Windsor bridge story).

The smart border policy seemed to work. Bradbury (2010) reviewed the free and secure trade (FAST) program introduced under the 2001 Smart Border Action Plan and concluded that it "has reduced the average border wait time at four of the five busiest crossing ports," but, she added, "the benefits were unevenly distributed among the ports, as determined by their ability to accommodate infrastructure improvements, and among firms, with larger trucking companies and exporters reaping the benefits" much more than small and medium-sized trucking firms burdened by higher costs (ibid., 367).

Hale (2012) traces the later developments about smart borders and perimeter development and whether these represented a new paradigm or just an incremental shift in Canada–US security and trade relations. He describes the 9/11 event as producing a near-immediate crisis response, but afterward, up to and including the 2008–12 global recession which represented a second crisis, further joint approaches by Canadian and US authorities in transport security and trade amounted to experiments or, in other words, incremental developments. He shows how "the Smart Border process resulted in efforts to assist larger firms to introduce supply chain security and traveller screening measures in return for more efficient processing at the border" (ibid., 109). But these policy measures brought the speed of crossing the border with cargo back to about where it had been prior to 9/11. As crucial as that restoration was, the gains from the new transportation policy measures, taken in the name of security, more or less offset the losses precipitated by the security measures themselves. And anyway, according to Hale, government reorganizations on both sides of the border "undermined both the political momentum and mutual trust necessary for effective administration" (ibid., 109).

The Obama Administration and the Harper government, motivated by economic considerations in the midst of the recession, pushed through two agreements to improve the border security-trade-transport dynamics. The first was Beyond the Border: A Shared Vision for Perimeter Security and Economic Competitiveness and the second centred on the creation of a bilateral Canada–United States Regulatory Cooperation Council (CURCC) (Canada 2011). The most significant policy development they contained, Hale argues, was a commitment to "work towards a common entry–exit system" (ibid., 113). The CURCC was designed to promote joint study and reform of bilateral regulatory realms. The Beyond the Border Action Plan (BTAP) (United States, Department of Homeland Security and Canada Privy Council Office 2011), which was contained in the first agreement, may be a brief document but as Hale points out it drives home "the size, diversity and complexity of border management issues in each country, along with the legal and administrative complications of coordinating different legal and administrative processes" (Hale 2012, 115). The BTAP extended existing programs and promised new ones. The latter were ambitious and complicated. All of this work and bilateral deal making was aimed at transportation. And its goal in turn was to enable trade and economic activity. The economic imperative of transporting goods, and the immediacy of the danger to its continued movement, pushed Canada–US deal making on this policy space to the top of the agenda after having languished previously.

We conclude the security, transport, and bridges part of the Canada–US section in this chapter with a story characterized by the incredible cross-border dynamics of events, decisions, and nondecisions involving the Windsor–Detroit crossing, whose Ambassador Bridge is the largest and most important piece of transport infrastructure in Canada–US trade and in the transport of goods. More than 25 per cent of Canada–US merchandise trade by dollar value crosses that eighty-seven-year-old span. Every weekday it handles 10,000 or more trucks that carry 60 to 70 per cent of all cross-border truck traffic in the region. There is no realistic fallback crossing anywhere if the span were closed on account of structural fatigue or if hit by a ship. Often congested, it has little potential for growth of traffic in future. A lot of Canada's economic eggs are in that one basket (Anderson 2011). Building a second span has been on Canada's transportation policy agenda for years.

The main decision came in 2012: to establish a Windsor–Detroit Bridge Authority (WDBA). A not-for-profit Crown corporation, it reports through the minister of Transport. Its function is to "manage the procurement process for the design, construction, operation and maintenance of the new bridge between Windsor, Ontario and Detroit, Michigan through a public–private partnership (P3)" (Windsor–Detroit Bridge Authority 2016a).

The new bridge will be built and operational by 2020. It will be named the Gordie Howe International Bridge, after the late NHL hockey legend from Floral, Saskatchewan, who played most of his career with the Detroit Red Wings. The bridge is described as the "largest and most ambitious bi-national border infrastructure project along the Canada–United States Border ... and consists of a new six lane bridge to be a component of a new end-to-end transportation system that also includes associated border inspection plazas and connections to the freeway systems of Ontario and Michigan. This project will provide an essential additional crossing option at one of the busiest Canada–US commercial border crossings" (Windsor–Detroit Bridge Authority 2016b, 2).

The WDBA website's history of the project is cryptic in the extreme, failing as it does to portray the nature and intensity of the ten-year-plus battle just to get the new structure built: the Ambassador Bridge is owned by a private billionaire businessman, Matty Moroun, who, having bought controlling interest when the bridge's shares were traded on the stock market and thus secured for himself a monopoly, fought the proposed project relentlessly in a process that played out as Detroit, a city, and Michigan, a state, were both bankrupt and in political and social disarray (Savage 2015). After prolonged but unsuccessful efforts to secure bilateral financing by both the Chrétien–Martin and Harper governments, and to strike a deal that was widely considered to be vital for the Canadian economy, Prime Minister Harper in February 2015 "gave up and made an extraordinary announcement: Canada would build a new $4 billion bridge benefitting both sides of the river, but without any financial participation from the state of Michigan or the US government" (ibid., 2). Canada undertook to pay for the entire infrastructure, even on the American side of the bridge including roads, plazas, and buildings and facilities for US Customs and Border Services! The twists and turns in the plot are amazing. As the owner of the existing Ambassador Bridge, Moroun used every financial, legal, and political measure and ploy in the book, and even invented some new ones, to block the approval, financing, and building of the new structure, which had been initiated by Canada. He appears now to want to reach some kind of cooperative agreement with the Justin Trudeau Liberal government (Diebel 2016). Moroun's case was ultimately weakened and ended by a Michigan court decision that overruled his appeal, because it was four years late.

Recent developments, however, have added to the complexity and politics of the bridge story (Gollom 2017). As Gollom reports, proponents "of both the Ambassador Bridge and the Gordie Howe Bridge often cite the need for redundancy that with so much trade occurring between the two countries, another bridge is vital in case one had to be shut down temporarily" (ibid., 2). The Justin Trudeau government approved a permit for Moroun but subject to the requirement that he "must tear down his current bridge within five years of his new $1 billion span being built, preventing any plans he might have had to control 10 lanes of bridge crossing" (ibid., 1). Not surprisingly, this development has led to sharp predictions that this will kill the Gordie Howe Bridge and blow the federal money spent on it or that, alternatively, the strategy will ultimately be positive for the needed two-bridge solution. On 18 July 2018 Canada's Infrastructure minister and the governor of Michigan held a groundbreaking ceremony on the Gordie Howe International Bridge site

(Fraser 2018). The US Trump administration supported the new bridge on the grounds of economic prosperity and security, but the impact of recent Trump trade tariffs on Canada meant that no one had a firm sense of what the actual cost of building the bridge would be. In short, progress had been made, but as a huge bridge infrastructure project, its actual costs still had to be finalized for Canadian and American governments and for bridge construction firms and consortia on both sides of the border.

While this bridge story is remarkable in many ways it is important to note that the ownership of cross-border infrastructure rarely involves one private owner. The system in fact is typically complex because border facilities can involve federal–state, provincial–state ownership, and/or statutory linkages and partnership arrangements. In most cases (e.g., Cornwall–Messina, Alexandria Bay, Queenston–Lewiston, Peace Bridge, and Sault Ste Marie) ownership and governance of bridges is shared between either (in most cases) Canadian federal and US state governments through structure specific binational bridge commissions.

Whether or not the above two-bridge scenario materializes, it is a remarkable feature of Canada–US trade and transportation policy that so important an international artery as this should be owned by a single person and that his personal financial interests and political influence should have held so much sway in delaying and almost preventing the construction of an asset of such strategic value to not one but two countries. Were it not for a transportation policy held onto with grim determination by the federal government, particularly the Harper administration, in support of Canada's trade policy, the new bridge would still be going nowhere and billions of dollars in economic activity would remain in a very susceptible state with no fallback in sight.

CABOTAGE AND INTERNATIONAL VERSUS NATIONAL TRANSPORT REFORM AND MODAL INTRICACIES

Our first three international and Canada–US policy lenses and examples each deal with individual major cross-border policy imperatives and reforms: economic deregulation, free and liberalized trade, and security and terrorism. The fourth lens needing attention in this chapter centres on cabotage and international versus national transport reform and modal intricacies. Cabotage refers "both to the transport of goods from one point to another within a country and to the requirement that the transport of goods or people from one point to another within a country be carried out by a domestic carrier" (Blank and Prentice 2012, 1).

Cabotage policy and protectionist practices were not ended when economic deregulation occurred, when most of the free trade agreements Canada signed were adopted, or when security and terrorism crises occurred and were the impetus for new laws and institutions. The failure to eliminate cabotage policies and practices and produce free trade or full deregulation in transportation is seen as a seriously unfinished agenda by some but to others it is not necessarily a problem, given the need for a national transportation system that to some continuing but changing extent supports Canadian modal transportation industries, firms, and employees. The policies, actions and inactions can show up in any number of linked policy fields and arenas including customs and border measures, tax policy, immigration, jobs and employment in the transport sector and system, and concepts of national defence and security (Brooks 2008; Transport Canada 1982, 2003).

While cabotage is a centuries-old practice starting in marine shipping but then extending to trucking and air transport modes, the more recent focal point for major policy change aimed at limiting such practices is the EU. Indeed, the EU first as a much smaller set of member countries and now as an entity comprised of twenty-eight member countries, was compelled to have such cabotage-limiting policies if it was to have any chance of becoming a vast new internal market. In this sense it can be seen as a later version of the US when the American constitution conferred strong interstate commerce powers on the US federal government, powers that are much stronger than Canada's interprovincial internal trade market powers.

In the EU road cabotage is governed by Regulation (EC) 1072/2009, which replaced earlier 1992 and 1993 regulations. The purpose of the regulation "is to improve the efficiency of road freight transport by reducing empty trips after the unloading of international transport operations" (European Commission 2016, 1). More specifically,

Article 8 of the Regulation provides that every haulier is entitled to perform up to three cabotage operations within a seven days period starting the day after the unloading of the international transport. A haulier may decide to carry out one, two or three cabotage operations in different Member States and not necessarily the Member State in which the International transport was delivered. In this case only one cabotage operation is allowed in a given Member State to be carried out within three days of entering that Member State without a cargo. (Ibid., 1)

It is important to note that the stated purpose is not unlimited free trade but rather improved efficiency via some managed trade liberalization. But the Article 8 example and its three cabotage operations also shows how complex it is to monitor and enforce, given the volume of haulage traffic across and within twenty-eight member states. We return to the EU example below with regard to the current Canada–European Union Comprehensive Economic and Trade Agreement (CETA) discussions, and we also refer very briefly to the Trans Pacific Partnership Agreement (TPP) that involves a different complex array of Pacific countries and which was being negotiated concurrently with CETA.

We also need to see what cabotage involves in a Canada–US context, historically and at present. For example, the Canada–US Free Trade Agreement did not deal at all with free trade in transportation services and thus cabotage issues were not addressed (Prokop 1999; Doern and Tomlin 1991). The North American Free Trade Agreement that followed involved discussions about cabotage but mainly between Canada and Mexico and thus again progress was limited. In both cases within the US the reasons for nonaction were centred on the protectionist power anchored in Congress and centred in continued support for the Jones Act, legislation passed in 1920 regarding US shipping. Recent analysis has made the case in the US for significantly changing the Jones Act on the grounds that it has seriously harmed the competitive advantage of the US in shipping and maritime-related industries (Slattery, Riley and Loris 2014).

Some of the arguments for cabotage changes and for the practicalities involved in the cabotage puzzle are found in research by Beilock and Prentice (2007) that is centred on their advocacy of the "open prairies proposal" as a single potential North American trucking market experiment. The proposed experiment would involve all or part of the "Canadian Prairie Provinces and the US Upper Great Plains," hence a cabotage experiment called "open prairies." This proposal has not yet been adopted, but the case for it and the analytics are instructive. The analysis begins with the fact that US law precludes cabotage and also that Canadian customs and immigration laws produce analogous restrictions. The EU is a better model, and Beilock and Prentice cite evidence that in Europe cabotage for trucking "has yielded benefits" and that "there is no evidence of disproportionate bias against or favour of any country. Notwithstanding regulatory inconsistencies, the more liberal approach has few problems that are not already being dealt with including considerations (such as), labour laws, weight and size limits, and tax regimes" (ibid., 3).

Beilock and Prentice begin by saying that it seems almost self-evident that free trade in transportation services "would facilitate greater economic efficiency in the trade of goods and services" (ibid., 3) but they also, when mapping and designing how the "open prairies" model might work, highlight potential variants. Thus, among the issues is the fact that "the location and duration of work (on each side of the border) would be difficult to predict. To deal with this, systems would have to be developed to address relevant tax issues" (ibid., 10). But other issues should not be seen as "problem factors" because they would be "materially unaffected from allowing cabotage" (ibid., 10). These other issues include national security, vehicle standards, and traffic safety.

When we switch back to maritime or marine cabotage policy (also known in Canada as coasting trade policy) the issues are partly the same but also different because this transport mode is different, as is its industrial political lobbying structure. Analysis by Hodgson and Brooks (2012) is useful here both in its overall account of the field but also regarding Canada in a North American cabotage context (Hodgson and Brooks 2007). These analyses again show the EU as the exemplar in that since "the late 1980s substantial efforts have been made to reduce protective barriers in Europe to the point where now any EU flag ship that is eligible to engage in its own coasting trade is able to engage in coasting trade activities in any other EU State" (Hodgson and Brooks 2012, 6). But it is also the case that "the relaxed restrictions on the registration of vessels engaged in maritime cabotage do not preclude the imposition of requirements in relation to crew and the location of the ownership of the vessel in question" (ibid., 6). In addition, EU member states offer "important fiscal aid, usually in the form of a 'tonnage tax' which effectively reduces corporate taxation to levels approaching zero" (ibid., 6).

These basic circumstances "are in sharp contrast to the substantial barrier between domestic and international sectors that exist in

Canada" (ibid., 6). Regarding Canada, Hodgson and Brooks conclude that, "beyond providing artificial protection for hard-pressed and expensive domestic fleets, there is little evidence that the present regime is providing an optimum environment for domestic shipping operations" (ibid., 7).

When weaving in OECD and other Canada–US issues (where in the latter context much less progress is evident, again because of continuing US protectionism but also due to Canadian lethargy), the above study nonetheless concludes "that it may be assumed that Canada's cabotage policy objectives overall "are to ensure economic efficiency, adequacy, safety, environmental integrity and fair employment standards" (ibid., 8). But these kinds of expressed transport policy content imply overall the concept of modal "neutrality," in short "the construction of a level playing field among domestic modes that has been a cornerstone of Canadian transportation policy since the 1960s" (ibid., 9). On the other hand, it is clear regarding cabotage that modes are different and thus such a "level playing field" metaphor regarding equality and equity actually involves treating some players and interests in equal situations equally and treating other players and interests in unequal situations unequally (Coleman and Doern 2014). So neither the politics nor the policy is simple as various interests jockey for advantage in different arenas across and within borders.

Meanwhile, the EU had been progressing on cabotage in both the trucking and maritime modes and also in air transport (see more in chapter 7). Not surprisingly the CETA trade negotiations between Canada and the EU did include cabotage. The final CETA agreement completed in the Harper Conservative era involved, compared to the earlier CUSFTA and NAFTA agreements, many more closed, secretive processes for the negotiations. Once key provisions became known, and even earlier to some extent, various interests assessed and commented on key provisions, including those on transport and cabotage.

The Canadian Centre for Policy Alternatives' (2014) analysis of marine transport provisions drew attention to several CETA provisions for intra-coastal shipping, where the CETA will allow:

- EU-based or EU-owned firms to ship empty containers between ports in Canada on a non-revenue basis by using vessels of any registry;

- The shipping of freight between the Ports of Halifax and Montreal on EU-registered vessels. This includes both bulk and container cargo for continuous service using vessels on EU first registries;
- EU contractors to bid on any federally procured dredging contracts exceeding the procurement thresholds for construction services (5 million SDR or about $8 million);
- EU contractors to bid on private dredging contracts of any size. (Ibid., 79)

The authors of this study concluded that the "CETA would have significant negative consequences on the Canadian marine transport sector, including lost jobs in domestic freighting.

A coalition of Canadian organizations has formed a committee called the Canadian Maritime and Supply Chain Coalition (CMSCC) to raise public awareness of these concerns" (ibid., 79). They also suggest that if these "provisions liberalizing cabotage in marine shipping are approved in the CETA, it will likely open the door to similar liberalization of rules in air, rail and road transport" (ibid., 80). Regarding CETA and air transport, this study expressed minimal concerns about CETA largely because air transport had already been liberalized by the 2009 Air Transport Agreement, but an array of concerns about that agreement and also various "open skies" provisions are expressed by the above authors as being potentially or likely harmful to the Canadian airline industry and market (ibid., 80–2). But other analyses of air liberalization internationally argue that major progress has occurred and cabotage *per se* is scarcely even mentioned (International Transport Forum 2015).

Other analysts such as Ryan (2015) show the diversity of Canadian support for and opposition to CETA by marine industry interests. For example the ports of Montreal and Halifax see "promising opportunities for growth in North Atlantic trade" (ibid., 1). So has the Shipping Federation of Canada. The Seafarers' International Union of Canada (SIU), on the other hand, has mounted a campaign to "stop CETA from sinking our ships" (quoted in Ryan 2015, 1). On these matters, the various interests may be eyeing the value or lack thereof in quite specific and particular situations and also whether protests now may be crafted as battles yet to be fought in the medium and longer time periods.

Also present on the agenda is the above mentioned TPP trade agreement. Given its greater diversity of Pacific-based countries rather than any kind of EU involvement, and also the greater scope of the TPP agreement's subjects, cabotage does not directly appear much by name. The TPP agreement's chapter 10 is on "cross-border trade and services" and it leads off with provisions that deal with air services, including ground handling services at airports, the selling and marketing of air transport services, the place of speciality air services, and networks of services in connection with the supply of a service. These relate often to cabotage-like situations but mainly to ensure that liberalization is encouraged but also monitored.

Cabotage as both an international and domestic feature and practice of transportation warrants separate treatment because it has a long history and is in important ways entrenched in an intricate manner. It involves trade-offs between national interests and protection and international needs to foster more efficient and liberal transport services across borders and within nations by international carriers based in other countries.

THE ST LAWRENCE SEAWAY, BILATERAL GOVERNANCE, AND RELATED GREAT LAKES MARINE AND ENVIRONMENTAL POLICY

In this, our fifth, example and lens we mainly focus on international governance as bilateral Canada–US governance of the seaway, The Canadian lead agency is the St Lawrence Seaway Management Corporation (SLSMC) established in 1998 as a not-for-profit entity and successor to the previous St Lawrence Seaway Authority (Jenish 2009). Its counterpart in the US is the Saint Lawrence Seaway Development Corporation (SLSDC), which is a wholly owned US government corporation (SLSDC 2014). Together, and by agreement, this is an international case of bilateral Canada–US seaway governance with inexorable ties to Great Lakes marine and also environmental policy and, as we see later, the earlier historical impetus provided by the Canada–US International Joint Commission (IJC).

Though the St Lawrence Seaway is in crucial ways a Canada–US governance story it was also a global and international one from the outset, now with ever more complex international dynamics and challenges. Historian D.G. Creighton's initial book (1932) examined the St Lawrence River from 1760 to 1850 in terms of the "commercial empire of the St. Lawrence" when it served as a transport conduit to Britain and Europe. The second edition of Creighton's book (1956) still cast it as an empire but by then and having changed it in major ways with more intra-North American politics and commerce. Then came the building and operation of the St Lawrence Seaway as a major infrastructure project and engineering achievement, which took a decade to build and opened in 1959 and will celebrate its sixtieth anniversary in 2019.

The seaway itself is a 189-mile system between Montreal and Lake Ontario. It involved the building of seven locks, five in Canada and two in the US, in order to "lift vessels to 246 feet above sea level" (Great Lakes St Lawrence Seaway System 2016, 1). The project also involved a deepening of the Welland Canal in Ontario. There were also earlier links with water policy where the Great Lakes were already also a focal area for Canada–US cooperation regarding water transportation and increasingly related environmental concerns.

On the US side its SLSDC annual report for 2014 initially stresses its work in maintaining and operating the two US seaway locks in Massena NY (SLSDC 2014, 2) but then immediately refers to how it "directly interacts with numerous Canadian government and private entities" (ibid., 2) particularly regarding "rules and regulations, overall day-to-day waterway and lock operations, traffic management, navigation aids, safety and environmental programs" (ibid., 1). Later in the report, SLSDC draws attention to how it "maintains 100 percent inspections of foreign vessels entering the St Lawrence Seaway" (ibid., 8), work carried out in Montreal before they enter the seaway and US waters. This program is jointly administered with Transport Canada. Also given attention is continued US support for the joint Canadian–US "Green Marine" program aimed at achieving a higher level of environmental performance (ibid., 10). The program began in October 2007 and sought, via self-evaluation reports by participants, "to build and maintain strong relations with key stakeholders and to develop greater awareness of the maritime industry's activities, benefits, and challenges" (ibid., 10).

With regard to Canada's seaway policy governance there has been from the outset analytical interest in what Sussman (1978) called the "joint water highway." Interestingly, in 2003, Canada's SLSMC began a branding and marketing campaign called Highway H2O that "started with public-awareness billboards on Ontario's 400 series highways. They informed motorists that one seaway-sized vessel can haul as much cargo as 870 trucks and made the point that marine transport is one way of reducing congestion on the roads" (Jenish 2009, 21). The US SLSDC agreed to join this campaign, including seeing it as a green alternative to rail and road. SLSMC also saw its then sluggish 60 per cent capacity performance being greatly improved if it could move from its reliance on stable commodity shipments of grain, iron ore, and coal to have a greater capacity to ship-container traffic.

Another interesting dynamic between the two national seaway entities occurred in the 1996–98 period. As we have seen, Canada opted in 1998 for a not-for-profit entity as its new seaway governance model. But in the run-up to this decision, there had been pressure in Canada to privatize the seaway authority and there appeared to be one or two willing buyers/bidders (Jenish 2009, 88–90). However, the US seaway authority was a public corporation (a Crown Corporation to use Canadian terminology) and it and other parts of the US transportation government structure were not ready to see Canada's entity become private if that meant it only had to behave like a private firm without public interest responsibilities.

Another relevant Canada–US process was the work and report of the Great Lakes St Lawrence Seaway Study (GLSLS) (2007). It involved seven departments and agencies as sponsors of and contributors to the study: Transport Canada, US Army Corps of Engineers, US Department of Transport, the SLSMC, the SLSDC, Environment Canada, and the US Fish and Wildlife Service. Its research and analytical work was carried out over three years by three working groups of subject matter experts: economic, environmental, and engineering (ibid., 1). The central question the GLSLS was asked was, "what is the current condition of the GLSLS system, and how best should we use and maintain the system, in its current physical configuration, in order to capitalize on the opportunities and face the challenges that will present themselves in coming years" (ibid., 1). A decade after it came out, the GLSLS report should still be essential reading for its quality regarding the subject matter of the three working groups. It offered several key conclusions and observations, only a sample of which are cited here.

On its economic role, it noted that, "while grain still moves through the GLSLS, its volumes have been overshadowed by huge shipments of iron ore" (ibid., 2). For these and other shippers, the system "offers significant savings" and also "it offers shippers considerable spare

capacity," an issue of growing importance given road and rail congestion (ibid., 2). The GLSLS can relieve some of these pressures "by
offering complementary transportation routes through less busy ports
and by moving goods directly across lakes rather than around them"
(ibid., 4) such as via so-called "shortsea shipping."

The study provided an inventory of environmental impacts and
costs of the system presented as varied and complex environmental
stressors, both navigational-related and non-navigational-related
(ibid., 3). Action is needed on the former but such improvements will
not themselves deal with growing broader environmental impacts
and hence are "unlikely to result in gains to overall environmental
quality" (ibid., 4).

Regarding GLSLS infrastructure and its engineering systems consisting of "locks, shipping channels, ports, bridges, control and communication systems" (ibid., 5), the key was the continued maintenance
of the system. In particular the study stressed that, "Reliability is critical
because the GLSLS is essentially a series of structures that must be
transited with no alternatives. ... As a result, closure of one of the
structures in the series closes the entire system" (ibid., 6). Increasingly
a "proactive maintenance strategy" will be needed.

While the GLSLS report is valuable and had seven government
entities involved, it was not very good at examining the governance
implications *per se.* A study by Jetoo et al. (2014) maps and assesses
"governance and geopolitics as drivers of change in the Great Lakes–
St Lawrence basin." They begin with the not uncommon view that
"the basic characteristic of governance is the migration of power
from the central state up into supranational institutions, horizontally
to non-state actors, and down to sub-national levels of government
and non-state actors" (ibid., 1). The analysis focuses on four central
problems: institutional fragmentation, the changing relationship
between federal and subnational levels of government in Canada and
the US, the governance capacity to implement decisions made within
a governance regime "which includes expertise, resources such as
funding and personnel, and an informed and engaged public" (ibid., 2),
and the "effect of geopolitics on Great Lakes region governance"
(ibid., 2).

This kind of broadened scope of analysis about the Great Lakes is
also found in different ways in the ecological history offered by John
Riley (2014). His comprehensive analysis begins in 1500 and ends
with the current imperatives of growing cities and changing climates

and the challenges of restoring a "new native landscape" (Riley 2014, 278–301). Overall it is not difficult to say that, as the St Lawrence Seaway heads towards its sixtieth anniversary in 2019, the entry points for its analysis are numerous and complex with Canada–US intermodal transportation–marine policy as one policy realm but conjoined inexorably with water policy, environmental policy, economic policy and trade and governance, and changing systems of political power.

In many ways this was not the first time the seaway and marine policy had been in these complex Canada–US governance worlds. Early formal cooperation began with the 1909 Boundary Waters Treaty, administered by one of the longest serving Canada–US bodies, the International Joint Commission (IJC) (Clamen 2013). The IJC, under its governing treaty, was mainly concerned with water quantity (i.e., water levels), but it has since addressed water quality related to pollution protection and restoration. The massive St Lawrence Seaway project also flowed from this bilateral cooperation. The project has been associated with major adverse socioenvironmental impacts due to major planned flooding and water diversions (Macfarlane 2014; Alexander 2009). Indeed, in hindsight, it is possible to say that if the building of the seaway were being planned now, the proposal would not proceed due to environmental concerns and opposition.

In terms of institutional legitimacy, the IJC earned considerable support because it was a truly bilateral entity with both the giant more populous US agreeing that it and the smaller Canada would each appoint three members to the commission. Early on, and in the decades since, water quantity and levels were vital because major economic and population growth occurred (especially in the US) in cities and elsewhere threatened the viability of such water resources. Thus a fairly principled view emerged that neither country should take actions unilaterally that might have adverse impacts on the other. As a result the IJC for the most part functioned as a consensus-oriented and expert body. But requirements for all of its decisions to have prior approval by the two national governments limited the IJC's practical autonomy. It also evolved to develop complex relations with numerous state and provincial governments and with social and environmental NGOs. It would also arbitrate between the two countries when asked. The IJC, however, was subject to criticism about the quality of some of its decisions on certain sensitive and often large-scale projects (Botts and Muldoon 2005; Kehoe 1997).

The 1972 Great Lakes Water Agreement between Canada and the US was signed just as Environment Canada was being created (Sproule-Jones 2003; Doern and Conway 1994). It had been preceded by joint scientific research on water quality by the two countries and also by considerable cooperation by Canadian and US environmental NGOs as they lobbied for an agreement, especially those in the Great Lakes bordering US states and Canadian provinces. Given the more than forty joint water boundary areas – and changing pollution threats and water-level concerns – at play with the Great Lakes, not all challenges were solved or even addressed. Great Lakes issues saw improvement in water quality but then also new pollution threats with the lakes as both an economic and social resource including their importance to tourism and to ecological biodiversity. These ongoing challenges are apparent in the seaway-related toxic algae bloom that spread in parts of Lake Erie in August 2014 and threatened wildlife and drinking water for communities such as Toledo, Ohio.

The St Lawrence Seaway provides an analytical lens and focus on international governance as bilateral Canada–US governance of the seaway through two linked cooperating agencies on each side of the border and the seaway. The analysis shows as well that it did not arrive at an empty Canada–US governance realm in that other institutions and challenges related to the Great Lakes and to environmental and water policy were already present and/or quickly became a part of the overall policy and governance dynamics and will remain so.

INTERNATIONAL TRANSPORTATION INSTITUTIONS: A PROFILE OF THREE AGENCIES

Last but not least in the chapter's international contextual discussion, we briefly survey some of the international transportation institutions in which Canada has membership. Our focus here is on three government bodies, but it is also important to mention that there are also transport *business* international organizations that both lobby governments and share power, knowledge, and governance. These business lobbies and cogovernance entities include the International Air Transport Association (IATA), the International Chamber of Shipping (ICS), the International Shipping Federation (ISF), the International Road Transport Union (IRU), the International Union of Railways (IUR), and the International Freight Forwarders Association (IFFA).

The three international *governmental* agencies more explicitly pro-filed here are the International Maritime Organization (IMO), the International Civil Aviation Organization (ICAO), and the International Transport Forum (ITF) affiliated with the Organization for Economic Cooperation and Development (OECD). The first two entities are the dominant international modal agencies, and the ITF presents itself quite validly as the only global cross transport multimodal entity *per se* (see more below).

Transport Canada's International and Intergovernmental Relations Directorate "in keeping with Canadian Foreign policy objectives ... coordinates and facilitates Canada's relations with these bodies but also international multilateral forums such as the Asia Pacific Economic Cooperation (APEC), the Summit of the Americas, the OECD, the European Ministers of Transport, and the Arctic Council" (Transport Canada 2011). In 2007, when the directorate created a new Coordination Unit, the impetus was said to come from the need to "support such high-profile initiatives as Gateway and Corridor work, key bilateral relations, including relations with China, and work with the Department's increasing role vis-à-vis the International Transport Forum" (Transport Canada 2011).

The International Maritime Organization (IMO) is a United Nations specialized agency composed of 171 member states, and as the oldest international transport mode it can trace its origins back to the mid-nineteenth century and onwards as several maritime treaties were adopted. When the United Nations itself was established in 1948, an "international conference in Geneva adopted a convention formally establishing the IMO (the original name was the Inter-Governmental Maritime Consultative Organization, or IMCO, but the name was changed in 1982 to IMO)" (International Maritime Organization 2016a, 1). Its history of further conventions captures its core and broadening mandate agenda: the 1960 reformed version of the International Convention for the Safety of Life at Sea (SOLAS); the disastrous 1967 shipwreck of the *Torrey Canyon* oil tanker raised sharply the issue of the pollution impacts of large oil tankers; the resulting 1973 Convention for the Prevention of Pollution From Ships, later amended to cover pollution by chemicals, goods in packaged form, sewage, garbage and air pollution (ibid., 1). In the 1980s and 1990s, the IMO developed a maritime distress and safety system and the International Safety Management Code. In 2004, a new comprehensive security regime was adopted, including port facility security (ibid., 2).

Though member states anchor the IMO, consultative status is given by application to nongovernmental organizations (NGOs) if "they have the capability to make a substantial contribution to the work of the IMO" and can "demonstrate considerable expertise" (IMO 2016b, 1). Such consultative status has been given to seventy-seven such international NGOs. In addition, sixty-five other intergovernmental organizations (IGOs) have signed agreements of cooperation with the IMO (ibid., 1).

The IMO's Strategic Plan for the Organization (for the six-year period 2016 to 2021) (IMO 2015) reiterates the IMO mission statement, namely "to promote safe, secure, environmentally sound, efficient and sustainable shipping through cooperation" (ibid., 3). In its identification of key "trends, developments and challenges" that it must face, the IMO lists in an implied priority order the following

- Globalization and sustainable development (including the UN's 2030 Agenda for Sustainable Development)
- Hightened maritime safety concerns
- Heightened maritime security concerns
- Heightened concerns about piracy and armed robbery against ships
- Heightened environmental consciousness
- Promoting the efficiency of shipping
- Shifting emphasis onto people (regarding safety chains of command)
- People at Sea
- The Importance of capacity building in ensuring universal and uniform application of IMO instruments. (Ibid., 3–7)

Also mentioned is technology as a major driving force for change in the maritime sector.

The International Civil Aviation Organization (ICAO) was established following a 1944 conference in Chicago that resulted in the Convention on International Civil Aviation (the Chicago Convention) signed by fifty-two states. Based in Montreal, the ICAO is the only UN international agency with its headquarters in Canada. The ICAO's initial purpose was to foster "cooperation and the highest possible degree of uniformity in regulation, procedures and organization regarding civil aviation matters" (ICAO 2016) with an initial technical focus on air navigation with means of increasing safety in flight. As a United Nations specialized agency, it has evolved and expanded to include 191 member states, and in its mandate tasks those members in keeping with the changed challenges of international civil aviation policy and governance. Two overall interpretations of the ICAO's origins and evolution (Mackenzie 2010, 328–43; Braithwaite and Drahos 2000, 454–71) are pivotal. The analysis by Mackenzie provides a Canadian perspective and the Braithwaite and Drahos account is a broader mapping of, as the title states, global business regulation. These analyses also drew needed explicit attention to the ICAO's continuing battles over jurisdiction and regulation with the International Air Transport Association (IATA) which was and is an industry association for airlines (not located in Montreal) and a de facto competing "regulator" with ICAO. We also need to stress, as highlighted on the agency's website (ICOA 2018) that at present there are seven regional offices of ICAO that function in a massively more complex international airline industry and policy and governance realm than it was when Montreal became the ICAO headquarters, after considerable and successful Canadian lobbying.

The ICAO council 2014 annual report discusses its five strategic objectives. In rank order these are safety, air navigation capacity and efficiency, security and facilitation, the economic development of air transport, and environmental protection. Its project summaries and their implementation issues are grouped into these priority areas. That safety should be the highest strategic objective is not surprising. But safety dynamics can be both broad in relation to air navigation overall and also quite specific as new hazards and threats are discovered and reported. For example, at time of writing, the ICAO's navigation commission "recommended banning cargo shipments of rechargeable lithium batteries from passenger airliners because they can create fires capable of destroying planes" (*The Guardian* 2016, 1). Some of the evidence for this came from fires and pilot deaths on destroyed cargo planes. So the issue partly centres on whether there should be bans on both cargo and passenger planes or just on passenger plans. In addition, another ICOA panel on the transport of dangerous goods voted 11–7 against such a ban (ibid., 2).

A larger recent ICAO decision is its path-breaking airline emissions policy, six years in the making, which has been agreed to in relation to the Paris climate change agreement and a resulting soon-to-be-completed Montreal Protocol (Mouawad and Davenport 2016). It provides for binding limits on CO_2 emissions, which would apply to all new airplanes delivered after 2028. Critics have argued that such emission reductions should apply to all aircraft currently in use. While the initial decision is pivotal and has been announced as an ICAO decision, it still must go through further internal ICAO decision stages before it is binding.

ICAO's security and facilitation strategic objective clearly flows from security rather than just normal safety challenges and is tied globally in both developed and developing countries to terrorism, in part flowing from ICAO's No Country Left Behind (NCLB) campaign. The facilitation features include an ICAO "traveller identification program" tied to travel document security and identification management. This in turn includes the capacity for each ICAO member state to systematically report and register all stolen or lost passports in Interpol's data base (ICAO 2015).

The International Transport Forum (ITF) at the OECD in Paris describes itself as an "intergovernmental organization with 57 member countries" that "acts as a think tank for transportation policy and organizes the Annual Summit of transport ministers. ITF is the only global body that covers all transport modes." Its mission "is to foster a deeper understanding of the role of transport in economic growth, environmental sustainability and social inclusion and raise the public profile of transport policy" (International Transport Forum 2016a, 1). The ITF acts "as a platform for discussion and pre-negotiation of policy issues across all transport modes" (ibid., 1).

Although created in 2006, it was forged in 1953 out of the European Conference of Ministers of Transport (ECMT) itself formed via treaty from sixteen European nations. The legal core of the current ITF still resides in the ECMT. The IFT has one regulatory role via its management of the multilateral quota system of licenses for road haulage operations. The IFT stresses that it "started as a regional organization, but it has looked to the world from the outset" with "the United States and Canada ... invited to become associate members." Both countries joined in 1975 and 1977, respectively (ibid., 1).

The IFT is administratively integrated with the OECD and the latter remains in its own terms as a well-known and influential international policy and governance entity composed mainly of wealthy democratic countries. The OECD, formed in 1960 and now consisting of thirty-four member countries, produces a wide range of diverse public policy and managerial reform reports and discussions (Pal 2012). There is little doubt that the IFT profits from and feeds off this kind of common research and think tank location and exchange. But equally, both entities stress their political independence and different membership.

The fact that transport ministers are central to its structure is what makes it attractive to ministers compared to other international bodies where officials are dominant, and as UN bodies they are also in the purview of national foreign policy ministries. At OECD annual meetings, however, transport ministers are joined by approximately 1,000 other transport experts from businesses and NGOs. The IFT also draws attention to the fact that it has regular links with the IMO and ICAO. When the IFT renewed its mandate via its 2014 "declaration by ministers," ministers "expressed satisfaction in particular with the success of the Annual Summit and the opportunities it presents for Ministers to engage with one another bilaterally and multilaterally, as well as with leaders from industry, civil society and academia" (International Transport Forum 2014, 4).

As a global transport policy think tank, researcher, funder, and online publisher, there is little doubt that it is multimodal and intermodal in its scope. Its twenty-three studies published in 2015 and eleven in 2014 represent a considered and broad effort to address key present and future transport policy (see International Transport Forum 2016 b,1–24). These include, for example, research and related reports on improving safety for motorcycle, scooter and moped riders; public transport provision in rural areas; road infrastructure safety management; the impact of megaships; big data and transport; automated and autonomous driving; and the liberalization of air transport. In 2012 and 2013, the ITF also attempted to foster thinking based on the discourse of "seamless transport" which variously meant or included integration between routes, schedules and fares across modes; complete connectivity, including better connectivity between people and markets, and international border crossings and security threats; and seamless transport for greener growth (International Transport Forum 2012a, 2012b, 2013).

The three international government agencies profiled here capture some key common features. They all have broad state membership at their core but with the IMO and ICAO being international regulatory bodies whereas the ITF is primarily a policy "prenegotiation" and research body. Transport ministers are not at the pinnacle of the two UN agencies but they are a continuous presence in the ITF. All three of the international entities reveal the broadening scope and complexity of the transport field beyond initial safety and economic development ideas and into security, environmental, and technological imperatives. The IMO and ICAO are modal in their birth and focus, but their mandates and governance concerns are also necessarily intermodal in some key respects. The ITF is multimodal but of course mainly in a research and think tank sense rather than a direct regulatory sense.

The structure of political power is by no means fully revealed in this kind of basic profile. Mentioning the broad state membership of these entities on its own does not tell us much about the influence and power of leading counties or blocs of countries. The agency heads of these institutions have leadership and managerial influence and impact how agendas are set and communicated. There are also dynamics among those within the organizations regarding their generalist policy or legal experience in international relations and also those with technical, engineering, and science experience with their own professional knowledge networks.

CONCLUSIONS

This chapter has provided a needed contextual look at the multidimensional nature of Canada–US and international transportation policy and institutions. The six reasonably representative lenses and examples examined show growing international influences and imperatives, greater governance complexity, intermittent success and failure, and intense political conflict as social, economic, technological, and political pressures and change have to be interpreted, decided upon, implemented or ignored or postponed.

We have surveyed some core features of Canada–United States transport policy relations across the decades being covered. The US, as a global super power and as Canada's closest and most important neighbour but with a complex and different political system, has had diverse impacts on Canada's transportation policy. Our account has been partly chronological, but it is also clear that overall there are overlaps and collision points among these developments and that there are diverse modal and multimodal dynamics and interests involved. The institutional and policy lenses and values have included economic deregulation and privatization ideas and actions always tied to transport safety concerns; trade liberalization and free trade internationally and internally; major security concerns and new rules following the 9/11 crisis; cabotage and international versus national transport reform and modal intricacies regarding protection and liberalization; formal bilateral Canada–US governance as seen in the formation and evolution of the St Lawrence Seaway; and finally, the combined agendas of key international agencies which Canada seeks to influence and support, occasionally lukewarmly, or oppose with regard to some rules, standards and enforcement strategies.

These bilateral and other multilateral international dynamics inform in different ways and degrees the structure and analysis of our seven domains mapped and analyzed in part 2 of the book. They produce successes and failures but also yield irritants and challenges about the primacy of policy ideas in and about transportation; the nature of economic and social power in varied arenas and agenda-setting situations, modal-specific or more broadly transportation policy oriented; and as impacted by changes in transport and related technology. We can only understand these varied policy challenges, irritants, and puzzles more clearly and accurately after we have examined each of the seven transport policy and governance domain chapters that follow.

PART TWO

Analysis of Seven Transport Policy and Governance Domains

4

The Transport Canada-Centred Domain

INTRODUCTION

The first transport policy domain to be examined is the Transport Canada-centred domain, defined as the federal transport department *per se*, headed by the minister of Transport as its elected cabinet minister. Transport Canada employs 4,700 persons and clearly has the largest concentration of transportation policy and technical expertise in the government of Canada. The notion of it being "centred" for our purposes also refers to the fact that Transport Canada is responsible for and/or assists in more than sixty laws and 483 sets of regulations regarding transportation matters (Transport Canada 2016d). It also is the lead federal transport policy and program spender and also carries out various kinds of transport-related research and analysis.

If this domain covers the centre defined in this way, then our first task is to briefly understand the stated core mandate of the department and its minister. The core central aspects of the domain can be seen via an initial summary look at how Transport Canada's mandate evolved and has been described across the five decades since it was formed. The versions of this mandate have been expressed in core statutes; statutes where the department shared roles with other departments; regulations; and agreements of diverse kinds, including funding agreements. Later, as the internet emerged and as websites became commonplace, mandates were also expressed as "visions" and multilevel "mission" statements, based on core statutes, but also with core values and approaches often embellished in aspirational ways well beyond statutory provisions and language.

Nonetheless, the Transport Canada website provides an initial useful sense about what the mandate is and seeks to achieve within the department, across government, and into transport markets. It describes the current Transport Canada portfolio as consisting of "Transport Canada, 12 Crown Corporations, an Agency, and a fund," and "42 Shared Governance Organizations, including 18 Port Authorities, 21 Airport Authorities, the Buffalo and Fort Erie Public Bridge Authority, NAV Canada, and the St. Lawrence Seaway Management Corporation" (Transport Canada 2016a, 1). As we have seen in chapter 1, this latter set of forty-two de facto "not-for-profit" organizations "are corporate entities without share capital for which Canada, either directly or through a Crown corporation, has a right pursuant to statutes, articles of incorporation, letters patent, by-laws or any contractual agreement to appoint or nominate one or more members to the governing body. These organizations do not report to Parliament" (ibid., 1). We discuss some of these further in chapter 7 on the air transportation policy and shared-governance domain and with regard to other domains as well.

Transport Canada's stated mandate vision is to establish "a transportation system in Canada that is recognized worldwide as safe and secure, efficient and environmentally responsible" and its mission is "to serve the public interest through the promotion of a safe and secure, efficient and environmentally responsible transportation system in Canada" (Transport Canada 2016b, 1). Later, the department reiterates that, "a safe and secure system protects people from the loss of life and from loss of or damage to health and property." It also

- enables the efficient flow of people and goods;
- protects people from accidents and exposure to dangerous goods;
- protects the environment from pollution that can result from such events; and
- contributes to a healthy population, a high quality of life and a prosperous economy. (Transport Canada 2016c, 1)

With this initial basic definitional notion of what the Transport Canada-centered domain is and a currently expressed sense of its mandate, we explore this as our first analytical domain through four selected and quite diverse policy and related governance histories spanning the last fifty years (with some brief reference to even earlier periods and events when needed).

But it is imperative to stress that more about Transport Canada and its ministers and central versus arm's length governance is also present in each of the further transport policy domains examined in chapters 5 to 10. Thus no overall definitive verdicts about Transport Canada and its ministers' successes and failures can be offered in this initial domain chapter alone. Indeed, we have seen additional evidence in chapters 1, 2, and 3 that must also be drawn together with the book's seven domain analyses in the book's conclusions. In chapter 1, for example, we have already previewed the current Justin Trudeau and Transport Canada and its minister Marc Garneau's stated and proposed legislative plans under Bill C-49, the Transportation Modernization Act, and its key component parts (Transport Canada 2017c, 2017d, 2017e).

The first policy and governance history examined regarding the current initial domain centres on the "ministry" of Transport era as it morphs from a ministry into the Department of Transport "with portfolio" era. The ministry era in the 1960s and 1970s (indeed earlier as well) implies a policy and governance era in transport (and in other policy fields) when there was greater detailed control by the minister or in the name of the minister, a feature that was relatively common in many policy realms in the federal government. The department "with portfolio" era (including now) implied greater arm's length independence by many of its various agencies and units (Doern and Phidd 1992, 1983). For our purposes, this shift is captured in the late 1960s to late 1980s period centred in part on core policy and power relations of the department and minister with two of its main regulatory agencies, the Canadian Transportation Commission (CTC) and its immediate successor the National Transportation Agency (NTA). The current Canadian Transportation Agency (CTA) that succeeded the CTC and NTA is introduced briefly as one "portfolio" era example but our main discussion of it comes in chapter 6 where its mandate is related to the Rail Freight and Competition-Market Dispute domain and to arguments by some that the CTA is too independent or perhaps has become so.

Our second policy and governance history is centred on Transport Canada's own regulatory policies, processes, volumes, and forward plans from 2006 to the present. We have already seen in chapters 1

and 3 Transport Canada and its ministers' roles in the economic deregulatory Freedom to Move policy era. But Transport Canada's core mandate is also one of continued and expanded regulation of other kinds.
This is partly driven internally but also governed by more recent
and fast developing Cabinet-, Treasury Board-, and Canada Gazette-
centred requirements for regulatory assessment and approvals.

Our third policy and governance history covering the period from
1990 to the present then examines core features of the transport safety
regulation story but with a focus on the Transportation Safety Board
of Canada (TSB). In a sense this history deals with safety policy and
structural change designed to confer an even more independent status
regarding the TSB's accident investigation mandate. It is overwhelmingly about transport safety but the agency does not report to the
minister of Transport but rather to the leader of the government in
the House of Commons.

We then turn to a fourth policy and governance history centred on
a broader examination and comparison of the expressed overall
transport policy mandates in the Chrétien–Martin and Harper governments in the period 2001 to 2015 as revealed through policy
mandate statements crafted by Transport Canada and revealed
through accountability reports on strategic plans and priorities. This
fourth policy and governance history also takes note of the core
recommendations of the Canada Transportation Act review presented
in early 2016 as policy and governance reform advice to the current
Trudeau Liberal government.

Finally, we look at overall summary evidence from the four policy
and governance histories and the challenges they raise as they relate
to domain development and the three domain *elements* that anchor
the book's overall analytical framework. Conclusions then follow.

FROM "MINISTRY" OF TRANSPORT
TO TRANSPORT CANADA WITH "PORTFOLIO":
LEVELS OF CONTROL VERSUS INDEPENDENCE

Our first policy history is about transport policy and governance
and hence the essence of the ministry-versus-portfolio story. The
Department of Transport (Transport Canada) was formed in 1936
to replace an earlier Department of Railways and Canals but the
"department" is a continuing part of the otherwise two-stage institutional and policy story on which this policy history focuses. Our

focus here is policy and institutional development where a Ministry of Transport is named as such and is described as a ministry with significant detailed ministerial policy control over its many constituent branches, directorates, arm's length agencies, crown corporations, and units. We trace this government structure from roughly the late 1960s to the late 1980s when the current Transport Canada "with portfolio" designation emerges as the descriptor (and continues to this day).

Is this "ministry" versus "portfolio" a distinction without a difference? And if this is not enough as a two-part story, why, as we see later in chapter 7 do we need to title the air transport domain, with the add-on of "shared governance" as a feature of its domain name and structure? The portfolio designation is intended to evoke considerably reduced degrees of political and ministerial policy control. As we have seen earlier "shared-governance authorities" *per se* are defined as not-for-profit entities, which are a particular feature of air transport policy and governance, but we have also seen their importance in chapter 3 in our discussion of St Lawrence Seaway policy and governance.

A useful starting point for this overall analytical history is the scholarly work of John Langford (1976, 1982). His 1976 book *Transport in Transition* examines transport policy and government as Transport Canada was already starting to move away from its earlier levels of detailed ministerial control, partly as we saw in chapter 1, under the influence of Royal Commission recommendations about the emergence of a truly multimodal transport system needing more competition among modes. (See also Baldwin 1977; Janisch 1977; Kroeker 1981; Hill 1988.) Langford's 1982 analysis focuses on transport spending and the attempt to "retreat to basics," in short, to greater competition and less regulation.

Langford begins somewhat curiously by arguing that, "Transport Canada is little more than a catchy phrase" (ibid., 148). He lists its many satellite agencies as of 1982 and notes that "even in its most bloated informal manifestation, it does not encompass all of the spending components of the ministry" (ibid., 148). Langford (ibid., 150) concludes overall that,

The traditional position on transport policy is that it is one of the major instruments of nation-building, national unity, and federal government involvement in the economy. ... The new thesis was that the national transportation system had matured to the extent that it was becoming increasingly competitive on the intermodal level ... basis and therefore it was largely capable of meeting the needs of the economy without a high level of government intervention across the entire system.

The focus of this account, however, was also on Transport Canada and ministry expenditures as projected into the mid-1980s (with growing federal deficits), and thus Langford also drew attention to what might be in store if the transport ministry was seen more as an operator and that it "can be subjected to savage cost-cutting exercises when the need arises" (Langford 1982, 170), such as in transportation safety.

Other parts of the ministry-versus-portfolio story is told and commented on in accounts of the department's evolving relationship with the Canadian Transportation Commission (CTC), formed in 1967, and its successor regulatory body, the National Transportation Agency (NTA), established in 1987 (McGuire 2004; Hill 1999). This institutional progression is also relevant regarding the Canadian Transportation Agency (CTA), established in 1996 (and examined in chapter 6), and the Transportation Safety Board of Canada (TSB), established in 1990 (see more below). Indeed, Hill (1999) characterized the overall departmental CTC, NTA, and CTA battle as a "30 year war" in recasting the federal transport regulator.

The CTC emerged in the National Transportation Act of 1967, which was itself forged by the MacPherson Commission of the early 1960s. The CTC mandate was to "direct all forms of transport under federal control-railways, shipping, airlines and interprovincial trucking (McGuire 2004, 32) It was also given a research branch so that it could be better informed and more proactive when needed. It was also, in concert with the 1967 legislative change, charged along with the department to gradually reduce transportation subsidies.

Jack Pickersgill, a legendary Liberal cabinet minister spearheaded the changes and then immediately became the head of the new CTC. There were policy reforms and some deregulation in the full package but also the new head was a politician par excellence. Organizationally, the CTA established separate modal committees to show its movement away from early railway dominance eras and to deal with greater competition among modes including air and trucking. Throughout the 1967 to 1987 period, however, there were power struggles between the CTC and the Ministry of Transport as a set of bureaucracies, and as new ministers came and went and the CTC had become itself quite a large organization with 800 staff.

As we have seen·in earlier chapters, when Don Mazankowski became Transport minister he initiated the 1985 Freedom to Move policy paper in the early Mulroney government era which pushed for regulatory reform, but it also paved the way for the replacement of the CTC with the National Transportation Agency (NTA) in 1987, headed by Eric Nielsen, also a former Mulroney Conservative government cabinet minister. It was to be a considerably smaller agency of 500 staff compared to the CTC, and it was organized into functional/managerial branches rather than modal ones and no longer with a proactive policy role. The new legislation also elevated transport safety to a high priority focus and to ensure responsiveness to the public interest (ibid., 49) but all of this in concert with competition as the main stated policy mandate.

Under the Canada Transportation Act proclaimed in July 1996 by the Chrétien Liberal government, the Canadian Transportation Agency (CTA) was created as the successor to the NTA. It was known immediately that it would be streamlined to have half the staff of the NTA and thus currently in the 230 person range. It would continue at that level in the combined quasi-judicial tribunal and economic and social regulator role of the NTA. The requirement "of regional representation among the (CTA) Members was removed along with regional offices" (ibid., 56). The CTA was also mandated to provide a greater consumer protection role (again, see detailed critical discussion of the CTA in chapter 6 in relation to freight rail regulation and adjudication).

TRANSPORT CANADA REGULATORY POLICY, PROCESSES, VOLUMES, AND FORWARD PLANS (2006 TO PRESENT)

Our second policy and governance history centers on Transport Canada's own regulatory policy and machinery, with a particular focus on the last decade where its own regulatory volumes have been better mapped and its regulatory planning dynamics are better understood, including the need to relate them to overall federal government-, cabinet-, and Treasury Board-centered regulatory policy – in effect the government's rules about rule-making.

Transport Canada describes its own regulatory machinery (Transport Canada 2010, 2016e) as a "complex structure," largely because "each mode of transportation has its own particularities, which renders its regulatory process unique" (Transport Canada 2010, 3). But it is also complex because, procedurally, each regulatory change proposal must go through not only its internal modal processes and then the department's coordination processes but also the full set of steps called for in federal regulatory policy and streamlining approaches. International agencies, rules, standards, and exceptions are also a part of the process as we have seen in chapter 3.

At present, under its published "proposed regulatory initiatives," thirty-one further sets of regulations were considered for the 2015–17 period (Transport Canada 2016e). Since statutes contain rules in the law itself rather than just in delegated law ("the regs") flowing from these statutes, there can be little doubt, despite the presence of economic deregulation bursts and eras, that Transport Canada overall is still very much a regulatory department but also a realm of considerable "unruliness" defined as situations where rules may not be easily developed or become complex regarding enforcement or are not supported by relevant staff resources and expertise (Doern, Prince, and Schultz 2014). Regulation also involves the increased use of guidelines, standards, and codes. Some of these overall dynamics are brought out further and in more detail in later domain chapters.

Transport Canada is one of the two or three largest federal government regulators in terms of volume (Doern 2010). The regulations refer basically to regulatory proposals and projects subject to the Cabinet Directive on Regulatory Management (CDRM) and the *Canada Gazette* process and related consultation dynamics as discussed further below. Rule-making volumes occur in a larger sense and also refer to major occasions of statutory change. The latter are normally much less frequent, but as mentioned earlier, rules do show up in statutes/laws themselves and Transport Canada has more than sixty of these under its primary jurisdiction or where it assists other departments.

Transport Canada processed about thirty to thirty-five new regulations per year between 2007 and 2010 (Doern 2010). In 2010, 147 projects were in the queue. About 90 per cent of these dealt with proposed safety and security measures. Among the modal and regulatory areas of the department, about 80 per cent of regulatory proposals historically and at present come from civil aviation and maritime safety, in that order. Road safety and dangerous goods are next in volume but well behind the first two modal realms. The list of 147 projects in place in 2010 was prepared to give senior Transport Canada managers a better idea of how many regulatory projects were queuing up in the department and hence what the department's regulatory agenda might or could be.

There is the possibility, in this process (then and now), that senior managers would delay action at any given time on some files and direct others to be expedited based on their risk-priority profile or other factors. But it must be stressed that a large number of Transport Canada's regulatory projects are technical in nature, relating to such things as construction standards for transportation craft, etc. With these kinds of technical standards, the department would have no choice but to put them in place because transportation safety and the integrity of the transportation system itself depend on uniform standards throughout the world.

While Transport Canada has its own regulatory dynamics, it is also governed by the changing features of overall federal regulatory policy governance. These features and processes include, at a minimum the Cabinet Directive on Regulatory Management (CDRM), the Statutory Instruments Act, the *Canada Gazette* consultation processes, constitutional provisions, and several oversight and challenge functions. We focus here on the CDRM, in effect since 2012. Under the CDRM, the federal government commits when regulating that it will

1 Protect and advance the public interest in health, safety, and security, the quality of the environment, and the social and economic well-being of Canadians, as expressed by Parliament in legislation.
2 Advance the efficiency and effectiveness of regulation by ascertaining that the benefits of regulation justify the costs, by focusing human and financial resources where they can do the most good, and by demonstrating tangible results.
3 Make decisions based on evidence and on the best available knowledge and science in Canada and worldwide, while recognizing that the application of precaution may be necessary when there is an absence of full scientific certainty and a risk of serious or irreversible harm.
4 Promote a fair and competitive market economy that encourages entrepreneurship, investment, and innovation.

5 Monitor and control the administrative burden (i.e., red tape) of regulations on business and be sensitive to the burden that regulations place on small business.
6 Create accessible, understandable, and responsive regulation through engagement, transparency, accountability, and public scrutiny.
7 Require timeliness, policy coherence, and minimal duplication throughout the regulatory process by consulting, coordinating, and cooperating across the federal government, with other governments and jurisdictions in Canada and abroad, and with business and Canadians. (Treasury Board Secretariat 2013, 2)

These seven expressed commitments in the current CDRM, developed and approved by the Harper government in 2012, are much more elaborate than the two commitments in the previous 2007 Harper government Cabinet Directive on Streamlining Regulation (CDSR) which were to

• Protect and advance the public interest in health, safety, and security, the quality of the environment, and social and economic well-being of Canadians as expressed by Parliament in legislation.
• Promote a fair and competitive market economy that encourages entrepreneurship, investment, and innovation. (Canada 2007, 1)

The seven CDRM commitments suggest somewhat more "managerial" content, but, at their core, they still set out policies and values about regulation that if anything lean towards variously expressed social and public interest purposes but also related norms about rule making and compliance. Evidence, knowledge, science, and precaution in the face of a lack of absolute scientific certainty are mentioned in that order in item 3 of the CDRM, but so also are potentially conflicting notions of regulations being understandable and timely (in items 6 and 7).

The CDRM also contains provisions whereby departments and agencies must prepare annual regulatory plans and priorities and practice a life-cycle approach to regulation. This includes managing the life cycle of the measure, including provisions requiring reevaluations of all regulations every five years, a policy that built on earlier spending program evaluation requirements. The CDRM encourages harmonization and mutual recognition initiatives (both federal–provincial and international) and advances the principle of regulating only if there is evidence that regulation is necessary and beneficial, confirmed through the greater use of quantitative cost–benefit analysis.

Later domain chapters on air transport and on dangerous goods also show the way in which particular further regulatory advisory bodies have been created and play a role overall or in reviews of particular regulatory proposals. These include entities such as the Canadian Aviation Regulatory Advisory Council (CARAC), advisory policy groups on dangerous goods, and also, bilaterally, the Canada–United States Regulatory Cooperation Council (CURCC). Their work is also partly better enabled because of the above noted changes regarding proposed regulatory plans as a form of more overt regulatory agenda setting or at least informing interested parties what proposed regulations are queuing up for review and possible/likely approval (Doern, Prince, and Schultz 2014).

SAFETY POLICY, REGULATION, THE TRANSPORTATION SAFETY BOARD OF CANADA, AND INDEPENDENT TRANSPORT ACCIDENT INVESTIGATIONS (1990 TO PRESENT)

The Transport Canada-centered domain has always had to deal with issues of transport safety. Our third policy and governance history briefly traces concerns that emerged with regard to transportation accident investigations and the need for greater independence in such matters. This analytical story centers on the formation and work of the Transportation Safety Board (TSB) of Canada. The TSB was established in 1990 with the passage of the Canadian Transportation Accident Investigation and Safety Board Act but, as we have seen in earlier chapters, transport safety policy and regulation predates the TSB and extends to more than one safety regulatory body and statute in the transportation policy field overall.

The TSB is an independent agency composed of five board members and a staff of 220 employees. It "advances transportation safety by investigating marine, pipeline, rail, air and aviation occurrences, and communicating risks in the transportation system" (Transportation

Safety Board of Canada 2016a, 1). Its mandate description stresses that the TSB "does not assign fault or determine civil or criminal liability, and its findings cannot be used in legal or disciplinary proceedings. Coroners and medical examiners, however, may use TSB findings in their investigations" (ibid.). Since 1990, the TSB has conducted "thousands of investigations across the modes for which it is responsible (Transportation Safety Board of Canada 2015, 4).

The TSB notes that "each year about 3,200 transportation occurrences (accidents and incidents) are reported" to it but that "they vary hugely from aircraft part failures and ship fires to pipeline ruptures and train derailments" (ibid.). (See discussion below of the 2013 Lac-Mégantic rail disaster.) The TSB first assesses the situation to determine if an investigation is needed. It "investigates an occurrence when there is a high probability that it can advance transportation safety and reduce risks to persons, property or the environment" and each investigation proceeds through "the field phase, the examination and analysis phase, and the report phase" (ibid.).

Crucially, while it was established by Transport Canada, the TSB does not report to Transport Canada, but rather it reports to Parliament through the leader of the government in the House of Commons. This accountability feature was adopted by Transport Canada to ensure absolute independence via the arm's length nature and thoroughness of the investigations, report findings and conclusions, and so that "there are no real or perceived conflicts of interest" (Transportation Safety Board of Canada 2015, 3). The TSB mandate also ensures that when the TSB investigates an accident, "no other federal department (except the Department of National Defence and the Royal Canadian Mounted Police) may investigate for the purpose of making findings as to causes and contributing factors of the incident. Transport Canada and the National Energy Board may investigate for any other purpose such as regulatory infractions" (ibid.).

Over twenty-five years, the TSB investigation history reveals its needed attention to both smaller/minor events and also to major ones as well as other kinds of guidance documents about safety threats and solutions. These investigations included a 1994 *Safety Study on the Survivability of Seaplane Accidents*; a 1997 *Key Safety Issues* document which lead to later periodic *Watchlist* reports such as that in 2009–10 which posited the greatest risks to Canadians; investigation of the 2 September 1998 crash of Swissair Flight 111 off Peggy's Cove and the later release in 2002 of the full accident report; the publishing of recommendations calling for an equivalent level of safety for fare-paying balloon passengers as those for commercial air services; release of a report on the *Safety Issues Investigation on Fishing Safety*; and the 2014–15 report on the Lac-Mégantic rail disaster (Transport Safety Board of Canada 2016b).

As it looks ahead to its 2016–17 to 2020–21 period of operations and planning, the TSB's key priorities include "improved information and data management," stressing that as a safety entity its "work is fundamentally reliant on the collection, retention, management and analysis of occurrence information" (Transportation Safety Board of Canada 2015, 5). It seeks to complete "the identification of investigation records that have enduring business value versus transitory value" but also to expand "the provision of online public access to occurrence data" (ibid., 5). With regard to risk analysis, the TSB argues that its "volume of activities is influenced by the number, severity and complexity of transportation occurrences and the volume cannot effectively be predicted" (ibid., 6). In these continuing contexts and uncertainties, the quality and knowledge of its workforce is pivotal but also ever changing.

Without doubt, the transport accident that received the greatest attention in recent years was the July 2013 disaster in Lac-Mégantic Quebec in which forty-seven persons were killed by an out of control train carrying a shipment of oil in seventy-two tank cars. The resulting derailment, explosions, and fire also destroyed the town center. It seemed almost unbelievable for the accident to have happened in the way it did. As the disaster involved hazards and risks related to transportation and to dangerous goods cargo, it immediately raised issues about what risk regulation means, an issue central to all safety regulation not to mention liability and compensation for damage and loss of life. Questions were raised from the outset about long-term federal transport safety regulations but also regarding the immediate peculiarities of the accident itself and whether it proved, as a single case, the inadequacies of past and current regulatory policies (Bishop 2013; Mackrael 2013).

The TSB's investigation of the Montreal, Marine & Atlantic Railway (MMA) train involved in the disaster showed that it was carrying 7.7 million litres of petroleum crude oil in seventy-two Class 111 tank cars. The TSB report identifies several key issues that were investigated (Transportation Safety Board of Canada 2016c) including fire in the locomotive; the braking force which included hand brakes plus two types of air brakes (automatic and independent brakes), the Class 111 tank cars manufactured between 1980 and 2012; the safety culture at M M A, Transport Canada's own monitoring and auditing practices regarding M M A, the issue of single-person crews, and the issue of dangerous goods and inadequate testing, monitoring, and transport.

Safety actions following the accident included the TSB communicating "critical safety information on the securement of unattended trains, (and) the classification of petroleum crude oil, and rail conditions at Lac-Mégantic" (ibid., 7). Transport Canada introduced an "emergency directive prohibiting trains transporting dangerous goods from operating with single person crews" among other initiatives (ibid.). The TSB final report "identifies 18 distinct causes and contributing factors, many of them influencing one another" (ibid.).

In 2015 the federal government laid criminal charges against six members of the M M A, under provisions of the Railway Safety and Fisheries Acts (Atkins and Stevenson 2015, 1). There was also a $430 million settlement claim for victims' families. The Fisheries Act actions were partly based on an "unprecedented spike in fish deformations in the wake of the accident" (Woods 2016, 1).

The TSB was basically an initiative of Transport Canada and a needed transportation investigative entity that has undoubtedly done good work that lives up to its structural independence from Transport Canada by not having any real or perceived conflict of interest as it investigates occurrences and accidents. But boundary dynamics, discretion, and choices nonetheless arise since it cannot prosecute or determine legal liability. It can prevent or minimize future adverse events with its risk advice and communication activities, but these are, as with other regulators, often necessarily "non-events" or things that fortunately do not happen and cannot be fully traced in performance terms. The Lac-Mégantic accident and report also showed that it had to find ways to report possible or actual failures in other Transport Canada regulatory realms (Robertson 2016). Indeed, an auditor general of Canada (2013) report on the oversight of rail safety by Transport Canada had been quite critical of the department's oversight actions and capacities, in staff and other terms, in a system which since 2001 had been focused on a safety management systems approach (ibid., 1–3). And it was Transport Canada and Environment Canada that had to bring criminal charges (although unstated in the TSB report), which also involved Justice Canada, since the minister of Justice is ultimately the government of Canada's lawyer.

EXPRESSED TRANSPORT POLICY MANDATES AND
MACRO REFORM AGENDAS AND PRIORITIES
(2001 TO PRESENT)

Having drilled down into the fully independent TSB as a domain policy history, we now complete our analysis of the Transport Canada-centered policy domain by moving back to a broad cross-domain look at Transport Canada-expressed transport policy mandates and macro reform agendas and priorities, revealed in more formal accountability occasions such as the annual submission of reports on plans and priorities. We look first, with the aid of table 4.1, at the expressed transportation policy mandates in the Chrétien–Martin and Harper governments as revealed in such documents. Then we sample some key macro policy and governance recommendations of the Canada Transportation Act review report submitted to the Trudeau Liberal government at the same time as the Trudeau Liberals were forging their own agenda, as partly previewed in chapter 1 regarding Bill C-49, the Transportation Modernization Act, and its key component parts, and in chapter 2 regarding its priorities as expressed in its initial speech from the throne and four budget speeches.

Overall, the categories of expression – vision, mission, and priorities and principles – evoke different levels of ultimate Transport Canada-centered purposefulness but also political and managerial wiggle room. The vision statements are similar in aspiration, and for the Martin Liberals in 2005–06 and the Harper Conservatives in 2015–16, they are identical. The mission statements of the Martin era lead off with notions of the public interest and with no mention of an efficient system; the Harper statement refers to three principles that are somewhat more discursive and managerial, with mentions of "targeted use of regulation and government funding" and then "selective use of regulation and government funding." For both the Martin Liberals and the Harper Conservatives, the policy ideas ranked first are safety and security.

In the longer mandate and highlighted priorities sections of these kinds of accountability statements, safety and security emerge first in all three statements. Other expressed priorities diverge in other partly expected ways, given what we have already seen in chapters 1 and 2. The Harper government in its final statement gives second priority status to its Responsible Resource Development agenda and then to

Table 4.1
Expressed transport policy mandates and priorities in Chrétien–Martin and Harper governments (selected years)

Levels of policy and mandate expression	Chrétien (2001–02)	Martin (2005–06)	Harper (2015–16)
VISION	The best possible transportation for Canada and Canadians	A transportation system in Canada that is recognized worldwide as safe and secure, efficient, and environmentally responsible	A transportation system in Canada that is recognized worldwide as safe and secure, efficient, and environmentally responsible
MISSION	To develop and administer policies, regulations, and services for the best possible transportation system	To serve the public interest through the promotion of a safe and secure, and environmentally responsible system in Canada	Three guiding principles are to work towards • the highest possible safety and security of life and property, supported by performance-based standards and regulations • the efficient movement of people and goods in support of economic prosperity and a sustainable quality of life, based on competitive markets and targeted use of regulation and government funding • respect of the environmental legacy of future generations of Canadians guided by environmental assessment and planning processes in transportation decisions and selective use of regulation and government funding

MANDATE AND HIGHLIGHTED PRIORITIES	Transport Canada is the federal department responsible for most of the transportation policies, programs, and goals set by the government	Plans and priorities by strategic outcome include	Five priorities are
	Our focus is on developing a modern and relevant policy and legislative framework, one that will ensure the safety, security, competitiveness, and sustainability of Canada's transportation system	• a safe and secure transportation system that contributes to Canada's social development and security objectives	• refining and strengthening its safety and security oversight
	Challenges and Priorities:	• an efficient transportation system that contributes to Canada's economic growth and trade objectives	• contribute to the government's Responsible Resource Development agenda
	• maintain and enhance the safety and security regime	• an environmentally responsible transportation system that contributes to Canada's sustainable development objectives	• continue to help improve Canada's competitiveness by strengthening its transport infrastructure
	• foster competitiveness in a global economy		• ensure that its policies, programs, and activities meet the long-term needs of the transportation system. This priority will ensure that our approaches meet the needs of the transportation sector, and consider social, economic, and environmental objectives; and
	• complete the divestiture program (re: airports and ports)		• work to adopt the government of Canada's efficiency and renewal measures. To reflect the importance of innovation, agility, and productivity, combined with the goals of improved service and greater efficiency, Transport Canada will strive to serve the public with excellence
	• facilitate transition to knowledge-based economy		
	• support infrastructure development		
	• advance sustainable development		

Sources: Transport Canada 2001–2002 Estimates: Report on Plans and Priorities, 2005–2006 Estimates: Report on Plans and Priorities, and 2015–2016 Estimates: Report on Plans and Priorities

enhancing competitiveness by strengthening its transport infrastructure and ensuring that its policies meet the long-term needs of the transport system.

In the 2001–02 context, the Chrétien Liberals sought to develop a modern and relevant policy and legislative framework regarding safety, security, competitiveness, and sustainable development. But it also drew attention at that time to complete the divestiture program regarding airports and ports. The Martin Liberal era 2005–06 statement also gave attention to transport policies that contribute to Canada's economic growth and trade objectives.

Also of some interest (but not shown in table 4.1) is the manner and extent to which the 2005–06 statement revealed the Transport Canada "portfolio" without calling it that. All three statements/reports mentioned some feature of its governance structure, but the 2005–06 statement listed in massive and quite revealing detail Transport Canada's "co-delivery partners" (Transport Canada 2005–06, 7), described as "hundreds of other organizations with an interest in transportation issues" (ibid., 7). They included other federal organizations (twenty-one); provincial, territorial and municipal governments, particularly regarding the maintenance of the highway system; transportation sector industries (twelve itemized); agencies and associations (regarding transportation infrastructure) (twenty-four entities listed); and international organizations (twenty listed) (ibid., 7–8).

The Canada Transportation Act review's overall strategy announced in 2016 has already been previewed in chapter 1. For the purposes of this final policy history and first domain chapter, central features of its chapter on governance are especially germane regarding expressed policy reform. The review argues that,

Canada does not have an ongoing private–public sector framework that considers the entire national system and is geared to strengthening its contribution to economic prosperity. Divergent but critical interests such as infrastructure investment, research, innovation and the environment need to come together with a transportation focus. While Transport Canada is the main entity responsible for the sector, there is no mechanism to integrate the breadth of interest in transportation across departments, sectors, or in terms of federal-provincial dialogue. (Canada 2016, 16)

The statement above maps out the need for a transportation dialogue and collaborative approach that includes "the entirety of Canada's multimodal system" (ibid., 18). It would develop a National Framework on Transportation and Logistics and also a Transportation Infrastructure Plan and Projects Pipeline for the next ten to thirty years. It proposes that an Advisory Committee on Transportation and Logistics should be created to include "representation from the entirety of Canada's multimodal transportation system" (ibid., 18). The advisory committee "should be assisted in its work by a new Centre of Excellence in Transportation Logistics and Innovation that provides expert policy advice aimed at enhancing the state of the transportation sector in Canada and marketing its position as an international hub" (ibid., 18). The latter would develop an Integrated Data Platform and Multimodal Data Dashboard as a means of "gathering supply chain data to support evidence-based decision making" (ibid., 30) and that "consideration should be given to housing this new entity within the Canadian Transportation Agency" (ibid., 31).

In essence, this set of recommendations seeks institutionally and in policy and research terms to elevate the macro transportation policy and governance role beyond Transport Canada and the federal government. If, in our terms, the Transport Canada-centered domain is the macro transport policy maker, this approach would yield a supra-macro reach in and beyond the federal government and to cover hoped-for time frames of twenty to thirty years. The Justin Trudeau Liberals, via the Transport Canada and Marc Garneau Bill C-49 approach (the Transportation Modernization Act) and its component parts, has shown this as discussed in chapter 1. We will have further opportunities as we proceed to later domain chapters to comment on these understandable aspirations.

THE THREE DOMAIN ELEMENTS

In the context of the above domain mandate and the four policy and governance histories we can now, with the aid of table 4.2, provide a closer summary of the three domain elements being used as a part of the book's analytical framework. We analyse and comment briefly on each element in turn and of course will return to these elements in chapter 11, once the evidence from other transport domains is assembled in other domain chapters.

Table 4.2
The Transport Canada-centred domain and the three analytical elements: Highlights

Policy and governance histories	Policy ideas, discourse, and agendas	Analytical elements	
		Economic and social power	Technology and temporal realities and conflicts
From "Ministry" of Transport to Department of Transport with "portfolio" (late 1960s to late 1980s)	Movement from nation building, national unity, and federal government intervention in the economy To foster transport competition at intermodal level Reduce subsidies Strengthen focus on safety in a competitive context Freedom to Move ideas and paper Reduce detailed ministerial control as per portfolio concept	Extensive and then reduced federal economic and social power due to business pressure regarding need for deregulation Deregulation occurs but not uniformly and often gradually as department remains a significant regulatory entity Power exerted through deficit imperatives and deep expenditure cuts Modal committees in governance structure of CTC but then shift to functional/managerial branches under NTA	Transport ministers often leave office but then quickly become heads of regulatory agency As agency mandates change amidst budget cuts, the three transport regulatory agencies examined shrink from 800 to 500 to 200
Transport Canada regulatory policy, processes, volumes, and forward plans (2006 to present)	Each mode has own particularities which makes its own regulatory process unique Unruliness and complexity Proposed regulatory plans Deregulation and new regulation Safety and security CDRM values and requirements applied also to Transport Canada E.g. protect and advance the public interest in health, safety, economy, and the quality of the economy	Transport Canada top two or three regulatory departments Internal modal processes Department's coordination processes Steps in federal government processes Rules in laws as well as in delegated law (the regulations) 80% of new regulations in civil aviation and maritime safety Canada Gazette process via Treasury Board	Large number of regulations are technical in nature Requirements for publishing new regulatory plans Requirements for regular reviews of existing regulations every five years

Transport Canada regulatory policy, processes, volumes, and forward plans (2006 to present) (*continued*)	E.g., social and economic well-being of Canadians E.g. efficiency and effectiveness of regulations Fair and competitive markets Monitor and control administrative burden Accessibility, engagement, and transparency	CDRM requirement for departmental regulation proposal plans Thirty to thirty-five new regulations per year in 2007 to 2010 Thirty-one new regulations for 2015–17 period Key role and influence of international agencies re: modal rules, standards, and exceptions Rule making and policy through several departmental modal and general regulatory councils including Canada–US	
Safety policy, regulation and the Transportation Safety Board of Canada and independent transport accident investigation (1990 to present)	Advance transportation safety by investigating transportation occurrences Communicating risks to users and transport modal providers Ensure through its independence that it acts to ensure no real or perceived conflicts of interest Does not assign fault or determine civil or criminal liability	A transportation agency but reports to Parliament through the leader of the government in the House of Commons rather than minister of Transport Exhortative and power of persuasion including via guidance documents about safety threats, risks, and solutions Lac-Mégantic accident and report assessed MMA train company responsible for the disaster but also Transport Canada and its regulatory compliance inadequacies Criminal charges against offenders made by Transport Canada and Environment Canada but with involvement also of Justice Canada	Occurrences and accidents as major, minor, and high volume overall Reports and reporting advice on those with long-term relevance and potential for safety advancement within and among modes If preventive, then, as in many regulatory fields, there are challenges regarding how to assess "nonevents" Effort and need to focus public investigative data and records of enduring business value versus transitory value

Table 4.2
The Transport Canada-centred domain and the three analytical elements: Highlights (*continued*)

Policy and governance histories	Analytical elements		Technology and temporal realities and conflicts
	Policy ideas, discourse, and agendas	*Economic and social power*	
Safety policy, regulation and the Transportation Safety Board of Canada and independent transport accident investigation (1990 to present) (*continued*)			Need for greater online public access to occurrences data Challenges due to fact that the volume of occurrences cannot effectively be predicted
Expressed transport policy mandates and macro-transport reform agendas and priorities (2001 to present)	Levels of ultimate purposefulness expressed as visions, missions, and principles Priorities as well in multiyear plans and priority documents Ranking of ideas, priorities tends to put safety and security first ... but linked closely to competitiveness of the economy and the transportation system Infrastructure receives increased separate emphasis Environment is listed but typically near the end and expressed mainly as sustainable development Canada Transportation Act review calls for new national framework on transportation and logistics	Communication as required accountability reporting and plans, with ministerial and departmental involvement and preferred discourse Each government in the three sample years related core priorities also to particular agenda items (e.g. airports, Responsible Resource Development) Canada Transportation Act review calls for macrogovernance for transportation involving the provinces and cities via a proposed Advisory Committee on Transportation and Logistics	Infrastructure for transportation seen and advanced as longer-term issue Canada Transportation Act review advocates overall for a needed twenty- to thirty-year focus for new transportation governance Includes new Transportation Infrastructure Plan and Project Pipeline for next twenty to thirty years

Policy Ideas, Discourses, and Agendas

Across the fifty-year period examined in the four policy histories, the policy ideas and discourse exhibit considerable change but also considerable staying power. The nation building and national unity ideas are prominent early on and well into the 1960s but are gradually complemented by concepts of competition among modes and the need to reduce subsidies to enable Canadians the "freedom to move." Later when we explore the expressed macro transport policy mandates since 2001 there is a strong tendency to stress ideas and discourse tied to safety and security but with these ideas quickly and concurrently linked to ideas regarding the competiveness of the economy and of the transportation system. Support for needed infrastructure as transport capital assets is increasingly present as agendas shift. The environment and sustainable development are continuous add-ons to the overall mixture of ideas.

In the two regulatory histories, the first on overall Transport Canada regulatory policy linked necessarily with overall federal regulatory requirements and the second on the TSB, the ideas and necessary discourse build on the past but need targeting for the specific modal and intermodal policy and governance tasks involved and also for required regulatory plans via the CDRM. The analysis of the TSB shows the emergence of normative ideas about what proper safety investigation involves as well as the importance of risk communication and how these tasks ought to be separate from the responsibilities to assign fault or determine criminal liability.

Economic and Social Power

The exercise and evidence regarding these dual features of power are trackable across the four policy histories, but they are also complex. In the first more macro "ministry to portfolio" history there is reduced federal economic and social power under the impetus of markets and deregulation reform and hence reduced ministerial intervention *per se*. But deregulation is by no means uniform and thus shifts in power are also subtle. Power exerted through expenditure cuts is also in evidence. The fourth policy history on macro mandates and priorities is more coordinated as an exercise in formal accountability reporting, but here the instinct of governments, of all party persuasions, is to express some kind of considered balance of social and economic power, including issues of safety and security.

In the two regulatory policy and governance histories, economic and social power presence and dynamics are somewhat more specific. In the Transport Canada and related CDRM regulatory story they are shown in quite specific ways with a focus on modal technical and other kinds of uniqueness but then branch out with an expanded list of requirements forged in the Harper era that are multiple in nature but also more managerial including provisions for the efficiency and effectiveness of regulations. Regarding the TSB policy history, aspects of power centred on social concerns are evident regarding the need to keep the investigation process strongly independent from Transport Canada and its portfolio. The reliance on public data and reporting of risk situations and solutions is also an expression of social power and justice.

Technology and Temporal Realities and Conflicts

The presence of this element in the Transport Canada-centered domain mainly reveals the dynamics of time and temporal realities and conflicts rather than technology *per se*. There is, however, some reference to the fact that a large number of Transport Canada regulations are quite technical in nature. Aspects of technology and insufficient technological capacity are present in concerns about greater online data for public access to occurrences data, and it is pivotal in the Canada Transportation Act review report for new transportation and logistics data and research capacity.

It must also be said, however, that this analytical element requires considerable detective work. Temporal features are certainly present across the policy histories such as in relation to some transport ministers shifting quickly to become heads of regulatory bodies they advocated and fostered while ministers. The temporal rhythm of budget cuts and pressures on regulatory agency staff and size and also mandate are present. The presence of a Forward Regulatory Plan requirement was adopted to foster a public medium-term regulatory agenda. An even longer explicit twenty to thirty year time span is seen as crucial for infrastructure funding and project planning.

CONCLUSIONS

The Transport Canada-centred domain has been defined as the federal transport department *per se*, headed by the minister of Transport as its elected cabinet minister. Its core mandate, large staff, and transport expertise place it at the centre of the federal transport policy and governance system. The initial survey of its statutory base indicated a role in sixty statutes (and dozens of sets of regulations and regulatory plans queuing in line). Transport Canada has certainly had an explicit economic deregulation history, but it is also very much an expanding regulatory department. The four policy and governance histories give us an initial sense of its central role but also of complex policy challenges. Regarding the larger story of federal and national transportation policy, this is our important starting point, but more is needed given what other kinds of transport challenges and proposed legislation are engaging Transport Canada and the current Justin Trudeau Liberal federal government. It is thus imperative to stress that more about Transport Canada and its ministers and central versus arm's length governance is also present in each of the further transport policy domains examined in chapters 5 to 10. Thus, no definitive verdicts about Transport Canada and its ministers' successes and failures can be offered in this first domain chapter alone. Indeed, we have also seen other evidence in chapters 1, 2, and 3 that must be drawn together with these further domain analyses in the book's conclusions.

5

The Grains and Trains Transport
Policy Domain

INTRODUCTION

"Well, why should I sell the Canadian farmer's wheat?" With this rhetorical question, Trudeaumania ended in Western Canada in 1968. Although taken out of context, Prime Minister Pierre Elliott Trudeau was vilified for asking a legitimate question and one that is no longer asked fifty years later. In our theme, "from here to there," the history of grain transportation is instructive, not so much as an example of transportation policy but of the use of transportation as an instrument of broader policy objectives. In Western Canada, it is often said that wheat is "13% protein and 87% politics." The grains and trains transport policy domain presents a story punctuated with wars, protectionism, technological revolutions, and depressed farm incomes but above all transportation policy that is trumped continuously by the politics of grain embedded in an era of strong Prairie populism forged especially in the 1910 to 1945 period (Laycock 1990).

Few sectors of the economy have witnessed such dramatic economic changes as the grain industry of Western Canada. In 1967, 5,032 small wooden grain elevators dotted the Prairies. No farm was more than ten miles away from a grain delivery point and, by extension, a railway track to serve their needs. All the grain was transported in small farm trucks and loaded into boxcars. Most of the grain was handled by three large farmer-owned cooperatives; all wheat, oats, and barley had to be sold through the Canadian Wheat Board, and wheat represented 68 per cent of grain production. Today, Western grain is handled through 336 primary elevators, of which 149 are inland terminals with greater than 20,000 tonnes storage capacity, commercial tractor trailers have largely replaced farm trucks, unit trains of covered hopper railcars move grain to the ports, the cooperatives have been replaced by a handful of multinational grain companies, the Canadian Wheat Board is gone, and, in most years, the canola crop exceeds the value of wheat production.

Despite these productivity improvements, the Canadian grain supply chain still lags behind its US counterpart in technology and regulation. The newer US railcars carry 10 per cent more than the aging fleet of government-owned covered hopper railcars. Loop tracks are only now being introduced into Western Canada, and rail transport of grain still remains subject to economic regulation that stifles the incentive to modernize or expand the transportation system. Grain transportation may no longer be the "third rail" of Canadian politics that it once was, but when the political pressure arose in the wake of an unexpected surge in demand for rail transport in 2014, new economic regulations were hastily enacted (the Fair Rail for Grain Farmers Act) to appease frustrated farmers.

Before addressing "from here to there" in our present context, it is necessary to review the "here" that PM Trudeau started from. Our first policy and governance history on the globalization of grain presents an interpretation of the Western Canadian grain sector as caught in a Nash Equilibrium of trading nations suffering an oversupply of exportable grain. This is followed by our second policy history on the gradual deregulation and reduction of subsidizes for Western Canadian grain farmers. The grains and trains domain analysis then looks at the three analytical elements in the book's analytical framework: policy ideas, discourse and agendas; economic and social power; and technology and temporal realities and conflicts.

THE GLOBALIZATION OF GRAIN (1897 TO PRESENT)

A Nash Equilibrium exists where no party has an incentive to adopt a strategy that could make anyone better off, given the known equilibrium strategies of the other parties. A Nash Equilibrium characterized the world grain market for most of the twentieth century. All major grain exporting countries suffered low commodity prices, subsidized their farmers directly or indirectly, and exercised blatant trade protectionism. No country was prepared to abandon efforts to export its way to profitability, which ensured that all grain exporters would suffer a "tragedy of the commons." Perpetual exportable surpluses depressed farm prices leading to support for output-increasing production strategies. During the course of the twentieth century, it is unlikely that Western Canadian farmers made an adequate return on investment in more than twenty-five of those years.

Canada was not alone in its use of border strategies to sustain the incomes of grain farmers. Both exporting and importing countries enacted programs to protect their markets from competition and increase the efficiency of their grain production. This is how Western Canadian farmers found themselves, awash in excess wheat inventories with no one willing to pay a sustainable price, when PM Trudeau's speech ignited anger and protest. Paradoxically, the part of PM Trudeau's remarks that did not get attention was his commitment to the government's export strategy and institutions, including the Canadian Wheat Board, that were devoted to assist grain farmers to compete in world markets.

The roots of agriculture's economic malaise are very deep and stretch back to the original policy decision to build a transcontinental railway across Canada. The economic development power of transportation innovations was exemplified in the nineteenth century railway boom. Prior to the building of the Canadian Pacific Railway (CPR), furs were the only exportable product that could bear the transportation costs (canoes) from Western Canada. With the arrival of the railways, the extensive grasslands of the Prairies were converted to cereal crops and livestock production for trade with the outside world. Immigrants flooded in to take up the "free land" and so began the modern history of Western Canada (Gwyn 2011).

On paper, the settlement of Western Canada looked good, and many fortunes were made settling the west, just as was occurring in the United States and many other parts of the world. The railways gave access to the continental interiors that allowed settlement and the export of grain from the US Great Plains, the steppes of the Ukraine, the Argentine pampas, and the arable parts of Australia and South Africa, as well as the Canadian Prairies. By the time that nineteenth century railway expansion had run its course, the oversupply of grain was permanent. Even as more land was being settled in Western Canada, grain import markets were deluged and barriers were being erected to protect the incomes of European farmers (Feinman 2016).

Once the economic impact of settling the Prairies had past, the reality of this "irrational exuberance" became obvious. Two

	$/bu.
1908–10	0.80
1911–15	0.75
1916–20	1.48
1921–25	0.91
1926–30	0.85
1931–35	0.46
1936–40	0.64
1941–45	1.04
1946–50	1.60
1951–55	1.42
1956–60	1.23

Adapted from E.P. Reid, 1960

Figure 5.1 Average farm price, Prairie provinces, 1908–60

transcontinental railways went bankrupt during World War I, and were amalgamated into the Canadian National Railway (CNR). The war demand sustained profitable export prices, but subsequently grain prices began a secular decline. In the 1920s, farm incomes dropped as wheat prices declined and continued to fall in a staircase fashion until the 1930s when the floor collapsed. Drought then combined with the Great Depression to make a bad situation deplorable. Relief did not arrive until World War II and its aftermath, which again created a short period of buoyant export demand before wheat prices began to fall again. Reid (1960) provides a record of nominal wheat prices on the Prairies. In constant dollars, farmers were receiving less for their wheat than fifty years earlier.

The Canadian Prairies were marketed to prospective immigrants under the ironic slogan, "The Last Best West." Located at the northern margin of agricultural land in the centre of North America, Prairie farmers are the farthest from an ocean port of any major grain exporting area in the world. While the average distance to an ocean port of competing grain exporters is less than 200 miles, the farmers of Western Canada are more than 1,000 miles from the coast. The inland shipping distance makes a great deal of difference to profitability when everyone is facing the same port prices for grain. From a transportation perspective, the Canadian Prairies would have been more appropriately entitled "The Least Best West."

The economic problems confronting Western Canadian agriculture after World War I had no solution. The over expansion of grain production spurred on by railway building could not be reversed. Political solutions to economic problems seldom make for good transportation policies. Under pressure to do something, in 1924 the government of Canada made it statutory that freight rates for shipping grain by rail to export locations would remain at the level previously agreed to in the 1897 Crowsnest Pass Agreement. This regulation, which came to be known as the Crow Rates, remained in place until it was replaced by the 1984 Western Grain Transportation Act (see also Kroeger 2009).

The Crow Rate was not the only measure used to help support farm incomes. During World War II, the Canadian Wheat Board (CWB) was made a regulated monopsony, mainly to help limit the costs of the government of Canada's pledge to provide wheat to the United Kingdom (Wilson 1978). Farmers' support for the CWB was strong in part because of their experience with a forerunner of the CWB during World War I and the mistaken belief that the CWB could sustain above-market wheat prices. Other measures included storage subsidies and publicly supported research to improve crop yields. In addition, commercial farmers began to depend on purchased inputs that further increased production, in particular mechanization of agriculture, artificial fertilizers, and pesticides. Grain surpluses that had been initiated by the expansion of agriculture into previously virgin grasslands were subsequently sustained by productivity improvement and subsidies.

Coming out of World War II, the railways were confronted with the need to renew plant and equipment, at the same time that technological advances in other transportation modes were creating serious competitive challenges. During the 1950s and 1960s, the trucking industry siphoned away the better-paying general freight from the railways, while the growth of the airlines, and in particular jet airplanes, took over the passenger market. Although the CNR had retired its last steam engine in 1960, the changeover to diesel-electric locomotives could not compensate for these revenue losses. Worse, grain transportation represented a large share of the total volume, and it was losing money. By the late 1950s the Crow Rate was yielding only about half of the necessary return.

The railways have told the Commission that in 1958 some
8 percent of the carloads of freight they originated was statuto-
rily rated grain traffic; that such traffic comprised 10 to 15 per
cent of their loaded car-miles, 19 to 26 per cent of their revenue
ton-miles, and 6 to 9 per cent of their freight revenue. All these
percentages are more than doubled when statutory traffic is set
against only that originating in Western Canada. (Reid 1960, 385)

In addition, the railways reported that fully 30.4 per cent of their
track in the three Prairie provinces was "solely-related" to the carriage
of grain. These grain-dependent branch lines were to become a greater
burden because the railways were not allowed to abandon such tracks
despite their money-losing character.

The general economic plight of the railways was recognized by
the Royal Commission on Transportation (1959–61) that was led
by Murdoch MacPherson. The MacPherson Commission operated
under "the premise that competition was now the major factor in
Canadian transportation" and recommended that the railways be
freed from regulatory controls in order to compete effectively with
other modes – especially trucking. It identified four areas where the
railways were providing services at a loss and recommended subsidies
to cover the shortfalls: uneconomic passenger services, unprofitable
branch lines, the statutory grain rates, and statutory free transportation (see Earl and Prentice 2016). The MacPherson Commission
accepted the railways' contention that they were losing money carrying grain and set these losses at $11 million for each railway (Currie
1967, 18–22).

The principles that MacPherson laid down were generally carried
into law in the 1967 National Transportation Act. The first section
of this legislation defined a new national transportation policy, declar-
ing that "an economic, efficient and adequate transportation system"
would "most likely" develop "when regulation does not impede competition, each mode of transport bears its fair share of facilities and
services provided at public expense," and is compensated for services
provided as "an imposed public duty." Three such duties were identified in the legislation: passenger services, uneconomic branch lines,
and grain movement.

Politics, once again, trumped rail policy. Clause 50 of the bill dealt
with grain, but to many people in the West and their representatives
in Parliament, this clause was nothing more than a ploy to allow the

railways to escape its sacred obligation to preserve the Crow Rates "in perpetuity" (Earl 2011).

The bill was sufficiently sensitive and controversial that, in committee stage, it was referred to "the committee of the whole," meaning that it was to be debated by the whole House of Commons. Just before 6:00 p.m. on 16 January 1967, the House turned its attention to clause 50. Debate continued for much of the following two days, at the end of which the official opposition proposed an amendment to delete clause 50. Whether the government party whip was asleep, or someone miscounted, will never be known, but the amendment carried, 59 to 58, and the National Transportation Act (NTA) was left with an enormous inconsistency, providing subsidies for branch lines and passenger service, while leaving the railways to cover the losses on grain – and, as an unintended but not unpredictable result, bringing railway investment in grain to a halt.

At roughly the same time, the federal government protected more than 12,000 miles of rail lines in the Prairies – about two-thirds of the total – from abandonment. In theory, this worsened the railways' losses by making rail rationalisation impossible. In practice, however, the inconsistency in the NTA distorted the branch line subsidy program, turning it into a hidden subsidy on grain movement. The situation, in summary, was that the branch line subsidies provided for in the legislation were determined by calculating revenue earned from moving traffic from origin to final destinations and deducting the cost of moving the traffic plus the fixed costs of the line. If the net revenue from moving the traffic covered the fixed cost of the line, the line was considered to be profitable and could not be abandoned. If a loss was determined, the line was then either abandoned or kept in the public interest and subsidised to the level indicated by the calculation (Earl and Prentice 2016). As the Hall Commission (1977, 55) noted,

> It failed in its objective. Grain dependent lines were allowed to deteriorate in condition and service. The subsidy was originally intended for the maintenance of branch lines. In reality it became a subsidy on grain on all the 19 thousand miles of railway lines in Western Canada and not just for grain that originated on the 12,000 miles of subsidized lines.

It is difficult to understand the seemingly wilful blindness with which, in the 1960s and 1970s, the defenders of the Crow Rates ignored the perverse effects that this regulation had begun to have on the grain handling and transportation system, impeding its modernisation, stifling efficiency, and undermining the grain industry's competitiveness in international markets. The frozen freight rates removed the incentive of the elevator companies to replace their obsolete network that was largely built prior to World War II. This was reinforced by grain storage subsidies that gave the grain companies a return on these old assets. When the opportunities to expand exports to China and the former Soviet Union developed, the grain supply chain proved unable to respond.

A report by the Canada Grains Council in 1973 finally called a spade a spade. "The Federal Government must come to terms with the statutory rate issue by recognizing that [the Crow Rate] is an income support measure for the producer. Its level is not in accord with the fundamental principles of rate setting. It can strain the evolution towards the least cost system for producers (Canada Grains Council 1973, 184). Decades of using grain freight rates as a means of bolstering farm incomes ultimately led to an uncompetitive grain supply chain and a monumental task of modernization. However, the support of Prairie populists would not be overcome easily. The Saskatchewan minister of Agriculture, J.R. Messer, introduced a motion in 1975 to send the following message to Ottawa: "The Legislative Assembly of Saskatchewan protests suggestions by the Minister in charge of the Canadian Wheat Board that the Crow's Nest rates be discontinued and requests your assurance that this historic right of Western Canada will continue to be guaranteed by the Federal Government" (Legislative Assembly of Saskatchewan 1975).

DEREGULATING WESTERN GRAIN (1970S TO PRESENT)

Over the past fifty years, a slow and halting process of deregulation has characterized the grain supply chain in Western Canada. The first hurdle confronting the Pierre Trudeau government was to obtain agreement that the status quo was unsustainable. By the mid-1970s, a rancorous debate raged about the Crow Rate as a "birthright" of Prairie farmers and questioning whether or not the railways were losing money hauling grain. Added to the economic issue was a fear of the social adjustment that reform might bring. Many Prairie residents feared that the closure of railway branch lines and shuttering of the local grain elevators would lead to the demise of their communities. Stabler (1986, 215) observes, however, that, "the relatively large number of [rail branch line] abandonments during the 1970s, followed community decline rather than caused it." He considered this aspect of the debate to be misplaced. Proximity to larger centres, a paved road, and institutions like hospitals and schools were more important than the rail lines, but this was an emotional issue that inflamed the resistance to change.

The political situation left no palatable options for ending the Crow Rate, but doing nothing was not an option either. The reality facing the grain handling system can be encapsulated in one railway statistic collected during this period: standing derailments. In some cases, the branch line sidings had been allowed to deteriorate to the point that standing railcars could simply topple off the track. The rolling stock was also falling to pieces. In 1972, the Canadian government began buying covered hopper cars and providing them to the railways for the exclusive use of grain carriage. They also entered a cost-shared program with the railways in 1974 to rehabilitate 7,400 boxcars. The federal hopper car purchases continued until the mid-1980s when the fleet reached 13,500. To this, the CWB acquired 4,000 railcars at the producers' expense, and the governments of Saskatchewan and Alberta each purchased 1,000 railcars. These railcars were divided evenly between the CNR and the CPR. Of all the measures used to assist the cost of grain transportation, the publicly owned railcar fleet has been the most enduring. General attrition and the expiry of railcar leases have reduced the remaining fleet of publicly supplied railcars to about 10,900. Pratte (2016) calculates that the rate of contraction will accelerate after 2020, and the fleet will be virtually gone by 2035.

Protecting railway branch lines from abandonment continued to be a hot issue that clouded any progress towards modernization. Approximately 6,300 miles of branch lines were not protected, and an inquiry under the chairmanship of a former Supreme Court Justice, Emmett Hall, set about to access the state of grain transportation and which branch lines should be preserved. The Hall Commission, which undertook a wide-ranging consultation, did more to sustain the status quo than rationalize the system when it released its recommendations in May 1977. Abandonment was recommended – in stages from 1977 to 1981 – for 2,165 miles of grain-related Prairie branch lines and the retention of the other branch lines until 2000 (Canadian Transportation Agency 2016d).

The Hall Commission recommended that certain lines be placed under a review agency that gave rise to the Prairie Rail Action Committee (PRAC). The designation of these lines under the PRAC created an indeterminate status. The grain companies and the railways would not commit to further capital investment while the PRAC studied whether the line should be part of the permanent network, abandoned at a certain date, or given priority for upgrading. This did more to slow adjustment than it did to facilitate technological rationalization.

An equally important initiative during this period was the appointment in 1975 of a Washington, DC-based transportation consultant, Carl Snavely. He was directed to calculate the costs and revenues associated with the movement of statutory grain during 1974. This study provided an independent answer to the debate whether or not the railways were being fully remunerated. The Snavely inquiry found that the railways had lost $103 million carrying grain in 1974. "The producer paid 38% of the total cost of the railways in the movement of statutory grain, the Federal Government paid 24% and the railways absorbed 38% in uncompensated losses" (Rothstein 1989). But the farm community in Western Canada disputed the validity of these findings. Consequently, Snavely was commissioned to update his numbers. Rapid inflation during this decade resulted in a finding of $244 million by 1980. Between the Hall Commission and the Snavely report, it was clear that the long-denied losses of the railways could no longer be sustained and the Crow Rates would have to change.

The Trudeau era was interrupted in 1979 by the short-lived election of a minority Conservative government under Joe Clark. When the Liberal government under Trudeau returned to power in 1980 (without any Liberal MPs elected from Western Canada), the rising costs of the various direct (branch line) and indirect (railcar) subsidies added impetus to finally deal with the Crow Rate issue. In 1982, Clay Gilson, a well-known and highly respected professor of agricultural economics from the University of Manitoba, was appointed to conduct negotiations with the various western agricultural interests. He was instructed, "to recommend a common set of principles and a clear and workable framework for a new and comprehensive approach to the western grain transportation system" (Tyrchneiwicz 1984). Dr Gilson started his work in the spring of 1982, and by June had submitted his final report. It recommended that the federal government absorb the railways' current annual financial shortfall on grain (which the report set at $650 million), that future cost increases be shared between the federal government and the farmers, and that task forces be established to work out the implementation details of the package.

In late 1983, the Crow Rate was finally replaced by the Western Grain Transportation Act (WGTA). The details of the WGTA had been hotly contested with regard to how the payment, referred to now as the "Crow Benefit," should be paid. Ultimately, the proregulatory side convinced the government that the payment should be made to the railways and based on distance. A concern of some farm groups was that a subsidy paid directly to farmers would be too easy a target for elimination. The Crow Benefit was initially fixed at $658 million with freight rates set by the Canadian Transportation Commission (CTC) on a cost-recovery basis. Under the WGTA, producers were responsible for any inflationary cost increases up to 6 per cent. By 1989–90, the Crow benefit was $720 million. This covered approximately 70 per cent of total freight costs with producers paying the remaining 30 per cent.

The WGTA resolved the financial bleeding of the railways and encouraged consolidation of the primary elevator numbers. From 5,031 elevators in 1967 the number had diminished to 2,800 by 1983. During 1984, a further 833 elevators closed. After this, the pace slowed because the extensive branch line rail network was still in place and the marketing of wheat, oats, and barley through the CWB provided no incentive to haul beyond the nearest delivery point – the price was always the same. Prentice et al. (1996) observe that farmers were more likely to truck the CWB grains to the nearest elevator and use commercial trucks to sell non-CWB field crops to more distant locations.

The National Transportation Act (NTA) of 1987 was introduced under the Mulroney administration. The NTA contained extensive regulatory reforms for all modes of transport, including the sale or abandonment of rail lines, but the grain-dependent branch lines under the WGTA were specifically excluded until the year 2000. The WGTA provided for an averaging of all costs, including the retention and maintenance of grain-dependent branch lines. The more important achievements of the Mulroney era were the signing of the Canada–US Free Trade Agreement, the subsequent North America Free Trade Agreement (NAFTA), and the Uruguay Round of the GATT (now World Trade Organization). Export subsidies and free trade agreements are incompatible with each other, and this laid the

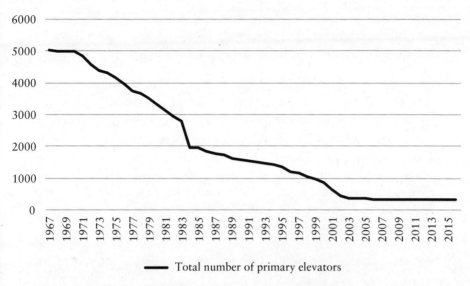

——— Total number of primary elevators

Figure 5.2 Total number of primary grain elevators in Western Canada, 1967–2016

Source: Canadian Grain Commission

groundwork for change when the Uruguay Round came into effect in 1995.

Although trade obligations were used as an excuse for ending the WGTA, it was fiscal pressure that ultimately weighed heavily on the Chrétien government. "The Crow benefit was scaled back in 1993/94 and 1994/95 as part of the legislation enacted to reduce the deficit. By the time of its demise in 1995, the Crow benefit had been reduced to $565 million and farmers were paying almost half the cost of transporting grain" (Doan, Paddock, and Dyer 2003). As compensation, farmers were given a one-time payment of $1.6 billion to offset the expected fall in land values. Following the passage of the Canada Transportation Act (1996), the Canadian Transportation Agency was charged with setting grain freight rates based on distance, known as the Maximum Rate Scale, but now these costs were borne entirely by shippers.

The deregulation of the grain handling and transportation system (GHTS) was then well underway, and in December 1997 the minister of Transport appointed Justice Willard Estey to conduct a comprehensive review of the efficiency of the GHTS. The Estey (1998) report contained fifteen recommendations that envisioned an increasingly commercial transportation environment, including the tendering of CWB-administered grain shipments, repeal of the statutory rates in favour of contracting, and disposal of the government-owned hopper car fleet.

Opinion divided on the role of the CWB in grain transportation. Arthur Kroeger, who had served as deputy minister of Transport during the end of the Crow Rates, was asked to undertake a second consultative process during 1999 to implement Estey's 1998 report, *Grain Handling and Transportation Review*. Kroeger was unable to bring about any consensus on Justice Estey's recommendations (see Kroeger 2009). The result was a feared "cherry-picking" that Estey had specifically warned against. On 10 May 2000, the government announced measures to respond to the Estey–Kroeger work.

- Introduction and gradual expansion of tendering for Canadian Wheat Board shipments to port
- Replacement of the current maximum rate scale for grain with a cap on the annual grain revenues of railways
- Improvements to the branch line rationalization process
- Improvement to the Final Offer Arbitration (FOA) process
- Five year $175 million transitional fund for prairie roads
- Mechanism for continuous monitoring, measurement and reporting on the overall performance of the GHTS system. (Transport Canada)

On 1 August 2000, Bill-34 amended the Canada Transportation Act to replace the Canadian Transportation Agency rail freight rates with a revenue-cap form of regulation, called the Maximum Revenue Entitlement (MRE). A memorandum of understanding that came into force on 1 August 2000 directed CWB to organize a tendering program that turned out to be largely ineffectual. The branch line rationalization and final offer arbitration were done through further amendments. One of the most enduring and valuable changes was the creation of the Grain Monitor. Instead of opinions governing the day, accurate statistics became available to inform decisions.

The MRE is based on the railways' activities in the 2000–01 crop year and a costing review completed in 1992, adjusted for inflation and productivity gains. The MRE sets a statutory limit on the amount of revenue a prescribed railway can earn from the movement of regulated grain in Western Canada. It applies to revenues earned by CN and CP on export shipments from Western Canada routed through the west coast ports of Vancouver and Prince Rupert. Revenues from grain shipments east are also included in the cap when routed through Thunder Bay or Armstrong. Grains exported through Churchill and the US are excluded from the MRE. Unlike the Crow Rate, the MRE has an input cost adjustments called the Volume Related Composite Price Index (VRCPI). The VRCPI formula sets the maximum revenue that a prescribed railway can charge all shippers, subject to the volume and distance of grain movement in Western Canada. Railways are free to charge different rates by season, cars, scheduling, loading, and other variables but when all receipts are summed their revenues cannot exceed the MRE. If the MRE is exceeded, the railways involved would receive a fine and have to pay the excess revenues to the Western Grains Research Foundation.

The MRE was successful in promoting the modernization of the GHTS because it aligned the interest of the grain companies and the railways toward an efficient, low-cost system. Large high-throughput grain terminals have replaced most of the wooden elevators. Unit trains with large blocks of railcars have reduced the car cycle times, and expansions of terminal elevators have occurred at the ports. However, the MRE, always envisioned as a transitional measure, has now been in place for sixteen years. The problems inherent in this form of regulation stem in part from its requirement for the retrospective accounting by the railways of each year's shipments once they are completed. In theory, the railways are free to charge different rates by season, cars, scheduling, loading and other variables, but, to repeat, when all receipts are summed the railways' revenues cannot exceed a maximum amount adjusted annually by the VRCPI set in regulation. Consequently, the railways cannot vary their rates with the ultimate level of demand, which leads to railcar rationing during the peak harvest shipping months and chronic customer service complaints. Moreover, customer service failures at the beginning of the supply chain get translated into customer service failures for the end receiver, with a negative impact on Canada's reputation as a reliable supplier, which leads to price discounts and lost sales (Prentice 2015).

The economic distortions created by the MRE are not as severe as they were under the Crow Rate, but they have similar impacts. Rate regulation discourages efficiency-enhancing investment and technological improvements in grain handling. The Crow caused boxcars to be used in Canada long after they were abandoned in the US. Today,

Canadian grain is carried in hopper cars that have been replaced by more efficient cars in the US. As one of the quirks in the MRE, the railways get credit for the value of the earlier generation government-owned hopper car only if they replace it with the more-efficient current generation. Moreover, the railway that bears the cost must share the benefit with its competitor. Regulated rates get more out-of-date while technology and costs change. Given that the basis of the MRE consists of a 1992 costing, an *ad hoc* productivity adjustment, and a formula, it would be remarkable if it represented actual market returns. It is impossible to know how the railways set investment priorities, but opportunities to improve lower-yielding traffic are very unlikely to be seen as important as competing opportunities for investment in more lucrative freight.

The MRE includes no provision for the movement of grain in containers. Transloading grain into containers at the coast always adds cost and removes the benefits that accrue from traceability and product specificity that loading containers at source would otherwise provide. Worse, the MRE discriminates against source-loading of containers with grain on the Prairies. And because the movement of containers costs more than bulk grain in hopper cars, it needs to be charged at higher rates. But any extra revenue charged for transporting containers merely reduces headroom in the revenue cap faster than before. This in turn creates a near-total disincentive for railways to carry any containers identified with grain.

The deregulation of the GHTS continued under the Harper government with its termination of the CWB monopoly as of 1 August 2012. While not an owner of transportation or grain handling facilities, the CWB had exerted tremendous influence on the movement of wheat and barley. A significant portion of the railcars had been reserved to move CWB shipments and to serve some export points, like the Port of Churchill, that commercial operators now ignore. Today the CWB lives on as G3 Canada, a grain company, but its power to control the delivery of grain into the GHTS and its domination of grain movements has ended. In one respect, the timing of the CWB's end proved to be problematic. In the 2013–14 crop year, Prairie farmers were blessed with ideal growing conditions that delivered the largest crop on record and cursed with one of the worst winters to try to move a record crop. Without the CWB delivery quotas to restrain (i.e., meter-out) the shipments, farmers rushed to obtain available space in the elevators and quickly overwhelmed the capability of the railways to move their grain to port.

Once again, politics trumped policy. Literally nothing could be done to alter the physical reality that a surge in demand cannot be accommodated in a GHTS designed for a smaller crop maximum. Moreover, the railways lose efficiency and carrying capacity very fast when the temperatures drop below -25° C, which was common in the winter of 2014. But this did not stop the criticism that the government had to "do something." Complaints about the lack of rail service reached a crescendo by mid-winter as the severely cold weather accentuated the limits of the railway network to respond. In an effort to appear to be doing something, the Harper government passed Bill C-30, the Fair Rail for Grain Farmers Act, on 29 May 2014 – long after the worst of the problem was past. The two major provisions in the legislation were, first, introducing the regulatory authority to extend interswitching distance in the Prairie provinces to 160 kilometers and, second, giving cabinet the authority to set minimum amounts of grain to be moved by each railway. Perhaps in recognition that these were not well thought through polices, they were scheduled to terminate in two years, unless made permanent.

The Canada Transportation Act Review (2016) led by the Hon. David Emerson recommended changes to the MRE including that the extended interswitching measure under the Fair Rail for Grain Farmers Act be allowed to sunset. With respect to the MRE, some immediate changes were recommended to remove anomalies like the disincentive for using containers to move grain, interswitching, and railcar-replacement biases. However, the larger recommendation was a move to terminate the MRE in favour of an unregulated market within a seven-year time horizon. This last point draws on the observations of the prior 2001 CTA Review chaired by the Brian Flemming that asked why grain transportation should be treated differently than all other commodities.

On 23 May 2018, the Transportation Modernization Act (Bill C-49) received Royal Assent. Despite the recommendations of the Emerson-led CTA Review, the MRE is destined to continue as an exception to transportation policy that is based on market forces. It also extends the pattern of agriculture bending transport policy to serve its (the agriculture sector's) interests.

As expected, the anomalies of the MRE associated with railcar purchases and interswitching revenues were remedied. Containerized grain was taken out of the MRE, while soybeans were added as an eligible crop. The new Act also adds some measures for reciprocal penalties and data collection. The newest regulatory twist is the creation of the Long-Haul Interswitching (LHI) remedy for "captive shippers". LHI will allow shippers that located beyond the 30-kilometer radius of an interchange point at origin or destination to apply for a regulated rate for the local railway to connect to another carrier.

By creating individual VRCPIs for the railways, they will receive full credit for railcar purchases. Effectively, this ends the responsibility of the Government to maintain a publicall owned covered-hopper car fleet. Almost immediately, the railways announced plans to purchase new equipment. Thus ends a long-standing indirect subsidy for the transport of grain to export points. Full economic deregulation of grain transportation will have to wait until a future review of the CTA.

THE THREE ANALYTICAL ELEMENTS

Policy Ideas, Discourses, and Agendas

The two policy histories in this chapter trace their roots back more than one hundred years, to the settling of Western Canada and the grand bargain on which that monumental human enterprise was based and when the seeds of many of the "grains and trains" problems were planted. Table 5.1 gives the highlights. It is organized by the three elements of our analytical framework and shows the causes and effects of change and inertia in this fertile policy space. There is a lot of change and inertia to go around.

Probably the foremost de facto policy idea is that of bolstering farm incomes. There is a direct line to it from the grand bargain on which the settling was based. And from that one idea, almost everything described in this chapter springs. Why? Because there is, or at least was, an implied obligation on the part of governments to indemnify farmers when the opportunity for prosperity they thought they were buying into with the promise of "free land" turned out to be rather illusory. That is because grain production got caught in a Nash Equilibrium that arose when over-production worldwide depressed prices and when the distance from Prairie farms to tidewater in Canada made it clear just how much the overhead accounted for by rail transportation ate into their margins – margins already so thin

Table 5.1
The grains and trains transport policy domain and the three analytical elements: Highlights

Policy and governance histories	Analytical elements		
	Policy ideas, discourse, and agendas	Economic and social power	Technology and temporal realities and conflicts
The globalization of grain (1897 to present)	Rail transport induced perpetual immigration and "free land" in Western Canada as nation-building	Strong export strategy institutions, including National Wheat Board	Railways as the embodiment of a new technology that gave rapid access to continental interiors and allowed settlement and export of grain
	Nash Equilibrium in world grain markets for most of twentieth century, built-in "tragedy of the commons"	Oversupply of grain permanent	Post-World War II need to renew plant and equipment at the same time as new technology emerged in trucking, etc.
	Transportation as an instrument of broader policy objectives, under overall prairie populism ideas	Subsidizing farmers directly and indirectly	Crow Rates impede modernization
	The Canadian West as the "Last Best West" globally versus the "Least Best West"	Grain freight rates made Statutory (1924) at the 1897 level	
	1959–61 MacPherson Royal Commission on Transportation advocacy of competition as the key policy needed	Drought and Great Depression of 1930s	
	Distorted branch-line subsidy ideas and outcomes persisted	1897 Crowsnest Agreement held in the main until replaced by Grain Transportation Act 1984	
	Wilful blindness to Crow Rate's adverse impacts	National Wheat Board as regulated monopsony	
	Hall Commission 1977 study showed grain-dependent lines had been allowed to seriously deteriorate	Storage subsidies emerge as partial reforms	
	Grain freight rates as a means of bolstering farm incomes	Grain-dependent branch lines becoming greater burden to railways	
		1967 National Transportation Act included some deregulation but also inconsistencies	

Policy and governance histories	Analytical elements		
	Policy ideas, discourse, and agendas	Economic and social power	Technology and temporal realities and conflicts
Deregulating Western grain (1970s to present)	Slow and halting process of deregulation in grain supply chain in Western Canada	Canadian Wheat Board (1980s) acquires 4,000 railcars at producers' expense	Rail infrastructure deterioration best illustrated by "standing railcars could simply fall off the tracks"
	Crow Rate as a "birthright"	Hall Commission 1977 consultations do more to sustain the status quo than change it	Feds as buyers and suppliers of hopper cars for railways
	Feared demise of Prairie communities	Prairie Rail Action Committee (PRAC) established as review agency but inertia was its main result	Maximum Rate Entitlement (MRE) has helped modernization but seen as a transitional measure that has now been in place for sixteen years
	The "do nothing" option was not an option either	Snavely report in 1975 and later also the Hall Commission showed the long-denied losses of the railway companies could no longer be sustained	MRE contains no provisions for the movement of grain in intermodal containers
	Protecting rail branch lines from abandonment was still key issue	1983 Western Grain Transportation Act replaces the Crow Rate	
	Canada–US free trade, NAFTA, and WTO elevate free trade as idea and set of rules in Mulroney era	Mulroney-era 1988 National Transportation Act reforms regulation for all modes of transport including sale or abandonment of rail lines	
	Fiscal deficit realities and ideas in Chrétien era lead to deregulation of the grain handling and transit system (GHTS)	Harper government ends Canadian Wheat Board as monopoly. CWB lives on as G3 Canada, a grain company, but its power ended	
	Canadian Transportation Agency (CTA) in 1996 charged with setting grain freight rates based on Maximum Rate Entitlement (MRE) with costs borne entirely by shippers	Harper government passes the Fair Rail for Grain Farmers Act as its "solution" for dealing with the massive record Western grain crop and alleged transport failures in handling it	

that grain production was a financially unsustainable proposition in something like seventy-five of those one hundred years. The result were subsidies and blatant trade protectionism that created a "tragedy of the commons" and led to the kind of policies that usually arise when everyone is in a precarious situation with few apparent options for escape.

Supporting this idea was a second component, the subordinating of transportation policy to serve other policy objectives: rail freight rates were driven primarily by the imperative of putting more money into grain producers' pockets. (Transportation aficionados will not be cheered to learn that this kind of subordination shows up in various other chapters and policy and governance histories in this book.)

A third component is that of Prairie populism. It grew in fertile soil from 1910 to 1945 (Laycock 1990) but flourished especially during the Great Depression and drought of the 1930s, aided and abetted by a number of inducements like the asymmetric freight rates charged for many years by the railways in general and the CPR in particular, and all manner of other sociopolitical developments that led Western Canadian grain producers to think they were getting a raw deal. That in turn supported a fourth component, a belief in the Crow Rates as a birthright. And from that sprang decades of inertia – in the form of not decreasing transportation subsidies, not modernizing the rail transport system and the grain elevator infrastructure that fed it, and not removing the CWB's monopoly and its inefficiencies and instead introducing counterproductive policy measures like the Fair Rail for Grain Farmers Act, from which the "grains and trains" holy deadlock still has not recovered.

The second main policy idea in this domain is closely related to the first, that of settling the Prairies. It was a product of railway development, nation building, and what was imagined at the time to be immigration in perpetuity. Of course it didn't last, but by the time immigration had cooled other pressures began taking its place. One of the most powerful in recent decades has been the fear of Prairie communities dying from branch line abandonment. The fear seems to have been aimed at the wrong culprit, but that is not the point. The point is that it contributed significantly to inertia in the evolution of rail transportation policy and the pursuit of competitiveness for Canadian grain in world markets.

Probably the third most significant idea in this policy space is that of the protection of monopolies and the slow and halting process by which some of them were removed. The first was CPR's monopoly over much of the transportation of Western grain and the continuing monopoly of CN and CP in serving those farms not within feasible reach of both railways by truck. But the replacement of small farm trucks by large commercial tractor trailers has changed the game considerably. The second component was the MacPherson Commission's appreciation that competition had become a sufficiently powerful force in transportation that the days of policy measures predicated on government regulation of monopolies were coming to an end. Yet five decades later, MacPherson's principles are still not fully implemented. The MRE and the Fair Rail for Grain Farmers Act are exhibits A and B in that regard. The third component was the idea of supporting high prices and large export sales through an agency that turned out to be the CWB. Its monopoly lasted more than half a century before succumbing to freer-market principles. The trend to removing monopolies wounded, but did not kill, another tacit one, that of the federal government protecting Canadian industries, in this case grain, with export subsidies. The rise of free trade agreements and the mathematics of federal deficits put a dint in the usefulness of that monopoly but they have not yet altogether neutered it.

Economic and Social Power

The primary feature of economic power in our grains and trains history is probably the fluctuation and frequent long declines in grain prices and thus farm incomes. Table 5.1 shows the brutal numbers. The resulting paucity of economic power on the part of Western Canadian grain farmers was arguably the main impetus in creating the CWB, in constraining most (if not all) increases in rail freight rates, first by the Crow and then by the MRE, and in consolidating farms to achieve economies of scale and diversifying crops to protect against the tyranny of single-crop production in volatile world markets. Some of these measures led to railway losses – in effect transferring money from railway's pockets, which were perilously shallow in the years leading up to deregulation in the 1980s and 1990s, and putting it into grain producers' pockets, which, as noted above, was precisely the basis on which transportation policy was subordinated to some other policy. Virtually all of these measures led to marketplace distortions whose effect was to prolong inefficiencies in rail transportation, some of which remain with us today.

Probably the most significant feature of social power over much of the century-long story in this chapter has been Prairie populism and its manifestation in politically driven decisions that continually trumped good policy. Rooted in the grand bargain by which the Western provinces were settled and in the abuses farmers faced at the hands of railways in the late-1800s and in the hardships from drought and Depression in the 1930s, this form of power shows up at the ballot-box and in the often-disproportionate clout within cabinet of ministers from the Prairies (especially of agriculture ministers relative to transport ministers), in the number and vociferousness of grain associations like the Prairie Rail Action Committee and dozens of others, and in the extent and vigorousness of the grain lobby on Ottawa. Another way of looking at this power is through its manifestation in the susceptibility of governments to subordinating transportation policy to serve the income problem of Western Canadian farmers. Trudeaumania ended with an indiscreet comment, the National Transportation Act (1967) passed with an enormous inconsistency, the Hall Commission and several others had to be formed to calm the political waters, and the MRE is still in effect. And when an ostensibly probusiness, free-market government like the Harper Conservatives enacts an absurd bill like the Fair Rail for Grain Farmers Act, chances are good they were pressured into it.

Technology and Temporal Realities and Conflicts

This analytical element has four highlights. First is the rise in global production of grain and the resulting determination of exporting nations to subsidize their farmers, engage in blatant trade protectionism, and ultimately trap Canada along with all the others in a Nash Equilibrium. At first the surpluses were driven primarily by the expansion of agriculture into previously virgin grasslands, but when that form of expansion levelled off another one took its place, driven in part by productivity improvements from technology in the form of mechanization and improvements in crop genetics. Future prospects seem a little brighter, with the continuing growth of world population and a probable reduction in arable land turning the historic problem of global grain surpluses into a possible shortage with attendant benefits for Canadian farmers.

The second highlight is the rise of competition for railways from trucking and jet aircraft in the years following World War II. We describe and analyze the phenomenon more fully in chapter 6, but suffice it to say that it precipitated an end to the railways' ability to contribute all the money needed to keep farm incomes at the levels they had been in the past. That in turn triggered the move to government subsidies, branch line abandonment, the elimination of CWB's monopoly, and the halting (and still incomplete) wind down of the Crow and it's successor, the MRE.

The third highlight is the long tail of regulatory measures that got introduced when conditions seemed appropriate for them, like the statutory freight rates in 1924 (Crow Rates), the CWB during World War II, and the MRE in 2000, but that were held in place by politics or inertia (or both) long after the prevailing conditions had changed and they had become dysfunctional in ways that were often not hard to see. Anyone driving across the Prairies not that long ago could see this dysfunction in physical terms, in the form of more than 5,000 small wooden grain elevators that had become obsolete decades before most of them were replaced with far-more-efficient inland terminals. And even today the dysfunction can be seen in the form of grain hopper cars whose design is based on fifty-year-old technology.

Our fourth highlight is the seasonality of grain growing. That is a temporal problem with few solutions in sight. It manifests itself in massive seasonal fluctuations in the amount of grain to be shipped by rail, which, according to optimization theory, is almost certainly the primary cause limiting the railway network's throughput capacity. And so unless (and until) "winter wheat" refers to grain that actually grows in the winter, the only solutions are to vastly increase grain storage capacity on farms or at inland terminals – these act as "buffers" in the system – or to invest in so much surge capacity on railways that it (the unused railway capacity) fulfils the role of buffer, or to manage railway traffic so that other commodities are shifted to months when grain is not moving. Unfortunately, the latter is probably about as realistic as growing wheat in winter.

And finally, looking to the future, the evolution of crop production, formerly dominated by wheat but now far more diversified with canola, pulses, and special crops, represents a change in agricultural practice and developments in biotechnology that seem likely to improve farm incomes more, and with far less market distortion, than the traditional approach of subordinating transportation policy to a policy designed to transfer money from one industry sector to another ever could.

CONCLUSIONS

Unlike the other chapters in this book, this one on the grains and trains transport policy domain is explicitly and crucially about a mode of transportation, railways, serving a single (and historic) industry, the grain industry in Western Canada. (In chapter 6 we will extend the rail freight analysis to look at railway and shipper relations beyond a single industry. It includes a multiplicity of shippers and industries and shows how an early twenty-first century model adopted by Canada's principal railways, based on a new optimization strategy, raises important issues about what a market duopoly of CPR and CNR actually means.)

The thesis of this "grains and trains" chapter is that transportation policy with respect to grain has been bent to serve the income problem of Western Canadian farmers. It is worth reviewing whether or not the basis for the use of transportation as an instrument of agricultural policy still remains. Certainly, all countries defend their agricultural sectors and, notwithstanding the advances made through the World Trade Organization and other treaties, protectionism and subsidization have not gone away. What has changed, however, is the supply–demand balance of the world market.

The United Nations' demographic forecasts and future outlook scenarios all suggest that the world's population will grow from more than 7 billion people today to between 8.3 and 10.9 billion by 2050, an increase of between 1.3 and 3.9 billion people, providing a steady increase in the demand for grains, oilseed, pulse crops, and special crops. Climate change threatens to challenge global crop production and cause it to contract. For example, rising sea levels could flood some of the most agriculturally productive multicropping deltas of the world, while droughts are predicted to hit with greater force. The northern location of Western Canada may be one of the few areas that stands to benefit from rising global temperatures.

For much of the twentieth century, the incomes of Western Canadian farmers were subject to major shocks because of the dependence on one crop – wheat – that accounted for more than 90 per cent of their exports. This began to change with the expansion of canola acreage and the popularity of pulses and special crops. The change has been helped by changes in world import demand for these crops. The agricultural base is now more diversified and stable as a result. The effects can be seen in the larger picture of the economies of Western Canada.

Agriculture is still important, but resources, manufacturing, and food processing are being integrated with a large service economy that can weather commodity cycles much better.

When the Crow Rate was formed, the railways were the only means of surface transportation. Farmers were truly captive shippers. It is not particularly clear that such terms are still valid in the twenty-first century. While grain shipments to overseas markets may have no other economic option than rail, trucks can haul grain to the domestic processing facilities and to US markets. The US accounted for 17 per cent of grain exports in 2015 and 25 per cent of these deliveries were made by trucks (Quorum 2016). As a volume-driven business, railways have an interest in minimizing any leakage of traffic to truck and local markets.

These and other kinds of developments are important as we shift to our next transport policy and governance domain in chapter 6 where modern rail freight is examined on a multiindustry basis.

6

The Rail Freight and Competition-Market Dispute Domain

INTRODUCTION

We now turn to the rail freight and competition-market dispute domain and how it has been reshaped over the last thirty years. In chapter 5 we covered rail policy and governance for the transport of grain, but that was over a longer period, one that began much earlier, and it focused on a single industry. In this chapter our focus is on rail freight transport in general, but we also note how other transport modes, mainly trucking, compete with rail freight. Indeed, it is important to note that in contrast with other modes, the two main railways own their own (albeit regulated) infrastructure, but trucking and other modes do not.

The rail freight story has three main threads. First is the theory and practice of economic deregulation that invites (and even encourages) an industry sector to become more vibrant, energetic, and hungry to serve its customers and make money. Second is the means by which regulation discourages or prevents firms from abusing their market power. And third are the forms of redress made available to players who feel abused or unfairly treated in the marketplace. All three of these threads involve a mix of transportation policy on one hand, and policy and law for dealing with competition and the settling of market disputes on the other. In dealing with the latter we look at the mandate and some performance aspects of the Canadian Transportation Agency (CTA), as well as the potential for an alternative system, centred on the federal competition commissioner and the Competition Bureau, to deal with competition issues and market disputes in rail transport.

We briefly described the CTA's 1996 origins in chapter 4. Here we will focus on its role in arbitrating disputes between freight railways and shippers. That role has undergone considerable flux as rail policy (and its expression in federal regulations) changed over the past three decades as the two main railways, CP and CN, changed their system-optimization strategies, as shippers adapted their own strategies for lodging complaints when they perceived themselves to be treated unfairly or just not served the way they needed or expected, and as the CTA evolved (or failed to evolve) to meet the changing market conditions or the expectations of government.

One thing that has *not* changed much for more than a century is the legal obligation placed on railways to provide service to shippers. Known popularly but not precisely as "common carrier obligations," they have, as shown in chapter 1, morphed into "level of service" requirements under the Canada Transportation Act and now form the basis on which many or most disputes are arbitrated. We discuss them below because in the last fifteen to twenty years they have become a growing source of contention and arguably an impediment to progress.

In some key respects the starting point for this chapter is the Freedom to Move policy that we traced earlier in chapters 1 and 3. The policy dates from 1985, but the seeds of it were planted many decades earlier. Government regulation introduced in the late 1800s to curb flagrant railway abuses grew in subsequent years to what in retrospect seems an astonishing level of federal control over railway routes, services, schedules, operations, and even the minutiae of railway business practices. For example, by the mid-twentieth century it was illegal for railways *not* to collude in price-fixing led by government on virtually every route! Railways, like Gulliver, were tied down by thousands of tiny ropes and were neither incentivized nor allowed to respond to growing competition from trucking, airlines, and automobiles. Years of excessive government regulation had "locked railways into unproductive practices and money-losing operations" (Coleman and Doern 2014, 3) that drained their financial lifeblood. Despite initial economic regulatory relaxation in 1967, the entire rail industry was deep in a capital-starvation hole by the 1970s and its physical infrastructure nearly collapsed from lack of reinvestment (Coleman and Doern 2015, 8).

A turnaround began when the National Transportation Act took effect in 1967. Although modest and slow acting, it gave legislative expression to new thinking embodied in the MacPherson Commission report of 1961, i.e., that competitive forces could now do at least as good a job as federal regulation in providing some aspects of governance over the rail freight marketplace. But it was the even stronger promarket ethos embodied in the 1985 Freedom to Move policy that really turned the tide. When made law in 1988, it untied enough Gulliverian ropes that railways began the long climb back to competitiveness and financial health. With a second wave of economic deregulation eight years later, railways' "productivity rose, freight rates dropped, and traffic climbed as shippers voted with their wallets" (ibid.). Railways came to figure prominently in national programs for growing intermodal international container traffic, most notably the Asia–Pacific Gateways and Corridors Initiative, launched in 2004 to invigorate Canadian supply chains and boost the economy.

The story is not quite that simple, though, because economic deregulation of rail is entangled with safety regulation and other policy developments, many of which, as discussed in chapter 4, have been growing in what we broadly consider to be a late-1990s to 2018 story. And so, despite the rail freight marketplace and political dynamics revolving mainly around CN and CP and their customers and federal politicians, it is a complex brew of at least four other vital interest groups – rail freight interests and lobby groups such as the Freight Management Association of Canada, the Coalition of Rail Shippers, the Western Grain Producers Association, the Railway Association of Canada, and many others; the tens of thousands of large and small firms and industries who are the customers of the railways; the many communities served by – or sometimes not served by – rail transport; and the communities located on or near rail lines where people are concerned about rail safety in general and the transporting of dangerous goods through their towns and cities in particular (see chapter 9).

So, while the rail freight sector was genuinely becoming more competitive it was also turning more disputatious and difficult to understand. It was not even clear where the greatest market power actually lay. The lingering regulatory ethos from the late 1800s assumed that railways had greater economic clout than any of their customers. But many shippers can hardly be described as "little guys" these days because they include auto manufacturers, large mining and energy companies, giant retailing firms, powerful grain brokerages, influential terminal operators, and other businesses whose economic footprint and control of events in their supply chains is larger than that of the railways. But despite these other players' economic and lobbying clout (including during formal reviews of federal legislation), individually as well as collectively through industry coalitions and associations, the default presumption remains that railways have, and too often use, excessive market power that, therefore, needs to be curtailed by government, at least partly in the name of fair markets.

This chapter is divided into two policy and governance histories. The first one deals with rail freight policy from the mid-1960s to the present and how it developed in three main thrusts, all of them hinging on beliefs and convictions on the part of federal ministers about the way in which railways and their customers would respond to fundamental changes in the economic regulatory regime. The second policy and governance history deals with the policy and governance of competition and the settling of marketplace disputes from the mid-1990s to the present. The two stories need to be told separately, but they are interconnected because both shed light on how disputes are handled (or avoided) by the current private arbitration system as supported in law and how they might be changed if there was a greater role for independent federal competition authorities.

IN SEARCH OF OPTIMIZATION: FEDERAL POLICY AND THE FREIGHT RAILWAYS' BUSINESS MODELS (MID-1960S TO PRESENT)

Usually, changes in "public" policy represent that which has been decided and acted upon by governments. But that was not the case in rail freight policy. Instead, it emerged in an iterative *pas de deux* whereby governments periodically experimented with new regulatory principles by enacting them in law and waiting to see how railways would respond, and railways responded by modifying their strategies and their optimization principles in light of the new opportunities and constraints presented to them. Then government, gauging the degree to which the previous measures had worked as intended, updated its regulatory approach and made corresponding changes to the law. And so it went, over three main iterations beginning with the Freedom to Move policy statement in 1985. The upshot is that government positions represent only half the "public" policy evolution about which this chapter is concerned. The progression of railway optimization strategies and business models represents the other half, including issues leading to broader use of competition policy as discussed in our second policy and governance history.

We first look at the hypothesis on which the government's half was based and the circumstances that enabled it to be enacted in law. Then we look at the railways' operational and service performance in response to the legislative changes and how it contributed to the iterative dance. The first two steps were generally positive, but the third one was not. At the time of writing, a fourth step is emerging in the form of Bill C-49, an act to create the Transportation Modernization Act and its component parts currently before Parliament and as previewed in chapter 1.

The Government Half:
How the Hypothesis Became Law

We take a quick look back to 1967 when the economic deregulation ball started rolling with the passage of the National Transportation Act. Although too modest to have much effect on railways' business performance or financial viability, it established in legislation a new premise, introduced in principle by the MacPherson Commission six years earlier, that Canada's economic well-being is best served by an efficient, competitive transportation system. This was the first serious challenge to the orthodoxy that had settled over, and almost smothered, rail freight transport – that government should determine the basis on which commerce was transacted without much, if any, reference to the dynamics of the marketplace. This was not a popular new policy direction for the government to take when regulating railways, which were still suffering widespread opprobrium well earned in their robber baron days decades earlier. In strictly political terms, that meant there was a lot of risk in deregulating railways but little advantage. Moreover, after more than a half-century of micro-level government control, apart from principles argued in the MacPherson report there was no accepted policy template to which government could turn to validate the legitimacy or wisdom of what it contemplated doing.

That meant the hypothesis of improved railway performance under a relaxed regulatory regime was technically still that: a hypothesis. It took two things to turn it into legislation. First was a compelling need. In 1967 that need was *not* to give freer rein to market forces as a means of optimizing the rail transport system – it was to save the government money! The second thing it took was a forceful transport minister, Jack Pickersgill, willing to expose himself and his government to the possibility that the new approach might fail spectacularly but who was influential enough to carry the government along with him despite the political and policy risks. As to the compelling need, Pickersgill later wrote that the new legislation "began a reversal of the mounting subsidization of the [money-losing operations of] Canadian railways" whose "payments ... had risen to in excess of $100 million per year. ... This process could not continue indefinitely. The increasing subsidies would have reached astronomical proportions" (Pickersgill 1994, 85–6). So Pickersgill and his colleagues took something of a leap into the unknown. With respect to the risk, even two years after the legislation was enacted he wrote, "Whether we are on the right road in the way we are now approaching the problem, experience will tell" (ibid., 86). His convictions, supported by those of MacPherson, turned out to be well founded, as we discuss further below.

The government's next policy step in deregulating railways – and where the meat of this policy history really begins – was an announcement in 1985 by the relatively new Mulroney Conservative government (twenty-two months old) of a bold set of reforms. Far more extensive than the 1967 reforms, it was led by Minister of Transport Don Mazankowski. As we have seen in chapters 1 and 3, he began with a position paper called Freedom to Move that signalled in no uncertain terms his displeasure with the way the transportation sector had evolved and his determination to take things farther in the direction Pickersgill had started in a modest way – towards competition and market forces – in part by changing the policy expectations surrounding regulation, and in part by adding new tools to the regulatory toolbox, for example introducing confidential contracts for the first time and final-offer arbitration to "prompt the contestants to negotiate in good faith and attempt to reach their own resolution" (Canada 1985, 57).

Yet apart from the MacPherson Commission report, which by then was twenty-four years old, and whatever downstream effects could be measured or observed from the very modest changes embodied in the NTA (1967), there was *still* no accepted policy template to which government could turn to validate the legitimacy or the wisdom of what it intended to do.

So the hypothesis of improved railway performance under a relaxed regulatory regime was still largely a hypothesis. Again it took two things to turn that into legislation – a compelling need and an influential transport minister. In this case the compelling need was a mix of three things: the Staggers Act, which had boldly deregulated US railroads five years earlier and raised the stakes for Canada to keep pace; how unacceptably Mazankowski thought the rail transport system was performing (the preceding chapter on the grains and trains domain gave a flavour of how bad some things had become); and a deeply held Conservative (and neoliberal) principle of relying heavily on market forces and competition to achieve key public policy aims. In Freedom to Move Mazankowski left no doubt about the third point when he wrote that, "our regimes of economic regulation in transportation have kept pace with neither changing circumstances in our economy nor the transportation system itself" (Canada 1985, ii). In short, "the existing regulatory regime represents an obstacle to economic growth" (ibid.). "The legislation assumes that transportation markets are immature and carriers need protection. Users, too, are over controlled with regulatory authorities establishing the terms and conditions on which business may be done with carriers. The regulatory regime has restricted competition and enterprise" (ibid., 1). "The government wants a new legislative framework for transportation that will minimize government control over shippers and carriers, while ensuring that the public interest is met" (ibid., 2). "The thrust of these proposals, reliance on competition and market forces rather than regulations, is clearly the wave of the future" (ibid., 3).

The second thing that was needed to turn the hypothesis into legislation was, once again, an influential transport minister – Mazankowski soon became deputy prime minister – willing to expose his government to the possibility of serious political damage in view of the fact there was no guarantee that upping the ante on competition and market forces wouldn't fail spectacularly in this oligopoly-dominated sector. Evidence was accumulating that this was indeed the right direction in which to go, but entrenched interests and vocal lobby groups, particularly in agriculture, were vigorously resisting. The government acted anyway. Freedom to Move was given legislative expression in the National Transportation Act, which took effect in 1988. As we show further below, Mazankowski's convictions turned out to be well founded.

One of Freedom to Move's critical (albeit low profile) features was an explicit statement that "the transition from the existing regime to the new one will require adjustments on the part of all concerned" (ibid., foreword). That brought out into the open for the first time a previously unwritten premise – that neither railways nor government would shield or indemnify shippers from the consequences of having to adapt their business operations to changes in railway practices. Despite its subtlety, that point was highly significant. It meant that in Mazankowski's mind, at least, railway customers bore considerable, if not primary, responsibility for adapting to changes in the transportation marketplace. In other words – provided that railways were not breaching their common carrier obligations (see more below) – considerable onus would be placed on shippers to adapt to changes in railway business models as the railways themselves responded to changes made by government in the legislative and regulatory framework and to constant changes in the global marketplace. That was a very indirect way of saying that the health and performance of the railway network *as a system* was more important than ensuring that every single shipper individually benefitted from the new regime. We describe the significance of this further below. The larger meaning of "the goal" embodied in Mazankowski's statement is a crucial concept in system optimization and therefore one of great importance in this chapter about rail freight policy and governance because it affects the degree to which rail transportation serves the Canadian economy as a whole.

The next step in this policy history occurred soon afterwards, under another influential cabinet minister, Doug Young. As inaugural minister of Transport in the Chrétien government, he perceived deep-seated problems in the transportation industry and in the way it was regulated. In June 1994, barely seven months into office, he made a policy statement in Parliament calling the existing regulations "outdated, unnecessary, and often stifling" (quoted in McGuire 2004, 69) and leaving no doubt how unacceptably harmful he thought that was to the Canadian economy. Less than a year later he tabled a revised Canada Transportation Act in Parliament. Passed in May 1996, it reduced or removed many remaining subsidies, allowed railways to shed unprofitable branch lines more expeditiously, and took economic deregulation still farther in the direction of relying on market forces and competition.

Young was thus continuing a pattern started modestly by Pickersgill and driven seriously by Mazankowski. Every decade or two the regulatory regime grew obsolete and needed the government of the day to hit the reset button. It took a strong minister to hit it hard enough and with enough political skill to avoid doing serious political damage to the government. In Young's case, as before, there was no guarantee that further upping the ante on market forces and competition wouldn't fail spectacularly in this oligopoly-dominated sector, with interest groups arguing vigorously against it. But again the government screwed up its courage and decided to act (albeit after removing some of the more contentious measures in the draft bill). In essence, three strong ministers saw a compelling need and, relying on their convictions about a lighter governmental hand on the tiller and an intuitive sense of the right direction in which to go, went through a window of opportunity.

Their sense of direction paid off. With the regulatory burden considerably lightened, railways staged a remarkable recovery from the hardscrabble years of the 1960s and 1970s. Especially in 1988 and 1996, the changes in regulatory policy set in motion a chain of events by which railways further optimized their strategies to achieve far greater operating and financial performance, and provide better service that attracted more business from shippers. These in turn led to subsequent government policy to deregulate economically farther and so on in a mutually reinforcing circle. Evidence of the validity of their changes came in a statutory review of the Canada Transportation Act completed in 2001. It painstakingly examined, and then set aside, most arguments it had received that railways were routinely abusing their market power and needed to be regulated back into line. Its report, "Vision and Balance," said that the freight rail transport system was not fundamentally anticompetitive and "works well for most users most of the time" (Canada 2001, 56).

The Railway Optimization Half:
How Railway Strategies Affected "Policy"

While governments were changing the regulatory regime, Canada's railways were not sitting around doing nothing. In the early years after the Freedom to Move reforms of the 1980s they shed unprofitable services and, most of all, set about improving what in hindsight had become appallingly inefficient operations. Originally manifested in what they called "the scheduled railway" and "precision railroading," the new strategy consisted of maximizing the "fluidity" and "velocity" of their traffic movements. The historic randomness of train schedules and freight car movements was replaced by planned and disciplined execution in operations much more tightly choreographed than ever before. Regulatory reform by governments had given them the necessary latitude to make the transition, and they responded more or less as policy-makers had hoped. Their response encouraged the next deregulatory step in a mutually reinforcing progression. But two surprises lay ahead.

The first came when the major railways took optimization into a whole new level. Introduced in the early to mid-2000s, this new model for the twenty-first century – we call it Model 21 – was based on what used to be counter-intuitive principles, like removing locomotives and, especially, freight cars from the network to drive out (and prevent) congestion, particularly in classification yards. The concept also included driving relentlessly to keep the freight cars moving to destination and back for reloading faster and faster. It was the application of a concept called lean production that had been transforming the manufacturing world for about three decades; CN was the first railway in North America to do it.

Lean production is based on optimization theory. It holds that variation is the primary culprit in preventing the optimization of any system of production (including railways). That is because variation constrains throughput and capacity by causing bottlenecks to manifest themselves, which in turn creates six negative outcomes: decreased throughput (hence economic output), decreased quality of what the system produces, increased work-in-progress inventory, stretched out delivery times to end customers, longer lead times for customers, and reduced efficiency (Coleman 2015b, 57–8).

These constraints affect everyone in the supply chain, not just the railways participating in it (ibid., 58). With railways, the strategy for minimizing variation begins with striving for conveyor-belt consistency all the time. That is the essence of Model 21. But it can never be achieved completely, so lean production requires one or more "buffers" somewhere (ibid., 58–9). Buffers consist of productive resources not always being used, hence available to help overcome bottlenecks when they appear (ibid., 58).

A side effect of lean production is to drive railway networks towards maximum utilization but, crucially, without triggering congestion (Coleman and Doern 2015, 2). The ideal is to have little spare capacity except that needed to cope with the inevitable perturbations that otherwise would trigger congestion – along the lines that people can see every day with automobile traffic on expressways at rush hour – as well as to accommodate projected growth. Despite shipper complaints that arose from its introduction, there is nothing inherently wrong with Model 21. It was inevitable and frankly overdue. It brings major financial benefits to railways and their shareholders *and* to the Canadian economy *and* to railway customers: shippers get their goods moved at lower cost because inefficiency in railway operations is driven out. Transit time to destination is, on average, less variable and generally faster because delays from congestion and from excessive cushions in the schedule are systematically removed. And railways attract private investment for recapitalizing their plant and equipment, which increases their capacity to meet growth opportunities in trade, and that builds the national economy.

This new model turned conventional thinking about railway optimization upside-down. Some shippers, negatively affected by the abrupt change but not grasping the concept, started demanding that government instruct railways to add more cars to their networks, anticipating it would increase railway capacity and improve service when in all likelihood it would do exactly the opposite.

Model 21 caused a problem with railway service that had almost nothing to do with lean production *per se* and almost everything to do with the way it was introduced (Coleman 2015b, 29). The lead railway, CN, introduced it with far too little good-faith negotiation with other players in supply chains or, perhaps more accurately, in some cases with no negotiation at all. Its drive to introduce Model 21 pushed responsibility for providing many or most of the buffers on to the other players. But many of them were already lean and did not by themselves have all the buffers needed to sustain their business operations. That was a huge problem. Other players simply objected in principle to the idea that they might have to adapt their business operations to changes in railway practices, notwithstanding the benefits those changes might create for everyone in their supply chain, including themselves. By 2010 the din from shipper complaints had grown too loud for government to ignore.

The second surprise was the government's response. This occurred initially during the Harper administration. With little or no grasp of what was going on with the application on railways of optimization theory (in the form of lean production), it was caught napping. It had no regulatory measures in place to deal with Model 21 nor to respond to the new type of conflict arising in the rail freight marketplace – a conflict primarily about railway service not railway prices, the traditional source of conflict. Nor did government have competence in figuring out whether adding locomotives, cars, and additional traffic to the rail network would help or hurt, but it responded sympathetically to shippers' demands that government empower the CTA to overrule railway decisions in that regard anyway.

The Harper Regulatory U-turn

As Model 21 began to bite, shippers claimed that railways were abusing their monopoly power. (In the lead railway's case that almost certainly was true.) The chorus of complaints grew so loud that government intervened. Five significant developments followed, starting with the commissioning of a rail freight service review panel. Appointed by the government in 2010, it reported its findings early the following year (Canada 2011a). Its recommendations took a broad pluralist fair-market position about what needed to be done in the short- and medium-term future. Among other things it recommended that railways develop "commercial measures to improve rail service [in] … four key elements related to service changes, service agreements, dispute resolution, and enhanced reporting" (ibid., 49). But the panel did not seem even remotely to understand or relate to the concept of optimization in the railways' Model 21 strategy as described above. And anyway, the evidence strongly suggests that even before the review began, the government had made up its mind to regulate the railways back into line (Coleman 2015b, 30–2). The second main development was an announcement by government in March 2011 that, in light of the panel's report, new legislation would be introduced.

Third came the commissioning of a mediation process led by former Alberta cabinet minister Jim Dinning to help railways and shippers find common ground on issues of service. It was set up in a way that virtually guaranteed it would not succeed, and indeed it did not (ibid., 31). And fourth, as the government had announced earlier, was the introduction of new legislation. One of its main features was to give authority to the CTA to arbitrate the content of service agreements between railways and shippers if the negotiations to create an agreement did not result in a deal the shipper liked. That meant regulating what were supposed to be voluntary agreements. That is a contradiction in terms. The legislation took effect as the Fair Rail Freight Service Act in June 2013 (Statutes of Canada 2013). It reversed the trend towards lower regulatory constraints begun in 1988 by increasing government intervention in business-dealings between railways and shippers. That almost certainly was a mistake (Coleman 2015b, 39).

And so began a regulatory U-turn. The railway–shipper relationship, always complex, succumbed to politicization at the expense of optimization and the overall commercial performance of supply chains. Worse, it set in motion a failure mechanism described further below. In effect, the government, and especially its transport and agriculture ministers, lacking an intuitive sense of the right direction in which to go (except perhaps in the narrowly political sense) and lacking a proper understanding of how railway networks function, had made up their minds to go through a window of opportunity opened by shipper complaints and were bent on heading in the opposite direction from all of their predecessors as to where the balance ought to lie between government regulation on one hand and market forces and competition on the other.

Failure Mechanism

Canada's transportation network involving railways and shippers is a large, complex system. With government's direct involvement there is a "positive feedback loop." The term originated in electronics engineering, but it applies to a large number of other fields including psychology and economics. A run on the bank is a good example. The phenomenon is sometimes called a vicious circle or a self-fulfilling prophecy. It makes a system inherently unstable. Unless there are robust safeguards built into the system's architecture, it will progress to a state of collapse with an accelerating swiftness that takes everyone by surprise. Government regulation contributes to the positive feedback loop because it empowers the CTA to instruct railways to add a given shipper's traffic to their networks when they may well be (and probably are) rationing their services on certain corridors to avoid traffic congestion. But the CTA does not – and almost certainly never can – know enough about the susceptibility of a rail network to congestion and it is likely to misjudge situations (Coleman and Doern 2015, 11; Coleman 2015b, 33). And so, in essence, the regulatory system introduced during the Harper years was designed in such a way as to make the railway network eventually fail (ibid., 85).

The fifth step in the failure progression was taken in 2014 when grain shippers prevailed on government to enact new legislation. The bill further empowered the CTA – and even cabinet – to instruct railways to·add more traffic to their networks without the slightest possibility that the CTA or cabinet could understand the effect their decisions would have on railway congestion and throughput. Called the Fair Rail for Grain Farmers Act, it had other seriously retrograde features as well. Some have already been referred to in chapter 5 on the grains and trains domain. Moreover, it came fast on the heels of the previous bill, the Fair Rail Freight Service Act, and so there was no evidence about whether the previous bill had been helping or harming rail–shipper relations. In other words, this market space was being changed by legislation before anyone knew what the effect of the previous legislation was. It looked like a recipe for confusion. It still does.

There can be no doubt that the dissatisfaction of many shippers was, and is, real and partly legitimate. That is a serious problem and railways need to fix it. But transportation policy does a poor job of establishing what constitutes legitimacy in these kinds of circumstances. The current process for dealing with such questions, being so dependent on government intervention, is causing a failure in the system of governance (Coleman and Doern 2015, 12).

Perhaps the most insidious feature of the regulatory regime is the premise on which it is based: that shippers should be exempt from having to adapt to the consequences of the rail transport system's transition to lean production. That reverses the crucial premise of Freedom to Move, as mentioned earlier. And it puts a lid on growth in the efficiency and performance of rail transport in Canada, to everyone's detriment.

In Search of the Goal

Probably the most important phenomenon *not* recognized in rail regulation is the effect of a primary goal on the system that serves it. We refer to it as "the goal." Public policies almost never have just one goal because policy setting invariably consists of juggling disparate interests and balancing conflicting needs and aspirations. But it would be an amazing coincidence if all the different goals in a given situation ended up being perfectly balanced with each other. That means one of the goals will be primary. Then optimization theory comes into play. It says that whatever the primary goal happens to be (whether consciously chosen or not), it becomes the key driver for the optimization of any system with constraints (Goldratt 1984, 1990). That includes railways. A complex system can be optimized in more ways than one. So unless the primary goal happens to be synonymous with the most desired outcome, the work of optimization usually will end up optimizing the wrong things. It gets trickier when multiple goals have to be recognized and accommodated, but that does not reduce the importance of optimization theory's principle that a primary goal drives the direction in which the system performs and evolves. Choosing not to set a primary goal is tantamount to not driving anything and letting things evolve more or less of their own accord. We will say more about that further on.

Many of the problems with the government's involvement in railway–shipper disputes arose because the CTA has received no unambiguous guidance in its decisions affecting the functioning of the railway network. It depends on whether the primary goal is to have railways keep the greatest *number* of individual shippers satisfied or to get the greatest *economic value* out of freight through supply chains to reach customers who want to buy it. This represents a choice between two different policy paradigms.

The first of these choices constitutes making as many local optima as possible. The latter consists of optimizing the system as a whole. The two are not the same. That is because *"the end result of many local optima is certainly not the optimum of the total system"* [emphasis added] (Goldratt 1990, 121). Many shippers believe the regulatory system is intended to do the former, and so does the CTA, but railways believe it is the latter. Rail freight policy in Canada has not reached a conclusion on this. That enables and sustains conflict in this marketplace because optimization theory says that railways cannot do both. No wonder the regulatory system has become so contentious.

Dealing with this question is arguably the most important remaining step in the twenty-year *pas de deux* between government rail freight regulatory policy and railway optimizing strategies. It has been on the table at least since the early 2000s when Model 21 was first introduced, but the issue remains unresolved and almost undiscussed.

We have seen no indication that government even recognizes the fundamental nature of the conflict – yet it (the conflict) is explained by optimization theory that emerged more than three decades ago. And so, for about fifteen years now, the governing legislation has been silent on what we think is the most important thing it could say (Coleman 2015b, 55). The legislation's silence on that issue produces "satisficing," the accepting of second-best solutions, and the perpetuating of conflict among players whose differences inevitably boil over into the policy and political realms of government. Aspects of this remain under the Justin Trudeau Liberal plans and policies under the Transportation Modernization Act now passed by Parliament (see discussion in chapter 5) (Standing Senate Committee on Transport and Communications 2018; Tomesco 2018).

This brings us back to a point raised earlier in this policy and governance history: without a consciously chosen and robustly defended primary goal that transcends political and economic eras, public policy in rail transportation regulation is susceptible to whatever political pressures or convictions or intuitive sense the minister and the government of the day happen to have. And because those things change from time to time, the regulatory framework vacillates between policy paradigms. Transport ministers Mazankowski's and Young's convictions proved beneficial at least until the mid-2000s, as demonstrated by railways' financial performance and shippers sending them more traffic. But with the transport and agriculture ministers of the Harper era, things went the other way. And by allowing itself to make politicized decisions, so did the CTA.

The "Common Carrier" Principle: Railway Level of Service Requirements

As discussed in chapter 1, this principle had its origins in the 1820s when railways were first being built. It was embodied in statute to prevent railways from abusing shippers, e.g., by withholding service from those they wanted to break. The principle almost certainly was a net benefit in terms of public policy at the dawn of rail transportation. But that was one hundred years before the concept of lean production, and it has become an impediment to optimizing the rail system in ways that would maximize Canada's economic performance.

The principle as originally conceived has become at least as dysfunctional as it was meant to be helpful. There are seven main reasons why.

First, it contains the premise that there should be no casualties of the transition by railways to lean production (Coleman and Doern 2014, 22). That is economic nonsense – in effect wanting creative destruction (Schumpeter 1942) without the destruction. Second, it is blind to the need for buffers (Coleman 2015b, 59). In a system of lean production it is essential that buffers be negotiated among the players in the supply chain. But the common carrier principle says in effect that shippers do not need to negotiate anything with railways. Third, it requires that railways provide suitable and adequate service to all shippers, even those who bring their cargo to a railway without any prior commitment or even a forecast of volume, which turns the management of network traffic into a guessing game. With the tabling in Parliament in May 2017 of the Transportation Modernization Act (Bill C-49, to amend the existing Canadian Transportation Act), the dispensation historically given shippers who make no traffic commitments seems about to change. But this is by no means guaranteed, given key reform provisions in the policies for "growing Canada's economy with modernized rail transportation" (Transport Canada 2017e) which includes new data reporting requirements for railways on rates, service and performance; new clearer definitions of "adequate and suitable rail service"; and "more accessible and timely remedies for shippers on both rates and service to support fair negotiations" (ibid., 1).

And fourth through sixth, the common carrier principle says in effect that shippers bear no responsibility in the eyes of the law for (4) helping to reduce variation or (5) helping to prevent or eliminate bottlenecks or (6) helping maintain uncongested flow of traffic on the rail network. Together those last three things represent nonsense from the standpoint of maximizing the economic benefits to Canada as a whole.

Seventh, shippers have argued the common carrier principle is sacrosanct and have insisted it be equally applicable to all of them – even to the point of disallowing the possibility of some of them paying a premium price to get premium service. That was a position to which shippers held adamantly during the 2011 Dinning-led facilitation process mentioned earlier – which, not coincidentally, failed to reach much, if any, accommodation between railways and shippers. The position was tantamount to shippers being allowed to negotiate prices with railways but not levels of service. That is commercial nonsense because price and service are inseparable in every business transaction.

In fact, the Canada Transportation Act no longer refers to the principle *per se* (Doern 2015). Instead it speaks about levels of service (LOS) that railways are required to provide (Statutes of Canada 2014, section 113). But these requirements are anything but specific. They use qualifier words like "adequate and suitable," "customary or usual," and "reasonable compensation." These invite all kinds of socioeconomic differences of view and interpretation, as well as challenges and disputes in negotiations between shippers and railways. Moreover, the level-of-service provisions are public in statute but very private in commercial cases involving railways and shippers most of the time. And two of the provisions effectively say that infrastructure is the responsibility of the railway, but shippers and terminal operators are assigned no comparable obligations to be efficient businesses functioning in a modern rail network. That means, for example, that shippers and terminal operators bear no statutory responsibility to furnish adequate infrastructure for loading and unloading rail cars, even at country grain elevators or elevators at the Port of Vancouver (Coleman 2015a) where shippers own the infrastructure. Yet even if *their* capacity for loading and unloading is causing the bottleneck in a supply chain, shippers are still at liberty to file, and may well win, a complaint against the railway for providing inadequate service. Issues like this should be resolved through good-faith negotiations. But, as noted earlier, the level of service provisions in law say in effect that shippers and terminal operators do not need to negotiate anything.

The imprecision of this language, and the invitation it gives to disputes, would not be particularly worrisome if there were a shared and generally accepted view of the primary goal to which everyone in this transportation space should be working. But as mentioned above, no one in a position of authority has articulated a primary goal. As Doern argues "The common carrier concept is now simply a residual unmentioned concept and … service levels are used to define something that is no longer mentioned as a principle. It makes little practical sense unless all parties recognize publicly that the new North American model of system interrelationships among capacity, congestion, system optimization, and levels of service is the overriding feature of Canadian freight rail transportation" (ibid., 17).

We conclude this policy history by noting that it suggests the presence of both "regulatory breakdown" (Coglianese 2012) and "unruliness" (Doern, Prince, and Schultz) as previewed briefly in chapter 1.

It also suggests a failure to choose between two competing policy paradigms. One of them says the goal is for railways to satisfy the greatest number of shippers individually, and the other says the goal is to get the greatest amount of economic value through supply chains.

THE POLICY AND GOVERNANCE OF COMPETITION AND SETTLING MARKETPLACE DISPUTES (MID-1990S TO PRESENT)

Our second policy history deals with the CTA, whose existence and performance has considerable influence on the level and nature of competition among carriers – and on the degree to which that competition actually helps maintain and grow the national economy. It also affects the degree to which marketplace disputes are resolved in accordance with commonly accepted notions of fair and effective market power.

Competition is an important issue primarily because Canada's two main railways, CN and CP, constitute a duopoly. No matter how vigorously they do or do not compete with each other, or with other modes of transport available to shippers (like marine and trucking, and US railroads in some parts of Canada), duopolies are not what a competitive market space is usually understood to be. That makes it unrealistic to think there is no need for at least some kind of regulatory system.

As we discussed in chapter 4, the main transport regulator has had various names and mandates over the years (McGuire 2004). In this chapter we speak mainly about its incarnation as the CTA and its performance in fulfilling its governance role since 1996. In light of that performance, we ask two supplementary questions. The first is whether the premise on which it operates (that dispute settlement is a *private* matter between the disputing parties) should be replaced by a more public process, in recognition of the fact that the CTA's function amounts to one of dispensing administrative justice. And second, we ask whether an altogether different approach would make sense – one based on regulating *competition* as the primary macro consideration (and situating the transport sector within it) rather than the other way around by regulating the transport *sector* as the primary consideration (and making reference to principles of competition within it). The latter is what we have now. The former would imply making greater use of the Competition Bureau, the Commissioner of

Competition, and the Competition Tribunal and hence the principles of market framework competition.

In 1996 the current agency, the CTA, came to have three main statutory functions: regulatory, quasi-judicial, and facilitating accessibility in transport by the handicapped. The judicial portion of its role had been in existence for many years, but it was expanded in the mid-1990s to include that of being a mediator whose role was to encourage marketplace dynamics. However, the prominence given to that new function did not last very long.

In retrospect we see a pattern in the transport regulatory agency's development since 1967. Whenever it was given major new policy direction by government, it would then be left more or less to its own devices for years at a time, only to fall behind in its competence, performance, or responsiveness to the changing political environment or to the constantly evolving realities of the transportation marketplace. Then its mandate and scope of operations would be rewritten and its resources cut back by a new government dissatisfied with the way things had been going.

Again, we begin with Freedom to Move. It was implemented in part by removing what Mazankowski clearly believed was an unacceptable degree of latitude enjoyed by the then existing agency and the intrusiveness of the regulatory role it had been given to fulfil, as a result of which he perceived the problems had been growing. By the time his legislation was tabled in Parliament, Mazankowski's place as transport minister had been taken by John Crosbie, who was no more impressed with how things were going than Mazankowski. He sharply curtailed the agency's powers, for example by requiring it to take policy direction from the government. That ended its role in policy-making. Probably the most vigorous changes came from Erik Neilsen, a former deputy prime minister whom Crosbie appointed chairman because he (Crosbie) was reportedly "fed up" with the way regulatory functions were being discharged (McGuire 2004, 62). Neilsen wielded a sharp axe. Eighty-five per cent of the agency's commissioners were fired (ibid., 63), the organization was thoroughly restructured, its staff was cut by one-fifth – down from almost 1,000 people (ibid., 61–2) – and its budget was cut as well. From this it would be hard *not* to conclude that the agency, created some twenty-one years earlier, had failed to evolve with the changing realities of transportation and with the expectations placed upon it by government. Even the current CTA's own historical account of earlier agencies says that the CTA's predecessor body "had become obsolete" (ibid., 61).

Minister Doug Young's changes to the transport regulatory regime in 1996 did not end with legislation – he radically changed the agency too. Its research group was removed, its role in managing transportation subsidies was taken away, its safety function was transferred to the Transportation Safety Board, its staff was cut by almost half (ibid., 72), its powers were curtailed, and the number of its members was reduced by almost half. "What made these changes exceptional was the magnitude of their impact" (ibid., 71). As with the Crosbie–Neilsen shake-up seven years earlier, it would be hard *not* to conclude from this that the then existing agency had failed, again, to evolve with the realities of transport and the expectations placed upon it by government. Tellingly, a new chair with business experience; Marian Robsum, was installed. She led the organization's development for the next ten years.

Those years seem like the CTA's golden decade. In response to Young's shake-up and the new chair's direction, the CTA started thinking outside the box more often. It undertook all kinds of pilot projects and experimented with new ways of encouraging negotiated settlements between disputing parties (ibid., 3). It introduced alternative dispute resolution processes, started offering mediation in marine disputes, began training mediators, developed codes of practice, established an air travel complaints commissioner to resolve disputes through facilitation and persuasion, and used public awareness campaigns as a means of encouraging carriers to treat passengers fairly. Innovation and risk taking became the norm.

But after a change of chair in 2006, the CTA's emphasis shifted back to judicial determinations. That probably was not a coincidence. A new government had just been elected, and the incoming chair had a background entirely within government (in the government of Canada and the government of Ontario), not in industry. Apparently comfortable in sticking to a role that did not call for much innovation, and lacking external governance to keep it sharp, the CTA slipped back into a pattern of failing to evolve with the realities of transportation.

Meanwhile, the railways' shift to Model 21 was starting to bite, and the agency seemed to have missed that fundamental transformation in the railway–shipper marketplace – a marketplace it was commissioned by statute to regulate. While competent in economics and financial issues – the disciplines that mattered in arbitrations when shipper complaints against railways were nearly always over *pricing* – the agency acquired little or no competence in science and engineering, disciplines that matter when adjudicating disputes over railway *service*. (The abolition of the CTA's research group in 1996 almost certainly did not help in that regard.) Yet with the arrival of Model 21, service had replaced price as the primary source of contention between railways and shippers.

A lot of things boil down to the kind of people you hire. As of 2015 the vast majority of the CTA's arbitrators – including most of its members and forty-seven of its fifty-one external arbitrators – are lawyers (Coleman 2015b, 83). That means its arbitration proceedings can be expected to show high respect for due process, the rules of evidence, and the legal meaning of provisions in the Canada Transportation Act. But it also means the members and external arbitrators are susceptible to getting things fundamentally wrong when a case hinges on grasping the implications of technological change or principles from science and engineering. As a result, when evaluating a level-of-service complaint, an arbitrator has little choice but to ignore the possibility of his or her decision causing congestion and loss of throughput capacity on the railway, or to ask the railway whose case is being arbitrated to furnish that vital information.

Probably just as important, a shipper whose case is being arbitrated will not know whether the information provided by the railway is accurate. That means the shipper cannot know whether the arbitrator's decision is based on fact. That is a *huge* problem because it means trust in the system of arbitration is impossible. Then the only remedy is the one mentioned above – for arbitrators to ignore the effect of their decisions on other users of the network whenever they decide in favour of a shipper. But in some cases that would contravene the requirements in the act and would push railways towards congestion on their networks (Coleman and Doern, 13).

Amazingly, there are no provisions in transportation law regarding the knowledge or expertise that arbitrators must have. So federal legislation permits the agency to reach arbitrated decisions that instruct railways to add a shipper's traffic onto their networks without knowing whether that will cause congestion, drive down throughput capacity, and reduce service for everyone. In short, by missing the change to Model 21 the CTA was resting on its laurels and failing to innovate and adapt to changing times. That showed up alarmingly in the Dreyfus case. We turn to that now.

In October 2014 the CTA, following the government's new direction as manifested in the two recent legislative changes described in our previous policy history, rendered a decision (Decision No. 2014-10-03) in a complaint filed against CN by a grain shipper, Louis Dreyfus Commodities Canada Ltd. (Canadian Transportation Agency 2014). The decision violated the laws of physics, revealed the agency's ignorance of systems dynamics, contradicted more than one of its own other decisions, ignored its apparent obligations under the Canada Transportation Act, contravened the common carrier principle, and signalled a flagrant disregard for the principles of how market economies are supposed to work (Coleman 2015b, 36).

In the CTA's defence, CN had put itself in a tough contractual position with Dreyfus and the agency demanded CN respect. Yet the discourse in the CTA's ruling is astonishing. For much of it (Canadian Transportation Agency 2014, §1–69 and §76–164) the document, although peppered with non sequiturs, is not egregiously illogical. But from that point on the logic falls apart. It says in effect (ibid., 34, §165–7) that CN, responding to financial incentives which discouraged it from expanding its fleet of grain cars, had failed to serve the interests of grain shippers over and above its own and therefore was in breach of its obligations. Yet the disincentives to which CN responded were embodied in federal law! (See our earlier discussion in chapter 5 of the Maximum Revenue Entitlement.)

By this, the CTA is saying three things: (a) adding more cars to CN's fleet would have increased its throughput capacity, (b) CN under-invested in grain cars, and (c) CN had a duty in law to acquire more cars prior to the surge of grain traffic which it could not have predicted, notwithstanding the fact that, under the Maximum Revenue Entitlement, to the degree that surge capacity is not fully utilized, the railway could not have earned a return on such an investment.

The first point signifies that the CTA believes it knows better than CN how to get the greatest volume of throughput from a freight railway network. That is technical nonsense. The second and third points are tantamount to the agency saying that, by declining to make an unrecoupable investment in acquiring additional grain cars, CN earned more profit than the agency thinks it was entitled to – and therefore CN deserved to be penalized by a ruling in Dreyfus' favour. That means the agency is saying that *it*, not the markets, will determine what constitutes a sufficient rate of return on the railway's equity and its shareholders' investment. That is a stunning over extension of the CTA's role in doing financial analysis – one that takes it into the realm of substituting its own judgement, and the personal judgement of its members, for the railway's shareholders in particular. From now on, the agency was effectively saying, its members will set the rate of return that shareholders in a publicly traded company can look forward to earning.

CN appealed the Dreyfus case to the federal court of appeal and lost. The court upheld the CTA's decision (Federal Court of Appeal 2016), ruling that the CTA had not misinterpreted the law but, citing judicial deference in favour of the agency, declined to comment on the facts of the traffic situation on CN at the time or on the inferences the agency made about quasi-technical railway terms in the contract between CN and Dreyfus.

Dreyfus seems unlikely to be the last of the CTA's seriously flawed determinations unless it makes nontrivial changes going forward. The agency described the approach it developed in its Dreyfus decision as intended for its own future use (Canadian Transportation Agency 2014, §35–7). Moreover, it developed a set of criteria for its own use in determining whether, in any given case, a railway had legitimate grounds for not meeting its "level of service" obligations – criteria that represent flawed proxies for what is actually desired and that will cause the agency to err, possibly heavily, on the side of finding railways in breach of their obligations even when they are not (Coleman 2015b, 85–7). This flawed thinking probably reflects another downstream effect of the CTA's research group being abolished in 1996.

There are several inferences to be drawn from the CTA's involvement in the marketplace. First is the very premise on which its role is based. It is aimed at constraining a railway's market power regardless of whether it ever abuses that power or not. The mere existence of market power – even the *presumption* that it exists – is enough to involve the agency in many cases and determine their outcome. Little or no evidence is required as to whether the alleged abuse actually occurred. In fact, a shipper can successfully prosecute a complaint before the agency without even making such an allegation. The underlying premise is that abuse should be prevented before it occurs, not remedied if and when it does.

Unfortunately, this approach suffers from an inability to tell the difference between (a) the shipper's and the railway's respective market power and (b) their respective negotiating skills. Yet negotiating skills are essential in a market economy. Canada should want all of its businesses to be extremely good at it. Railways generally are. That means that in the average case, the agency is predisposed to conclude that railways are acting abusively. By contrast, remediation revolves around curtailing the abuse of market power but only if it can reasonably be found to have occurred. Prevention suggests a role for a *transport* regulator. That is what we have now. Remediation suggests more of a role for a *competition* regulator.

The significance is that the CTA has not been used effectively to get closer to the heart of what economic regulation of railways is really all about – curbing undesirable business behaviour. Things are different in the US. There, freight railroad regulatory policy is designed "to prohibit predatory pricing and practice, to avoid undue concentrations of market power, and to prohibit unlawful discrimination" (Transportation Research Board 2015b, 27). This policy is applied by US law at a macro, economy-wide level – not in case-by-case determinations by a transportation regulator, as is done in Canada.

Here, railways are judged on whether they have adequately served each shipper's needs. That is an important test of meeting the "public interest." But ever since 1985 the test of public interest in the US "has been greatly narrowed to mean whether the incumbent carrier has acted in an anticompetitive manner" (Pretto and Schulman 2015, 8). In other words, US railways are not exposed to before-the-fact presumptions of having abused their market power the way that Canadian railways are.

In a world where governance and external oversight are widely considered essential for any organization, the CTA, surprisingly, has little if any. It is a quasi-judicial tribunal with the authority of a superior court, and its decisions carry very significant legal weight. Although its decisions are subject to being overturned by cabinet or a higher court, in any given case the courts will rule only on whether the CTA correctly interpreted the law, not whether it understood or correctly interpreted the facts of the case or their significance. In those matters, the courts give the CTA judicial deference. But the courts have no specialized technical expertise in subjects like systems dynamics and network performance, and so they are not equipped to evaluate the agency's performance or competence in those disciplines. In other words, the agency is liable to be accorded deference by the courts for expertise it does not have.

Nor does it seem that Transport Canada provides much external governance of the CTA in that respect. It is beyond the scope of this chapter to discuss the matter in any depth, but the department's capacity in substantive policy expertise has atrophied over the past two decades to the point where its ability to inform the minister about technical errors and omissions, and more generally about the significance of any deficiencies in the agency's competence in specialized technical disciplines, means that an alternative form of external governance (i.e., alternative to the courts) is not in place either.

Things are hardly more auspicious at the cabinet level. For years, virtually no minister has had the technical background to frame and defend a solid case on those grounds for his or her colleagues to overturn a decision made by the agency. The current minister of Transport, with a doctorate in electrical engineering, is probably the only one in living memory who does. So, apart from the current fortuitous situation, cabinet's governance of the rail transport regulatory mechanism has potentially serious holes.

Those holes showed up with a vengeance in 2014, when complaints by grain shippers about railway performance ended with the minister of Agriculture, who had a background in farming and construction, winning a disagreement in cabinet with the minister of Transport, who had a background in science, law, and the running of complex organizations. The result was the absurd Fair Rail for Grain Farmers Act described in chapter 5.

In effect there is no proper oversight body for the agency – the regulator is unregulated. That can be seen in the degree to which the agency's performance and its results get measured. To a first approximation, at least some of its most important results do not get measured at all (Coleman and Doern 2015, 18). Even so thoughtful a document as the agency's one-hundred-year history (McGuire 2004) covering it and its predecessor regulatory agencies is silent on the *results* the organization has produced by way of improving (or *not* improving) the performance of the rail freight system or the state of transportation in Canada or ultimately the nation's economic and social well-being. The upshot is simply that there is little if any oversight or governance being applied to some critical elements of the administration of Canada's rail transport regulatory system. That seems like a serious omission and seems likely to continue under some features of the planned Justin Trudeau era Transport Modernization Act which gives the CTA more to do without a word being said about the CTA's lack of relevant capacity and technical expertise.

One possible remedy would be for Transport Canada to strengthen its capacity for policy analysis in technical matters at a sufficient level to provide oversight of the agency's performance. Another would be for the CTA to acquire the technical competence needed to evaluate railway performance at a systems level. That would let it discharge its regulatory functions in a more credible way than it has in the past. But the prospects of that happening are not auspicious. It takes more than highly competent people and advanced software models to determine what is happening on a complex railway network – it takes mountains of rapidly changing data being processed in almost real time, but no one player has it all and the technical and legal hurdles for the CTA to acquire and use it effectively are daunting.

There is another problem. In performing its quasi-judicial functions, the agency is or should be practicing a system of *administrative justice*. That is not uncommon in regulatory policy, especially in fields where scientific and technical expertise needs to be embedded in the system (Doern, Prince, and Schultz 2014). So far, so good. But administrative justice is expected to be public and transparent, not private, especially when its legitimacy depends on a reasonably widespread perception of the regulator's fairness in using its authority and in the effect its decisions have on the disputing parties (Jones and de Villars 2014; Van Harten, Heckman, and Mullan 2010). The CTA's handling of level-of-service complaints is public, but its arbitration-centered process is close to being private and secret, and, as noted earlier, it lacks the scientific and engineering competence to do its job – and to be *seen* to be doing its job – with enough expertise to ensure fairness. As a result, the apparatus set up by government to administer the provisions for dealing with arbitrations under the Canada Transportation Act and now in the Transportation Modernization Act (Bill C-49) has no way of understanding many of the most critical aspects of how the current rail transportation system actually functions. That is not how good public policy and regulatory governance is supposed to work.

There is another problem. It involves the underlying premise of the regulatory construct. It came to light at a Carleton University discussion among shippers and railways: "Many participants noted that [the Act] is a potentially useful mechanism to deal with railway–shipper relations but it lends itself mainly to large- and medium-sized shippers and does not provide particularly useful tools for smaller ones" (Regulatory Governance Initiative 2015, 5). In other words, shippers who have the least negotiating clout are the ones least protected by the legislation and the way it is administered.

In spite of the CTA's having missed the shift to lean production (i.e., to Model 21) and, as a result, falling short in maintaining peace in the railway–shipper marketplace – the rail freight service review and the acts passed in 2013 and 2014 are clear manifestations of that – it has not been seriously called to account for its performance in more than twenty years, including the most recent decade under the Harper administration and also, in some ways, in the current Justin Trudeau era thus far. In effect the act instructed the CTA to stay relevant in this market space and it did not. Yet amazingly the report of the 2014–15 statutory review of the Canada Transportation Act and now the Transport Modernization Act follow-up budget support gives the agency more resources, more independent authority, and more powers – all without more external governance. That looks like a mistake. Pal's central idea, that public-issue management in turbulent times tends to show a pattern of crises and elongated responses – a pattern we previewed in chapter 1 – is also relevant here (Pal 2014).

Competition Policy as Framework versus Sectoral Policy

We end this policy history by asking, should there even *be* an economic competition regulator assigned exclusively to transportation? That represents a sector-based approach. There are alternatives. As Doern, Prince, and Schultz (2014) argue, a marketplace-based framework competition policy is intended "to govern horizontally across the economy with rules and guidance approaches and indeed to ensure that *sectoral* industry preferences are not encouraged. Otherwise, one is essentially fostering *industrial* policy rather than marketplace framework policy" [emphasis added] (ibid., 207).

As shown in chapter 1, competition policy is designed to promote rivalry among firms, buyers, and sellers. It does this by restricting anticompetitive activities like mergers, cartels, conspiracies in restraint of trade, misleading advertising, and other offences (Competition Bureau 2015a; Doern and Wilks 1996). The underlying premise is that a marketplace free of these abuses will function more or less the way a competitive market should.

In principle there should be no sectoral preferences in a framework competition-based approach to policy. But, "as in most areas of law and policy there are ... exceptions ... which arise out of political pressures or realities and ... out of arguments about the nature of competition" (ibid., 212). Unfortunately the two approaches do not often coexist easily in the same market. Industries with natural monopoly or oligopolistic features – for example, telecommunications, energy, and transportation (each with its own sectoral regulator) – have historically been exempt from charges of anticompetitive behaviour (Janisch 1999), even if some of the participants engaged in it.

For their part, competition authorities in Canada usually refrain from intervening in areas subject to sector-specific regulation. That is because the regulators assigned to those sectors (NEB, CRTC, and the CTA) are also, at least partly, competition regulators. But the separation of authority over macrocompetition and authority over sectors is not airtight. For example, the Competition Bureau intervened, and secured a resolution, in a case in which Air Canada and United Continental Holdings Inc. "announced plans for a joint venture that would effectively merge their flight operations on high-demand Canada–United States (US) routes" (Commissioner of Competition 2013, 6). In other words, the commission ventured onto someone else's turf: i.e., transportation. That is noteworthy because a macrocompetition regulator is supposed to depend in part on how a given effective market is defined or about which complaints have been raised.

Is one approach better than the other? Sometimes. A study done for the Canada Transportation Act review panel on consumer protection for airline passengers found that the

> existing Canadian model [a sector-based approach] provides inconsistent and inadequate protections ... and recommends a model based on Canada's Commissioner for Complaints for Telecommunications Services, an industry dispute resolution model that customers appear to be very satisfied with, that operates at low cost to the public/users, and that has made extensive efforts to be transparent regarding the structure of the organization, senior staff, its complaints process, complaints statistics,

as well as the identification of systemic industry issues. (Public Interest Advocacy Centre)

Most areas of competition law deal with offences or behaviours that have already occurred or are alleged to have occurred. As noted earlier, that differs from the CTA's sector-based approach, which is aimed at constraining a railway's market power in advance of it abusing that power and regardless of whether it ever does – an approach that unfortunately cannot tell the difference between (a) a railway having better negotiating skills than a shipper and (b) the railway abusing its market power. Moreover, a sector-based approach requires the regulator to be competent in all the necessary technical subjects, like network optimization and systems dynamics, *and* to have access to independent and extremely detailed databases whose content changes every few seconds. It is doubtful that could ever be achieved and sustained at a level sufficient for a sectoral regulator to do the job properly now that Model 21 has arrived and almost certainly is here to stay.

And Model 21 almost certainly *is* here to stay, for at least the next decade or two. No transformational technology that would alter the fundamental characteristics of railcar movements is anywhere in sight. That means freight cars will continue to be assembled at classification yards into trains pulled by locomotives with a single crew. The resulting economics drive railways inexorably towards longer trains and lean production with buffers in supply chains continuing to be needed in the same way they are now. No other broadly accepted theory has emerged to refute the underlying premise that variation is the fundamental cause of constraints on throughput and the need for buffers. Yet, as described in Coleman (2015b, 62–3) on the science of lean production, that premise is the foundation of Model 21. In terms of staying power through major economic cycles, Model 21, first introduced on CN, came through the global economic meltdown in 2008 in robust health, then spread to CP and reached full expression there, and now is taking hold on US Class 1 railroads.

So the question arises: should the Commissioner of Competition involve himself in rail freight competition issues, where he can apply his greater expertise than the CTA in determining what competition is in defined markets and how a competitive market ought to function? The commissioner has already signalled he intends to move in that direction. His annual report for 2013 stressed the "beginnings of a shift toward greater transparency and more frequent use of strategic regulatory interventions to encourage fair and competitive practices" (Commissioner of Competition 2013, 4). Among other benefits, that would make it possible for railways and/or shippers to explore issues in a more-public way than they can under the CTA. But in that regard, amendments to the act as proposed in Bill C-49 currently before Parliament leave things pretty much as they were.

THE THREE ANALYTICAL ELEMENTS

We close this chapter by discussing, with the aid of table 6.1, the rail freight and competition-market dispute domain in the context of the three elements of the book's analytical framework.

Policy Ideas, Discourses, and Agendas

Our policy and governance histories cover roughly a thirty-year period. During that period the foremost idea and discourse consisted of railway economic deregulation that began in a major way with Freedom to Move in 1985 and ended with a U-turn after railways did something unexpected (introduce Model 21) and the regulatory system was caught unprepared and evidently unaware. There are four main components inside this idea. First is competition and market forces. There was a consistent premise in the economic deregulatory steps of 1988 and 1996 that a competitive marketplace in which there is rivalry among firms, buyers, and sellers, and that is free of anticompetitive behaviour, will function more or less as it should. But as a result of the railway's abuse of its market power when introducing Model 21, the applicability of that premise was largely pushed aside in the Harper era U-turn that began with the rail freight service review in 2010 and culminated in the legislative and regulatory developments of 2013 and 2014 whose effects are with us still.

The crux of "market forces" is largely a reliance on negotiation between businesses when they deal with each other. But the railway that introduced Model 21 brooked far too little negotiation with shippers between 2003 and 2009, and ever since then many shippers have been saying it is almost pointless to negotiate with railways over anything. That is almost certainly not true, but many think it is. And they have no compelling need to try to make it work because the common carrier principle says that shippers do not need to negotiate anything with railways. Collectively, shippers have

Table 6.1
The rail freight and competition-market dispute domain and the three analytical elements: Highlights

Policy and governance histories	Analytical elements		
	Policy ideas, discourse, and agendas	Economic and social power	Technology and temporal realities and conflicts
In search of optimization: Federal policy and the freight railways' business models (mid-1960s to present)	Historic role of railways in nation-building	Rise of trucking, airlines, and automobiles takes away railway market share	Rise of competition to railways from airlines, passenger automobiles, and trucking, all arising from technology developments
	Freedom to Move based on "competition and market forces" (i.e., negotiation) starts economic deregulation legacy for freight rail	Power of CN and CP as a duopoly	Two-to-three decade delay by governments in lifting regulatory constraints that prohibited railways from responding to competition
	Model 21 as rail optimization strategy for lean production	Notion of "competition and market forces" puts market power in hands of those railways and shippers who are good negotiators	Introduction of Model 21 enabled system-optimization theory and supporting logistics practices, along with more powerful locomotives, longer trains, and IT systems
	Uniformity and consistency of traffic but less "surge" capacity	Responsibility on shippers to adapt to changes in rail marketplace	Greater speed, consistency, and throughput of rail traffic, with higher revenues on average for players in supply chains
	"Just-in time" production in concert with supply chains	Rail-freight interests and lobby groups – Freight Management Association of Canada, Coalition of Rail Shippers, Western Grain Producers Association, Railway Association of Canada, and many others	Need for supply chains to participate in temporal-driven "just-in-time" production and shipping
	"Required service" levels as replacement for "common carrier" idea per se	2010–11 Rail Freight Service review at the behest of vociferous shippers	
	Railways concentrate on long-distance hauls (their forté) but "first-mile, last mile" service is not stellar	Large versus smaller shippers, and their relative influence when negotiating with railways and government	
	Differences in service levels		

Duopoly of CN and CP as unstated discourse, but in fact an underlying reality

"Failure mechanism" in form of positive feedback loop set up in response to Model 21

Idea of "the goal" versus multiple goals

Fairness in rail–shipper relations/markets

Creative destruction, but without the destruction

"No shipper left behind" as overt or fairness resultant

"Third parties" and their needs – including shippers' customers

Communities that depend on rail service and municipalities concerned about rail safety and dangerous goods policy

Vision and Balance report in 2001 uses logic to argue against favouritism sought by lobby groups with political clout

Securing of "head of queue" position by grain shippers re: rail service in a congested supply chain

Relatively low influence on policy or railway operations by third parties (shippers' customers and local communities)

Relatively low (or no) influence on policy by experts and authorities in systems dynamics and network optimization

Supply chains applying discipline to their own participants, acting as de facto governance systems

Absence of rail–shipper marketplace public monitoring

Lack of influence by railways to improve quality of shipper's forecasts (shippers are shielded from this by "common carrier" provisions in the Act)

Slow recognition by government of fundamental change in rail marketplace caused by shift to lean production

Creation of "positive feedback loop" in governance system that makes it unstable and prone to collapse

Response by government to a one-in-one-hundred-year grain crop in 2013 (and railways' inability to handle all of the temporary surge) by introducing the dubious Fair Rail for Grain Farmers Act

Bill C-49 currently before Parliament would let the *Fair Rail for Grain Farmers Act*'s most dysfunctional provision – empowering cabinet to set quotas for railway to haul grain in preference to all other commodities – remains unsettled

Table 6.1
The rail freight and competition-market dispute domain and the three analytical elements: Highlights (*continued*)

Policy and governance histories	Analytical elements		
	Policy ideas, discourse, and agendas	*Economic and social power*	*Technology and temporal realities and conflicts*
Policy and governance of competition, and of settling marketplace disputes (mid-1990s to present)	Competition but in a duopoly market	Rail–shipper power relations as reflected in Fair Rail Freight Services Act	Serial falling-behind by the regulator, that precipitated major housecleaning by government to the organization and its powers
	"Fair" rail service as expressed in Fair Rail Freight Service Act of 2013	CTA primarily an adjudicator, notwithstanding its two other roles as regulator and supporter of accessibility rights in transportation	Nonresponse by the CTA and Transport Canada to need for technical expertise in network performance and optimization with introduction of Model 21
	Private contract ideas as in many markets but …	CTA as an adjudicative body with its own staff among the adjudicators	Very short specific time limits and metrics in 2013 Fair Rail Freight Services Act
	Private (nonpublic) rail freight arbitration decisions	Influence of the CTA's arbitrators in disputes	Arbitration as speedy vs slow moving private justice process, e.g., in the courts
	Public dispute settlement idea and system as "administrative justice" as in other marketplace regulatory systems	Absence of systems-optimization experts in rail–shipper disputes and monitoring	Considerable uncertainty regarding ultimate impacts of Transportation Modernization Act
	Competition-based approach to policy as a marketplace framework (possible), contrasted with sectoral approach (current)	Awarding by CTA of head-of-queue position to a single grain shipper (Dreyfus), even ahead of other grain shippers	
	"Regulated industry" defence	Rail and shipper lobbies and unknown rate of uptake of CTA's new dispute provisions	
		Influence of shippers in advocating greater gathering and publishing of railway-based data, despite seldom if ever explaining what it would be used for, and how	

US rail regulatory law concentrates on competition, is much more stringent in that regard than Canada's

US rail law pays little or no attention to level of service a shipper receives from railways, but Canada's concentrates on that.

Caseload and volume of disputes or their disposition not made public by the CTA especially vis-à-vis new adjudication rules since 2013

Advocacy by shippers and railways in Canada Transportation Act review process, reflected in its report recommending that CTA be given more scope, more authority, and more funding

Provisions in the Transportation Modernization Act give CTA more authority but without dealing with its weaknesses regarding technical and logistical expertise and competence maintained the common carrier principle as an inviolate part of their agenda in dealing with government policy about freight rail economic regulation, so it does not seem likely that there will be be much voluntary movement from shippers towards a rejuvenated process of economic deregulation.

The second main component is the idea of creative destruction without the destruction. What began with Mazankowski's overt statement that shippers would have to adapt to changes in the freight railway market, turned into "no shipper left behind" – i.e., no casualties from Model 21 or any other innovation for that matter – during the U-turn of the Harper era.

Third is the idea of setting a primary goal. In the deregulatory steps taken by Mazankowski and Young, the underlying principle was essentially one of letting railways and shippers figure that out among themselves, with an increasingly lighter hand on the tiller by the federal regulator and even-handed changes to the legislation. But during the Harper-era U-turn, the CTA was instructed to ratchet up the idea that railways were responsible for making many local optima. Optimization theory says that is incompatible with optimizing the total system from a "get the goods to market" point of view. The latter is the underlying premise of lean production, and it generates the greatest economic benefit for Canada as a whole. But as mentioned earlier we have seen no evidence that policy makers recognized the significance – or even the existence – of that fundamental choice. They seem to have been content to hand the matter over to the CTA in hopes it could figure out how to make acceptable choices in the face of two different policy paradigms whose ascendance had not been resolved. But those ambiguous instructions to the CTA may be changing. Proposed changes to the act in 2017 include several requirements that the agency take into account: in effect, a railway's performance *as a system*. That means at least some of the more dysfunctional aspects of the Harper era regulatory U-turn would be left behind.

And fourth is the idea of whether a sector-based approach to regulating the freight rail marketplace, which is what we have now with the CTA, is preferable to a competition-based approach, which would involve the Competition Bureau and the Commissioner of Competition. The latter has gotten little attention in the transportation sector over the past three decades. As a result, many players seem to accept the notion without thinking that a governance system which cannot differentiate between two parties' respective negotiating skills on one hand and abuse by railways of their market power on the other, is an acceptable price to pay for having a regulatory approach that (a) assumes railways *might* behave inappropriately and tries to prevent that possibility and (b) gives shippers an avenue of redress based on the service they receive rather than on whether the railway engaged in bad-faith negotiations or abused its market power in other ways.

There are obviously other issues in this complex policy field, including fairness in rail–shipper relations and services. Is it "fair," say, to let some shippers receive poor service and possibly go out of business, while the total system is being well-optimized because a primary goal calls for system-level optimization to maximize the economic benefit for Canada as a whole?

Economic and Social Power

The primary feature of *economic* power in the two policy and governance histories is the duopoly of CN and CP in the freight rail marketplace. That, however, is not as straightforward as it seems because the market for rail services overlaps with the market for trucking services, a service that in some situations is extremely competitive with rail (and thus reduces or removes the duopoly effect). There are three main elements in all of this. First is the progression of economic deregulatory steps starting in a major way in 1988 that gave railways increasing room to exercise their economic power and the degree to which they used or abused it. By and large they were circumspect during the first fifteen years, as shippers voted with their wallets and the statutory review of the Canada Transportation Act in 2000–2001 reported in "Vision and Balance" that the marketplace was not fundamentally anticompetitive and was working reasonably well for most users most of the time. But all that started changing as the new century began and Model 21 was first introduced, precipitating vigorous shipper complaints that led to the policy U-turn described above.

Second is the degree to which the economic power of *shippers* was expected to play out when the advent of "competition and market forces" obliged them to duke it out with railways when negotiating business deals. Despite lack of any guarantee that things would work out well, governments took the plunge in 1988 and 1996 at least partly because they expected the economic power of shippers – and railways' hunger for more business – to produce generally positive results. Government's risk in that regard was cushioned by its willingness to let some shippers fail if they could not adapt to changes in the rail transport marketplace.

Third is the introduction of regulatory measures in 2013 and 2014 that reversed the expectations described in the previous paragraph. Those two pieces of legislation were designed to curb the economic power of the railway that introduced Model 21, even though it had made substantial and acknowledged progress in its dealings with shippers starting four or five years earlier. The legislation supplemented, and in some cases rendered moot, shippers' economic power because it furnished a government-backed assurance that no shipper would be left behind.

The primary feature of *social* power in our domain analysis consists of the clout of shippers and their customers with political influence – clout that counteracts railways' ostensible economic power. It showed up primarily in the late Model 21 era and in several forms in the government's predisposition to increase rail regulation even before the rail freight service review had begun, in shippers' refusal to agree to anything in the Dinning-led facilitation process that would require them to negotiate with railways, in the absurd Fair Rail For Grain Farmers Act, in the CTA's appalling Dreyfus decision, and in the absence of any serious consequences for the CTA from the Harper government despite the evident need for it. It is too soon to say how shippers' social power will affect the Transport Modernization Act examined in chapter 5.

Finally, we mention the social power that might be expected from a vast array of affected third parties like the customers of shippers, the citizens, and the communities that depend on the presence and quality of railway service. Most of these players have remarkably little social power in this market space. Nor do scientific and engineering experts have much social power despite their ability to help policymakers analyze complex networks and differentiate between things that improve, optimize, and stabilize networks on one hand or do the opposite on the other hand. The main reason they have little social power is that neither Transport Canada nor the CTA seems to have any of them in house, and external experts seldom get asked about issues like these by policy makers and do not seem to be very effective in volunteering their knowledge.

Technology and Temporal Realities and Conflicts

This analytical element has four highlights, mentioned here in chronological order. First is the rise of transport modes that began to compete with railways including jet aircraft, automobiles, heavy trucks, and the building of highways that enabled cars and trucks to flourish and take away railway market share and revenues. All four were technology-based developments that caught policy makers off guard, leaving railways trapped in a century-old regulatory regime that almost caused their infrastructure to collapse in the 1970s for lack of reinvestment. It was not until 1988 that the regulatory regime started to be updated in a major way.

Second is the introduction of lean production (Model 21) by railways which caught many if not most shippers unprepared and set off a chain reaction of events described earlier in this chapter.

The third highlight is the serial falling behind by the CTA – twice when it missed fundamental shifts in the transport marketplace and political landscape and had to be restructured, downsized, and redirected by transport ministers in 1988 and 1996 and once when it missed a fundamental technology-based shift in the mid-2000s as lean production took hold on railways. As a result of the latter shift, network congestion and volume throughput became prime determinants of railway performance, and issues of system optimization driven by a primary goal displaced other issues in terms of importance from a "get the goods to market" standpoint. But the CTA did not acquire competence in the necessary technical disciplines to handle these new developments (and given its budget constraints, perhaps it could not). Anyway, it has received no significant consequences as a result of that, and its current fifteen-year-long episode in falling behind has not yet begun to be corrected. In fact, the Transport Modernization Act will expand the agency's powers in various ways without adding to its governance and without requiring increases of its competence in fields, which have been absent in the past.

The fourth highlight is the government's (presumably unwitting) setting up of a "positive feedback loop" in railway/shipper governance when it enacted the Fair Rail Freight Service Act in 2013 and then went one better with the Fair Rail for Grain Farmers Act. These have *huge* temporal significance. The performance of any system with a positive feedback loop – in this case, Canada's freight rail network – is prone to collapse with exponentially increasing swiftness. Despite the freight rail system appearing to be in more or less stable condition now – because the failure progression set up by these two acts has not yet accelerated enough to be easily discernable – the rate of failure will become increasingly significant as time goes by. The problem was masked by a temporary downturn in rail traffic in the mid-2010s, but when the economy is growing strongly again the regulatory chickens will come home to roost. The new Transportation Modernization Act may or may not stop the failure progression because it refrains from exacerbating the vicious circle mentioned earlier. It might even start things in a positive direction. Why? Because it would enhance the (admittedly thin) requirements for the CTA to regulate railways *as a system*, introduce at least two promarket incentives in dispute settlement adjudications, prevent long-term damage to railway solvency that might have resulted if Harper-era interswitching provisions were extended nationwide, and thread the political needle about tricky grain transport issues. But it does contain provisions for a new mechanism, "long-haul interswitching," intended to provide captive shippers across all sectors and regions with access to a competing railway, to insure they have options. Still, it is a fragile proposition at time of writing as indicated in reports by the Standing Senate Committee on Transport and Communications 2018b and Tomesco 2018). This is because its downstream effect will be strongly influenced by the behaviour and performance of the CTA. Yet the agency still has the same gaps in technical expertise and the same limited range of competence among its members and arbitrators and the same governance shortfall as it had in the past.

CONCLUSIONS

Probably the most fundamental issue in the rail freight and competition-market dispute domain has been that of government setting and vigorously espousing a primary goal. Despite the railway optimization goal, there hasn't been a governmental one. All manner of other issues flow from that omission. Foremost is the regulatory dysfunction that has grown from no one knowing whether railways are expected to satisfy the greatest number of shippers individually or to get the greatest amount of economic value through supply chains that depend on rail. The two are not the same. Optimization theory makes it clear that railways cannot do both.

All of the following problems trace at least some of their roots to the absence of a vigorously espoused primary goal: the recent regulatory dysfunction, the Harper-era U-turn, the positive feedback loop; the CTA's freelancing in a benchmark case like Dreyfus, and the susceptibility of government to acquiescing when lobbied by interest groups for head-of-queue status.

The absence of a consciously chosen primary goal also leaves everyone without guidance when it comes to determining what constitutes "fair" rail service – and fair to whom. And without a clear understanding of that, regulatory policy suffers from a shortfall of legitimacy. Moreover, the absence of a consciously chosen primary goal exacerbates the tricky question of whether the regulator should adjudicate complaints on the basis of a railway's service (and if so, in private), as is the case now, or on the basis of whether a railway abused its market power or behaved in an anticompetitive manner, as is the case in the US.

Thus we have asked whether the Commissioner of Competition can and should involve himself in rail freight competition issues, where he can apply his greater expertise than the CTA in determining what competition is in defined markets, and how a competitive market ought to function? The commissioner has already signalled he intends to move in that direction. Among other benefits, that would make it possible for railways and/or shippers to explore issues in a more public way than they can under the CTA. There is a lot to recommend the latter, but there has not been much discourse on the choices and their consequences.

Perhaps most of all, without a consciously chosen primary goal that transcends economic and political eras, regulatory policy in rail transportation has been, and still is, susceptible to whatever political or personal beliefs or intuitive sense and convictions the government of the day happens to have. It boils down to government failing to choose between competing policy paradigms in a clear and unequivocal way. The sense of transport ministers Mazankowski, Crosbie, and Young generally proved beneficial for Canada. But under the transport and agriculture ministers of the Harper era, things went the other way. And now, judging from the content of the Transportation Modernization Act it appears that transport minister Garneau is intending to take things back to a more economically productive direction – albeit without remedying the shortfall of external governance over the CTA's performance and technical competence and also by including new measures regarding long-haul interswitching and also new definitions of what constitutes adequate and suitable rail service.

7

The Air Transport Policy
and Shared-Governance Domain

INTRODUCTION

Our attention now shifts to the air transport policy and shared-governance domain. We have already seen in chapters 2 and 3 some features and dynamics of air transport including rapid airline deregulation in the US in the late 1970s and its slower progression in Canada, and also the International Civil Aviation Organization (ICAO), based in Montreal, whose role is pivotal in airline safety and security policy and regulation worldwide.

Our domain analysis concentrates on four policy and governance histories that span the past fifty years. We begin with the policy and governance dynamics of Air Canada and the way in which regulators and ministers worked to manage competition to its benefit and tried to establish an airline policy based on *regions* when new carriers, mainly in Western Canada, challenged Air Canada for business – initially when it was struggling but even now that it has achieved sustained profitability and a strong national and global presence. The second history looks at airport policy. It covers national, regional, and urban dimensions of its shared-governance features. A watershed moment occurred in 1992 when "airport authorities" across Canada were established on a "commercial" but not-for-profit basis after decades of these airports being federally owned, financed, and operated. The third policy history focuses on NAV Canada. It had its own watershed moment at the time of its creation in 1995, as a private not-for-profit air navigation service provider – but a "service provider" that simultaneously functioned as an air safety regulator. To no one's surprise, NAV Canada was structured quite differently than the air navigation services and air traffic control organization from which it emerged inside Transport Canada. In the fourth and final policy history, our focus is on airline security policy and especially the role of the Canadian Air Transport Security Authority (CATSA). It was created in 2001 shortly after the 9/11 crisis and amidst the perceived threat of rising terrorism, and it lives on to the present day in the role of an air security and safety regulatory body.

The chapter then compares all four policy and governance histories, examining each of them through the lens of the three elements being used in the book's analytical framework. And finally we offer some conclusions on the air transport policy and shared-governance domain in total.

To begin, we look at the way in which air transport policy is structured and situated inside Transport Canada. The department describes air policy by stating quite simply that it "works with many partners both here at home and around the world to protect and maintain our air safety and security record, and to make air travel more environmentally responsible" (Transport Canada 2016f, 2). The Air Policy Directorate develops policy with the principal objective of "encourag[ing] a healthy and competitive air industry, including airlines and infrastructure providers, to ensure that Canadians have reasonable and economic access to air services. This objective recognizes the importance of air transport to other sectors in the Canadian economy and to Canada's competitiveness abroad" (Transport Canada 2016g, 1).

There are several groups within the department's Air Policy Directorate. One is National Air Services, which concerns itself with policies effecting Canadian air carriers and domestic air services, as well as Canada's Blue Sky international air policy mentioned briefly in chapter 3. Another is the National Airports Policy group, which develops policy frameworks and legislation for airports and air navigation infrastructure (the latter including NAV Canada). A third is the Civil Aviation Directorate, whose role is to develop policy that "promotes the safety of the national air transportation system through its regulatory framework and oversight system" (Transport Canada 2016h, 1). In addition, there are directorates for safety and security, and for airport programs and divestiture, that we refer to briefly in the policy and governance histories that follow. Those are not all. Other relevant parts of the department include the Canadian Aviation Regulation Advisory Council (CARAC), which we discuss in chapter

10, and the National Aircraft Certification group that "establishes and regulates standards for aeronautical products designed and operated in Canada, and guides the aerospace industry with respect to certification in highly technical fields" (Transport Canada 2016i, 1).

In statutory terms, the air policy domain is anchored by seven laws (Transport Canada 2016d, 1–2). The overarching statute is the Aeronautics Act, a one-hundred-page law that contains the core powers of the minister of Transport on air issues and specific provisions on security matters. Unlike the Canadian Transportation Act, it does not begin with a type of "whereas clause" setting out the purposes of the law overall. A large number of sets of regulations (185 at the latest count) emanate under this statute, most dealing with airport zoning rules and provisions (Justice Canada 2016a, 2–10). Other relevant statutes include the Air Canada Public Participation Act, the Canadian Air Transportation Security Authority Act, the Carriage by Air Act, the Civil Air Navigation Services Commercialization Act, and the Secure Air Travel Act.

A final point in this introduction comes in terms of how air policy is expressed for official accountability purposes, as laid out in the Transport Canada Report on Plans and Priorities (Transport Canada 2015b), a formal accounting of the department's undertakings and covenants to government and the Canadian public. Air policy is expressed as an element of a strategic outcome under the broader rubric of "a safe and secure transportation system" (ibid., 47). In other words, air policy in this form of accountability is subordinated to the service of safety and security not to the aviation sector's economic performance. Transport's aviation safety regulatory framework calls for a "balance of tools (policies, guidelines, regulations, standards, education and awareness activities) based on risk, to promote a harmonized aviation safety regulatory framework for Canadians and Canada's aviation industry" (ibid.). The aviation safety oversight sub-program is also presented as being "risk-based" with supports for compliance through "services, assessments and validations, inspections, audits and, when necessary, enforcement" (ibid.).

AIR CANADA, MANAGED COMPETITION, AND REGIONAL AIRLINE POLICY (1970S TO PRESENT)

Throughout its history Air Canada has been the nation's dominant player in air transport (Pigott 2014; Iacobucci, Trebilcock, and Winter

2006; Stevenson 1987; Corbett 1965). From 1937 when it was first formed as Trans-Canada Air Lines (TCA) it quickly became the country's national carrier. Its name was changed to Air Canada in 1965 but it remained a federal Crown Corporation until 1989 when it was privatized. Its life as a Crown Corporation has been well chronicled and analyzed by Langford and Huffman (1988). It received both political and patronage support from key Liberal ministers beginning with C.D. Howe. But the airline found its close association with government to be as much a liability as an asset. By the late 1970s, it often argued that it was obliged to operate as a normal private airline even though the Air Canada Act of 1978 termed it "an instrument of national policy" (Langford and Huffman 1988, 99), which in reality meant the government could intervene at will in the company's business decisions for reasons that often had little or nothing to do with business.

The idea of "managed competition" and, as a direct result, the policy and politics of making hay with regional (east–west and north–south) splits in the country were in full swing when Canadian Pacific Airlines (CP Air, subsequently renamed Canadian Airlines International Ltd, or CAIL) emerged in Western Canada. They were still there when substantial charter airlines such as Wardair and other provincially based ones emerged. They (the policy and politics of regional pressures) had an effect. A report by the Competition Bureau (2014a) on competition in the Canadian airline industry said that, "by the 1990s, the market had effectively developed into a duopoly, divided between Air Canada and CAIL" (ibid., 2). But policy doesn't necessarily trump the marketplace for long. In 1999, CAIL became insolvent and its acquisition by Air Canada made the latter "the dominant carrier with more than 80% of domestic passenger traffic and close to 90% of domestic passenger revenues" (ibid., 2).

The merger of Air Canada and CAIL needed regulatory approval by the federal Competition Bureau (and by the minister of Transport). To get it, Air Canada made binding commitments to foster market entry, including relinquishing "takeoff and landing times at slot congested airports and to refrain from operating a discount carrier in eastern Canada for a period of time" (ibid., 2). That mattered. WestJet's subsequent growth as a strong competitor, and that of other rival carriers in key routes, was made possible by Air Canada's undertakings. So they (the undertakings) were abolished by law. If this looks like a policy flip-flop, that's because it was. But the market and market power will have its way. The Competition Bureau reported in 2014 that the airline industry "has returned to a duopoly structure" (ibid., 2) in which Air Canada "has 55% of the domestic market based on available seat miles, WestJet 36% and other 9%" (ibid., 2).

Air Canada in the 1970s and 1980s still had a huge advantage from route monopolies arranged on its behalf by the federal government (Langford and Huffman, 99–100). Following air policy changes in 1984, Air Canada's ability to take over smaller airlines helped it to grow further and take more market share (ibid., 105). But politics has a way of showing up, too. Political–economic battles ensued between Air Canada and Québec-based air carriers.

While Air Canada was growing in revenues and market share, its profitability was bouncing around. From 1937 to 1987 it compiled a record of thirty-four profit-making years and seventeen years of net losses (ibid., 103). Even traffic fluctuated a lot. In 1987 the airline carried 11.0 million passengers, a drop of 1.8 million (14 per cent) from 1979 (ibid., 103). Things got worse. In 2003 Air Canada filed for bankruptcy protection, a state of perilous corporate and financial affairs that lasted for eighteen months and was expected to possibly reoccur (Kirby 2013). Only very recently did Air Canada publicly express confidence that its profitability is sustainable and likely to be even better in the future airline market (Air Canada 2015).

Meanwhile, the federal government was endeavouring to explicitly create a regional air policy, with the government even going so far as to suggest that the federal transport regulator might have to regulate its licensees' aircraft purchases so as to give effect to its policy! One of the big problems with that, as Stevenson noted, was that the five operating regions to which the regionals were to be confined were "arbitrary, artificial, and, most significantly, for the future health of the industry, unequal" (Stevenson 1987, 75). But even so, there might not have been a problem with the objective of using licensing to plan the air sector were it not for one major development.

Provincial governments, which had largely ignored the air transportation field prior to the 1970s, began to mirror the federal government's nation-building air objectives by promoting their own regional champions for provincial policy and political purposes (Schultz and Alexandroff 1985; Stevenson 1987). Disputes developed involving all five regional airlines, with the regulatory agency caught in the middle of a wide-ranging series of intergovernmental conflicts. On one occasion, involving Alberta's purchase of Pacific Western Airlines, the province successfully challenged before the Supreme Court the authority of the then-existing regulator, the Canadian Transportation Commission (CTC), to review the purchase. In other decisions where the CTC invoked the government's policy statement to deny provincially supported route applications, the provinces successfully appealed to the federal cabinet to overrule its regulator, with the result that cabinet undermined its own policy statement.

Nothing demonstrates the turmoil in federal air regulation as much as the policy flip-flops that occurred in the first half decade of the 1980s. In 1981, the federal minister of transport, who could not persuade his cabinet colleagues to endorse his preferred policy, released a policy paper that sought to reestablish a version of the now-discredited regional air policy. Canada was to be divided into two regions with controls on the length of flights regional carriers would be permitted, supplemented by Canadian Transport Commission (CTC) regulation on the types of aircraft that carriers could purchase. Almost every concerned interest group criticized the new policy, including the federal Department of Consumer and Corporate Affairs and the Economic Council of Canada. Indeed, a parliamentary committee review objected to it on the grounds that "the prospect of competition is the principal inducement to efficient performance in the airline industry" (quoted in Schultz and Alexandroff 1985, 58). Although the then minister rejected the call for deregulation, his immediate successor in 1984 released his own policy statement that called for the effective end to the use of economic regulation to control airlines and to replace it with competition, at least for southern Canada. The president of the CTC told the minister that he would give effect to the new policy, notwithstanding the fact that the minister lacked legislative authority to compel the CTC to do so (Stevenson 1987, 191).

More specifically, for air policy purposes Canada would be divided into two geographic zones, North and South, with the South completely decoupled from the regulatory machinery noted above. Rather than employing the anticompetitive test of "public convenience and necessity," would-be entrants need only establish that they were "fit, willing and able," which granted very limited discretion to the regulator. There would be no route, schedule, or fare regulation in the South, and airlines could discontinue routes subject to a minimal amount of formal advance notification. But there would be residual regulation for airlines serving the North because it was presumed that competition at the time was not possible nor likely in the future. Even in retrospect, the logic behind that presumption is not entirely clear or thought through.

The airline industry in Canada has changed since then, first with the emergence of WestJet, the Calgary-based airline, and then with the launch of Porter Airlines. WestJet was founded in 1996 with a very different business model than Air Canada. It provided low fares combined with excellent customer service, modelled to some extent on emerging US low-cost carriers. WestJet was nonunionized, but its leaders developed a highly participatory culture and approach with its employees that featured a role for them in corporate decision-making and opportunities for employee share ownership (Kirby 2013; Sorenson 2010). It offered only economy class in its airplanes and all flights were direct – there were no connecting flights. Its business model involved flying only one kind of airplane, the Boeing 737, partly to keep maintenance and pilot training costs down but also because initially WestJet was going to focus on the North American market and the 737 was ideal (Sorenson 2010). WestJet also established a small regional airline, WestJet Encore, which in 2014 made its first foray into trans-Atlantic travel (McCullough 2014), thus complicating the policy situation even more.

There is little doubt from the outset that WestJet fought hard for market share with Air Canada, competing on the basis of lower oper-ating costs and its growing reputation as an airline with enthusiastic and friendly staff. But WestJet was also caught practicing illegal com-petitive practices (CBC New 2004, 2006). In a lawsuit brought by Air Canada against WestJet, the lawsuit centred on "allegations that WestJet management used the password of a former Air Canada employee to access a website maintained by Air Canada to download 'detailed and commercially sensitive' information" (CBC News 2006). WestJet apologized and agreed to pay $15.5 million to settle the lawsuit. Initially in 2004, Air Canada had sought a $220 million suit, but WestJet countersued, charging Air Canada with a separate differ-ent corporate espionage offence (CBC News 2006, 2004).

By 2013 WestJet had about 36 per cent of the market share in Canada and was aiming for 50 per cent and more, with most of the gains intended to come at Air Canada's expense. So in essence, a regional airline was yet again becoming a contending national carrier. But as its competitive horizons broadened, WestJet was buffeted by market forces. Late in 2015, the airline suffered a 30 per cent decline in profits in an otherwise very good year. This was partly due to

Alberta's collapsing economy from low oil prices but also from the decline of the Canadian dollar and resulting losses for WestJet on foreign exchange as its venture into becoming a global carrier turned around to bite it (CBC News 2015, 1). It is not hard to imagine federal transport policy makers working late into the night to ascertain the significance of this.

The situation for Porter Airlines is quite different. It was established in 2006 but, in a daring move, chose its operating hub as Billy Bishop Toronto City Airport, the island airport just off downtown Toronto (Spaeth 2014). The limited flight paths and other restrictions on using that airport mean that the number of available slots for all carriers is limited to 202 a day (in effect, 101 return flights), 85 per cent of which are allocated to Porter and 15 per cent to Air Canada. Porter uses the Canadian-made Bombardier Q400 propeller-driven aircraft, whose range of about 2,414 kilometres (1,500 miles) does not permit transcontinental nonstop flights (though other links are possible). Still, Porter has built up a strong market in the Toronto/Ottawa/central-Canada region with service to some key US cities as well.

Porter is campaigning to buy and use up to thirty of the new Bombardier C Series jet. These aircraft have a longer flight range than the Q400, but Porter's plans have encountered stiff local opposition in Toronto over the anticipated jet noise. The Justin Trudeau Liberal government has promised it will not allow the new jets to fly from the Island airport because of past agreements with the City of Toronto about noise and related issues. Overall, Porter Airlines has done well as a business and built a strong base of loyal customers, but it may not have a workable base for sustained future growth. Transportation policy and politics were useful initially but now seem to be the main impediment.

An Air Canada executive, Ben Smith, shed light on how Air Canada views WestJet and Porter Airlines as competitors for the title of Canada's biggest airline (Moore 2016). Smith says his airline considers WestJet "as a very fair competitor, they started business 20 years ago with a clean sheet, none of the legacy that we have; they have no defined benefit pension plan, aren't unionized and have much simpler work rules. And they put on a great show. I mean they are a very tough competitor, they have taught us a lot and they have forced us to evolve and that's what competition is and we like that" (quoted in Moore 2016, 2). With respect to his other main domestic competitor, Porter Airlines, Smith says "Porter was basically handed a monopoly position at a public facility and we continue to fight that. When it comes to Porter, I think they have a great product," but the "slot allocation process was done in a way that we've never seen in the Western world ... the Porter position stands in the way of competition" (ibid., 3). This is an odd complaint from Air Canada because it got preferential slot and route allocations for itself for years without much objection from its own senior management. Competition authorities are expected to take into account many more factors than that when judging anticompetitive treatment. For some markets, locations like Billy Bishop may be crucial, but for others it may be flight paths or access to regions, nations, or groups of nations. In other words, Mr Smith picked a very constrained issue to which to object.

The basis for the initial air market duopoly ending was partly due to the presence of bankruptcy and threats of bankruptcy. The seeming emergence of the new duopoly due to WestJet (plus Porter) may or may not hold. WestJet pilots are seeking unionized status in law, and overall unionization and other factors are dependent, as well, on whether genuine "ultra-low cost carriers" (ULCCs) finally succeed in Canada. WestJet is planning to enter this market with a new name – Swoop (Johnson 2017). Other Canadian ULCCs seem to be on the verge of serious entry, but there are no guarantees of market success and a new market duopoly situation given what a WestJet executive is quoted saying, namely that "Canada's population density is a challenge – we're too big a country and not enough people" (ibid., 3).

AIRPORTS POLICY AND SHARED-GOVERNANCE AUTHORITIES (1992 TO PRESENT)

Our second policy and governance history is probably the most complex of the four being examined in this domain chapter and possibly in the book as a whole. It revolves around the National Airports Policy (NAP), which was introduced in 1994 (Transport Canada 2016j) although the policy changes on which it was based actually began in 1992 when the first four local airport authorities (LAAs) were established in Montreal, Calgary, Edmonton, and Vancouver (Lovink 2001). Until then, all airports in Canada were federally owned and operated, but the 1994 NAP was intended to provide "a framework that clearly defines the federal government's role with airports" (ibid., 1) – and a different one it would be, based on two levels of federal involvement, not just one, as air travel was expected to grow in major ways and new investment and infrastructure were badly needed to enable the growth as a new century dawned.

The first level was the National Airports System (NAS). It was comprised of a set of twenty-six nationally significant airports, including all those in national, provincial, and territorial capitals. The set was already serving 94 per cent of all scheduled passenger and cargo traffic. The federal government began a process of commercializing them "through the transfer of responsibility for the operation and development of NAS airports to Canadian Airport Authorities (CAAs)" (ibid.). Each CAA would be required to be financially self-sufficient for both its operating costs and capital expenditures within five years. The CAAs would be not-for-profit corporations headed by a board of directors (see more on this key governance feature below). They would lease their airports from the federal government, a key feature of the "commercialization" premise of the new system. The second level of federal involvement was designed to deal with all the smaller and remote airports and of course some of these smaller airports feature networked commercial and practical relations with their larger cousins in the NAS.

The Canadian policy was unique – and it was put into operation as air traffic volumes were rapidly increasing and as other countries were adapting and reforming their systems, some of whose airports were competing with Canadian hubs like Toronto Pearson. As the new airport policy and governance system was being phased in, all kinds of comments and critiques bubbled up. There was considerable support for the approach, but criticism was voiced about its governance model and its implicit economic model. The auditor general of Canada (2000) report raised concerns about governance accountability, arguing that Transport Canada had left it vague or was silent about what its own role was supposed to be as lessor of the airports and supervisor of the NAS. That is not a trivial matter. Concerns were raised, too, about the use of "airport improvement fees" which are usually described in hard-to-criticize language as a form of "user pay" but in fact are a form of taxation levied by airports using their monopoly power.

The comments, lobbying, and lessons learned from several years of actual operation had some effect. The federal Liberal government introduced Bill C-27 in 2003 to reform the legal framework of the system. But it died on the order paper when the 2004 federal election was called. A further Bill C-20 was tabled in 2006, but it also died when the 2008 election was called by the Conservative government. A comprehensive study in 2014 of airport governance noted that even though Bill-20 was not passed, it became a reference and guidance document and "several airport authorities have adopted its main recommendations" (Institute for Governance of Private and Public Organizations 2014, 10). (See further discussion below.)

Gillen examines the changing overall and mainly economics model of the airport business from one platform to "two-sided platforms" (Gillen 2011). He argues that airports "have traditionally been viewed as public utilities serving the needs of airlines. More recently in many developed countries they are seen as modern businesses pursuing their own objectives and serving the demands of carriers and passengers. Regardless of which view one takes, it is a perspective of one-sided markets ... [in other words,] the "sources of revenue came from one side, from the airlines." But now "airports have recognized ... that non-aviation revenues are important and can be large ... [and so] airport revenues are [coming] from two sides, from airlines and passengers." But, he says, "this thinking also requires that we consider airports as platforms lying between passengers and airlines: it brings the two together. Airports add value to both sides by internalizing network effects which exist between the two demand groups" (ibid., 11).

Assessment and reform of the system has varied more recently in the relative emphasis accorded to its governance institutions and its changing market structure. A penetrating study by the Institute for Governance of Private and Public Organization (IGOPP) looked at the policy of governance in principle and examined a sample of airport authorities in seven cities (IGOPP 2014, 29–41). Speaking mainly about the composition of airport boards, it concluded that "current airport governance exhibits shortcomings in terms of effectiveness, transparency and vigilance ... and that major changes are required" (ibid., 55), arguing that "it is essential that the boards of directors be composed of legitimate and credible directors." The study spoke directly about Canadian airports, saying that "the number and variety of the non-governmental organizations that can propose candidates to the boards of Canadian airports should be increased to ensure greater representation of the community," that the directors "must be independent from the nominating organizations that suggested that they be appointed," and that no "nominating organization can recommend more than two of the directors, in order to avoid certain organizations having predominance on the board" (ibid., 56–7).

The IGOPP analysis covered more than governance in the abstract. It examined the ways in which airport facility investments were having to be financed "by a substantial increase in the indebtedness of the airport authorities, a debt which is largely repaid by fees imposed on users (such as the airport improvement fees) which "have increased spectacularly in recent years" (ibid., 58). Clearly concerned, the authors emphasized "that's when their governance becomes an issue as the boards and management of airports do not have to give any accounting, or ask for any authorization, for their investment decisions or the increases in airport fees" (ibid.).

With airports as major drivers of economic growth, the IGOPP study saw another problem: "the provinces and municipalities [need] to play a more significant role in the development and strategy of airports in their proximity, including facing up to the competition from American border airports" (ibid.). The authors even thought the federal government could "offer to sell the airports to the relevant provinces and major municipalities" (ibid.). In short, the study put its finger on some deep-seated weaknesses and ambivalence in the model as currently constructed. It was intended to be complex and it is. Indeed, it is easy to see in the airports governance story the value of the insights of Agranoff (2007) as previewed in chapter 1 and the reasons why "managing within networks" is both promoted as necessary and inevitable and then needing change but always against the views different players. Foucault's notion of "governmentality" is also of some analytical use given its meaning regarding quite literally, different "mentalities" (Foucault 1991) by those who have to function amidst complexity that is obvious to them.

The Canadian Airports Council (CAC) has had relevant things to say. Its members represent more than a hundred Canadian airports and its extensive submission to the Canadian Transport Act review panel (Canadian Airports Council 2015) presented a long-term Vision 2040 program that would draw from a still-to-be-created aviation policy agenda "for competitiveness and economic prosperity." It included suggestions for a national air travel and air trade strategy, expressing concern for a "lack of policy alignment" (ibid., 9) across government agencies that would be needed for current and longer-term competitiveness internationally, and pointing out a wider array of misaligned policies that obstruct airports from reaching their full potential, including CATSA security screening services and the Transit Without Visa processes. But what "policy-alignment" might actually be in practice does not leap convincingly out of its report.

CAC also pointed to "end of lease issues" as a particular problem for some airports because they (the airport authorities) "are open to moving to a fully privatized model" (ibid., 13, and see also 54–7) but without any "clear arrangements for the transfer of airport assets and contracts back to the federal government when airport authority leases expire" (ibid., 13). Still, most CAC members are reportedly of the view that the "current non-share capital corporation model continues to be the best governance structure for the long term" (ibid.). That means the model is likely to be kept, but the deficiencies with which it was endowed need attention. But rushed reforms can also be problematical. For example, it has been reported that Transport Canada, under orders from the current Trudeau Liberal government, anxious for new sources of funding for its massive overall budget 2016 infrastructure commitments, are eyeing the sale of airports to private owners as an untapped source of such new investment cash (Campion-Smith 2016). But under such a change, the chief executive officer of the Vancouver Airport Authority, Craig Richmond, argues that "in five years you would not recognize Canadian airports ... you would see cutbacks on maintenance, cleaning, you would [see] them become much more crowded because of the pressures on the management to deliver that return" (quoted in Campion-Smith 2016, 2). There has since been further study by the federal government regarding the sale of major Canadian airports (Beeby 2017) and such sales are also part of discussions about what the new Canada Infrastructure Bank might or might not do (Infrastructure Canada 2017).

We close this section of the chapter by discussing a report from a Public Policy Forum (2015) roundtable event convened with Toronto Pearson airport. Among its main concerns was the enduring problem of significant airfare differences between Canadian and US carriers. As a result, "as many as five million Canadians annually chose to travel through what is sometimes referred to as the 'missing airport', airports in the US" (ibid., 5). The Canadian airports' funding model – the one they inherited by federal transportation policy that saw their creation as CAAS – were at the center of these price differences because in the US "key elements of airport infrastructure are owned and operated by US municipal governments" (ibid.) and their costs are not charged back to travellers as they are in Canada. In other words, Canadian airports are facing subsidized competitors just across the border. Still, the roundtable did "not [suggest] that one system was obviously preferable to the other. Rather, both systems have good and bad qualities" (ibid.). That means the problem of price differences seems likely to endure.

Air policy as of late 2018 has introduced a new level and extent of support and protection for air passenger rights. Minister Marc Garneau announced changes in the Transportation Modernization Act that will "mandate the Canadian Transportation Agency to make new regulations to strengthen Canada's air passenger rights" (Transport Canada 2017d). While the agency will "develop precise details through a regulatory process, the new initiative would establish clear standards of treatment for air travelers in common situations as well as financial compensation under certain circumstances. The announcement gave examples such as denied boarding (including in case of overbooking), delays, and cancellations; lost or damaged baggage; tarmac delays over a certain period of time; seating children near a parent or guardian at no extra charge. Of interest, given our discussion of the CTA in chapter 6 regarding freight rail, is the decision to hand the CTA a lead role, despite its past and current institutional weaknesses, along with one under ministerial direction, on air passenger reforms and rights when it had none before and indeed no expressed interest.

While the above air passenger rights item was the lead-off initiative, it was in fact one of several "travellers initiatives." One of these dealt with the "international ownership of air carriers" whereby the Canada Transportation Act was to be amended to "liberalize international ownership restrictions from 25 to 49 percent of voting interests for Canadian air carriers with accompanying safeguards." There was also a provision regarding joint ventures whereby the minister could consider and approve such ventures "between two or more carriers" with the process undertaken in consultation with the Commissioner of Competition regarding "both competition and the public interest" (Transport Canada 2017d).

NAV CANADA AS NAVIGATION SERVICE PROVIDER AND AIR SAFETY REGULATOR (1996 TO PRESENT)

We begin our look at NAV Canada in 1996 when it was created. Canada naturally had an air navigation system well before then, but it was housed within Transport Canada. A defining event in its history was the bilingual air traffic control conflict of the mid-1970s (Borins 1983). This turned into a high profile national unity crisis when francophone controllers and pilots sought to use French as well as English in Québec aviation. An airline pilots' strike in June 1976 in support of their counterparts in air traffic control led to an agreement with the pilots' and controllers' unions, but French Canadians in general saw it as a humiliating defeat. By 1979, the newly elected Clark Conservative government ruled that bilingual air traffic control was in fact safe. That ended the crisis but its resolution has a direct legacy in the subsequent structure and governance of NAV Canada because it gave union representatives direct participation on its board of directors. (See further discussion below.)

By the early 1990s, many alternative governance ideas and dynamics were underway, as we have seen in the airports policy history earlier in this chapter. But the impetus for the NAV Canada change had a partly different policy trajectory. Some of the concerns about the 1980s system were discussed in a 1992 ministerial task force on the air navigation system (ANS). NAV Canada's account of its gestation is of interest here (NAV Canada 2015a). It said that the 1980s ANS was "not working well" (ibid., 2), reflecting a view held by virtually all the key players and interests. Much of the problem had to do with money:

> While there were areas of excellence, such as its operational people and its safety record, infrastructure was in need of renewal and major system projects were falling further and further behind with escalating costs. Delays and decreasing service levels had become unacceptable to the various operators of the system, especially commercial airlines. The cost of the system was high and increasing at a faster rate than revenue from the ticket tax, which did not cover all ANS costs. There were air traffic control shortages and government wage freezes and there was an inherent conflict of interest with the service provider essentially regulating itself in respect of safety. (Ibid., 2)

Transport Canada was operating the ANS system. By the late 1980s and early 1990s the system – run as a unit within the department – was buffeted along with the department as a whole by repeated staff and budget cuts, resulting especially from the massive reductions of the federal program review that started to bite in 1995. Flowing from the ministerial task force and discussions lasting three years, an announcement was made on 31 October 1996, that NAV Canada would be established and "given a legislated monopoly in perpetuity to operate the system. In return, the Crown received a payment of $1.5 billion" (Standing Committee on Public Accounts, 1998, 1). At a single stroke this ended the conflict-of-interest problem and opened the door to solving the money problems, although of course it just transferred the obligation of paying for the service to those who could not refuse – air travellers themselves, not their government via tax-payers. User pay won out.

NAV Canada was also a particularly intriguing example of a larger new public management (NPM) reform ethos emerging in the 1990s that involved several types of new public organization (Kernaghan, Marson, and Borins 2000, 106–9). We first set out how NAV Canada describes itself and then reflect on some of its service and regulatory features.

NAV Canada calls itself Canada's Air Navigation Service Provider (ANSP) "managing 12 million aircraft movements a year for 40,000 customers in over 18 million square kilometers – the world's second largest ANSP by traffic volume" (NAV Canada 2016a, 1). It points out that it is "the world's first fully privatized civil air navigation service provider, created in 1996, through the combined efforts of commercial air carriers, general aviation, the Government of Canada, as well as our employees and their unions" (ibid.). It says that "safety is our first priority" and "our safety benchmark [see further discussion below] has seen a steady reduction since 1996, and our record is now among the best in the world" (ibid.). It does not say whether that represents a better trend line than air navigation had in Canada before NAV Canada's creation.

Its governance consists of a board of directors in which "all key stakeholders are Members of the Company, and elect the Directors" who must be Canadian citizens (NAV Canada 2016b, 1). The fifteen member board consists of

- four directors elected by commercial carriers through the National Airlines Council of Canada (NACC);
- one director elected by business and general aviation through the Canadian Business Aviation Association (CBBA);
- three directors elected by the government of Canada;

- two directors elected by employee unions;
- four independent directors elected by the board through the director;
- the chief executive officer. (Ibid.)

NAV Canada has no shareholders. Its stated vision "is to be the world's most respected ANS: in the eyes of the flying public for our safety record; in the eyes of our customers for our fee levels, customer service, efficiency and modern technology; and in the eyes of our employees for establishing a motivating and satisfying workplace with competitive compensation and challenging career opportunities" (NAV Canada 2016c, 1). Its stated mission is "to facilitate the safe movement of aircraft efficiently and cost-effectively through the provision of air navigation services on a long term sustained basis" (ibid.).

The organization's first two overarching "objectives" (of six) are maintaining a safety record in the top decile of major ANSPs worldwide and "maintaining ANS customer service charges, on average, in the bottom quartile (lowest charges) of major ANSPs worldwide by ensuring that the growth in costs of providing air navigation services does not exceed the growth in revenues, thereby resulting in a decline in customer service charges over the long term" (ibid.). The other four objectives deal with cost-efficient ANS technology, value to customers' operational efficiency, creating a productive and fulfilling workplace, and reduction of the environmental footprint of the aviation industry (ibid.).

As to its financial structure, NAV Canada is incorporated as a nonshare capital corporation and its long-term financing is done "with publicly traded debt"; its "bonds and notes payable currently total $2 billion" (NAV Canada 2016d, 1). That, it says, makes it "entirely independent of government funding." But things are not so simple. If NAV Canada ever ran into serious financial difficulty it almost certainly would be bailed out by the federal government. In other words, it has an implicit guarantee of solvency from the state – a fact surely not lost on creditors – and so it is *not* entirely independent of government funding. With regard to its day-to-day financing, the organization is largely funded by charging "airlines and other aircraft operators for air traffic control flight information, and other air navigation services" (ibid.). What that really means is air travellers pay, albeit indirectly.

In many ways NAV Canada is a unique entity, even among the large array of shared-governance authorities for airports (and even the airline industry itself). Several of its features stand out. First, it calls itself a "privatized entity" but this is not entirely accurate because there is no share ownership (Kernaghan, Marson, and Borins 2000). In other documents, NAV Canada describes itself more accurately as a "private sector, non-share capital corporation" (NAV Canada 2015b, 4).

NAV Canada does not call itself a "regulator" but sees Transport Canada regulating *it* on safety matters. Yet key industry groups such as the Canadian Airlines Council (2015) identify NAV Canada second only to Transport Canada as a regulatory authority (ibid., 1). Indeed, a regulatory public engagement process convened by the Canadian Airports Council and NAV Canada led in June 2015 to joint measures "to ensure effective public engagement on changes to flight paths" (Canadian Airports Council 2015b, 1). That led to the Airspace Change Communications and Consultations Protocol, an agreement with a specified process to foster consideration of community noise issues in the design of flight plans. To some observers that must have looked a lot like regulation.

Some of these core functions are understandable. NAV Canada sees itself as providing air navigation services but stresses that it is, above all, a safety-first entity. So there can be little doubt that NAV Canada *is* a regulator. Look no further than what a key set of its employees do: they are air traffic controllers, engaged in communicating their organization's rules and practices to airline pilots in flight and during takeoff and landing. This may look like air navigation management, but it is one with rules and safety practices at its very core, and they carry the weight of law. NAV Canada even adopts new technologies and obliges airlines to do the same. Aireon, a major global system, is a recent example (NAV Canada 2014, ii).

SECURITY POLICY AND THE CANADIAN AIR TRANSPORT SECURITY AUTHORITY (2001 TO PRESENT)

As discussed in chapter 3, within days of the 9/11 attack by terrorists, the US began demanding that Canada join in the construction of a North American security perimeter (Gattinger and Hale 2010; Molot 2002). The Chrétien government quickly established a full-fledged cabinet committee on public security and antiterrorism. New antiterrorism legislation, the Public Safety Act, was introduced. It changed nineteen existing laws and greatly strengthened antiterrorism measures. Many of them were aimed at transportation. The federal government was empowered to collect air passenger data from airlines and reservation systems and even share it with foreign governments. These and other provisions in the law were criticized by opposition parties and privacy advocates for their (the provisions') intrusiveness into the personal details of people using the transportation system. In other words, international security issues found their way, via transportation policy, directly into the lives of individual Canadians.

Our focus turns to the Canadian Air Transport Security Authority (CATSA) but we also need to look at some of the debates about, and analytical underpinnings of, security policy as it surged onto the agenda and raised all kinds of complex values and ethical issues about risk, safety, and intelligence in security policy pertaining to air services. That means it is connected to regulatory governance as discussed in chapter 1 and in the Transport Canada-centered domain in chapter 4.

The International Air Transportation Association (IATA), mentioned in chapter 3, set a bold tone by requiring that all its member airlines and airports establish a security management system (SEMS) by March 2007. Not everyone knew what this meant. As Salter (2007) shows, many organizations had "to learn from safety and quality management systems. Without specific guidelines or best practices, organizations are forced to imitate these processes designed for different goals. Since safety, quality, and security environments operate on radically different principles, SEMS implementation must take a different tack" (ibid., 389). This was not easy. CATSA, for example, "illustrates the importance of a custom-designed program that meets public and corporate needs" (ibid.). In a subsequent article, Salter (2008a) argued that some of the inherent political problems of transportation security arise from "the dilemma of [dealing with conflicting] public/private security screening; policy coordination and market failure, and intermodal security" (ibid., 29). So, he argues, "the more governments and corporations spend on security, the greater perception of failure in the event of a low-probability disaster event, hence the greater the risk of investment; currently actors have an incentive to move transportation off the public agenda and avoid spending on security" (ibid.). In short, not everybody agreed on what security was worth.

In another article Salter (2008b) ties securitization and desecuritization to international relations theory and practice, and he examines CATSA in that context, arguing that "scholars have retained the statist view of securitization: actors identify an existential threat that requires emergency executive powers, and, if the audience accepts the securitizing move, the issue is depoliticized and is considered a security issue outside the rules of normal politics" (ibid., 321). That is a penetrating observation. He asks, "how are securitizing moves accepted or rejected? What are the politics of that successful process of desecuritization?" He argues that it is not just a binary process and that "securitizing moves take place within different sociological settings" (ibid.), which means the exact same problem can have entirely different solutions from one year to the next. Within this, CATSA's formation and early evolution can be seen and interpreted. The constant flux of sociological settings means that frequent innovation in securitization is needed, but as a "guardian" organization CATSA tends to be slow to embrace it. (See more below.)

Research shows the number of ways in which civil aviation can be represented as a threat to national security (Yates and Scrinivasan 2014). The list is long and creative. Issues that are regularly claimed to threaten national security include "privatizing national carriers, allowing foreign investors to purchase airports, carrying citizens who want to train with foreign militias, and transporting gold and drugs for criminal gangs" (ibid., 227). These authors point out that by "linking an issue with national security ... issues can become elevated to the status of national emergencies with all the attention that these receive" (ibid.) whether or not they actually deserve it.

Still other analysts point to the "unmitigated insider threat to aviation" (Loffi and Wallace 2014). Traditional "aviation security methods place a strong emphasis on managing the risks of aviation passengers and customers. [But] little emphasis is placed on monitoring and mitigating the security risks presented by industry employees" (ibid., 289). That means there was a remarkable hole in the fence. These "insider risks" have finally become important, including cases where private contract screening companies have their own employees on the airport premises, as CATSA does.

Without doubt the most comprehensive analysis of airport and aviation security is the book by Elias (2009) on the US system, looked at in the "age of global terrorism" both before and after 9/11 but with a focus on the latter. It discusses the US in a global context of broad and particular issues and concepts ranging from the evolving terrorist threat, the realities of "layered security," the need for and complexities of evaluating and managing security risks, the need but also the traps in exploiting intelligence information, passenger and baggage screening, and different notions of "perimeter security."

Almost all the post 9/11 analysis in Canada involved Canada–US comparison and context (Zaidi 2008; Lyon 2006; O'Malley 2006). Zaidi argues that both "Canada and the US have fostered aviation security by creating a multi-layered regime by forging partnerships between federal agencies and intelligence, law enforcement, and the private sector" (ibid., 30). That sounds pretty good. Lyon, however, links airport screening and surveillance with "social sorting" in Canada's response to 9/11 and with the "symbiotically growing 'surveillance society' and 'safety state.' Here, surveillance has become a feature not of specific monitoring of suspects but of generalized social sorting of populations, in this case in relation to their perceived levels of dangerousness" and in ensuring "that certain classes of person do not cross the internal border easily" (Lyon 2006, 423). That is a politically charged way of dealing with transportation safety and security.

O'Malley's work on airport security focuses on risks and ethics (2006), as airport security shifts from "a rule-based system" to "one based on risk." In his view, "rule-based or 'bureaucratic' security refers to a setting characterized by uniform practices in which every case is accorded the same degree of scrutiny. This implies that, in the absence of some specific issue that draws attention to a specific case, all cases will be treated as moderate risks" (ibid., 413). That is a pretty robotic way of looking at a highly nuanced environment. Risk-based models for security, he believes, are superior if done properly because they "would appear to focus on issues relating to selective attention given to high-risk cases" (ibid.).

CATSA powers were set out in the Canadian Air Transport Security Authority Act. The agency has two overriding responsibilities, namely

1   [to take] actions, either directly or through a screening contractor, for the effective and efficient screening of persons who access aircraft or restricted areas through screening points, the property in their possession or control, and the

belongings or baggage that they may give to an air carrier for transport; and

2 for ensuring consistency in the delivery of screening across Canada and for any other transport security function provided for in the CATSA *Act*, as well as air transport security functions that the Minister of Transport may assign to it, subject to any terms and conditions that the Minister may establish. (Canadian Air Transport Security Authority 2016a)

"Consistency" has a nice ring to it, but if it means in the *application* of security measures it falls into the trap of being a "rule-based system" that is blind to the context of the situation. CATSA is told it must function "in the public interest, having due regard to the interests of the travelling public" (ibid.). The question of what constitutes "due" is not mentioned. Further clouding things, CATSA is told that it "shares responsibility for civil aviation security with several federal government departments and agencies, air carriers and airport operators. Transport Canada is Canada's designated national civil aviation security regulator, and regulates pursuant to standards established by the International Civil Aviation Organization (ICAO)" (ibid.). When the chips are down, it seems unlikely that anyone will know who exactly is responsible for what and in what circumstances. Moreover, as discussed in chapter 3, as a member of ICAO, Canada (and therefore CATSA) has an obligation to comply with ICAO aviation security standards. Nothing is ever simple.

The CATSA corporate plan for 2014–2015 to 2018–2019 (Canadian Air Transport Security Authority 2015a) says its mandate and mission is to "protect the public by securing critical elements of the air transport system as assigned by the Government of Canada" and therefore to conduct screening in the following four areas

- Pre-Board Screening (PBS): the screening of passengers, their carry-on baggage and their personal belongings;
- Hold Baggage Screening (HBS); the screening of checked baggage;
- Non-Passenger Screening (NPS); the screening of non-passengers on a random basis; and
- Restricted Area Identity Card (RAIC): the administration of access control to airport restricted areas through biometric identifiers. (Ibid., 3)

In addition, it conducts screening of cargo at smaller airports. It is not clear if this screening, even if reliably performed, establishes a security perimeter with no holes. Given the creativity of malevolent players, it seems unlikely.

CATSA is a Crown Corporation with an independent board of directors. There are four positions for industry nominees, two nominated by representatives of the airline industry and two by representatives of airport operators. Its annual report for 2015 (Canadian Air Transport Security Authority 2015b) highlighted the CATSA key numbers for 2014–15 as being 57.3 million passengers screened at 89 airports across Canada by more than 6,000 screening officers at 102 checkpoints and in 306 screening lines (ibid., 4). The volume of passengers screened has increased from 47.7 million to 57.3 million since 2010–11.

Most of CATSA's screening function is carried out by its contractors and their workforce, which is unionized, but CATSA's own staff is not unionized. Its service delivery is clustered into four regions (Pacific, Prairies, Central and East) and its operational personnel are "stationed at Class I airports in each administrative region and responsible for the delivery of screening operations at over 80 airports across Canada" (ibid., 6). CATSA is required to regularly "report on its performance in accordance with a range of Acts and Standards" (ibid.) which include the Access to Information Act, the Privacy Act (see more below) and the Official Languages Act. Note these have essentially little to do with CATSA's *raison d'être* of directly helping keep people safe.

CATSA naturally has to work closely with many industry partners. This extends far beyond its primary screening tasks. It even means preventing itself from being the bottleneck in the continuous movement of people (hence even aircraft) through the system. Why? Because "delays at one airport can have ripple effects across the system" (Canadian Air Transport Security Authority 2015b, 15). This means CATSA has to devise approaches to manage "capacity risk" – the risk of becoming the bottleneck – even in the face of rising "screening contractor billing rates and rising passenger volumes." Unhelpfully, "its ability to purchase screening hours [from contractors] has declined in the last two years. Consequently, passenger wait times have increased" (ibid., 18).

The Canada Transport Act review (2016) report takes on CATSA. First, it was critical of CATSA, arguing that "it has not embraced technology and risk analysis to the same extent as the Canada Border Services Agency and so has not delivered the same process improvements. At airport security, higher passenger volumes have meant longer wait times" (ibid., 187). Later, the report states

> Throughout the consultations and submissions, the Review has heard near-universal condemnation of the existing state of security screening at Canadian airports ... the service and operational failings of the existing oversight and delivery model were consistently cited and observed first-hand. (Ibid., 201)

Three root causes were pinpointed: a growing revenue gap that does not allow CATSA to deal with increasing traffic, excessive control through regulation by Transport Canada, and a culture at CATSA that has been "relatively closed to outside criticism and new ideas" (ibid.).

The review did not discuss any of the issues mentioned above about the political nature of security or the multidepartmental securitization coordination in the Canadian government or the complex nature of risk analysis. That is a surprise because some of these issues had been raised explicitly by informed authors who examined CATSA as an institution in its own right and because of the imperatives of the Canada–US security system.

The previously mentioned recently proposed federal "travellers initiatives" included an initiative for new CATSA screening services on a cost-recovery basis. This would support "Canadian airports by creating new opportunities for smaller airports to attract new commercial routes, and by allowing the major hubs with an option of purchasing additional services to expedite passenger screening" (Transport Canada 2017, 2).

ANALYTICAL ELEMENTS

We now look, with the aid of table 7.1, across the four policy and governance histories through the three elements in the book's analytical framework: policy ideas, discourse and agendas; economic and social power; and technology and temporal realities and conflicts. They help us explain both change and inertia in the development of the air transport policy and shared-governance domain.

Policy Ideas, Discourses, and Agendas

Perhaps the dominant idea and discourse revealed across the last three of the four policy and governance histories in this chapter is that of shared governance. Shared governance was needed regarding the policies and involving airports, NAV Canada, and CATSA. Each of those were concerned with the need to end – for broadly similar reasons – the direct federal ownership and control of air transport by adopting shared-governance models, albeit of different kinds, to ensure that a wider set of players could be involved in not-for-profit and nonshareholding but nevertheless more "commercialized entities." This was due partly to the strong presence of fiscal deficits in the 1980s and 1990s and gave air cover to the divestiture process, but the federal government could not realistically afford it. In other words money (or, more accurately, the lack of it) drove an agenda that required some form of shared governance in order to work. But there was more. Concerns had been growing about the number of airports and the communities that needed to be involved in their governance, regardless of their ownership status. Also being interwoven in the early 1990s and onwards were ideas inherent in the emergence of a new public management ethos at the time, and new discourse and new varieties of public organizations that were emerging and being tested worldwide.

In our policy history stretching back to the 1970s and earlier, the predominant ideas, discourses, and agendas consist of struggling to work out a Canadian version of airline economic deregulation. It was not proceeding very well at all. The focal point of ideas in this history include Air Canada as a national carrier (initially state owned but later privatized) because throughout all the comings and goings in the domestic airline industry it (Air Canada) continued to function in basically a duopolistic market. Weaving its way into this set of developments were various notions, none particularly well developed, of what regional air policy might look like and be defined or operationalized as. They ranged from five regions to two regions and even a separation of South versus North/remote. Part of the problem was the government's limited imagination, daring, and willingness to keep its regulatory fingers out of the pie, except on a few bold occasions. In the end the dominant picture remains one of a duopoly in competitive terms, broadly playing out on Central Canada/Western Canada terms.

Table 7.1
The air transport policy and shared-governance domain and the three analytical elements: Highlights

Policy and governance histories	Policy ideas, discourse, and agendas	Analytical elements		
		Economic and social power	Technology and temporal realities and conflicts
Air Canada, managed competition, and regional airline policy (1970s to present)	National carrier	Air Canada (TCA) as dominant carrier with support from Liberal ministers (e.g., C.D. Howe and beyond)	Porter uses Bombardier Q400 aircraft based on a technology platform that restricts the carrier's range	
	Air Canada (formerly Trans-Canada Air Lines) as instrument of national policy	Canadian Airlines International (CAIL) formerly Canadian Pacific Airlines (CP Air) as Western Canadian-based airlines	Bombardier C Series jet technology platform with extended speed and range, but noise and other issues cloud Porter's right to operate from Toronto City airport	
	Managed competition			
	De facto duopoly			
	Regional airline policy	Provinces' belated role and interest in regional airlines and service (including Québec-federal disputes)		
	Privatization of Air Canada		National Aircraft Certification Group within Transport Canada	
	Arbitrary, artificial, and unequal regions emerge	WestJet established in 1996 as latest Western-based carrier but with nonunionized staff and with ethos of excellent customer service	Air Canada in bankruptcy protection for eighteen months and fears that it could happen again	
	North and South regions with south deregulated			
	"Fit, willing and able" criteria for would-be airline entrants	Porter Airlines established in 2006 based at Toronto City Airport as its (the airport's) dominant carrier	CAIL bankruptcy and Air Canada takeover but only under short-term conditions to enhance competition	
	Low-cost carrier and WestJet model	Rapid growth of passenger traffic		
	Sustainable profitability	Blue Sky international air policy	Air Canada overall growth, but this very unsteady with decline of passengers in 1979–87 period	
	Competitiveness abroad of Canadian airlines and their role in competitiveness of other industries as a result	Canadian Transport Commission (CTC) regulates types of aircraft that carriers can purchase		

Table 7.1
The air transport policy and shared-governance domain and the three analytical elements: Highlights (*continued*)

Policy and governance histories	Policy ideas, discourse, and agendas	Analytical elements	
		Economic and social power	Technology and temporal realities and conflicts
Airports policy and shared governance authorities (1992 to present)	Federally owned and operated up to 1992	NAS airports have independent monopolies as Canadian Airport Authorities (CAAs) leased from the federal government	Rapid increase in air traffic volumes
	1994 National Airport Policy (NAP)		Growth of indebtedness of Canadian airport authorities
	Air travel growth and thus new investment and infrastructure badly needed	Hub airports (e.g Toronto Pearson Airport) attract connecting flights whether passengers want them or not	Spectacular growth of airport improvement fees as main source of revenue
	"Commercialization" of the NAS airports	Airport improvement fees as key revenue source (paid mainly by airlines, hence actually by travellers)	Investment gap as airport authorities approach the end of their leases
	Airports as "not-for-profit" corporations		
	Federal jurisdiction retained over smaller remote and northern airports	Individual airports as a monopoly in most cities;	Unproven long-term viability of "guardian" monopolies running "trader" commercial businesses
		Increase of nonaviation revenues	
	Airport business as "two-sided platform"	Some community power representation in airport board of directors but criticism that more was needed	
	Airports as drivers of economic growth	Unionized and non-union labour (WestJet, CATSA airport employees)	
	Airports misconstrue their own importance vis-à-vis directly contributing to employment and GDP	Further permanent airport divestiture needed	
	Suggested Canadian Airlines Council (CAC) National Air Travel and Trade Strategy	Growing competition from American border airports because of their better financial base via city and/or state owner ship and subsidization	

NAV Canada as Air Navigation Service Provider and Safety Regulator (1996 to present)	Bilingual air traffic control conflict of mid-1970s as high profile national unity issue	Five million Canadians travel through US border airports to find cheaper fares	NAV Canada given legislated monopoly "in perpetuity"
	Safety concerns	Canadian Airport Council as chief airport lobby	NAV Canada is a regulator in fact, but overlooks or denies it publicly;
	Need for renewed infrastructure	1992 Ministerial Task Force on Air Navigation System	12 million aircraft movements a year
	Governance linked to "new public management" ethos of 1990s and resulting forms of new public organization (such as NAV Canada)	Ticket tax revenue inadequate for growing needs	Goal of providing air services on a long term sustained basis
	Air navigation system service-provider versus regulator	National Airlines Council of Canada as advocate for change	Aireon system as major new technology for ANS at NAV Canada and globally
	"Safety as first priority"	Transport Canada as NAV Canada's regulator after 1996: (previously TC was home where air navigation service was based)	
	Employee unions as elected board members	Core air traffic controller/airline pilots relationships and mutual dependencies during flights, take-offs and landings	
	NAV Canada as a "non-share-capital corporation"	2016 Canadian Airport Council joint work with NAV Canada to foster public engagement on changes to flight paths	
Security Policy and the Canadian Air Transport Security Authority (CATSA) (2001 to present)	"Security perimeter" as idea for North America in post 9/11 era	Cabinet Committee on Public Security and Anti-Terrorism formed	9/11 crisis as pivotal driver of global security and anti-terrorism agenda
	Public Safety Act as Federal focus on anti-Terrorism measures	Powers given to collect passenger data from airlines and reservation systems and share with other countries	Also cast now as an age of global terrorism

Table 7.1
The air transport policy and shared-governance domain and the three analytical elements: Highlights (*continued*)

Policy and governance histories	Analytical elements		
	Policy ideas, discourse, and agendas	*Economic and social power*	*Technology and temporal realities and conflicts*
Security Policy and the Canadian Air Transport Security Authority (CATSA) (2001 to present) (*continued*)	Privacy as growing concern as a result	International Air Transport Association (IATA) orders its airline members to establish a security management system (SEMS)	Multiple and changing technologies for security screening
	Risk, safety, and intelligence ideas in combination and conflict		Nontrivial ignorance of what an SEMS actually is
	Public–private security screening	Security cast a being outside of normal rule of politics – takes on a life and authority all its own	Increases in waiting times for passengers, sometimes causing flight delays that quickly reverberate through whole airline
	Intermodal security	"Securitization" viewed differently in elite, popular, scientific, and technocratic settings	Issues of continuous movement/ travel through the system
	Civil aviation seen as threat to national security	Surveillance society	CATSA criticized for not embracing new technologies the way Canada's road border agencies/ports have
	Insider threats to security and safety, initially not recognized or dealt with	CATSA mandate to "protect the public"	
	Layered security	Private security screening unionized contract companies as core staff	
	Social sorting of populations	CATSA must report on actions regarding the Access to Information Act, the Privacy Act; and the Official Languages Act (but not on its performance in terms of real security)	
	CATSA to function "in the public interest" having due regard to the interests of the travelling public"	CATSA is not an intelligence agency	

Economic and Social Power

There is a lot of variety in the ways and degrees to which economic and social power played out in our four policy and governance histories as well as in the broader domain from which they are extracted. Air Canada's economic power base was anchored in nation-building (mainly Liberal) expressions of government dominance, but challenges to Air Canada came in at least two waves, both from Western Canadian airlines whose success in national policy terms was based on regional power aspirations and concerns including support from provincial governments in the West. Passengers – the customers – finally emerged as an economic and social power element because of their growth in numbers and in their insistence on quality of service, price, and safety.

In the airports policy and governance history, the main story is one of conjoined socioeconomic forces. These forces drove many decisions by the federal government to cede extensive control of airports to new shared-governance authorities, largely because federal resources alone could not adequately pay for that control as passenger volumes grew along with federal deficits. The airport authorities involved a model of shared socioeconomic participation in their governance. US border airports also became a competitive and power source because they were funded differently and attracted Canadian travellers by offering cheaper fares.

The NAV Canada and CATSA histories involved different, more micro issues of socioeconomic power. NAV Canada was built on a complex air traffic controller/airline pilot relationship, in which both sought to ensure passenger and system safety. That gave it a regulatory function so circumscribed as to elude NAV Canada's awareness that it *is* indeed a regulator. Its work also extended to the need for local community processes for dealing with flight paths – again a circumscribed issue. Our analysis of CATSA showed a sudden, significant broadening of air security and safety governance and power beyond CATSA itself that takes in a large array of security departments and agencies at least partly surrounding it, much of it arising from tighter Canada–US relations in the post-9/11 era. Protecting the public retained its unquestioned validity, but the same could not be said for the security processes themselves when CATSA started incorporating private screening companies, social profiling, and the growth of a surveillance society.

Technology and Temporal Realities and Conflicts

The technology components of this element of the air transport domain vary considerably in their scope and importance. That may seem surprising because aviation is a thoroughly technology-intensive industry. Technology features modestly in our first policy history in the form of Bombardier's propeller-driven Q400 aircraft, as an enabler of Porter Airlines' starting business model, and the C Series jet, as a less certain enabler of Porter's new model thanks to noise and other considerations at Porter's hub airport. New technology systems for air navigation such as Aireon are a more far reaching technological disrupter because they affect *all* air navigation domestically and probably globally as well. The CATSA story lays out an equally transformative dimension of technology for security screening, on account of its direct and personal effect on travellers, and the evident failure of a critical element in the nation's safety and security apparatus, CATSA, for not embracing new technologies quickly enough.

The temporal aspects are equally varied across the four policy and governance histories. They include Air Canada's short-term bankruptcy protection and CAIL's fatal bankruptcy; the rapid growth of air traffic volumes, airport authority debt, and airport improvement fees as a main source of revenue for airports; the NAV Canada legislated monopoly being granted "in perpetuity"; the sudden change in priority for security and the formation of CATSA in response to the 9/11 crisis; and the drumbeat repetition from many sources about the dawning of an age of global terrorism. And finally, growth in passenger waiting times in the new screening process is temporal to the core and so is its impact on the rate of movement of people through the airport system.

CONCLUSIONS

This chapter's mapping and analysis of the air transport policy and shared-governance domain tells a complex story perhaps ultimately dominated by the inherent much greater speed of motion and movement in the air transport mode compared to other modes and also the rapid and massive growth in traffic, travel and passenger growth in an ever shrinking world. The policies in this domain include some that are similar to some of those discussed earlier in the book in that they involve national versus regional values, the continuous presence of safety and broadening security concerns and how to deal with those in an age of real or imagined terrorism.

Canada–US relations show up as a governance feature in this domain, especially after 9/11, but its most prominent governance feature almost certainly is the emergence in the early 1990s of shared-governance authority at each of Canada's airports, most noticeably at major hubs but also at major city airports and even smaller southern Canada ones.

We conclude by saying that the continuing role of Transport Canada in air transport policy and governance, with which we began the chapter, remains a critical but fast-changing part of this domain. Transport Canada has both advocated for and supported the shared socioeconomic governance system including the independent regulators examined here while simultaneously being unable to fully control or keep up with them. Global air travel will continue growing, and Canada needs to continue searching for ways to ensure its competitiveness in attracting traffic to this mode and enabling the competitiveness of the many Canadian industries dependant on it.

The 2017 "travellers initiatives" (Transport Canada 2017d) underway at time of writing show some considerable intent by Transport Canada to be much more energetic regarding the regulation of air passengers' rights with the CTA being given, somewhat surprisingly, a lead air policy role but under greater ministerial supervision. The provisions regarding the liberalization of international ownership of air carriers from 25 to 49 per cent of voting interests for Canadian carriers is also now underway as are the CATSA screening services expansion on a cost recovery basis.

8

The Transportation in Cities and Federal Infrastructure Policy Domain

INTRODUCTION

This chapter examines the nature and impact of transportation policy in Canadian cities and the effect of federal infrastructure spending on municipal transportation. Cities are hugely important for all kinds of reasons. First, 65 to 70 per cent of Canadians live in them. Second, cities are the country's primary engines and locations of economic activity. And third, they account for virtually all of Canada's transportation terminals, which means that most people and goods travel in cities or through them.

That is no accident. Virtually every major city in the world is located on a trade route, and those are usually at the confluence of two rivers, where a river flows into a lake or sea, at a natural harbour, where a railway line crosses a river, or at the uppermost point of navigation on a river. Cities grow in those locations because geography and the flow of commerce make it possible, necessary, or convenient for transportation to serve trade there. "Trade" includes people travelling on business, which has raised the contribution of airports and air travel to urban growth since the dawn of commercial aviation in the mid-1900s.

Cities come in all kinds of sizes and characteristics, and no two are identical. For the purposes of this chapter we concentrate on Canada's roughly seven to ten largest urban regions because there is a strong correlation between a city's population and the degree to which its transportation systems fall short of meeting the mobility needs of its residents. In other words, large cities almost always have more severe transportation problems than small ones. That makes larger cities useful objects of study about what works and what does not. But the basic phenomena are universal and vary only in degree. As anyone who has lived for years in an urban area that grew significantly will surely attest, congestion and travel delays do not suddenly appear out of nowhere – they emerge when the city is small and get steadily worse as it expands.

Infrastructure figures prominently in this chapter, especially the way in which it is influenced by federal policy and federal spending. As in earlier chapters, we take a broad view of "infrastructure" to include physical capital assets – like roads, bridges, parking garages, subway lines, intermodal terminals, and port facilities – and also the softer, intellectual/analytical side of infrastructure. By that we mean things like institutional competence in planning and managing city layouts, zoning, and traffic movement, and in setting policies for parking, collecting (or waiving) user fees, and dozens of other things that affect urban mobility. Both the hard and soft kinds of infrastructure are indispensable, but the former is the only aspect of infrastructure that most people see. Yet when city drivers are stuck in a traffic jam, their plight is usually caused by a failure on the soft side of things – poorly designed urban layouts, roadway designs that cause turbulence in the traffic flow, road maintenance that closes lanes at rush hour, unwillingness of governments to discourage over use of a finite asset (i.e., road capacity), and so on. In short, "soft" failures cause most cities to get far less performance out of their physical transportation infrastructure than they could and should. But unfortunately, that side of infrastructure does not get much shrift in transportation policy, a finding we discussed earlier in chapters 2 and 6.

This chapter looks at the domain through the lens of two policy and governance histories. The first is about the elusive quest for urban mobility covering a period from the 1960s to the present. Mobility is a sought-after goal but one that has, for decades, been sliding farther away as the rate of production, ownership, and use of passenger cars overtook road capacity resulting in what one author has called "carmageddon" (Monbiot 2016). The second policy history, covering a period from the mid-1990s to the present, deals with the financing of transportation infrastructure in cities by federal funding programs and the degree to which they actually contribute to real mobility benefits instead of merely satisfying the urge to practice retail distributive politics.

The analysis builds on our discussion in chapter 1 of the dynamics of congestion in cities as well as the emergence and nature of federal infrastructure policy in urban policy and governance. Some of the latter reaches back to the early 1980s and even before, when federal urban policy was intentionally fostered by the creation in the Pierre Trudeau era of the Ministry of State for Urban Affairs (Cameron 1974) and by policies on housing and infrastructure that appeared around the same time. There were impacts on municipal transportation infrastructure arising from changes to airport policy and governance, too, and even tourism, as we discussed in chapter 7. And in chapter 10 we will explore the impact of disruptive technology-enabled transport, for example, from ride-hailing services like Uber on the municipal taxi industry and the advent of probably even more far-reaching innovations like driverless cars. When technologies like these succeed in the marketplace, they have the potential to overturn traditional policy ideas and agendas in the development, use, and financing of municipal infrastructure depending on how cities and also provincial governments respond to or adapt governing institutions and how quickly and effectively, given democratic needs and views.

One of the most salient points we raised in chapter 6, on rail freight transportation, is the twin concepts of system optimization and primary goal analysis – in other words, the effect of a primary goal in determining the direction in which the optimization will go – and how both are affected detrimentally by policy inertia. The same two concepts apply to municipalities and mobility as well, hence their value in offering a complementary focus on complex multimodal transport policy analysis. In fact, their application is of greater significance here than it was in chapter 6 because the policy and governance environment in cities is even more complex than it is on railways. That shows up in this chapter's first policy history. It focuses on why mobility is increasingly elusive and why it resists policy and governance efforts to enhance it. It also partly explains why a simple focus on the reduction of congestion doesn't take anyone very far in the direction of improved mobility: because the reduction of congestion mainly represents an indicator of progress and not an actual solution. Policy inertia is the main feature in our second policy and governance history, too, but seen through a different lens – the dynamics of federal infrastructure funding directed to cities, both transportation and nontransportation alike, and how well it does or doesn't work.

The domain story in this chapter has connections to a much broader field of study, i.e., the politics and governance of Canadian cities and urban places and spheres including the above mentioned analytical approaches to city planning and land development policy. It is a large and growing field, as mentioned in chapter 1, but transportation seldom gets systematic attention in the core academic literature on the politics and government of cities. That is mainly because so many other policy fields intersect there (Bradford and Bramwell 2014; Graham and Andrew 2014; Filion et al. 2015; Broadbent 2002; Andrew 2001) and they take up most of the headlines. But urban transportation does get some coverage in the literature, for example, in general terms (Fowler and Layton 2001) and in terms of infrastructure (Andrew and Morrison 2001), federal infrastructure funding (Champagne 2014), and innovation in urban economics (Bradford and Bramwell 2014).

The intersection mentioned above makes it impossible to draw a clean line between transportation policy and urban policy. Leonardo da Vinci may have been right in saying "everything connects to everything else," but that aphorism is cold comfort because dealing properly with the urban policy aspects of transportation would double or triple the length of this book. In this chapter we choose to deal with urban transportation as it is – as a result of the way in which urban planning and land development policy have encouraged the growth of transportation demand – not as it might be if new paradigms for urban planning reduced the demand for mobility in the first place (which would not be a bad thing). Readers interested in the latter would do well to consult such thoughtful works as Litman 2017; Cervero, Guerra, and Al 2017; Giuliano and Hanson 2017; and Rodrique, Comptois, and Slack 2016.

In chapter 1 of this book we mentioned the effect on urban transportation of the *structure* of city governments, starting with Winnipeg and Halifax, to see how, if at all, structure affects transportation holistically as distinct from the way it affects components like roads, parking, sidewalks, cycle paths, and planning projects. Of course, differences in the sizes of cities and their growth patterns are important. We discuss large cities like Greater Toronto, Vancouver, and Montreal in this chapter as well as in chapter 10 where somewhat smaller municipalities like Edmonton, Calgary, and Ottawa enter the story in order to broaden the range of cities under discussion.

THE ELUSIVE QUEST FOR URBAN MOBILITY
(1960S TO PRESENT)

The essence of transportation is mobility. From a citizen's standpoint that means travelling with few (and ideally no) delays to his or her movement. From a business's standpoint that means moving its own goods in the least amount of time and with the greatest predictability. But from a *policy* standpoint, mobility means dealing with the collectivity of movements not just individual ones. There are crucial differences between the two. Optimization theory, as mentioned in chapter 6, holds that maximizing the mobility of people or goods individually actually *reduces* mobility for everyone as a whole. That is because "the end result of many local optima is certainly not the optimum of the total system" (Goldratt 1990, 121).

The big issue is traffic congestion, but, perhaps counterintuitively, avoiding congestion is not the same thing as achieving mobility. Congestion sets in when too many individuals access the transportation network at the same time. It is probably the single most serious constraint on urban mobility. Most city dwellers get trapped in it every day.

Congestion is likely to appear whenever separately driven objects are confined to a pathway, like cars on a road, trains on a railway line, ships in a canal, or aircraft in a flight path.

The notional graph below (adapted from Coleman 2015b, 48) gives a general idea. The dots represent hypothetical data points, and their scattering represents variability in what is being "measured." The two most important things to retain from the graph are (a) the curve's inverted "U" shape, beyond whose peak the flow of traffic starts going downhill and ultimately collapses, and (b) two "sweet spots" whose respective locations depend on the choice of primary goal – i.e., undelayed travel or maximum throughput. Those two goals are often used interchangeably in public discourse, but that promotes soggy thinking because they represent fundamentally different things. The users of an artery want undelayed travel. But its owners and financiers usually want maximum throughput.

The portion of the graph to the right of the peak is an operating zone where nobody gets any benefit at all. Every driver gets delayed in traffic, and the artery delivers little (and sometimes even no) throughput. Yet that is where things always end up whenever there is an overabundance of vehicles and nothing to constrain their use of

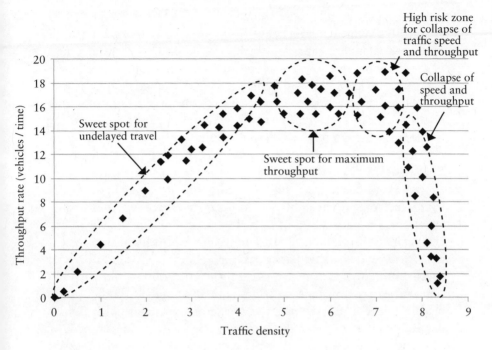

Figure 8.1 Notional throughput vs density on a traffic artery

the artery. Once the traffic density reaches the high-risk zone, mobility enters a fragile state because even the tiniest of perturbations can bring traffic to a standstill.

Managing congestion in real life is hard to do because, mathematically speaking, the phenomenon is highly nonlinear and highly stochastic. Traffic engineers work with those concepts all the time, but it seems doubtful that many city politicians keep them top-of-mind when (and if) they weigh the effect on traffic flow of the decisions they need to make. As a result, a lot of things that trigger traffic congestion – four-way stop signs, unsynchronized traffic lights, lane closures, "traffic calming" measures, and so on – get introduced by elected officials without fully appreciating the side effects on mobility. Unfortunately the side effects are seldom positive.

Once a city's core is designed and built, the downtown streets are generally fixed in width and therefore in carrying capacity, but as the city grows, the volume of traffic between the suburbs and the core goes up. So with each passing year, the roads leading into and out of the core get busier and more congested. One solution would be widening the downtown streets every so often, to keep pace with the growing demand for capacity, but that would mean demolishing most of the buildings every few years to make room for additional lanes.

Our premise in this first policy and governance history is that municipal transportation – in other words, the mobility of people and goods in cities – is caught in a seven-way trap that has been growing for decades and from which, despite recent signs of movement on the political front, most large cities in Canada seem unlikely to escape. That is what makes the quest to improve mobility so elusive.

The first trap is NIMBYism, a catchy acronym coined in the 1980s to capture some of the politics of location and place (not in my backyard) and certain aspects of the "free rider problem" that was first characterized by economists (Fast 2014). If the breadth of applicability is anything to go by, the "backyard" metaphor is a good one. It relates to all kinds of urban transport policy and politics, like airports (Dourado 2016), and is tangled up with any number of other policy fields that are a part of urban and federal–municipal policy, which makes it hard to disentangle from transportation in almost any kind of agenda setting. Worse, as published analyses of NIMBYism show, most citizens both support it and oppose it at the same time, depending on the nature of their personal interests (Innovative Research Group 2013; Keenan 2016a, 2016b, 2016c; Devine-Wright 2009). That makes it exasperatingly complex. Even the word "backyard" reflects the problem by connoting a fixed place without even acknowledging the existence or importance of personal mobility.

The second trap is related to the governance structure of many municipalities (Bradford and Bramwell 2014; Graham and Andrew 2014; Filion et al. 2015). City planning often works in ways that make growth-fuelled congestion worse (Fowler and Layton 2001) Especially in cases of the forced amalgamation of cities with their surrounding municipalities – a phenomenon in Ontario, Quebec, Nova Scotia, and Manitoba but not in Alberta, BC, Saskatchewan, New Brunswick, and Newfoundland and Labrador – the structure of city councils often gives disproportionate political weight to residents in the suburban and rural wards, as well as to land developers whose homebuilding on the city's periphery encourages people to live outside the core. That adds traffic to the road network used by those living outside the car-based core to commute to town and, because of lower property values, those in suburban and rural wards pay lower taxes, which, in turn, are insufficient to expand the capacity of the transportation network in proportion to the increased demand the new residents are placing on it (Stoney 2016). The only ostensible solution is a wholesale revamping of municipal governance, zoning, and taxation regimes. This is highly unlikely because each of those things is politically and democratically complex in the extreme.

The third trap is what we consider to be a widespread failure by governments to really understand the phenomenon of congestion. That is unfortunate because such an understanding is crucial for proper goal setting and for designing policy instruments needed to achieve whatever primary goal the city has decided upon. Yet we have seen no evidence in the literature (or elsewhere) of elected officials or policy advocates recognizing the "peaking" effect of traffic throughput or the existence of different sweet spots whose respective attractiveness depends on the primary goal actually being pursued.

As a result, even so thoughtful and refreshingly bold a report as "We Can't Get There from Here" (Ragan et al. 2015), which advocates widespread road pricing in Canada, argues that the primary goal (to use our terminology) should be to reduce congestion *per se*. It says that "the primary purpose of congestion pricing is to reduce traffic congestion" (ibid., 8) and that the "effectiveness" of a policy choice is synonymous with "reducing congestion" (ibid., 25, table 3).

But reduced congestion is not a "goal"; it is only a proxy for the goal of undelayed travel or maximum throughput of the artery. And congestion does not cause the problem; it is only a manifestation of the causes – i.e., the physics of vehicle performance, the characteristics of the roadway, the psychology of driver behaviour, and the dynamics of a complex system when exposed to perturbations. As a result, public discourse is, and probably always has been, sufficiently fuzzy when it comes to congestion that the selection of policy instruments to deal with it in Canadian cities is susceptible to misdirection. That is often what happens. The fact that many large cities are multiple city–municipal governments, rather than single organizations, does not help. The results do not augur well for the use of transportation infrastructure. To restate the issue, reducing congestion is nothing more than a means to an end. But what end? Undelayed travel ... even at the expense of reduced throughput?

The fourth trap is the historic unwillingness of governments in general, and elected officials in particular, to put a price on the use of roads. That idea is almost unanimously advocated by economists on the premise that people over-consume things that are underpriced and because the money raised would help recapitalize the infrastructure. For example, Flemming et al. (2013) argue for – and in six roundtables held across the country found general support for – road pricing (which, oddly, they refer to as "rationing"). But politicians have avoided or rejected the concept of tolling with almost equal unanimity on the premise that electors may turf them out if they try it.

Elected officials who ignored that premise in the past often paid a price at the ballot box. Flemming (2015, 9) describes the results: "The history of tolling roads and bridges in Canada is neither a pretty picture nor [one] that gives one much confidence that using tolls and road pricing are serious mechanisms to solve the ... problem." The provincial election in British Columbia in May 2017 seems to demonstrate the point. One of the sharper divisions among the three main political parties was over tolling of two major bridges in the Vancouver area. The NDP rejected tolls altogether, but the Liberals took a halfway position. Some observers, such as Meggs 2017 and Bailey 2017, considered this to be a battleground issue that cost the incumbent Liberals the election. That might not come as a surprise, in light of a three-fifths majority in a BC plebiscite two years earlier having rejected a 0.5 percentage point increase in sales tax to help fund a major transportation improvement program for Metro Vancouver.

Various bridges in Canada have been tolled over the decades. But the only tolled roads or highways of which we are aware are Highway 407 in Toronto, the Cobequid Pass in Nova Scotia, the Coquihalla Highway in BC, and the Canso Causeway in Nova Scotia (Flemming 2015). All were tolled from the outset, but none except Highway 407 has retained (or will retain) its toll beyond the date of paying off the debt that financed the original construction.

Those routes are provincial or federal. None is municipal. Other attempts at tolling have failed for political reasons. New Brunswick planned a toll on a new highway between Moncton and Fredericton in 2001 but cancelled it because of public outcry (ibid.). The City of Ottawa explored tolling part of an arterial highway in 2013 but the provincial minister of transport vetoed it (Willing 2016; Reevely 2016).

Economists are absolutely right about the effectiveness of putting a price on the use of transportation infrastructure. But the unwillingness of elected officials to do it, traps Canadian cities in a tragedy-of-the-commons situation in which users are constantly accessing public roads beyond the maximum carrying capacity of those very roads.

That disadvantages everybody, and it benefits nobody – except maybe politicians wanting to maintain their prospects of reelection.

And so, unless congestion is bad enough and infrastructure users aggrieved enough to compel daring remedies, as road pricing has been done with zone-based fees in London, Stockholm, Milan, Singapore, Norway, and on an experimental basis in New York City (Ragan et al., 13), not many municipal leaders, and essentially none in Canada, have yet been willing to bite that bullet.

But this is a fast moving story. The mayors of Toronto and Ottawa, both of whom stridently rejected the idea of road tolling, began championing tolls (Willing 2016; Reevely 2016; Coyne 2016). And the growing chorus from advocates like Flemming, Ragan, and others, may yet see this idea come into practice. From a policy standpoint that would be positive.

The fifth trap is related to the fourth. Even cities with the political leadership and courage to introduce user fees lack the authority to do so without provincial consent. That means there are always two potential vetoes facing every opportunity, not just one. The only exceptions are Vancouver and Toronto. No other Canadian city has delegated authority to apply road-user charges (Ragan et al., 8). In other words, the probability of a case for tolls succeeding is roughly the square of the probability of success if only one level of government has to approve it – for example, ¼ x ¼ = 1/16.

The sixth trap is the hoarding by provincial governments of various taxing powers and denying them to cities. Apart from property taxes, municipalities have no effective way of raising revenues for sustained investment in infrastructure, so they depend largely on transfers from higher levels of government – but those tend to come in spurts – and on capital loans that have to be repaid (Champagne 2014; Andrew 2001). It probably reflects provincial wariness of cities externalizing (to other jurisdictions) the cost of their policy decisions, but it is not a promising way to enhance urban mobility on a sustained basis.

The seventh trap is the intermixing by governments of multiple motives for introducing user fees. Historically, tolls were used to raise money for repaying loans that financed the original construction. But two other motives have risen to prominence in recent years. The first is to generate revenue for the repair of existing and failing infrastructure because increasingly cash strapped cities cannot afford to otherwise maintain that infrastructure (Bradford and Bramwell 2014). The second motive is to discourage people from over accessing the infrastructure. But, tolls will increase mobility only if the fees are set high enough to cause at least some of the drivers' financial discomfort. If the discomfort is moderate and drivers choose alternate routes, tolls will have helped suppress traffic volumes to around the sweet spot for maximum throughput. And if the fees, and therefore the discomfort, are set higher still, they will help suppress traffic volumes further, to around the sweet spot for undelayed travel.

The mayors of Toronto and Ottawa are acting on the first motive – levying tolls in order to raise money. No elected official of whom we are aware is advocating tolls for the purpose of reaching a sweet spot for mobility. Presumably that is either because they don't grasp the key concepts shown in figure 8.1 or, more likely, don't want to impose the amount of financial discomfort needed to actually discourage road usage. (The concession company managing Highway 407 is effectively pricing to reach a sweet spot for undelayed travel. Traffic on that artery nearly always moves freely.)

Unfortunately the two newer motives – generating revenue and discouraging overuse – tend to conflict with each other. A toll set high enough to raise revenues but low enough to at least try to avoid angering motorists almost certainly will not be enough to suppress traffic volumes to reach any sweet spot. As Coyne (2016) puts it, that approach would be terrible politics because "the worst way to sell road pricing is as another way for governments to pick your pocket, rather than cut their [own] costs. [Toronto Mayor John] Tory's plan may simply wind up discrediting the whole idea of road tolls." Then everyone would be further behind than they are now. Coyne's point is reinforced by Flemming (2015, 9), who says that surveys show a slim majority of Canadians support the idea in principle "but only if *tangible benefits* can be proved to emanate from tolling" [emphasis in original]. With no traffic sweet spot on offer from a municipal government, it's hard to imagine road users swooning over the benefit they will receive from having their tolls used to maintain distant infrastructure that the city formerly neglected.

There may be reason for optimism in greater Vancouver. Mayors there began exploring a more extensive plan in the works called "comprehensive mobility pricing." That may reflect the fact that in 2016, according to TomTom, a GPS navigation firm, Vancouver was the most congested city in Canada and fourth in North America, surpassing even New York. Meanwhile Ottawa, on at least a dozen of its main arteries, is introducing "complete streets" that feature wider sidewalks, semiprotected bicycle lanes, cycling stoplights, sculpted intersections, yield signs, stop signs, new driving patterns, "zig-zaggy white lines of uncertain meaning," and so on (Egan 2016). It will be amazing if that doesn't make citywide congestion substantially worse.

Unless congestion is debilitating enough to compel progress, about the only hope for greater mobility and for escaping the seven-way trap seems to be (a) greater amounts of courage from municipal leaders, (b) a significant transfer of tax points to municipalities, (c) infrastructure banks, (d) the rigorous setting and pursuing, by federal infrastructure funding programs, of goals for mobility sweet spots, and (e) driverless cars. We deal with infrastructure programs in the second policy history in this chapter and with the issue of driverless cars in chapter 10.

In summary, the use of, and the need for, financial incentives to improve urban mobility has been driven by the steady growth of automobile traffic that started in the years following World War II, aided by municipal governance structures that encourage commuting from the suburbs. Tolling has been used occasionally over the years, albeit mainly for bridges rather than roads, but, anyway, the associated fees were nearly always tied to paying off the original loans and then were removed. There has been little if any uptake by most Canadian municipalities of setting tolls high enough to discourage the overuse of transportation infrastructure or even the use of non-financial alternatives like ramp metering or variable-rate parking. Recent noises by Toronto and Ottawa mayors about applying tolls to selected roads are aimed at raising revenues not at discouraging overuse, and that is unlikely to produce a sweet spot of any kind.

All this represents policy inertia and the de facto acceptance of a continuing decline in urban mobility. Unless something bolder is tried, and succeeds, the credibility of user charges seems likely to be undermined. That would make the prospects of enhancing urban mobility even dimmer in future than they have been in the past.

FOLLOW THE MONEY:
THE DODGY EVOLUTION OF FEDERAL FINANCING OF URBAN TRANSPORTATION INFRASTRUCTURE (MID-1980S TO PRESENT)

The second policy history in our domain analysis deals with the federal financing of transportation infrastructure. It is not easy to separate urban from nonurban because everything is bundled together in government funding programs that make little or no distinction between one and the other. That in itself is an important part of the story.

While there are earlier 1980s features to the story as set out further below, our opening premise is that, beginning in about the mid-1990s with major budget cuts during program review (Doern, Maslove, and Prince 2013), the federal government has walked farther and farther away from taking a strategic interest in transportation infrastructure. The retreat initially was driven by budget cutting and the expedient downloading of costs onto lower levels of government, and by the divesting of ownership of federal assets, and it has been sustained by (a) the cash accounting practices of governments (Doern, Maslove, and Prince 2013; Auld 1985), (b) the continued elevation of retail distributive infrastructure politics above the pursuit of goals more relevant to transportation, and (c) a shortfall of competence in government with respect to the technical disciplines needed for sustaining and enhancing mobility.

We argue that federal financing has consisted primarily of spraying money around the country for political advantage with almost no strategic purpose in transportation. To the degree that some benefits actually accrue from federal "investments" along these lines, they do little or nothing to serve a primary goal in transportation. There are two notable exceptions: the Asia–Pacific Gateways and Corridors Initiative starting in 2006, which is still recalled by leading transport practitioners as a major success for mobility in general and railway traffic throughput in particular, and the Gordie Howe Bridge, which we described in chapter 3. Neither of those initiatives is primarily an urban story, although support for the Gordie Howe Bridge reflected in part the influence of a Windsor-based minister of Finance, Dwight Duncan, in the provincial government.

This policy history is really about money and, in particular, the policy frameworks surrounding federal government decisions to spend infrastructure money (or not), the conditions they attach to such spending, what the money gets used for, and the actual results and impact of having spent it.

The strategic retreat from transportation can be traced back to the completion of the St Lawrence Seaway in the 1950s. (See chapter 3.) There have been no transportation projects of such nation-building scope since then. In their place has come the practice of dispensing federal money for projects conceived by lower levels of government with the federal government acting as fiscal benefactor. (The increase in spending was also partly a result of the growth of lobbying clout in Ottawa of the Federation of Canadian Municipalities [Doern, Auld, and Stoney 2015, 260–7].) As Flemming (2015, 11) puts it, "more than 95 per cent of Canada's infrastructure spending is controlled by provinces, territories and municipalities. The federal government in 2015 is really a bystander." "Except for dispensing the money," he might have added.

Until about two decades ago, most infrastructure works funded by the federal government were announced one or two projects at a time, as we show in chapter 2's history of federal budget speeches. But subsequently, the federal government assembled various pots of money to which provinces and municipalities could submit proposals. One of the first, in 1994, was the Canada Infrastructure Works Program. It ran until 1999. A 1997 bulletin described the infrastructure projects it had supported. Of the twenty-two, only six were for transportation. Of those, four were mainly to repave roads; two involved adding road capacity, and one of those was for a logging road that probably should have been paid for by the forestry company that used it. Only a single project consisted of doing anything – adding road capacity – to increase urban mobility. The sixteen nontransportation projects paid for things like putting up an administration building, an art gallery, a fermentation facility, and a fire hydrant (Canada Minister of Infrastructure 1997). It is hard *not* to see the sheer ad hocery of the program.

Things didn't change much in subsequent programs. In 2001 the federal government created three new pots of money, aimed at "municipal rural infrastructure," "strategic infrastructure," and "border infrastructure." The latter had a strong de facto component of transportation, but the other two did not.

The lack of specificity kept recurring. For example, the background sections of budget 2004 referred to transportation as a "challenge" that municipalities were facing (Department of Finance Canada 2004, 163), and its section on budget measures spoke frothily about supporting them with federal money (ibid., 165). But despite the fact that the single largest backlog in municipal infrastructure, at 35 per cent of the total gap, was for transportation (Whiteside 2016, 65), the budget measures said nothing about making sure the money actually went towards that. Unfortunately, the enabling legislation for the new Canada Infrastructure Bank (Statutes of Canada 2017) (see more below) is no more specific than earlier statements on what that federal money is earmarked to buy.

In order to qualify for funding, projects have to fit into prescribed categories in these programs. That probably seems like a reasonable way of providing strategic direction, but the number of categories has ballooned to the point that not many expenditures *aren't* eligible, and anyway the criteria are vague enough to leave plenty of manoeuvring room, as we show further below. The result is an institutionalized version of what Flemming (2015, 11) calls "parish pump politics." Whatever strategic considerations there may have been in decades gone by, those have largely melted away. Soberman (2010, 8) says the funding of city transit has boiled down to "a chorus of pleas for more dollars."

Why such unquenched thirst by cities for federal and provincial money for transportation infrastructure? There are five main reasons. First, as seen in our first policy history, is the growth of urban population and car ownership. That began in earnest in the 1950s and eventually reached the point of traffic density being high enough to trigger congestion on more roadways, in more cities, for longer periods of the day – and most solutions to that problem cost money.

Second is the decades-long federal withdrawal from infrastructure ownership, leaving municipal and provincial governments with greater responsibility for transportation than in the past. Whiteside (2016, 67–8) shows that the proportion of Canadian capital stock owned by the federal government fell by 31 percentage points between 1955 and 2011, while the fraction owned by municipalities went the other way, climbing by 30 points. Associated with that are the disproportionate share of federal spending cuts often visited on transportation. In the February 1995 federal budget, for example, transportation took 51 per cent of the government-wide hit.

The third reason for municipal thirst is the broad downloading of financial responsibilities to cities from higher levels of government since the 1990s. Without commensurate increases in their taxing power, that leaves most cities short of money. Today they receive only 8 per cent of tax revenue in Canada (ibid., 65).

Fourth, and crucially, the continued use by most governments of "cash accounting" renders them largely blind to the growing liability for recapitalizing their assets, and it discourages or prevents them from accumulating a reserve for major investments coming due in future years (Canadian Chamber of Commerce 2013).

Fifth, federal funding programs support only new construction, which means the federal government "has no ongoing liability for projects financed by its Building Canada money" (Flemming 2015, 11). The bias in favour of constructing shiny new stuff is driven primarily by a "lack of political rewards for undertaking routine maintenance and rehabilitation" (ibid., 13). It leaves municipalities holding the bag for the cost of maintaining and recapitalizing their constantly growing stock of transportation infrastructure. No wonder they're thirsty for federal money. It's a dependency that won't go away. About 35 per cent of the liability for deferred maintenance of infrastructure in Canada is for transportation (Mirza, cited by Whiteside 2016, 65), the largest single category of all.

For a transportation funding program to be purposeful, strategic, and committed to delivering results of real importance, we would expect to see three things:

1   a clear statement of the primary goal the program is intended to achieve and a clear definition of what constitutes "success"
2   a requirement that each submission to the program include a solid analysis that demonstrates a *shortfall of mobility* (as manifested in travel times or throughput capacity) and the degree to which the project will achieve that
3   a requirement that each submission show a clear plan to measure the project's impact after completion

David Dodge, former governor of the Bank of Canada, described the concept of "purposefulness" with a useful analogy: "Shovel-readiness is not exactly the criterion you should use; the criterion the government should be using is 'What's going to produce the greatest opportunity for growth in the future?'" (Dodge 2016). In other words, he was advocating economic growth as the primary goal and urging the feds to keep other money-dispensing temptations in check while pursuing it. Specialists in systems optimization would cheer. Unfortunately that's not what has happened in transportation infrastructure over the years.

The screening criteria for the many infrastructure funds that cropped up since 2001 give little or no weight to the contribution a project is expected make to any primary goal. None of the three things that we would expect to see, listed above, is much in evidence in any of them. Most of their detailed requirements are about process, project management, due diligence, and other things to ensure prudence and probity in spending public money. No one doubts those are necessary. But they are not sufficient to ensure the accomplishment of anything strategic, except perhaps in terms of retail politics. When it comes to actually improving transportation, there is a gaping policy void.

Something important happened in 2008–09. As the recession started to bite, federal opposition parties demanded the minority Harper government commit to large-scale stimulus spending or they would trigger an election the Conservatives did not want (Pal 2011). The result was $30 billion of new money. The main targets were infrastructure in general, and transportation and cities in particular. The politics of the situation created a new primary goal – job creation-cum-economic growth. Useful as that goal may have been, it embodied only an incidental connection to transportation. So you could expect the results of dispensing the money to have no more than a coincidental effect on the mobility challenges described earlier in this chapter.

We have sampled several years of Infrastructure Canada's reports on plans and priorities for three major funds: the Canada Strategic Infrastructure Fund (CSIF), the Building Canada Fund (BCF), and the Border Infrastructure Fund (BIF). Those reports are submitted to Treasury Board as an integral part of federal accountability requirements, so ostensibly they represent the definitive government account. Two of the three funds predated the 2008 recession, but one arose from it. We describe all three below, then describe others that have proliferated more recently. There are so many of them that our account is almost certain to be incomplete.

Canada Strategic Infrastructure Fund

The idea for this program originated with the Chrétien–Martin Liberals in 2001, who, fresh from slaying the federal deficit, seemed awash with money that was burning a hole in their pockets. If this fund doesn't look like a licence to shill, nothing does. The eligible categories are infrastructure for highways and rail, local transportation, tourism or urban development, water or sewage, and "other categories approved by regulation" (Infrastructure Canada 2015a): in other words, potentially anything. There are *bon mots* about directing the money to things that are "vital" to economic growth and

Canadians' quality of life, but there is no mention of how those categories were chosen.

Transportation is intermixed with all the others, with no apparent priority assigned to any of the categories. Municipalities qualify, but so does everything else. There is no evidence of focusing on bottlenecks that restrict mobility or the things that are necessary and sufficient to reach any other transportation goal. The planned outcomes are to "facilitate" and "ensure" the safe and efficient movement of goods and people, "ease" congestion or reduce greenhouse gas emissions (GHGs), "continue to contribute to" the economic well-being of Canadians and "serve as a bridge" between Canada and the world, or "ensure" that drinking water is safe "at drinking water facilities" and that wastewater treatment is "sustainable." Anyone seeking a basis in those words to hold the government accountable for achieving something with the fund – in transportation or anything else (apart from spending money) – is likely to be disappointed.

We studied the fund's annual "Plans, Spending and Results" reports to Treasury Board each year from 2007–08 to 2014–15. Each one gives the number, value, and description of projects that received funding and how they contribute to the goals of the program. But the latter are hollow because they simply repeat the program's advertised outcomes, and nothing is mentioned about the projects' actual impacts. In other words, reporting on the fund has been set up almost as a tautology – the money is being spent on what the parliamentary estimates said it would be. That speaks to diligent program administration, but it says nothing – zero – about whether the program is serving the primary function of transportation in cities, i.e., mobility.

Building Canada Fund

This program was announced in the 2007 federal budget under the Harper Conservatives just as the economic meltdown started to bite. It was intended to run for seven years. Unlike earlier programs aimed primarily if not transparently at dispensing federal money for partisan political ends, this one was aimed at stimulating the faltering economy. Speed of spending suddenly mattered. It identified fifteen priorities, which is tantamount to having no priorities. They are just bins. Six of them were for transportation, of which three (public transit, regional and local airports, and local roads and bridges) were decid-edly municipal. In fact, more than half of its $33 billion total was slated to flow to cities (Department of Finance Canada 2008, 131). The BCF's largest component was the Federal Gas Tax Fund (FGTF), aimed specifically at cities. We describe it further below.

Over the following eight years the BCF went forth and multiplied, and it scooped up other funds that had preceded it. In addition to the FGTF, its daughters and step-daughters included the Infrastructure Stimulus Fund (2009–12, total $4 billion), the Municipal Rural Infrastructure Fund (2004–14, total $1.2 billion), the Border Infrastructure Fund (2003–14, total $600 million), the Canada Strategic Infrastructure Fund (2003–13, total $4.3 billion), the G8 Legacy Fund (2009–11, total $50 million), the Infrastructure Canada Program (2003–14, total $600 million), the National Recreational Trails Fund (2009–10, total $25 million), and the Public Transit Fund (2003–14, total $400 million). As of early 2015, all of these funds had stopped accepting new applications and were being wound down (Infrastructure Canada 2015b). But (quelle surprise) they were replaced by a bigger and better fund in 2014.

The BCF's expected outcomes were "to deliver infrastructure that matters to Canadians" and were aimed at "supporting broad federal priorities" (Infrastructure Canada 2015a). The fund has two compo-nents: major infrastructure and communities. The latter seems to be roughly synonymous with "nonmajor," which means that between the two categories not much is left out. And the major infrastructure com-ponent is split into transportation and nontransportation, which doesn't seem to leave much out either. But when it comes to pursuing goals, enhancing mobility, achieving results, and establishing accountability, similar problems apply here as those described above for the CSIF.

Border Infrastructure Fund

This is the third and smallest fund managed by Infrastructure Canada as a "horizontal initiative." It has little if anything to do with munici-palities, but we mention it anyway because it has a modicum of strategic targeting that the previous two lack.

BIF came into effect in 2003–04. Designed to fund infrastructure projects that "help sustain and increase the long-term efficiency" of Canada–US movements, its "focus was on projects at or near the busiest Canada–U.S. border crossings" (Infrastructure Canada

2011, 8). That means it was aimed at increasing mobility – i.e., unde-layed travel and throughput capacity – at potential bottlenecks. From a transportation standpoint, that is an excellent place to start. And a report on the projects that were funded shows that much of the money did indeed go to busy border crossings (Infrastructure Canada 2011; Bureau of Transportation Statistics 2011).

Even here, however, there are three concerns. First, the busiest or largest crossings are not necessarily those with the most significant bottlenecks or where investing money will do anything to increase mobility. Second, there are a few dodgy projects in the mix. At least three improvements were to highways that stop fifteen to forty kilo-metres short of the border, including one in central Vancouver. And third, the fund's annual performance highlights as submitted to the federal Treasury Board for 2011–12 to 2015–16 (e.g., Treasury Board of Canada Secretariat 2015) said that the progress of ongoing projects had been "monitored" and that various of the projects had been completed, but nothing is mentioned about their impact on mobility. For all we know, the impact may have been zero, which seems unlikely, but that is not the point. The point is that no one seems to be speak-ing to the primary goal that ought to be the basis on which money gets invested in transportation related projects, i.e., mobility. *En pas-sant*, we note that money from this fund was used to create a G8 Legacy Fund that paid for building tourist infrastructure (including gazebos) in the riding of then-president of the Treasury Board, Tony Clement, which is nowhere near a border (Auditor General of Canada 2011, chapter 2).

New Building Canada Fund

In 2014 the original Building Canada Fund was replaced by the New Building Canada Plan (NBC Plan). It includes the $14 billion New Building Canada Fund (NBCF), which, despite having fewer elements than its predecessor, has no apparent diminution of scope or coverage. It in turn has two components: national infrastructure and provincial–territorial infrastructure. Both are expected to "sup-port projects of national, regional and local significance" (Infrastructure Canada 2016b, 2) – in other words, potentially almost anything. Other funds contained in the NBC Plan are a $32 billion Community Improvement Fund (with two subcomponents, the Federal Gas Tax Fund, mentioned earlier and described below, and the incremental

Goods and Services Tax Rebate for Municipalities), and a $1.25 bil-
lion P3 (Public–Private Partnerships) Canada Fund (ibid.).

The plan is intended to support projects that "promote economic
growth, job creation and productivity." Unfortunately that doesn't
guarantee much focus because its twenty-plus eligible categories
pretty well cover the waterfront. Space does not permit listing them
all, but here is a taste: highways and roads, public transit, rail infrastructure, local and regional airports, port infrastructure, intelligent
transportation systems, drinking water, solid waste management,
connectivity and broadband, innovation, green energy, culture, and
tourism. Municipal transportation qualifies, but so does almost
anything else.

Gratifyingly, the national component says it supports increased
mobility, reduced congestion, "managed" traffic volume, and reduced
travel time (Infrastructure Canada 2016e, Annex A). Those are important for transportation. But again we have three concerns. First, amazingly, projects do not necessarily have to be a priority in the applicant's
longer term plans (ibid., 5). That probably removes much of the
discipline needed for dealing effectively with the continuing growth
of impediments to mobility. Second, some of the fund's elements
require applicants to demonstrate only that their proposal is based
on "current demand," not growth in future demand. That means city
governments are given a free pass if they don't bother trying to get
ahead of the curve. And third, it is unlikely that many of the applicants
have the internal capacity to assess what it actually takes to reduce
congestion. We say more about that further below.

Federal Gas Tax Fund

Introduced in 2005 and slated to run to 2014, the FGTF was made
permanent in 2008 and rolled into the NBC Plan when the latter was
created in 2014. Conceptually simple, it transferred money to municipalities. As of 2014, the rate of transfer was $2 billion annually. Cities
may spend the money on projects that fit into any of eighteen (!)
categories. The number and breadth should give governments no
shortage of manoeuvring room to fund just about anything.

Six of the categories relate specifically to transportation. Another
three might or might not, depending on the project. Nine do not. We
have found no explanation for why those particular categories were
chosen. They just were. It seems odd that a fund whose coffers are

replenished by a tax on fuel used specifically for transportation is not fully dedicated to improving transportation *per se* or to dealing with its side-effects like energy, emissions, and safety. The featureless inter-mixing of transportation with everything else is almost *prima facie* evidence that there is no primary goal of dealing with real-life prob-lems of mobility in Canadian cities.

The budget documents mention no criteria for accepting or turning down a given project. They say it is based on "merit" but with no elaboration on what that means. They speak about "partnerships" with municipalities, but the only basis of partnering seems to be the federal government agreeing to donate money and cities agreeing to accept it. They say the money is being spent on strategic things, but they don't say what "strategic" amounts to. They say the programs are proving to be successful, but there is no explanation of what "success" is. They do not mention any particular goal, which means that it is impossible to gauge success. The budget documents strongly suggest that the only real goal consists of pushing money out the door and that "success" consists of taking credit for doing so.

Naturally, there are supplementary documents to elaborate on the fund and its terms and conditions. They refer to "mobility," which is a good thing. Readers are urged to explore the documents with a critical eye, in search of a clear understanding of what the fund truly thinks "mobility" consists of and what it takes to deliver it. Our review strongly suggests a vacancy in that regard.

Retrospective reports on the F G T F's results give a further indication of how strategic the fund is *not*. In the public transit category, for example, Infrastructure Canada reports that in the "*spending trends indicate* that transit investments focus on expansion and renewal of existing service systems" [emphasis added] (Infrastructure Canada 2016a). In other words, the "results" consist of whatever the money happened to be spent on. That is a tautology. It is hard to find evidence of improvements in undelayed travel or throughput capacity – the only transportation goals of any significance.

P3 Canada Fund

We touch on the concept of Public–Private Partnerships (P 3 s) here because it became an integral part of the federal infrastructure agenda whose effect was to shift the financial burden from the public sector to the private (Whiteside 2016, 72–80; Demers and Demers 2016).

The idea of P3s gained currency in the 1970s and 1980s. Canada's first significant P3s were the Confederation Bridge (opened in 1997) and Highway 407 (sold to a Canadian-Spanish consortium in 1998). Both were transportation assets. The pace accelerated under the newly minted Harper Conservatives: "When new infrastructure funding was announced in 2007, the Canadian government decided to create a new P3 office – PPP Canada – to foster this development of the P3 market and to encourage consideration of the use of P3s" (PPP Canada 2009a, 6). The federal government obliged municipalities submitting proposals to the P3 Canada Fund – endowed with $1.2 billion for infrastructure investment – to evaluate P3s as an option to reveal if theirs was a good fit. But organizations similar to PPP Canada already existed in Alberta, Saskatchewan, Nova Scotia, and Prince Edward Island, and you don't have to look very far to see evidence that the premise behind PPP Canada's creation was largely imaginary.

Early documents seem to show that P3s were a solution in search of a problem. PPP Canada's corporate mission was "to further develop the Canadian P3 market" (ibid., 2), but its first annual report gave only a weak explanation of why the organization needed to exist in the first place and no evidence that P3s were needed to fill a strategic role. And the reports gave no hint that PPP Canada had any greater purpose than to follow an unquestioned belief by the government of the day in P3s and no evidence that in Canada there was P3 "market failure" – although that is usually the *ne plus ultra* test for governments to involve themselves in the marketplace at all.

On the contrary, PPP Canada's first annual report tacitly conceded that no market failure was known to exist: "The Corporation felt that in order to fulfill the corporate mandate outlined above, it was critical to **understand fully the dynamics of the market** and build on the best practices demonstrated by its provincial counterparts" [emphasis added] (ibid., 14). And the underlying premise for promoting P3s was largely debunked soon afterwards by PPP Canada's Amended Corporate Plan 2008 to 2012 which reported that "the use of PPP models to build and renovate Canada's public infrastructure is [already] increasing" (PPP Canada 2009b, 7) and that the "market for large ... and medium-size projects ... is well served by existing financiers" (ibid., 13). Moreover, none of the organization's six corporate objectives (PPP Canada 2009a, 12) speaks directly to its ostensible *raison d'être* of developing the P3 marketplace. *If* there is evidence in PPP Canada's early documents to suggest that the government's push for P3s was based on anything besides political dogma to favour the private sector's involvement in infrastructure, we have not been able to detect it.

And the future? PPP Canada, and the P3 Canada fund with which it was endowed, originally were presented as a gap filling measure that by rights you would expect to sunset when the "work to support the development of a dynamic and efficient P3 market" was accomplished (ibid., 6). But subsequent documents show the organization has taken on a life of its own. By 2015–16 its corporate plan did not even mention the original mission of developing the P3 market (PPP Canada 2015–16, 4), and it commits the organization to "strive to be the provider of choice" (ibid., 5), which is tantamount to an admission that competitors exist and are already doing roughly the same thing. Eight years after its launch, PPP Canada is still active and shows no sign of having achieved its original mission or of closing up shop anytime soon. It seems like an organization perpetuating itself long after its original mission was forgotten.

Should P3s be involved in financing municipal transportation infrastructure in the first place? Maybe. It is a relatively new idea that private-sector money could finance public infrastructure that traditionally was paid for by public institutions. Private sector companies are always investing in infrastructure for their own use, and much of it has public impacts (not all necessarily positive). But the idea of private money financing assets that are intended primarily or exclusively for use by the public is attractive for several reasons. It relieves municipal governments from having to drum up the money from taxes or bonds. And private-sector responsibility in the construction phase often works out better than government-managed operations do, probably because companies are more serious than governments about holding their construction managers' feet to the fire, which infuses the process with discipline that helps prevent cost overruns.

Yet not everyone is convinced the benefits are worth it. Whiteside (72–8) gives a penetrating critique of P3s that exposes serious flaws in the concept. And she points out that the P3 model actually "is a mechanism of infrastructure *financing*, not *funding*" [emphasis in original] (ibid., 74). That is an important distinction: it means that roughly the same people – those who use transportation infrastructure – are ultimately paying the bill under a P3 scenario just as they would in its absence. And finally, she observes that, in Ontario, the province most eager to use P3s for its public infrastructure, "there has yet to be any systematic analysis of the track record of risk and performance associated with traditional public procurement" (ibid.). In other words, much of the solid justification missing from public documents when PPP Canada and the P3 Canada Fund were created still seems to be missing today.

By the end of 2015–16 the federal government had spent or committed more than $1.3 billion in more than twenty P3 projects through the P3 Canada Fund, including in twelve municipalities, with an additional $6.6 billion from other sources (PPP Canada 2016, 6). Fifty-eight per cent of the projects were for transportation infrastructure, (ibid., 22).

Public Transit Infrastructure Fund

This is a recent addition to the smorgasbord of funding programs. Announced as part of the Justin Trudeau Liberal budget 2016, it is aimed specifically at city transportation. But it seems rather tentative, with an expiry date just two years after its launch on 1 April 2016. All three illustrative examples in the announcement are rail related (Infrastructure Canada 2016c). Gratifyingly, one of the categories is the expansion of soft capabilities – including "asset management capacity" and "demand management measures and studies." But there is no ongoing funding to sustain those capabilities, and, anyway, no explicit justification is mentioned in terms of increased transit ridership or urban mobility.

The fund is predicated on the idea that better transit systems will get more people out of their cars. That is not necessarily valid. Soberman puts his finger on a flaw in the premise that pouring large amounts of money into transit infrastructure will cause ridership to grow, and he says, "Massive investments in transit infrastructure ... are predicated on the assumption that they will generate profound changes in travel behaviour" and on "an optimistically large increase" in ridership by those who have a choice (Soberman 2010, 14). He argues that the supply of riders who do not have a choice and therefore *must* use transit is a relatively fixed number. That means the hoped for growth will come only from those people who *do* have a choice. Technology and equipment aren't the key to making those people switch to transit. Yet that is what the money will buy. What matters to them are good service and a positive experience, and money alone will not buy that. At the time of writing there is no information on which to base a comment about the program's uptake or its results.

When seen from the viewpoint of cities, the buffet of funding programs offers potentially unlimited opportunities to get money for things each city wants or needs. But all is not well. "Cities must still come up with iterative or piecemeal proposals for federal funding on a project-by-project basis. This discourages integrated long run planning and ensures Ottawa's commitment remains sufficiently vague as to what exactly will be funded, when, and to what degree" (Whiteside 2016, 70).

The lack of strategic focus by federal infrastructure programs on making solid improvements in mobility downloads the responsibility for providing such a focus onto the provinces and municipalities. Unfortunately the capability to do that doesn't seem to be there either. "Many municipalities, through limitations of staff and money, lack the internal capacity to assess the state of their infrastructure. A significant percentage report that they have no information on the condition of their assets nor do they have any programs to collect condition or capacity information" (Canadian Chamber of Commerce 2013, 9). So imagine the state of their internal capacity to assess such mathematically complex things as unsteady flow rates, nonlinear relationships, stochastic data sets, traffic perturbations, network optimization, and other things that are crucial for evaluating mobility. But cities continue to apply for the proffered money, even for projects of convenience. As a respected authority recently said to one of the authors, "City planning departments always have these kind of projects on the books so they can be 'shovel-ready' really quickly."

It's not just cities. The same respected authority pointed out that most "provincial transportation departments are really highway construction departments, filled with civil engineers, so there has been a built-in bias toward road construction. Yes, you get the odd arena or other local boondoggle, but mostly you just get asphalt."

The upshot is this: there is not much evidence of any level of government having the competence needed for determining precisely where to make infrastructure investments that improve urban transportation in a way that gets to the heart of mobility. Yet money flows to them from federal programs anyway, on account of the attractiveness to elected officials of practicing distributive retail politics.

Infrastructure Banks

Until the federal budget update in November 2016 the concept of creating one or more infrastructure banks (iBanks) in Canada did not seem to have legs, despite being advocated for some time by many individuals and think tanks. The idea is for private investors to underwrite large funds that invest in transportation (and other) infrastructure projects and get a return over the life of the asset. Flemming (2014) describes several iBank models that might work. Some already exist in the EU, Nigeria, India, Germany, the Netherlands, and about forty US states, and are being seriously considered in the UK and Thailand. There are several motivations behind them. Take demand, for example. Public sources of investment by themselves almost certainly cannot keep up with the need for recapitalizing the existing stock of infrastructure or sufficiently adding to it. Even if the federal government devoted the equivalent of 1 per cent of GDP (about $18 billion annually) the amount would come nowhere near solving the infrastructure deficit (Flemming 2014, 9).

Things seem to be moving fast. The federal Advisory Council on Economic Growth (2016) recommended the establishment of a Canadian infrastructure development bank (CIDB). Its central arguments emphasized transportation infrastructure. In the budget update of November 2016 the Trudeau Liberals announced their intention to go down that path with the creation of a Canada Infrastructure Bank. They linked that announcement soon afterwards to major meetings with global investors as well as key Canadian pension investment agencies such as Canada Pension Plan Investment Board, the Ontario Teachers Pension Plan, and the Caisse de Depôt et Placement du Québec (Shecter and Hasselback 2016; Wells 2016). Legislation to create the Canada Infrastructure Bank has been passed (Infrastructure Canada 2017a). Some of its provisions came as surprise.

They seem likely to compromise the basic concept, perhaps seriously. For example, the federal government's financial participation in, and its control over, the bank's investment decisions will perpetuate the fourth trap described in our first policy and governance history, i.e., the perennial avoidance for political reasons of putting a price on the use of roads and other transportation infrastructure. (See more below.)

At a global conference of the Canadian Council of Public–Private Partnerships, Transport Minister Marc Garneau focused on the $10.1 billion in trade transportation funding that had been announced in the November budget update. He stressed that the new funding did not need to await private funding and was designed to "remove bottlenecks that are currently slowing traffic at important export corridors" (Schecter and Hasselback 2016, 2). If bottlenecks really exist where he perceives them to, and if they are significant, and if the projects funded by the new program actually relieve the bottlenecks, that will be a very positive development. But because project funds are directed to export corridors they probably won't have much impact on mobility in cities. The same is likely to be the case for Minister Garneau's announced creation of a new $2.1 billion Trade and Transport Corridors Initiative (Transport Canada 2017).

The main conclusions we draw from this policy history on federal urban infrastructure funding are not encouraging, at least in retrospect. Canadian cities, needing constant "fixes" of money to pay for all manner of things, and federal funding programs, set up to provide them with hits, put no higher emphasis on transportation than on anything else. And even when transportation projects *do* reach sufficient prominence to secure government funding, they are rarely if ever driven by a primary goal that deals with the two fundamental purposes of transportation – undelayed travel and throughput capacity. Projects need to be planned and tackled with technical knowledge about the phenomenon of congestion. But at a policy level that knowledge is in short supply. Instead of a primary goal that relates to transportation, we have three weak proxies that vary in prominence depending on external circumstances – retail politics, job creation, and economic growth. The result is a mobility deficit in which Canadian cities now find themselves, with little prospect of escape unless a transformative concept and set of actions emerge.

Readers may wonder if this pessimistic account reflects terminal negativity on the part of authors who couldn't find a positive thing to say if they had to. But this is the way we would suggest viewing things: success in the job of enhancing urban mobility depends on getting a lot of things right – *all* of them, all at the same time – and, at least so far, not many government initiatives have managed to do that. This represents a lack of policy "coherence" among the instruments at play in this very tricky space.

But looking on the bright side, the steady decline of mobility and the unchecked growth of congestion sooner or later will make things bad enough, and infrastructure users aggrieved enough, to compel daring remedies. The failure of conventional policy tools is causing what researchers call "drift" – drift that can lead to crisis, shedding of political support for the status quo, and the creation of opportunities for patching or replacing the increasingly dysfunctional package of measures in which urban transportation has been trapped for decades (Howlett and Rayner 2013, 177).

THE THREE ANALYTICAL ELEMENTS

Policy Ideas, Discourses, and Agendas

The two policy histories in this chapter cover about a twenty-five-year period, but their roots go back much earlier. Table 8.2 shows the analytical story overall. Probably the foremost de facto policy idea, if not necessarily the subject of effective or continuous discourse, is that of *mobility* –and especially its decline – as populations, car ownership, and suburban living started increasing rapidly after World War II and have kept growing ever since.

There are four main components to the mobility idea. The first is that transport infrastructure absolutely must maintain its physical integrity to be of any use to anyone because otherwise it is unsafe. That means cities have to spend their first infrastructure dollars on repairs, not on expanding capacity. But, for lack of money, cities defer maintenance until roads and bridges are deteriorating at an increasing rate, which traps cities in a vicious circle of having to spend more and more dollars in an increasingly futile attempt to recover. So capacity enhancements get postponed or shelved, and urban transport mobility continues to decline.

The second main component is related to the first: the agenda of provincial and federal governments to retain exclusive authority over the taxing of income, and of goods and services, while restricting cities mainly to taxing property. That makes cities dependent on other levels of government for cash transfers (often made arbitrarily), and it contributes to the problem mentioned above.

The third main component is a lack of ideas about the physical phenomena that trigger the loss of mobility. It is rare for people in public policy to persuasively articulate a position that is grounded in

Table 8.1
The transportation in cities and federal infrastructure policy domain and the three analytical elements: Highlights

Policy and governance histories	Analytical elements		
	Policy ideas, Discourse, and agendas	Economic and social power	Technology and temporal realities and conflicts
The elusive quest for urban mobility (1960s to present)	Mobility as idea and feature of post-World War II growth of urban areas	Voters use electoral power to trap themselves in a "tragedy of the commons" of over-accessing transportation infrastructure by voting out politicians who introduce user fees	Growth of automobile production and ownership, in post-WWII era
	Declining mobility as reality		Rise of suburban living
	Rise of NIMBYism as idea and acronym, with analytical promise and limits similar in some respects to economist's ideas about the free-rider problem	Provincially imposed amalgamation of cities exacerbates loading of traffic on to municipal arteries	Fixed width of core city streets cannot accommodate rising commuter demand
	Belief that use of transportation infrastructure is "free" and ought to be	Multicity urban areas also create problems	Rise of urban congestion
	Widespread lack of understanding that mobility of traffic reaches a peak on each artery and then suddenly declines	Suburban and rural residents politically over represented on many or most city councils	Change in municipal dynamics from forced amalgamation
	Widespread lack of recognition that there are "sweet spots" for traffic movement and throughput on every artery	Municipal taxes, based on market value of property, favour suburban and rural residents at the expense of traffic mobility	Rise of NIMBYism itself fosters temporal complexity
	General lack of realization that while higher "induced demand" resulting from expanded road infrastructure will not cure congestion it nevertheless provides higher roadway throughput capacity	Land developers' power to build residential communities in suburbs despite local policies and efforts for densification	Daily variation in loading demand on municipal road infrastructure (i.e., rush hour) limits total throughput capacity of road network
	Widespread ignorance of the effect that unrestricted access to transportation networks has on congestion		Decline and sometimes collapse of mobility during periods of daily traffic build up

Table 8.1
The transportation in cities and federal infrastructure policy domain and the three analytical elements: Highlights (continued)

Policy and governance histories	Analytical elements		
	Policy ideas, Discourse, and agendas	Economic and social power	Technology and temporal realities and conflicts
	Popular notion that rationing of access to highway infrastructure is unfair and outrageous	Municipal traffic engineers who understand phenomenon of congestion are subordinate to city councils who almost certainly don't	Persistent lack of awareness of phenomenon of congestion, especially "peaking" characteristic of mobility as a function of traffic volume
	Near universal understanding by economists that user charges are essential to deter over-accessing of road infrastructure		Persistent lack of awareness of existence and significance of "sweet spots" representing a particular optimum in fostering mobility
	Inertia by elected officials to introduce user fees for transportation infrastructure because it can be political suicide		Failure by most governments to recognize significance of optimization theory – or at least to act on that recognition more frequently
	Traditional belief that tolls, if used, should be used only for paying off debts that financed original construction		
	Overlooking or rejecting of idea that tolls could be used to discourage over-accessing of road infrastructure		
	Idea that suburban and rural dwellers should have unrestricted access to core city roads while paying lower taxes		
	Idea that federal government should fund municipal transportation infrastructure on a project-by project basis, rather than on asset life-cycle basis		
	Idea of federal tax points transfer to cities as a nonstarter		

Follow the money: the dodgy evolution of federal financing of urban transportation and related infrastructure (mid-1980s to present)

Practice of ideas at federal level of infrastructure policy and funding as distributive "retail" politics No federal nation building vision for transportation since St Lawrence Seaway in 1959

Asia–Pacific Gateways and Corridors initiative of 2006 a template for government success, but not followed up

Concept of "user pay" infuses Harper-era policy agenda

... But "user pay" concept stops at provinces' and municipalities' doorsteps because of political risk

"Partnerships" involving multiple levels of governments lauded as a panacea to shortage of funds but they are not

Idea that federal government should fund municipal transportation infrastructure on a project-by-project basis, rather than as an integrated long term capital asset

Idea of transferring tax points to cities is not accepted at either federal or provincial level

Idea that starting with a primary goal of (a) gaining political advantage or (b) creating new jobs will accomplish any important transportation goal, except by accident

P3s often seen as panacea to all manner of transportation infrastructure problems when they are not

---

Open-endedness of criteria in federal infrastructure funding programs lets governments spend on just about anything

Role of the Federation of Canadian Municipalities as influential player and lobby in Ottawa from 2000 on

Intermixing of transportation with all manner of other issues in infrastructure funding program lets governments spend on just about anything

Broad refusal of federal government to transfer tax points to municipalities (except gas tax)

Provincial requirement that cities balance their budgets every year

Federal minister of Infrastructure's retention of power to approve all applications to funding programs

Parish pump politics

Municipalities not allowed to cover ongoing maintenance costs from federal infrastructure funding programs

Investment community pushes use of P3s, from which they stand to gain

---

Rising priority in recent decades for government spending on social programs that compete with transportation for funds

Declining physical state of municipal infrastructure

Federal government divestiture of transportation assets

Downloading since 1990s of federal responsibility for all manner of spending

Proliferation of infrastructure funding programs when federal budget returned to surplus in early 2000s

Further proliferation of funding programs when minority government began massive stimulus spending in 2008-09 economic meltdown

Disinclination or refusal of most funding programs to pay for "soft" infrastructure, e.g., analytical competence in mathematically complex things like flow rates, volume throughput, traffic perturbations, and network optimization

Rise of a new motive for funding infrastructure – stimulate a sagging economy – in addition to historical motive of retail politics alone

Table 8.1
The transportation in cities and federal infrastructure policy domain and the three analytical elements: Highlights (*continued*)

Policy and governance histories	Analytical elements		
	Policy ideas, Discourse, and agendas	Economic and social power	Technology and temporal realities and conflicts
Follow the money: the dodgy evolution of federal financing of urban transportation and related infrastructure (mid-1980s to present) (*continued*)	Ostensible, but dubious, need to "develop p3 market" in Canada	Federal government makes consideration of p3s a mandatory part of city applications for infrastructure funding programs	Rise of two new motives for road tolls – (1) generating revenue to pay for maintenance, and (2) discouraging overuse of the transportation network – in addition to the historical motive of repaying loans for original construction
	Idea that putting money into public transit systems will necessarily get people out of their cars	Investment community pushes development of infrastructure banks, which would create opportunities for themselves along with certain benefits regarding long-term asset and life-cycle funding	De facto federal acquiescence to pay for only those projects proposed by lower levels of government
	Idea that a federal Infrastructure Bank not only should be created but should mix private sector capital with public funds and have federal government oversight and controls on its investments	Federal government capitalizes new infrastructure bank with $35 billion of public funds and uses that as justification for requiring federal oversight and control, including over private funds placed with the bank	ppp Canada still active long after its original mission seems to be forgotten
			Possibility that infrastructure investment choices on which the feds insist will not generate long-term revenue streams,
			if, for example, road tolls are ruled out for political reasons – in which case the new Infrastructure Bank's viability will be short lived

understanding the "peaking" effect of throughput on traffic arteries or the causes of throughput collapse or the existence of sweet spots for the goal being pursued. The ideas embodied in the physics of vehicle performance, the psychology of driver behaviour, and the dynamics of complex systems subjected to perturbations, usually get overlooked – sometimes in discourse about congestion and nearly always in agendas for reducing or "calming" traffic in urban neighbourhoods, promoting bicycling, and so on. To the extent there is discourse about mobility at all, the facile nature of it tends to divert attention and effort away from dealing with the *root causes* of its decline on cities' main arteries. It induces inertia in transportation policy, not relevant change that would benefit cities and those who live in them.

The fourth and perhaps most significant component is the widespread belief that the use of transportation infrastructure ought to be free. That lies at the heart of public resistance to tolling and rationing. And it perpetuates a "tragedy of the commons" in which individuals, acting in their own self-interest, overuse a finite public resource and drive it to collapse. In this case, the finite resource is the capacity of each city's transportation infrastructure. The collapse is guaranteed by the "peaking" effect in the relationship between an artery's throughput capacity and the density of traffic using it, as shown by the inverted "U" shape of the graph in figure 8.1.

Economic and Social Power

The primary feature of economic power in our twenty-five-year history is the massive distributive politicization of decisions that affect municipal infrastructure funding. It shows up in five main ways. First is the federal downloading of costs to provincial and municipal governments. That began in earnest in the 1990s when the Chrétien–Martin Liberals started budget cutting under program review to deal with a spiralling deficit. Politically convenient for the feds, the downloading obliged lower levels of government to find the money for almost unavoidable expenditures, like health care, and to put the brakes on spending for things that could be avoided or postponed, like transportation infrastructure. This exercise of federal economic power contributed to the vicious circle in which cities are caught, as mentioned above.

The second main element is the paucity of municipal governments' economic power. Cities collect only 8 per cent of total tax revenues in Canada and in some cases are prohibited by provincial law from running a deficit. That puts them in a highly dependent position when it comes to money for infrastructure, of which transportation represents their largest single funding shortfall.

The third main element in the politicization of decisions is the rebounding of federal spending activity. That got underway in 2001 when the Chrétien–Martin government created three new pots of infrastructure money as we described in the first policy history in this chapter, and it ballooned under the Harper Conservatives. At first that was with a modest step (the Building Canada Fund) in 2007, but in 2009 it turned into a fire-hose approach to stimulate the economy and create jobs. The proliferation of programs since then is remarkable and so is the amount of money spent. It begs the question of why the feds don't just transfer tax points to municipalities because that's where most of the dollars end up being spent. But when viewed from a political standpoint the question answers itself. The feds control the money, so their economic power lets them control the categories of eligible expenditures, vet the applications, and take credit for all the projects that get announced.

Unfortunately the terms set by the federal government on how various pots of money may be used do not always embody sound public policy. For example, they disallow maintenance and repair, they often insist on "shovel ready" projects, they push P3s without considering their cumulative effect, and they give too little shrift to the development and sustaining by cities of analytical capabilities to tackle mobility problems from the "soft" side rather than defaulting to the pouring of concrete and laying of asphalt. That is not helpful to urban transportation or to the people and businesses that depend on it.

The fourth aspect of economic power is the general unwillingness of governments to tie their revenues to expenditures. That means, for example, that the Federal Gas Tax Fund gets spent on all manner of nontransportation things, which disadvantages mobility. And it induces municipal politicians like the mayors of Toronto and Ottawa to view road tolls as a source of revenue for unspecified infrastructure repairs throughout the city rather than as a way of creating tangible benefits for those paying the tolls on the roads in question. That is likely to be dysfunctional in the long run. Among other things, it will discourage road pricing at a level high enough to offer a disincentive and reduce the overuse of the infrastructure.

The fifth aspect of economic power is the influence of land developers on city planning and development. Often important contributors to municipal politicians' election campaigns, they undergo homebuilding on city peripheries that lead to disproportional loading of road networks without a commensurate increase in the tax base to solve the resulting delays from traffic and loss of roadway throughput capacity.

The primary feature of social power in this twenty-five-year story is that of a complex sort of political hedonism that arises when citizens become "more concerned with what's in it for me than with what's fair, [and] demand that politicians give them more than they have put in" (National Post 2015). There are three highlights. First is the rise of urban NIMBYism. It took root as a political slogan and analytical device in the 1980s but reached much fuller flower as highly diverse social movements developed new ways of altering public policy or fostering inertia through activism, aided in the last decade by social media tools. NIMBYism, as we have seen, is tied to concepts linked to the free-rider problem. These show up in all kinds of ways. In the 1960s and 1970s NIMBYism led some cities to abandon rail lines and remove unsightly tracks, at least in part so they could build urban parks and trails. But that removed future options for introducing light rail transit on the divested rights-of-way, which in turn constrained cities to stick with conventional (and increasingly congested) roads or to build elevated or buried public transit systems at huge cost. It also led to delays and cancellations in the building of new arteries, a proliferation of measures that intentionally slow and discourage traffic on arteries in residential neighbourhoods, a banning of truck traffic on important freight routes, and so on.

The second highlight of political hedonism is the resistance by motorists to the introduction of measures like rationing (e.g., with ramp meters) or tolls on roads at prices high enough to discourage overuse of the infrastructure. Their resistance traps municipal transportation in a "tragedy of the commons" situation in which the aggregate exercising of individual rights to use a finite resource leads to the collapse of the system as a whole.

And finally there is social power as manifested in politics that affects municipal transportation infrastructure (usually in negative ways); for example, the obligation provinces imposed on cities to amalgamate, the authority that provinces vest in municipal boards to overturn decisions made by city councils when attempting to slow or prevent land developments that would cause overloading of municipal transportation arteries, and the veto that provinces can and sometimes do exercise over municipal plans to introduce local tolling.

Technology and Temporal Realities and Conflicts

This analytical element has five highlights. First is the increase in vehicular travel and in particular the fact that its rate of growth exceeds the rate of growth in the capacity of cities' transportation infrastructure. The trend began in the post-World War II era with a rise in car ownership and in suburban living. It has continued almost unabated ever since. The difference between those two rates is a recipe for declining mobility.

The second highlight is the change of some financial ratios in an unhealthy direction, at least insofar as municipal transport infrastructure is concerned. Cities' revenue-to-asset ratio is one area of concern. Over the years, their revenues have declined relative to the value of their stock of infrastructure. Permitted by provinces to levy taxes on property (but not on income), municipalities inevitably reached the point of being unable to afford the maintenance of even their existing roads and bridges. Meanwhile the absolute value of that stock of infrastructure has risen, in part because federal programs continue to fund new construction. The net effect is to drive the ratio progressively farther off kilter, with negative effects on mobility.

Another ratio of concern is the fraction that cities' tax revenues represent of the national total. At only 8 per cent, municipalities have become increasingly dependent on federal and provincial infrastructure funding, which, as mentioned above, comes with political considerations that seldom do much (if anything) to maximize mobility.

A third development has not helped either – the growth in cities' responsibility for social programs and other priorities, some of them downloaded from federal and provincial governments. They compete with transportation more than they used to for the available money.

Fourth is the growth of unrequited pleas that governments introduce traditionally taboo measures like roadway access pricing and/or the use of rationing (e.g., with ramp meters) for transportation infrastructure. Economists' urging of the former grows steadily more full-throated and compelling, while technical evidence supporting the latter grows continually stronger. But so far political considerations have led mainly to institutionalized stasis, despite easily seen evidence that the problem of users over-accessing the transportation infrastructure keeps growing. The newly announced Canada Infrastructure Bank, compromised by its federal capitalization and governance and the ongoing politicization that almost certainly guarantees, seems unlikely to break the taboo anytime soon.

Fifth is the growing gap between what is technologically possible for improving urban mobility and what is actually being done. Developments in technology and the availability of intelligent transportation systems, advanced algorithms, analytical methods, computer models, and physical equipment for traffic control have made enormous progress over the past twenty-five years. But those developments are going largely unused in Canadian cities. Yes, there are large overhead signs on some expressways and cameras monitoring how bad the congestion is, but those are passive ways of dealing with mobility problems, and they depend on drivers responding to the information by making what amount to semi-uninformed decisions about using the infrastructure to its (and their) better advantage. It seems remarkable that in an age when GPS capabilities in cell phones can tell people their location almost in real time and when apps on tablet computers can tell people their bank account balance almost instantly, oral traffic reports are still a staple of morning and afternoon local radio shows.

Finally, there was the prospect of what many thoughtful observers anticipated would be potentially groundbreaking change with the creation of a federal infrastructure bank. If successful, the bank would take some of the purely distributive politics out of infrastructure financing and shift some to longer-term capital asset and life cycle asset management in transport infrastructure. That would be an unalloyed good thing. But after announcing the bank, the Trudeau Liberals explained that it would be set up with $35 billion of federal money and a governance model that involves a high degree of federal control. The prominence of government in the mix is likely to sustain the problem of distributive retail politics and perpetuate the lack of focus on doing anything that would actually improve mobility. Optimization theory says that by elevating the practice of investing (read, spending) money as a goal, over and above securing whatever the money is supposed to *buy* (like mobility), the bank will generate the latter only by coincidence, if even that.

CONCLUSIONS

The primary feature in this transportation policy domain as discussed in both of our policy and governance histories is a double dose of serious inertia for transportation in cities and the degree to which federal infrastructure funding has had beneficial impacts on urban mobility.

Our main conclusion about city transportation and the fostering of mobility is that its policy and governance is caught in a seven-way trap that has been growing for decades and from which, despite recent signs of movement on the political front, most large cities in Canada seem unlikely to escape – hence the "elusive" quality we ascribe to the quest for urban mobility. The seven traps are the dynamics of NIMBYism and the free-rider problem, the governance structure of cities and municipalities, the widespread failure by governments to actually understand the phenomenon of congestion and that its reduction is dealt with as a symptom rather than providing a solution, the historic unwillingness of city governments in general and elected officials in particular to put a price on the use of roads, their lack of authority to do so without provincial consent, the hoarding by provincial governments of various taxing powers and denying them to cities with the result that – apart from property taxes – municipalities have no way of raising revenues for sustained investment in infrastructure, and the intermixing by governments of multiple motives for introducing user fees.

When it comes to federal infrastructure funding policy and governance, by far the most important factor in urban transportation over the past twenty-five years has been the profound politicization of federal decisions about financing and construction. Not much gets done without distributive retail politics dominating all other considerations, including sound public policy. All manner of other problems flow directly from that. It enables motorists to over-access a finite resource – road capacity – and drive the transportation network to a state of failure, manifested by congestion. It makes countermeasures like rationing and the pricing of road usage almost unattainable. It invites (and even compels) short-term planning and thinking. It makes the building of shiny new assets more attractive than looking after existing ones, which in turn traps cities in a vicious circle of trying and failing to maintain their deteriorating transportation infrastructure. And it makes elected city officials obeisant to higher levels of government, which removes local accountability for ensuring (a) undelayed travel, which is the goal of infrastructure users individually and (b) throughput capacity, which is the goal of city officials representing their populations in aggregate.

In short, there isn't much to recommend the degree of politicization we have today, except perhaps what it does to help politicians maintain their reelectability. If we can get beyond that, there is hope. Infrastructure banks looked like a candidate in that regard, but the one established by the federal government in 2017 does not inspire confidence that we will make much progress. If we cannot get beyond politicization, hope for a significant turnaround from the ongoing overall decline of urban mobility seems unlikely anytime soon. In this domain overall, there is not much evidence of any level of government having the competence needed to determine precisely where to make infrastructure investments that will improve urban transportation in a way that gets to the heart of mobility. Yet money flows to them from federal programs anyway, thanks to the allure of distributive retail politics.

9

The Transportation, Dangerous Goods, and Environment Policy Domain

INTRODUCTION

We now turn to a mapping and analysis of the transportation, dangerous goods, and environment policy domain. Dangerous goods policy and governance challenges loom large and draw on some of our earlier chapters, including chapter 4 on transport safety policy and regulation. We also build on chapter 3's account of key international transport policy governance institutions. In particular, dangerous goods policy in Canada cannot be understood without an appreciation of Canada–US dynamics and imperatives. In the US dangerous goods are referred to as hazardous materials (Hasmat). Environmental policy is increasingly important in overall transportation policy but not necessarily in policy performance. Earlier parts of our analysis show how environmental policy dips in and out of transport agenda dynamics as revealed already in chapter 2 in both speeches from the throne and annual budget speeches and in chapter 1 in Transport Canada's own very selective and muted environmental reporting and discourse.

We examine the domain through three interacting policy and governance histories. The first policy history centres on the development of core dangerous goods policy anchored in the 1992 Transportation of Dangerous Goods Act and the regulations flowing from it. The second policy history shifts to a somewhat more recent and conjoined policy nexus when dangerous goods centre on the dynamics of transporting oil via pipelines versus its increasing shipment by train. Interestingly, the US has always regulated pipelines via its Department of Transportation and its Pipelines and Hazmat Administration (PHMSA). In Canada, the transport of oil has always been regulated separately by the National Energy Board (NEB). But these dynamics changed because of the growth of fracking technology-generated shale oil in the US and its increased shipment into Canada via rail (Prud'Homme 2014; Cairns 2013a, 2013b) and also in the aftermath of the Lac-Mégantic accident examined in chapter 4 which we pick up again at the end of this transport, dangerous goods, and environmental policy and governance journey in quite unexpected ways when US and Canadian bankruptcy law become the weapon of choice to avoid responsibility. A further looming possibility was the more extensive transport of oil sands products by both pipelines and trains (Cairns 2013b). The third policy history centres on environmental policy *per se* both as a part of dangerous goods policy and as encompassed in Transport Canada's responses to the changing policy and discourse of Environment Canada and its various environmental policies, including environmental assessment, sustainable development, and climate change (Doern, Ault, and Stoney 2015). Changing energy policy is also an entry point for environmental matters, including the issue of transport by pipelines versus by rail.

Before turning to the three policy and governance histories *per se*, we need to appreciate the institutional and governance locus of these policies, initially centred in Transport Canada's Transportation of Dangerous Goods Directorate (TDG) (Transport Canada 2016k) but then extending into other agencies whose mandates and research we also have to follow to have a clear sense of both policy boundaries and issues of complexity as the content of this domain is revealed. The TDG "serves as the major source of regulatory development, information and guidance on dangerous goods transport for the public, industry and government employees ... and works closely with other federal and provincial agencies to implement the safety program" (ibid., 3). Its staff also represent Canada "on international organizations for establishing uniform international requirements for classification, labeling and marking of means of containment, transport documentation and safety marks for vehicles carrying dangerous goods" (ibid., 3). Relevant international organizations include the UN Committee of Experts on the Transport of Dangerous Goods and the ICAO's Dangerous Goods Panel, to name only two. The US PHMSA in the US Department of Transport is even more crucial, as we see further below.

The TDGs Compliance and Response Branch functions in Ottawa and in five regional offices across Canada. Also pivotal is the Canadian Transport Emergency Centre (CANUTEC) whose scientists assist emergency responders in the event of a dangerous goods accident. The TDG, however, is only the starting point for Canadian governance in this domain. Given the scope and types of dangerous goods and their movement within and across modes and their varied presence in thousands of locations/situations, the role of other key players and interests is crucial in mapping and understanding the governance terrain in regulating dangerous goods.

For example, Transport Canada's Transportation of Dangerous Goods General Policy Advisory Council (TDGGPAC) has representatives from thirty entities and interest groups including those on transport modes but also ranging across players such as the Canadian Association of Fire Chiefs, the Mining Association of Canada, the Canadian Renewable Fuels Association, and the Federation of Canadian Municipalities (Transport Canada 2016l). Another good sense of the range of interests involved is also revealed in a 2015 report on dangerous goods by the Standing Committee on Transport, Infrastructure and Communities (2015) whose work involved witness testimony from fifty-seven entities and groups and eleven groups which also presented briefs to the committee (ibid., 59–65). As mentioned above, the Treasury Board also plays a relevant role in the development of policy both with respect to its regulation-making processes and analysis and also its requirements in risk–benefit policy for departments and agencies to publish and adhere to "safety management systems" (SMSS) as a complement to detailed enforcement and compliance.

As the key features of this domain emerge further in the second and third policy histories, the array of other institutional players widens and deepens. These include the Commissioner of the Environment and Sustainable Development (CESD), the above mentioned Standing Committee on Transport, Infrastructure and Communities as a vehicle of parliamentary review, and also, more broadly, Environment Canada (more recently renamed Environment and Climate Change Canada) but also the transport and environmental policy advice tendered by the 2015 Canada Transportation Act review report.

DANGEROUS GOODS POLICY AND REGULATION (1992 TO PRESENT)

In our review of overall dangerous goods policy and regulation, we take a three-stage approach. First, we look at the federal Transportation of Dangerous Goods Act 1992 (Justice Canada 2016). Second, we look at the policy links in the US and Canada between the transport of dangerous goods and the operation of the common carrier principle, an historic issue, as we have already seen in earlier chapters and one that resurfaced in the 2007 to 2018 period. Third, we look at the abovementioned 2015 report of the Standing Committee on Transport, Infrastructure and Communities (2015) and its research and policy and institutional recommendations.

The Transportation of Dangerous Goods Act was passed in 1992, but there was an incomplete framework for the legislation as early as 1985. This alone may seem odd given that dangerous goods had been a part of the Canadian transport system from the outset. Early transport safety policy had some crossover, particularly when accidents occurred, and of course there were private sector liability policy and insurance measures present. The 1992 law defines dangerous goods as "a product, substance or organism included by its nature or by the regulations in any of the classes listed in the schedule" (Justice Canada 2016c, 1). There are nine such classes (ibid., 35): 1) explosives, 2) gases, 3) flammable and combustible liquids, 4) flammable solids, 5) oxidizing substances, 6) poisonous, 7) nuclear substances, 8) corrosives, and 9) miscellaneous products, substances or organisms.

Dangerous goods, of course, also have positive attributes in that many are valuable parts of goods and are produced by Canadians in a large number of diverse industries. Indeed Transport Canada and other reports emphasize this positive feature as the dangerous goods rules *per se* are introduced. Thus dangerous products are a necessary element in the daily lives of Canadians. They range from gasoline used in motor vehicles to substances such as lead and mercury used in manufacturing electronics products. Industries that manufacture and use dangerous products provide jobs to Canadians (Commissioner of the Environment and Sustainable Development 2011, 2).

The US PHMSA's four year strategic plan published in 2012 begins with a similar baseline statement, namely that "hazardous materials underpin our economy. We use ... hazardous materials to purify our drinking water, fertilize crops, produce medicines, and manufacture clothing and many other products. ... They also introduce inherent risks to the public, the environment, and property when they are transported" (Pipeline and Hazardous Materials Safety Administration 2012, 1).

Of interest in this domain, and indeed in the book as a whole, is that the above 1992 Canadian legislation defines public safety as "the safety of human life and health and property and the environment" (Justice Canada 2016c, 2). The "environment" is not itself further defined in the statute, but we return to the boundary and normative issue of environmental impacts and policy discourse later in the chapter. These content and boundary issues are of practical and conceptual importance in literally decades of safety and public interest regulation (Doern, Prince, and Shultz 2014). For example, when occupational and workplace health law and policy was forged in the 1970s, one way to ensure that a workplace facility was "safe" was simply to dump any hazard into the "environment," which was defined by default as anything that was "outside" the workplace building. It is of no small import to note that the transport of dangerous goods has impacts on many workplace situations and locales (and thus "environments") for modal transport personnel as they drive/move in vehicles, for regulatory inspectors, for first responders, and for staff using diverse "means of containment" for dangerous goods etc.

The scope of the legislation, its complexities and its compliance and enforcement features are revealed at a glance by many of the titles of individual sections of the law such as agreement with the provinces, means of containment, inspectors, duty to respond, personal liability, disclosure of information, recovery of costs and expenses, regulations, measures and orders, evidence, and offences and punishment. The last of these regarding punishment specifies that "every person who commits an offence under subsection 1; a) is liable on indictment to imprisonment for a term not exceeding two years; or b) is liable on summary conviction to a fine not to exceed $50,000 for a first offence, and not exceeding $100,000 for each subsequent offence (Justice Canada 2016c, 31). So this statute has regulatory and enforcement clout at its core rather than just exhortative compliance, although the latter is also present. This is because it is self-evident from the nine classes of dangerous goods that they are potentially everywhere while the regulator cannot also itself be everywhere all the time in, on, and around key transport modes.

If the 1992 statute is the necessary key starting point, there are also other partial or different entry points, one of which is to relate such policies to both Canadian and US policy as they relate to, or emerge from, the idea of common carrier transport obligations. As noted in chapter 1, this link has reemerged in both the US and Canada in recent years and remains a long-term future issue as well because transport technologies and the nature of dangerous goods or hazardous materials will both change. Abel (2011, 973) points out in a US context that as a result "of the operation of the common carrier doctrine and the modal strengths of freight transportation via rail, railroads are prohibited from refusing shipment of dangerous cargo." In short, this prohibition against refusing to carry dangerous goods is unique to railroads.

Abel stresses that:

A direct result of the common carrier obligation is the specter of limitless exposure of railroads to financial liability in the event of an accident releasing hazmat shipments that the railroads had no choice in deciding whether to ship in the first place. The dangers of hazmat releases in any context, including rail transportation, implicate environmental, public health and anti-terrorism concerns. At bottom, an "unfunded mandate" of sorts surfaces, wherein railroads are forced to assume what they perceive as an unreasonable financial risk, while those benefitting from this policy, including hazmat shippers, the government, and the general public, assume few, if any, of the costs. (Ibid., 974)

A major release of dangerous goods in an urban area is probably the most feared scenario. Solutions to this policy dilemma in the US, as recommended by various interest groups, include the outright abolition of the common carrier doctrine, the localized regulation of the routing of dangerous shipments, and some kind of publicly or jointly funded liability backstop as, for example, found in the nuclear and marine industries.

Earlier, in 2008, a US review of the common carrier obligation as it applies to hazardous materials was conducted by the Federal Railroad Administration (FRA) for the US Department of Transportation (DOT). DOT argued that, "there is no reason to change this common carrier obligation" (Elby 2006, 2). Because of the value and necessity of such products to support essential services, "the transportation of these materials is unavoidable" and "the diversion of this traffic to the highways or other modes not practicable" (ibid., 2–3). The DOT report cites other efforts to deal with hazardous materials with several case studies, including one involving a CPR train derailment in Minot, North Dakota in 2002 that involved the release of anhydrous ammonia (ibid., 6).

A further review of the common carrier obligation (CCO), conducted in 2008 by the US Surface Transportation Board, led to a position announced by the US Department of Agriculture (USDA) (Knight 2008). It was broader than the hazardous materials study commissioned by DOT, and it concluded that the railroad industry was "actively discouraging the movement of hazardous materials and encouraging shippers to use safer substitutes" (ibid., 9). Safer substitutes are, in this sense, a form of advocated environmental policy. This report concluded that "the CCO and concept of public convenience and necessity must be fully considered in addressing cost and safety issues in the transportation of hazardous materials by rail" (ibid., 9). It also stressed that careful study would be needed of all options and in particular shipping by truck.

There are also related developments in Canada regarding the shipment of dangerous goods by rail in general and the inherent policy connections with the common carrier principle in particular. For example, Canadian Pacific CEO Hunter Harrison said publicly that CP is seeking authority to refuse dangerous shipments, and he linked this to an overhaul of "common carrier obligations" (quoted in Atkins 2015).

In 2014, following the Lac-Mégantic rail disaster, the Canadian Transportation Agency reviewed the safety and liability issues surrounding the transport by rail of dangerous goods (Krugel 2014). The Canadian Association of Petroleum Producers (CAPP) and the Canadian Fuels Association (CFA) said that the current framework is fundamentally sound and they stressed that the Lac-Mégantic accident was largely a result of issues with smaller railways. The Railway Association of Canada (RAC), however, sought changes in that regard because the common carrier obligation does not allow railways to turn down cargoes (Krugel 2014).

In February 2015, Transport Minister Lisa Raitt announced new legislation to ensure that any railway or company that transports crude oil will share accountability for the costs of cleanup and compensation in the event of an accident. (See more below in our second policy and governance history on pipelines and dangerous goods.) The new legislation will also impose mandatory minimum insurance levels on railways in amounts that depend on the type and volume of dangerous goods being transported.

When the Trudeau Liberals came into power in late 2015, its first Transport minister's, Marc Garneau's, initial transport policy initiative (Transport Canada 2016p) was on new measures to strengthen rail safety and the transportation of dangerous goods. Of considerable importance is that the initiative was announced at a meeting with the

Federation of Canadian Municipalities. Via a new protective direction thirty-six railways "will be required to provide municipalities and first responders with even more data on dangerous goods to improve emergency planning, risk assessments, and training" (ibid., 1). Such information can be shared directly with the Canadian public. While cities and municipal governments are a crucially linked feature, one also needs to stress the role of the provinces and their capacities and availability for monitoring compliance and enforcement, especially given Canada's obvious geographic enormity. Later in June 2016, Garneau also took increased action, including fining the railways for unsafe practices. This was linked to a significant increase in 2015 in the numbers of incidents regarding "runaway trains" with Garneau quoted as saying that reducing such incidents significantly is "my No. 1 mandate" (Robertson 2016).

While the above discussion links dangerous goods directly and indirectly to the common carrier principle *per se*, it is important to note that Transport Canada policy has focused on broader multimodal issues and also on emergency response processes and support. In none of its recent annual reports has Transport Canada explicitly linked dangerous goods to the common carrier principle *per se* (Transport Canada 2012, 2014).

The report of the Standing Committee on Transport, Infrastructure and Communities (2015) offers our third and final vantage point for seeing overall Canadian policy on dangerous goods. Early in the report the committee noted that in 2011 "approximately 70% of all dangerous goods were transported by road, 24% by rail, 6% by vessel and less than 1% by air" (ibid., 2). The minister of Transport assured the committee that "99.997% of dangerous goods shipments in Canada arrive safely without any incidents" (ibid.). But the committee itself drew attention to the fact that "over 72% of all reportable dangerous goods accidents across all modes of transport since 2008 happened in facilities where the goods were *prepared for transit, unloaded or stored* (e.g. transload facilities)" (ibid., 2). Thus final destination was not the key performance indicator. In addition "at 56%, human error was the main underlying factor contributing to these accidents followed by equipment problems (34%)" (ibid., 2). The committee had already reported Transport Canada's data showing that there are 40,000 dangerous goods sites in Canada (ibid., 1).

Interestingly, the committee report argued that the system "encompasses the entire supply chain for products identified as dangerous goods" including "the producers and consumers of the regulated products, the transportation services and transfer points between them, as well as the organizations that are involved in the production of the standardized means of containment used" (ibid., 1). Transport Canada informed the committee "that the department has 35 dangerous goods field inspectors who conduct approximately 3,000 inspections of the 40,000 dangerous goods sites across all modes per year" (ibid., 3). The TDG office also must review about 900 emergency response assistance plans (ERAPs) annually. The committee was told that, "approximately 60% of the dangerous goods sites inspected were found to be compliant" (ibid.). There were also 116 rail safety inspectors under the Railway Safety Act, some of who were trained to conduct dangerous goods inspections (ibid., 7).

It is not surprising, given the daunting scope and range of inspection tasks and sites profiled above, that the committee's first recommendation in its report is "that Transport Canada ensure that it has an adequate number of transportation of dangerous goods and rail safety inspectors to fulfill its oversight function" (ibid., 7). The committee report then went on to look briefly at the dangerous goods regime in the different transport modes, including air, marine, and trucking where a small set of further specific findings were noted and recommendations made for reform.

The committee report's focus in the second half of its analysis was on "safety management systems (SMSs)" to complement the regulatory focus profiled briefly above. Transport Canada had already decided that "simply making more regulations that address specific issues or events would not necessarily bring about improvements in the transportation system" and that therefore "the transportation sector must also be accountable for proactively and systematically addressing risks within its operations" (ibid., 22). SMSs are the key here and are defined as "essentially quality assurance processes that provide for responsibility and accountability for safety at all levels in the organization" (ibid., 22). In essence a safety and risk management culture is needed and can and must emerge. Again, the report then looked briefly at these kinds of SMS processes on a mode-by-mode basis regarding rail, air, marine, and road transport.

Related system-based thinking about reform has also emerged regarding training in the transportation of dangerous goods, both in a recent consultation process (Transport Canada 2016s) and in a preceding Transport Canada white paper on the subject (Transport

Canada 2016t). In the consultation process, participants were asked "what do you think of the existing definitions of 'competent person,'" and Transport Canada indicated that "it is proposing to clarify what it means to be 'adequately trained,'" the phrase used in the current regulations (Transport Canada 2016s). But it is clear from the white paper analysis, that the department thinks that the current system is seriously inadequate and that it seeks to put into place a "competency-based training and assessment" system (Transport Canada 2016t, 4, 8–9).

DANGEROUS GOODS POLICY AND OIL TRANSPORT VIA PIPELINES VERSUS RAIL (2010 TO PRESENT)

Our second policy and governance history centres on dangerous goods policy regarding oil transported by pipelines but crucially in recent years also by rail. We have already seen this to some extent in the House of Commons committee report referred to above, but here the policy–governance nexus is different and involves the policies and mandate evolution and enforcement capacities and weaknesses of the National Energy Board (NEB) (Doern, Prince, and Schultz 2014, 125–37). Also involved analytically is the work of the federal Commissioner of the Environment and Sustainable Development (CESD) (2011, 2015) through two reports: the 2011 report on dangerous goods transportation predates the Lac-Mégantic disaster, and the second, in 2015, is post-Lac-Mégantic and deals with federally regulated pipelines. The CESD is an auditor and thus cannot comment on policy, but it can and does comment on and assess policy implementation.

The 2011 report looks at both Transport Canada and the NEB as dangerous goods regulators. Not surprisingly, given its mandate, the CESD draws immediate attention to the fact that "acids and oils can result in the death of wildlife and the contamination of ecosystems" (Commissioner of Environment and Sustainable Development 2011, 5). The audit focused on whether Transport Canada and the NEB "have designed and implemented a risk-based approach to determine whether regulated organizations transport dangerous products in accordance with established legislation and standards" (ibid., 7). Covering the period from 2007 to June 2011, the CESD's main findings are that, "Transport Canada lacks a consistent approach to planning and implementing compliance activities. As a consequence, it cannot ensure that sites are inspected according to the highest risk" (ibid., 2). Regarding the NEB, the CESD concluded overall that while it has "identified gaps and deficiencies through its verification of compliance for the companies it regulates, there is little indication that it has followed up to ensure that these deficiencies have been corrected" (ibid., 2).

The CESD's later report, in 2015, was entirely on pipeline regulation and immediately stressed that the NEB-centred system pipeline sector had entered a period of rapid oil sands-centred growth, with several proposed pipelines including Northern Gateway, Trans Mountain Expansion, and Energy East on the agenda. The report said that the NEB defines its "public interest" mandate as "a balance of economic, environmental and social considerations that changes as society's values and preferences evolve" (quoted in Commissioner of Environment and Sustainable Development 2015, 2). The NEB, it stressed, regulates "approximately 73,000 kilometres of pipelines and about 100 companies" (ibid., 3). The CESD's overall findings as of 2015 are that the NEB's "tracking of company compliance with pipeline approval conditions was inadequate" (ibid., 5).

The CESD drew immediate attention to "pipeline approval" conditions because such conditions "may cover a range of topics such as protection of critical habitat, reporting on economic opportunities for Aboriginal groups, or safety and engineering requirements such as pressure testing" (ibid., 5). Most pipelines have to adhere to dozens of such approval provisions, including those on the environment. This kind of multidimensional public interest focus has been a part of other analyses of the NEB on environmental matters as it has evolved (Doern, Auld, and Stoney 2015, 146–86; Doern and Gattinger 2003, 95–113).

A full analysis of the NEB is not possible here but as combined shale oil and oil sands product is shipped by combined and linked pipeline and rail modes there will be a greater need for coordinated dangerous product regulation and enforcement. This will also be environmental regulation oriented for the further practical reason that the NEB, since 1995, has been a "responsible authority" under the Canadian Environmental Assessment Act and thus has to coordinate its assessments on a joint basis with Environment Canada's Environmental Assessment Agency. In the transition from the Harper pro-pipeline era and its central preference for environmentally muted "responsible resource development" to the Justin Trudeau era, and its potential greater caution about new pipelines and its climate change agenda, the role and mandate of both the NEB and Transport Canada as oil product and dangerous product regulators is now subject to greater scrutiny. Recent analyses also relate this to various roles of a wide and growing array of defined communities and the extent to which they trust and understand the kinds of values, choices, and evidence needed both for good governance and good democracy by energy bodies (Cleland, Nourallah, and Fast 2016).

The oil by pipelines versus rail developments and policy nexus raise two different core dynamics of change: first, the development and use of fracking technology to produce shale oil in the US (Prud'Homme 2014) and the movement of significant volumes of shale crude oil by rail since 2008 including into Canada and second, actual and potential issues of the role of rail versus pipelines in oil sands crude oil transport (Cairns 2013a). As Cairns points out, none of the latter is currently moved by rail but may well be so in the medium term. He shows that the recent growth in crude oil by rail is due to three factors:

- The rapid development of shale oil – particularly the Bakken formation in North Dakota, which has insufficient feeder pipelines
- Associated transmission pipeline capacity constraints
- The ability of rail to serve many markets across the continent, and to reach underserved markets. (Ibid., 11)

Cairns also argues that rail has other advantages such as that its "transload facilities do not require very significant capital investment ... unlike new pipelines, existing rail does not require very long term contracts" and "there is synergy in related crude oil products" (ibid., 11). The rail record in handling crude oil, in Cairns view, has been successful, with the exception of course of the Lac-Mégantic disaster (Cairns 2013b).

Cairns makes it clear that the issue of emerging and future rail service for the Alberta oil sands is very different but his analysis (Cairns 2013a) suggests that it is by no means an impossible development depending on the potential train capacity and equipment needed. He notes that bitumen "can be handled in heated tank cars without the need of diluent" (ibid., 12). (In pipelines the *in situ* bitumen is "typically mixed with a diluent in order to flow for pipeline distribution" (ibid., 3). Cairns notes that "short rail line build-ins" by CP and

CN may provide direct rail service near Alberta oil sands facilities and that "the construction of transload facilities is already underway" including one by CN at Fort McMurray (ibid., 12). It is likely that oil sands development and transport will eventually have some kind of joint rail and pipeline transport configuration, but of course these issues join others since the above analyses, including much lower global oil prices, the massive May 2016 forest and ecosystem fire in and around Fort McMurray, and the Trudeau government's pipeline policies and choices regarding the three new proposed pipelines mentioned above, which are now being cast in terms of energy policy, NEB reforms, indigenous policy, and climate change policy in highly combined and uncertain ways.

A further example of rail and dangerous goods policy is to take note of how it also involved the processes followed under the Treasury Board and *Canada Gazette*-centred regulation making process to amend, in the wake of the Lac-Mégantic disaster, the transport of dangerous goods regulations regarding TC 117 tank cars. The Treasury Board's required regulatory impact analysis statement was carried out after Lac-Mégantic but also built on the work on the Lac-Mégantic disaster by the Transport Safety Board (see chapter 4). The required Treasury Board process produced detailed amendments dealing with the TC 117 tank cars, but it showed also how it involved a cost–benefit analysis and statement, and requirements for domestic and international coordination and cooperation (Canada 2015). The latter international aspects involved discussions and joint work with the US Pipeline and Hazardous Materials Safety Administration of the US Department of Transport and were absolutely pivotal in developing the new rules because of the imperatives of the integrated Canada–US rail transport market (Pipeline and Hazardous Materials Safety Administration 2015, 2016).

Aspects of Les Pal's analytical insights into "public issue management in turbulent times," as mentioned in chapter 1 (Pal 2014), further show how the presence of crises and turbulence can indeed be normal. In this case it is the impact of numerous potential hazards regarding dangerous goods as defined overall in law but also in the above analysis of the Lac-Mégantic disaster as, first, a kind of normal accident but also quickly one that raised issues regarding the shipment of oil by rail as opposed to by pipelines. This was double turbulence and crisis management in very short order and involving different sets of players and institutions.

TRANSPORTATION POLICY AND ENVIRONMENT POLICY
(1995 TO PRESENT)

Transport Canada's expressed environmental policies and approaches are shown in its website and related reporting in three ways: its environmental programs, its compliance with federal environmental laws and rules which typically emerge from Environment Canada but are government-wide in nature, and other forms of summary environmental reporting. Unlike other of its mandate areas, at no point does Transport Canada indicate what number of staff (or their expert backgrounds) are devoted full time to these environmental realms. Under environmental programs, the department stresses how "with specifically targeted programs ... it ... aims to promote a more sustainable transportation system" (Transport Canada 2016k, 1). Examples cited include its ecoTechnology for Vehicles (eTV) program centred on testing a range of new and emerging advanced vehicle technologies for passenger cars and heavy-duty trucks, and its Shore Power Technology for Ports (SPTP) (ibid., 1–2).

Regarding its compliance with federal laws and rules, several are highlighted. One relates to "protecting the environment" under the Canadian Environmental Protection Act. Three "pillar" aspects are noted including the national environmental management system, national environmental monitoring and oversight, and emissions under the Clean Air Act (ibid., 2–3). The national environmental management system also includes a program on contaminated sites, including Transport Canada contaminated sites (Transport Canada 2016l).

Other broadly familiar policy and regulatory terrain includes the environmental assessment of projects under the long established Environmental Assessment Act but altered managerially by Harper era requirements via a cabinet directive that includes "strategic environmental assessments" and also a Major Projects Management Office based in Natural Resources Canada (Transport Canada 2016m). Sustainable development policy is also featured and refers initially to requirements since 1995 under the Auditor General Act that key departments submit sustainable development (SD) strategies every three years (Transport Canada 2016n). The Transport Canada website states that "the department's vision of a sustainable transportation system is one that integrates and balances social, economic and environmental objectives" (ibid.). The notion of integrating and balancing these three objectives is somewhat different than earlier expressions of s D policy whose test was the somewhat weaker one of "considering" social, economic, and environmental objectives in the policy process, the so-called "triple bottom line" (Doern, Auld, and Stoney 2015; Toner and Meadowcroft 2009).

The policy objectives related to climate change and greenhouse gas emission reductions do not feature centrally in Transport Canada's view of its role in transport policy but this may change. Its relevance may change under the Trudeau Liberal government, which took office and immediately made Environment Canada into the Department of Environment and Climate Change. The previously mentioned Canadian Transport Act review report released as the Trudeau government took office was the first such transport policy review to have a standalone chapter on climate change (Canadian Transport Act Review 2015, chapter 5).

Early on in its report, the review stated that, "an overwhelming certainty never to lose sight of is this: The more efficient the transportation system, the smaller the economic trade-off to achieve greenhouse gas objectives. A slow motion, fragmented system, punctuated with too much stopping, starting and idling will be an economic failure and an emissions disaster" (ibid., 88). But it also stressed that "there are no simple formulas where transport is concerned: The system is complex and responsibilities are dispersed across a broad spectrum" (ibid.). The report took note of some areas of progress in the transport sector but its two overall recommendations to the Trudeau government are 1) that the review's "proposed Advisory Committee on Transportation and Logistics work with Environment and Climate Change Canada to set objectives and report results impacting environmental stewardship in the transport sector" and 2) "that the Government of Canada develop performance-based emission regulations for all modes of transportation, while providing support for technological innovation" and that "North American harmonization should be the goal" (ibid., 93–4).

At the same time that the review report was released, the larger impetus from the global December 2015 COP 21 Paris Agreement on climate change initiatives was already triggering research on the decarbonisation of transport and the methodologies needed to deal with it over the longer term (International Transport Forum 2016; 2015). It was now clearer that transportation, "representing 23% of all energy-related emissions, now has an opportunity to play a leading role in climate change" (International Transport Forum 2016, 2).

While these developments reflect a kind of new aspirational high for transport environmental policy, one must remember that, in the current CTA legislation, environmental outcomes are linked to *outcomes* that can be "achieved *satisfactorily* by competition and market forces and do not *unduly* favour or reduce the inherent advantages of any particular mode of transport" (emphasis added) (Canadian Transportation Act 5b). Basic annual and multiyear reporting on the state of transportation needs to explicitly include, as environmental evidence and performance, the issues of sustainable development, climate change, and the safety–environment nexus inherent in the transportation of dangerous goods, including whether substitutes to those goods are available. Saying that something or some policy is "environmentally friendly" or "clean" never was or is a suitable kind of descriptor except when one does not want to produce much or any evidence about actual outcomes. Thus in key ways Canada remains in transport and otherwise an environmental laggard in policy and compliance terms.

Recent Transport Canada annual reports about the environmental aspects of each mode of transport are useful in some specific ways and occasionally mention broader ideas of the kind referred to above. For example, the air transport section reported as its lead "environment" item that "Canada supported the resolution on climate change" adopted at the previous 38th Assembly of ICAO (Transport Canada 2014, 12). The resolution "includes a goal of carbon neutral growth starting in 2020 to be achieved through a broad basket range of measures" (ibid., 12).

Regarding the marine sector, the same report gave prominence to the report of the federal Tanker Safety Expert Panel (TSEP) whose forty-five recommendations included "the development and implementation of a regional, risk-based model for spill preparedness and response in collaboration with local stakeholders" (ibid., 16). Also mentioned in the marine section is an Arctic Shipping and Assessment and Emissions Inventory conducted for the North (ibid.).

The rail sector of the report referred in its environmental initiatives to how Transport Canada and the Railway Association of Canada announced a new (third) memorandum of understanding (MOU). It encourages "RAC members, including freight, intercity passenger, shortline and commuter railway companies in Canada, to continue to voluntarily reduce locomotive emissions" (ibid., 20). In an earlier report, the rail transport section also stressed, in both environmental and safety matters, that Canada's rules were being aligned with US standards.

In the road transportation section, the environment data presented starts with the stark information that "the road transportation sector emitted (in 2011) 137.5 Mt of CO_2 accounting for 87.1 percent of domestic transportation-related GHG emissions and 19.6 percent of total Canadian emissions" (ibid., 25).

Two other features of regular Transport Canada environmental reporting are also important to note. The first is that the concept of sustainable development as a key way of thinking about and practicing environmental policy is in fact rarely highlighted, whereas it is commonplace in many other policy fields, and, of course, such policies and performance are assessed via reports by the CESD located within the office of the Auditor General of Canada. The second feature is that safety issues and environmental issues are too often separately discussed as if the boundaries are clear-cut when they typically are not. In many cases, where the safety-related dangerous goods spill or accident starts and the "environment" begins or ends is by no means clear-cut, as the Lac-Mégantic disaster sharply revealed.

The point to stress here is that while Transport Canada does report on environmental matters and often works with Environment Canada, its reporting and hence key aspects of its accountability, by mode and overall, are not often reported on in comprehensive ways and with evidence about outcomes on its full array of obligations clearly assembled.

The most recent department-wide notion of Transport Canada's way of thinking about describing environmental matters expressed as planned outcomes is found in Transport Canada's 2016–17 report of plans and priorities for the 2016–17 to 2019–20 period (Transport Canada 2016o) submitted by Liberal Transport Minister Marc Garneau. In it Transport Canada's three stated programs are presented and analyzed by "strategic outcomes." Strategic outcome 2: a clean transportation system is separated into "clean air from transportation; clean water from transportation; and environmental stewardship of transportation" (ibid., 45–52). The environmental stewardship program "fulfills Transport Canada's responsibilities in working towards an environmentally responsible and resilient national transportation system by ensuring compliance with the department's environmental obligations in relations to Acts, Regulations, policies and guidelines, and meeting the department's obligations towards Aboriginal peoples" (ibid., 51).

Early in the report the department writes that its "vision of a sustainable transportation system integrates social, economic and environmental objectives (ibid., 4). Three guiding principles are contained in the vision "to be worked towards," the third of which is "respect of the environmental legacy of future generations of Canadians, guided by environmental assessment and planning processes in transportation decisions and selective use of regulation and government funding" (ibid., 4). But all the "expected results for the first two programs" then use the term "clean" (ibid., 45–52). Curiously, however, Transport Canada in its initial discussion of "planning highlights" has three items centred on reducing "greenhouse gas emissions" (ibid., 47) but without mentioning specifically the idea of climate change.

Last but certainly not least in this domain story is the way in which the Lac-Mégantic disaster enters the ever-widening Canada–US institutional mix of court processes and decisions, Quebec government actions, and US bankruptcy law as a weapon of choice to protect the American rail company, MM&A, from accident liabilities (Laframboise and Brunette 2018; Rousseau and Rivest 2018; CBC News 2018, 2013). MM&A initiated "proceedings for Chapter 11 bankruptcy protection in a U.S. court while its sister firm in Canada presented a petition in Quebec Superior Court" (CBC News 2013, 1). The parent company said that it has between "$50 million and $100 million in estimated assets and between $1 million and $10 million in estimated liabilities" (ibid.). Quebec Justice Martin Castonguay granted an application for bankruptcy protection in Canada for its Canadian sister firm by saying "this decision is to prevent anarchy" but also that he was not impressed with the railway's application and believed that the people of the town "have a right to know what is going on" (ibid.). Quebec and town authorities meanwhile "had also sent legal notices to MM&A for almost $8 million in environmental mop-up costs" (ibid.).

Five years later on 19 January 2018 "after nine days of deliberations, jurors ... acquitted the three former MM&A railway employees" who had been "charged with criminal negligence causing death" in

the accident. (Laframboise and Brunette 2018). The acquittal was
supported by many town residents. But those residents, including
local businesses, bore the brunt of the massive costs of the accident
and there are still no decisions to rebuild the railway track in a way
that bypasses the town.

THREE ANALYTICAL ELEMENTS

With the aid of table 9.1 we now look across the three policy and
governance histories to see the nature of both change and inertia in
this domain via a summary sampling of the three analytical elements
featured in the book as a whole. We look at each element in turn.

Policy Ideas, Discourses, and Agendas

Across the domain policy histories examined, there are, at an overall
level, core policy ideas and discourse centred on public safety with
some diverse add-ons regarding environmental content. The core
concept of dangerous goods (or hazardous materials) as expressed in
the Transportation of Dangerous Goods Act, not surprisingly leads
to measures to protect public safety defined as the safety of human
life and property (but then also "environment"). We have seen as well
that those same dangerous goods (nine classes of them) are needed
by Canadians in everyday life and that they are vital to the industries
that develop, make, and sell them, which also needs to transport them.
Their historic link, however, to the common carrier obligation, also
means that transport modes (rail in particular) are not allowed to
decline to carry such cargo, although some are seeking change in such
provisions and indeed are advocating that new safer substitute goods
should be developed on a required basis.

As one moves into the pipelines versus rail dynamics of oil shipments, the ideas shift somewhat to encompass notions of safety-
management systems and, more broadly in the combined Transport
Canada and NEB cases, into concepts of risk–benefit policy and discourse. Sustainable transport also enters the policy lexicon, but there
is only limited embrace of the full meandering ideas that had emerged
in environmental policy *per se*, including environmental assessment,
sustainable development as the "triple bottom line," and, slowest of
all, over calls for climate change policy and the measured reduction
of greenhouse gases overall and in transport specifically.

Table 9.1
The transportation, dangerous goods, and environmental policy domain and the three analytical elements: Highlights

Policy and governance histories	Analytical elements		
	Policy ideas, discourse, and agendas	Economic and social power	Technology and temporal realities and conflicts
Dangerous goods policy and regulation (1992 to present)	DGs as "products, substances or organisms" in regulations (nine classes of DGs)	1992 Transportation of Dangerous Goods Act and regulations	Lac-Mégantic rail disaster in 2013 and subsequent rapid legislative change
	But DG also as necessary elements in peoples lives and for industries that produce them	Transportation of Dangerous Goods Directorate	Eventual use of bankruptcy law by guilty US railways
	US refers to DGs as "Hazard Materials" (Hazmat)	40,000 dangerous goods sites in Canada	
	"Public safety" in law as "safety of human life and health and property and environment" and also workplace health	Only thirty-five DG inspectors	
	Statutory features such as "means of containment," disclosure of information	Reviews 900 emergency response assistance plans (ERAPS)	
	Offenses and punishment etc.	Role of Dangerous Goods Policy Advisory Council (composed of numerous key DG players/interests such as Federation of Canadian Municipalities	
	Links with common carrier idea and obligations (and inability to turn down cargoes)	CP's CEO seeking authority to refuse dangerous shipment	
	Localized routing of dangerous shipments	Standing Committee on Transport, Infrastructure and Communities 2012 report	
	Encouraging shippers to use safer substitutes	Commissioner of Environment and Sustainable Development 2015 report (based on input from fifty-seven entities)	
	Multimodal issues	Canada Transport Act review 2015 report advocacy includes climate change chapter	
	DG and entire supply chain for DG product		
	Safety management systems (SMSS) as approach needed to complement the statutory regulatory focus		

Table 9.1
The transportation, dangerous goods, and environmental policy domain and the three analytical elements: Highlights (continued)

Policy and governance histories	Analytical elements		
	Policy ideas, discourse, and agendas	Economic and social power	Technology and temporal realities and conflicts
Dangerous goods policy and regulation (1992 to present) (continued)	Related approaches also needed in the transportation of DGs to establish training based on competency-based training and assessment	Treasury Board role regarding regulation approval process and also regulatory management and safety management systems Role of international DG entities, including UN Committee of Experts on the Transport of Dangerous Goods, and ICAO Dangerous Goods Panel	
Dangerous goods policy and changing oil transport via pipelines versus rail (2011 to present)	Risk-based approach by Transport Canada and National Energy Board (NEB) NEB's public interest mandate as "balance of economic, environmental social considerations that change as societies' values and preferences evolve" Pipeline approval conditions include protection of critical habitat, economic opportunities for Aboriginal groups Acids and oils as causes of death of wildlife and contamination of ecosystems Harper era "responsible resource development" as muted/weakened environmental approach Trust in array of defined communities Rail's ability to meet underserved markets re: shale oil	Shale oil growth and shipment by rail from US Transport Canada and NEB as joint regulator NEB dealing with 73,000km of pipelines and one hundred companies Oil sands bitumen shipped by linked pipeline and rail modes but future growth of dual modes not certain given oil sands market problems and lower oil prices But need for greater coordination of DG and enforcement NEB as joint regulator with federal Environmental Assessment Agency Direct shale oil rail link and exposure via Lac-Mégantic disaster in 2014; DG regulation passed re: TC 117 Tank Cars	Shale oil drilling technology via fracking as major impact/driver Transload facilities being developed by CN vis-à-vis oil sands rail transport but early stages only Sudden growth of shale oil production, use, and transport by rail since 2010 Rapid and strong growth of oil sands and need for new proposed pipelines

Transportation and environment policy (1980s to present)			
Trudeau Liberal's oil scrutiny concerning climate change and pipeline battles	US similar regulations as well	Fort McMurray fires of May 2016 have adverse impact on oil sands already affected by declining oil prices	
A more sustainable transportation system	Important to stress that US hazmat regulation is centred in its Pipelines and Hazardous Materials Safety Administration of the US Department of Transportation	"Respect for the environmental legacy of future generations of Canadians"; stated but fudged by no sense of what respect means and over what time frames	
Canada Transport Act environmental outcomes that can be achieved "satisfactorily by competitive market forces" and "which do not unduly favour or reduce the inherent advantages of any particular mode of transport"	Transport Canada's own environmental programs		
"Sustainable development" (SD) as "balancing" or "considering" the social, economic and environmental objectives	Transport Canada's compliance with federal environmental laws and rules		
The "triple bottom line"	Transport Canada's summary environmental reporting		
Climate change and GHG reductions not usually mentioned but is a chapter title in CTA review report of 2015	Contaminated site program		
	Federal Tanker Safety Expert Panel (TSEP) report leads to marine travel safety reforms		
	Transport Canada and Railway Association of Canada promote "voluntary reductions in locomotive emissions"		
	2016–17 Priorities and Planning report commits to "clean water" and "clean air" as two stated planned outcomes, along with "environmental stewardship"		
	Guiding principles include "respect of the environmental legacy of future generations of Canadians"		
	December 2015 COP21 Paris Agreement on Climate Change		
	Research brings out data that transport produces 23% of all energy related emissions		

Economic and Social Power

Tracking the dual and interacting power configurations of the domain story adds up to a complex account. The fact that it was not until 1992 that significant dangerous goods laws emerged testifies to the power of the industries involved in producing and shipping those goods. Other aspects of power and capacity are also in evidence when we take note again that there are 40,000 dangerous goods sites in Canada that have to be regulated and monitored but that there are only thirty-five Transport Canada DG inspectors who cannot, of course, be everywhere at once or always possess the right kinds of S&T and product and shipping knowledge.

In real terms, the economic power dynamic of pipelines versus railways from 2010 on was driven by the development of the shale gas industry in the US. Also important is the separate configuration of the fast-growing oil sands bitumen industry and the pressure for several new pipelines, especially during the Harper era, but then later and swiftly amidst declining oil prices. The Lac-Mégantic accident and disaster was also socioeconomicly pivotal in shaping the domain overall. The array of policy and accountability entities also widens overall and includes the CESD, the Treasury Board, and the National Energy Board, the latter having to coordinate its oil work with Transport Canada along with being, by law, a co-regulator of energy projects and pipelines with the federal Environmental Assessment Agency. Transport Canada's presentation of its three-part environmental role highlights its own environmental programs, its compliance tasks vis-à-vis federal environmental laws, and its summary environmental reporting.

Technology and Temporal Realities and Conflicts

The role of technology in this domain is somewhat less obvious than in some previously examined domains. In one sense, shale gas development via fracking technology had a major impact in developing the US industry and then, with its presence and shipment, in Canada via Canadian railways (including in the Lac-Mégantic disaster). Technology of a more modest scale was noted in the case of some early transload facilities being built to link oil sands shipment by both pipelines and rail (albeit at very early stages in Alberta). And of course there is science and technology knowledge inherent in some of the nine classes of dangerous goods in federal legislation.

In temporal terms, the domain reveals some varied dynamics where time is pivotal for good for ill. The Lac-Mégantic accident looms large here. It happened quickly and unexpectedly with a huge loss of life and community damage due to explosions and fire. It also triggered investigations that lead to new legislation. The shale oil industry's fast emergence was also pivotal and caught many unprepared. The Fort McMurray fire disaster also had major effects in human terms and in terms of oil sands development, certainly in the short term and possibly in the longer term as well. The analysis also took note of the expressed Transport Canada environmental policy and principle that it would respect the environmental legacy of future generations of Canadians, with no sense of what "respect" means or over what time frames for multigenerational accountability.

CONCLUSIONS

Our mapping and analysis of the transportation, dangerous goods, and environmental policy domain has been told through three related policy and governance histories. The dangerous goods policy and governance story is anchored first in Transport Canada but even here the statutory and policy governance extends significantly to an array of other entities interacting with the federal government but also, as per dangerous goods law and regulation, with the provinces and cities, and in complex spatial realms and transport modes as dangerous goods are moved and are needed in many diverse industries and sectors.

The story of dangerous goods policy and the transport of oil via pipelines versus rail has some core features similar to the first policy and governance history, but the array of core institutions broadens to embrace the National Energy Board and also includes closer links with environmental institutions such as the Canadian Environmental Assessment Agency, the Treasury Board, and the CESD. While the interactions among these bodies and the policy values at stake are observable in some ways, in other senses they are very tentative because the ways in which the twin dynamics of shale oil versus oil sands transport by rail versus pipeline are uncertain in their underlying economics and political support.

Environmental policy values and issues are present in each of the first two histories, but in our final policy and governance history environmental policy comes closer to taking center stage amidst an array of ideas that struggle for precedence and clarity. These include older ideas such as environmental assessment along with policies such as sustainable development or the "triple bottom line" encompassing social, economic, and environmental considerations and last, and usually least, climate change and greenhouse gas emission reductions. It is these that warrant our overall conclusion that in both transport and overall terms, Canada remains an environmental laggard.

10

The Disruptive Technology-Enabled Transportation Domain

INTRODUCTION

It is perfectly reasonable in one sense to refer to this final domain chapter as "the" disruptive technology-enabled transportation domain. This is because its three policy and governance histories examine, in turn, Uber ride-sourcing technology, autonomous vehicles, and unmanned air vehicles (drones), each major technology-driven instances with massive public and private decisions and means–ends dilemmas for diverse players, internationally and nationally and at multiple levels of government within countries.

It is an idea closely linked to Schumpeter's pivotal concept of "creative destruction" (Schumpeter 1934, 1954). The concept of disruptive technologies and also innovation has found its way into frequent analytical use for understanding and explaining how, for example, online digital businesses can grow with astonishing speed and quickly become an existential threat to established players in several industries that do not even see the disruptive wave coming (Doern, Castle, and Phillips 2016; Economist 2014a; Phillips 2007).

Other transportation domain analyses in this book have already brought these dynamics and features to the fore. These include accounts in chapters 9 and 4 of the Lac-Mégantic rail disaster that also had fast changing links to fracking and the quickly increasing use of the shipment of oil by trains rather than by pipelines in a Canada–US context. It also includes analysis in chapter 7 of Canada–US dynamics regarding post-9/11 air security and risk management requirements and also regarding increasingly digitalized borders and bridge infrastructures. We have seen in chapter 1 that technological disruption is also analyzed as "disruptive innovation," "innovation," and various complex reactions to attempted, partial, or failed regulation and continuous regulatory and guidance experimentation in complex governmental settings.

All three technologies examined in this chapter are disruptive. Notions of disruptiveness involve estimates as to when a technology gestates inside a private corporation, a government, or university research entity before it emerges or is imposed or rejected in markets or otherwise seeks or is given operational recognition and attention. Disruptive technology eventually must meet up with diverse public governing authorities that, as we see in some detail below, are multilevel in nature: international, national, provincial, and urban/local. The governance dynamics can also involve private entities such as business and consumer, labour, and environmental interest groups and related standard-setting bodies that function on a cogovernance basis. But what happens to disruptive technologies also confronts and has to find its way through or around several departments and agencies at each level of government, strategies within such levels as to which entity leads assessment and policy and regulatory processes and which others wait to see what happens and might act later, what kinds of fiscal budgets (taxes, spending, cofunding, operational funding, capital/infrastructure investment), and over what time frames.

When disruptive technologies emerge, legislative and regulatory policies are nearly always partial and largely experimental, as governments and societies try to figure out how to encourage these public and private socioeconomic innovations and regulate them in old and new ways. In the three policy and governance histories, we trace both US and international developments and also Canadian responses occurring at federal, provincial, and city governance levels separately and in varied coordinated or experimental trial-and-error ways. We then, as in our previous transport policy domain chapter analyses, look across the three policy and governance histories in relation to the three elements of our overall analytical framework. Conclusions then follow.

UBER RIDE-SOURCING TECHNOLOGY AND RELATED TAXI AND URBAN TRANSPORT MARKET GOVERNANCE (2005 TO PRESENT)

The development and rise of Uber (and its tech-company business model) as a ride-sourcing or ride-hailing service is having major disruptive effects on urban taxi and local transportation systems (*Economist* 2016b, 2016c) It has created a new supply chain, initially in the US but very quickly globally as well (Picker and Isaac 2015). An initial useful baseline account of the pre-Uber period taxi system is worth citing. Schaller (2007) explores the entry controls embodied in taxi regulation in forty-three cities and counties in the US and Canada. He looks at the industry's then two basic markets: the telephone-order (dispatch) market and the cabstand/street-hail market. The former has higher market share and is financially more successful, while the latter is weaker and over-supplied. Most interesting about the study from our point of view is that if it (the study) were conducted in the Uber-disruptive-technology era since 2010, it would have to be vastly different. Indeed, by 2016, initial economic assessments of the impacts of Uber on the taxi business in the US stressed the ways in which the Uber disruptive change had been beneficial in efficiency terms (Cramer and Krueger 2016). That is a reflection of how profoundly a technology wave – introduced in this case by Uber – can transform particular outcomes and related analytical considerations of transportation policy. When the sources of insight that scholars and practitioners need to consult in the literature become outdated almost immediately upon a technology's arrival, the change it brings is significant indeed (Fisher 2016).

Monteiro and Prentice (2016) also focused on the "closed entry" failures of earlier taxi reform processes and dynamics in two cities, Toronto and Ottawa, that covered more than six decades. This analysis concludes that the "two cities approached regulatory reform differently. Toronto paid very little or no attention to deregulation whereas Ottawa was more receptive to the idea but rejected it after severe public reaction" (ibid., 8). In a follow-up analysis Monteiro and Prentice (2017) looked at the basic continuing failure of closed entry but this time with more recent periods (the last two decades) as the temporal focal point. Again the staying power of closed entry emerges when the same two cities are looked at.

Uber was launched initially without formal regulatory permission in most cities whose market and power structure for the taxi industry is oligopolistic in nature. Usually that means at most a few core licensed firms, some with rights to access airports. The policies embodied in regulation and entry into the business are driven by all manner of criteria, some of them outdated. For example, in the pre–Sat Nav era, London's black cab market was regulated – in the name of safety and service – by testing drivers' detailed knowledge of London streets and routes (Jacobs 2015). The connection with safety *per se* seems tenuous, but the Uber story in London is complex now in different ways (Knight 2016). Still, taxis are frequently used as de facto ambulances that transport people to hospitals on an emergency basis and on occasion assist in the birth of babies.

The response to the Uber market penetration has been varied and complex. Uber drivers are attracted to the flexibility of part-time or full-time work. But many struggle with low pay and have begun organizing to protect their collective rights as workers. This is usually resisted by Uber, although Uber Canada said in 2015 it hopes for a "nicer approach" (Hui 2015), whatever that means. But there are labour-policy implications that will spill into the transportation policy field – and all of it is being driven by technology and tech companies such as Uber but with local closed-entry taxi industries being strongly unionized at either the city or provincial level.

The nature of Uber technology development in the US has been rapid and multifaceted and also continuously experimental as Uber and then other niche Uber-like companies formed and entered some urban markets but not others. UberPool, for example, was formed in late 2014 and its approach starts when a single rider starts a "one-time trip." The process is to "call up the app, specify your destination, and in exchange for a significant discount, UberPool matches you with other riders going the same way. The service might create just a ride for you, but just as often, it puts you in a ride that began long ago – one that has spanned several drop-offs and pick-ups, a kind of instant bus line created from collective urban demand" (Manjoo 2016, 1). The UberPool system and similar services by its competitor company Lyft work because of other related technologies, namely the "location sensors in smart phones (that) can precisely measure the whereabouts of drivers and riders and the companies' software that can efficiently match cars and customers" (Hardy 2016, 2).

Uber has also been pursued in the US courts by various opponents. It settled a civil suit in 2016 in Los Angeles and San Francisco "over claims that (Uber) misled people on its safety practices and the methods it used to screen drivers" (Isaac 2016). The suit required Uber "to pay $10 million to be split between the district attorneys of Los Angeles and San Francisco" and Uber "must reword the safety-related language around the fee that the company charges for each ride" (ibid., 1) and, moreover, "has to pay an additional $15 million if it does not comply with all the terms of the settlement within two years" (ibid.).

The Uber model has also begun in Los Angeles in smaller niche socioeconomic markets labelled by one author as "Uber for Children" (Zimmerman 2016, 1). Uber and Lyft policies are that drivers are not supposed to give rides to unaccompanied minors but other firms/ services such as HopSkipDrive have entered this niche market. It was started by full-time working mothers and "almost all of its drivers are women" (ibid., 2). Obviously parents have major concerns about the safety of their children, but HopSkipDrive and similar companies "provide a level of safety and security that the Ubers of the world do not, including fingerprinting and extensive interviewing, and they use software that monitors the drivers speed and conduct" (ibid.). In this growing urban market, "word of mouth marketing and referrals are crucial" (ibid., 3).

The Uber jobs/employment model is also contentious in relation to employment law and legal suits regarding Uber (and other firms dealing with the on demand economy or gig economy (*Economist* 2015, 2016a; Hutton 2016). Some analysts support the burgeoning need for a light touch, proinnovation approach rather than a hard regulatory one. This is because the Uber model demand economy, it is argued, has been "a dramatic success not just for consumers but for workers seeking flexibility. That is why Uber's number of drivers has been doubling every six months for the past couple of years" (*Economist* 2015, 58). Still others, and for good reasons, are deeply critical of the implications for workers in the "Uber Economy" and its claimed part of the commercially branded "sharing" economy on the grounds that little is "shared" in a normal social context but rather it is the exact opposite, namely one of exploitation via technology (Hutton 2016; Slee 2016; Hill 2015).

The savings in the abovementioned UberPool service amount to about half of a standard Uber trip and "although Uber made less from the single ride than it would have from multiple rides, the company benefitted by installing itself as a fixture in people's lives" (ibid., 2). Uber's cofounder Travis Kalanick argues that "when rides get cheaper, it means that for more people in more cities, Uber is cheaper than owning a car" and then "we can become a mainstay of transportation in that city" (quoted in ibid., 2). Manjoo concludes and conjectures that "Uber raises the stakes. Because it reduces price and increases volume, it suggests that if Uber ultimately succeeds, the company could have a much bigger impact on urban mobility, labour, the environment, local economies and the national transportation infrastructure than we've all supposed – and its effects could confound expectations of its harshest critics" (ibid., 2). Uberpool now operates in twenty-nine cities and in some major US cities accounts for more than half of the Uber trips, and "in China, Uber is running 20 million UberPool trips a month" (ibid., 3). Uber's main US competitor nationally, Lyft, has also introduced Lyft Carpool.

More recently firms such as Juno, operating in the New York market, have adopted a business and market model focusing on better treatment of drivers (Thomas 2016). Juno's owner, Talmon Marco, has adopted an approach whereby it takes "just 10% commission – compared to Uber's 20% and Lyft's 25%" and also plans to "give drivers an equity stake in the company" (ibid., 2). In Canada a new online taxi service, TappCar "was introduced as the responsible challenger to Uber [in that] you can call up, confident the driver will have appropriate insurance, a pension, and employment rights – and it only costs 5% more" (Hutton 2016).

Smaller innovative firms have sought to compete with Uber, but none of them have Uber's capacity to raise capital, which is itself a competitive $15 billion weapon. As Sorkin (2016) argues, "Every time Uber raises another 1 billion, venture capital investors and others may find it less attractive to back one of Uber's many rivals" (ibid., 2). Thus the market battle "is not just a rivalry over customers and drivers, it's a war of attrition, a mad scramble to starve the competition of cash" (ibid.). Ultimately, limits may also be emerging for Uber as well. The evidence for this came when Uber, which was not making a profit in the massive Chinese market, pulled out of China by selling its Chinese operation for $7 billion to its Chinese rival Didi Chuxing (Hern 2016, 1).

There is thus an array of related policy and governance issues in play. Concerns arise about the more lax (or nonexistent) training and qualifications of Uber's contract drivers. Women are often said to be more concerned about their personal safety in cars driven by Uber drivers. Uber fares tend to be lower than those of regular cabs, largely because Uber pays drivers less. Some argue that Uber makes money without itself having to do anything as a frontline transport provider. Whether or not that is true is almost immaterial in most disruptive technology-enabled policy contexts. More relevant, though, is the logical extension of that: Uber is not so much a transport company as a ride-sourcing company, and, perhaps even more germane, it is actually a tech company. The fact that it supports a transport function is secondary for Uber. Supporters consider it an example of what a knowledge-based innovation economy is all about: new products and services, and more choice for consumers at lower prices (*Financial Times* 2015). So where does that leave transportation policy making and governance?

Uber's business development and services are referred to here as "ride-sourcing" in concert with some of the literature (Rayle et al. 2016), but the notion of ride-hailing was also an early descriptor. A major US study by the Transportation Research Board (TRB) (2015) cast the relevant policy terrain as being a realm "between public and private mobility" populated by the "rise of technology-enabled transportation services." Uber, and its competitors such as Lyft in the US, was only one of these "transportation network companies." Policy issues were cast in this research in terms of an "economic framework for shared mobility services" and involved the need to consider and develop policies such as labour and employment conditions, personal security and public safety, insurance, equity, and access (ibid.).

The main policy laboratory for studying these transport-related issues are cities and local governments. But these policies and policy puzzles and challenges were also cast in terms of the above mentioned broader "sharing economy" since the same firms and others were pivotal in information and digital technologies involved in ordering and shipping food, restaurant meals, and many other local services (Rauch and Schleicher 2015). To others, and even more broadly, these and other developments in producer, labour, and consumer relations were also being cast as the "gig economy" (Sundararajan 2015; Hutton 2016). Uber's vast array of part-time drivers in cities are a key example of the gig-economy.

In an urban transport policy context, ride sourcing has been defined as a system that "dynamically matches supply and demand by allowing travellers to request car rides in real time from potential suppliers using a smartphone application. Distinct from ridesharing, ridesourcing drivers operate for profit and typically provide rides not incidental to their own trips. Ridesourcing is distinguished from traditional taxicabs by the use of smartphone technology and a dynamic matching algorithm – which some taxis also have adopted. It is also distinct because ridesourcing in the US has not been subject to taxi regulations, which in many cities limit supply, determine fares, and safety standards. Bolstered by support from customers, ridesourcing companies have grown quickly and received regulatory support across the US. However, they have provoked the ire of the taxi industry and generalized concern among many regulators. (Rayle et al. 2015, 168)

The battle between Uber and the conventional taxis industry has certainly been central in terms of political and media attention in the US, and policy disputes within many US cities, but analysis suggests that ride-sourcing trips also compete with and impact city transit and also that it "expands mobility options for city dwellers, particularly in large dense cities" (ibid., 177). Regarding US city regulation, US developments in the last few years were certainly raising issues about what the positives and negatives were, what kind of regulation and guidance might make sense, and what range of policy values are and should be at play (Transportation Research Board 2015).

The Canadian policy response to Uber has been slower but is now picking up speed on a city-by-city and province-by-province basis and with some initial expression of policy direction at the federal level. The federal Competition Bureau's white paper (2015b) places Uber in an interesting competition policy guidance context. Instead of calling for more regulation of Uber in Canadian taxi markets, the bureau argues broadly for deregulation of the conventional taxi industry to improve its competitive situation vis-à-vis Uber *and* make the overall industry more competitive and innovative, both economically and socially. A Monteiro and Prentice (2018) analysis considers "the Competition Bureau's advocacy of competition in the taxi industry, the theory for the competitive model, and the competitive struggle" (ibid., 1). They find theoretical support for the Competition Bureau's advocacy and that there is a case for the "removal of economic regulation" (ibid., 4). But Monteiro and Prentice, when examining recent developments in several Canadian cities, are prompted to add a cautionary note, namely that "while there may be good reason to advocate competition, it rarely comes without a fight" and that history "provides ample evidence that entry by new competitors is not received with open arms" (ibid., 5). They conclude that, "while the writing is on the wall what consumers want, regulators appear the last to see it" (ibid., 8). But in real terms that means that the regulators, competition bureaus and others, are themselves being lobbied. We have also seen this earlier in our overall account of competition policy in chapters 1 and 6.

A study by Victor Ngo (2015) prepared by UBC for the City of Vancouver is the most complete and integrated Canadian account of the Uber impact and its multilevel governmental policy options and dilemmas. Though focused on Vancouver and British Colombia, it also draws on key developments across Canada. Beginning in 2012, Uber operated in Vancouver only briefly after it was warned by the provincial Passenger Transportation Board (PTB) that, "it would pursue legal action if Uber operated in BC without the proper licenses" (ibid., 10). The Ngo study also took note of public opinion in other jurisdictions in Canada, concluding that:

> Uber finds the most support in larger jurisdictions where Uber has already established itself. Support is highest among younger people from 18 to 34 years old, and those 35 to 49 years old. Respondents generally agree that Uber should be regulated and operating with the same regulations as taxis. It is predicted that Uber has a moderate to potentially high support among Vancouver residents. (Ibid., 10)

The regulations and policies that Ngo (2015) show as being considered for ride-sourcing are:

- *Safety* (focused on regulations for driver safety, including background checks)
- *Driver training* (rules for driver training programs similar to taxis)
- *Accessibility* (provisions to ensure accessible vehicles are available to seniors or persons with disabilities)
- *Environment* (to favourably impact environmental outcomes from ride-sourcing such as via: vehicle, model year and engine year restrictions; minimum fuel efficiency standards; general anti-idling requirements
- *Data Sharing* (to support policy and planning)
- *Insurance* (Insurance for contingent liability and links to personal insurance)
- *Transit Integration* (steps to partner with Uber to provide an integrated multimodal system. (Ngo 2015, 46–52)

In terms of implementing such regulations and policies, the Ngo study examines four policy options: 1) do nothing, 2) permit entry with existing "taxicab" category, 3) permit entry with new "transportation network company" category, and 4) permit entry with shared vehicle for hire category (ibid., 54–60). Also discussed are the roles and financing of a potentially needed ride-sourcing transportation impact fund (ibid., 61–3).

Other Canadian cities initially responded to Uber and related developments in a variety of ways with their eye also on what was happening in the US. Regarding Toronto, Cohn (2015, 1) argues that, "UberX is the killer app that is driving taxis out of business and putting passengers in the fast lane. It also has most politicians running for cover, and lobbyists trying to hail cab companies as clients." Focus group research in Ottawa shows a highly favourable response to Uber and argues Uber is "here to stay" (quoted in Laucius 2015, 2). So the policy problems are not likely to go away anytime soon. For example, in 2015 the City of Ottawa conducted a taxi and limousine regulations service review and commissioned a study, Taxi Economics – Old and New (Hara Associates 2015). The study examined Uber operations and impacts in general and also in relation to concepts of the sharing economy. Interestingly, it also drew on research on the city taxi industry in the US in the 1970s when some cities deregulated suddenly, in keeping with US national deregulation urges. This supplied some avenues for examining situations when suddenly, there was a surge of new entrants to the taxi industry and how this could happen at some future time when, as is now happening, there is a surge of new Uber-like entrants.

Accounts of Uber as an aggressive lobbying and corporate juggernaut in several Canadian cities were available as front page and online stories and controversies (Haavardsrud 2016). Provincial transport ministers were cautiously aware of that and knew that the Uber issue was mainly a city governance and economy issue, but, as British Columbia Transport Minister Todd Stone pointed out, "These are services that would provide convenience and choice and certainly competition that I think would be welcomed by British Columbians" (quoted in Bailey 2016).

There has been considerable vocal opposition at city halls in most Canadian cities. In Quebec, the provincial taxi driver union representing 4,000 Quebec drivers announced early in 2016 that they would seek a court injunction against Uber to declare their services illegal under provincial law (Van Praet 2016). This and other developments resulted in the Quebec government's decision to establish a commission to study the issues (Richer 2016). Quebec's then premier Philippe Couillard has stated he would be "open to legalizing UberX-style means of transport, despite opposition from the taxi industry" (Remioz 2015). But in fact his government proposed legislation "that would kill Uber's business model in the province" (Boisvert 2016, 1) in that Uber's drivers would be forced "to work under the same restrictions as taxi drivers" (ibid.). Quebec courts were also involved via a ruling on whether, as alleged by Quebec tax investigators, Uber had destroyed data in its San Francisco headquarters and thus that "Uber wanted to shield evidence of its illegal conduct from the tax authorities" (ibid.). This was a separate smaller issue but was elevated as evidence that Uber's corporate practices were dubious.

The Toronto response is of particular interest because it is Canada's biggest city, indeed an amalgam of cities in the Greater Toronto Area (GTA). Toronto city staff proposed a system whereby "cabbies and UberX drivers would face different rules for vehicle inspections, police checks and more" (Rider 2016a, 1). Toronto's core taxi industry announced "an application for an injunction against all UberX drivers" that would ban them in Toronto (Pagliaro 2016). Initially, subsequent city committee meetings were highly combative. Neither the Uber or taxi sides of the debate are praised for their tactics, tone, and dubious sense of accountability to urban citizens. There are also particular concerns and dynamics in Toronto regarding which system is safer for women and whether women have a voice in the debate (Csanady 2016). On 3 May 2016 Toronto City Council eventually opted, by a vote of 27–15, for a new dual Uber and taxi system (Rider and Pagliaro 2016). A further interesting and multifaceted study looks at the issues regarding shared mobility in the Greater Toronto and Hamilton area and advocates a mainly proinnovation stance for policy makers involved (Ditta, Urban and Johal 2016).

In Edmonton, however, arguably the most significant benchmark city policy was announced even earlier, in March 2016. The press described it as the first "Uber-friendly bylaw" in Canada (Stolte 2016). Against the strong opposition of the Edmonton taxi industry, starting on 1 March 2016, Uber could operate based on several conditions (Rider 2016b). These include that private transportation providers (PTPs), including Uber drivers, "must have provincially approved commercial insurance and undergo car inspections and criminal record checks." PTPs and "traditional taxis all charge passengers a minimum $3.25 fare," and PTPs have no legislated per-kilometre rate, opening the door to Uber's 'surge' peak-time pricing with no maximum, while "taxis maintain city legislated rates" (ibid., 1). Edmonton's success in getting a policy adopted was also due to its speedier, more participatory city bylaw development and amending process (Rider 2016c).

Meanwhile, other policy routes that were interprovincial were taking shape on issues such as insurance. Ontario's insurance regulator, the Financial Services Commission of Canada, had approved a policy from Intact Financial Corporation for "private vehicles transporting paying passengers through the ride-hailing service" (Jones 2016). It covers "all Uber drivers, passengers and vehicle owners in Ontario when Uber is in use. When the app is turned off, the vehicle owner's personal auto insurance policy applies" (ibid., 1). Uber was now operating in forty municipalities in Ontario. The same kind of policy had just come into effect in Alberta under Alberta law.

An exception is Manitoba where the public car insurance agency (Manitoba Public Insurance) allows drivers to add on coverage for the time they drive but does not permit a blanket coverage policy. Neither Uber nor Lyft have begun operations in the province, but two independent ride-sharing companies (TappCar and Cowboy Taxi) are expanding services.

The dynamics of actual and attempted comparative regulation and innovation among cities and provincial jurisdictions is bound to continue. For example, new provincial rules in Quebec have been announced by the province's transport minister and include requirements for Uber drivers to have training, the only Canadian jurisdiction "where Uber operates that requires drivers to do training" (CBC News 2017). The government of Quebec also "wants Uber drivers to have criminal background checks done by police, instead of private companies that do them now and have their cars inspected every 12 months" (ibid., 1). Uber's response has been to threaten to cease operations, a strategy that is unlikely to be deployed. That same week, there was also the announcement in the UK that Transport for London (TFL) had rejected Uber's "application for a new licence in London on the basis that the company was not a 'fit and proper' private car hire operator" (Butler and Topham 2017, 1). The lack of corporate responsibility was said to be in relation to "reporting serious criminal offenses, obtaining medical certificates and driver background checks" (ibid., 2). The TFL was also said to be concerned about "Uber's use of Greyball, software that can be used to block regulatory bodies from gaining full access to its app and undertaking regulatory or law enforcement duties" (ibid., 2). There is both strong support for the new rules from the mayor of London and strong opposition from Uber drivers and users (ibid., 2–3).

The debate about Uber strategies and ambitions is now reflected by the resignation and removal of Travis Kalanick as its leader and CEO after numerous public controversies and battles within Uber centred on his style and aggressiveness. As Manjoo (2017) argues Kalanick's "expansive vision" was never "just about hailing rides" but rather "a gateway for a business model that he believed would upend the entire trillion-dollar global transportation, altering the way people and things mover around the world – and turning Uber into one of the handful of American tech giants that will lord over this century" (ibid., 1). Dara Khosrowshahi was chosen to replace Kalanick based on his related different experience as CEO "of the online travel company Expedia" and thus regarding ambition, "will the company still aim to become the Amazon of transportation, or will it settle for being the Expedia of its market – one of several players in the industry, but not expansionist and messianic, hell-bent on becoming the next great American technology behemoth?" (ibid.). Interestingly it was Khosrowshahi who had to respond to the abovementioned UK London license decision. He said he disagreed with the TFL decision but that "it was based on past behaviour" and added in his quoted note to Uber staff that "the truth is that there is a high cost to a bad reputation. ... It really matters what people think of us, especially in a global business like ours" (quoted in Butler and Topham 2017, 1).

AUTONOMOUS VEHICLES TRANSPORT TECHNOLOGY AND RELATED EMERGING POLICY AND GUIDANCE (2010 TO PRESENT)

The autonomous vehicles (AV) technology and policy development dynamics have been somewhat slower to emerge in the public media as a policy debate *per se* but as a disruptive technology and transport policy issue it is broader and deeper than the Uber ride-sourcing developments in world effects, benefits, and challenges that likely will soon be partially realized (*Economist* 2016b, 2016c; International Transport Forum 2015; Fagnant and Kockelman 2014; US Department of Transportation 2013, 2015). AVs involve both informational and technology giants such as Google and major car manufacturers with both sets now testing vehicles and some expecting AVs for sale in 2017–18 with a large market in place by 2030.

The International Transport Forum's 2015 study made several findings and offered several policy insights and challenges. Among the key findings are "road safety is expected to improve with vehicle automation. But this effect remains untested at a large scale and may not be immediate or linear," "there are many possible configurations for autonomous driving," and "there are two incremental paths towards full automation … the first involves gradually improving the automation … the second path involves deploying vehicles without a human driver in limited contexts and then gradually expanding the range and conditions of their use" (ibid., 5).

The policy insights and challenges highlighted in the study include AV as a part of a "much larger revolution in automation and connectivity" which means that "policies should account for this uncertainty and ensure sufficient resilience" (ibid., 6), AV will require changes in insurance and "as automation increases, liability could gradually shift from drivers to manufacturers and Original Equipment Manufacturers (OEMs)" (ibid., 7). Among the types of regulation possible/likely for automated driving are those that are public and private, and *ex ante* and *ex post* (ibid., 25). For example on the *ex ante* side, there could be public regulation regarding performance standards, process requirements, and entry barriers. On the private side, there could be rules/guidance regarding private standards, industry practice, and conditions of insurance (ibid., 25).

Policy development in the US, the early, main home base of the AV technology and industry, has been emerging but is also exploratory and tentative given the scale of the AV potential and its uncertainty. The US Department of Transport (2013) released an initial policy document cast as guidance for US state governments and based on research its National Highway Traffic Safety Administration (NHTSA) had been conducting for several years. Several states including Nevada, California, and Florida had already enacted legislation that expressly permits the operation of self-driving (autonomous) experimental vehicles under specified conditions.

In its guidance approach to state governments, the US Department of Transport set out five different levels of vehicle automation (from level 0 to level 4 at full self-driving automation). Its guidance recommendations relate to licensing drivers to operate self-driving vehicles for testing; regulations regarding the testing of self-driving vehicles; testing operations to roadway, traffic, and environmental conditions suitable for the capabilities of the tested self-driving vehicles; and establishing reporting requirements to monitor the performance of self-driving technology during testing (ibid., 11–13).

Interestingly, at a 2015 symposium on self-driving cars, the administrator of the NHTSA, Dr Mark Roseland, spoke of three features and needs for current and future policy on AVs. The first was the need for the industry to develop "a proactive safety culture" as a continuous part of product quality, especially given an AV future (Roseland 2015, 1). The second point was that "safety innovations" should not be developed "as an enticement for high end customers, but as a vital part of the industry's safety commitment to all of its customers" (ibid.). Roseland also argued that "immediate tangible action" is needed on cybersecurity because "failure to tackle the cybersecurity challenge would threaten the technology-driven safety transformation we all want to achieve. If drivers believe they are one virus away from a hacker taking control of their vehicle, they are not about to hand over the driving task to that vehicle's automated systems" (ibid., 1).

US policy has also emerged on the public spending side in an announcement by the departing Obama administration regarding proposed spending of \$4 billion on self-driving car projects and infrastructure. Also promised were policies to remove hurdles to developing AVs and that further guidelines for the industry would emerge within six months (Vlasic 2016a). Reports also emerged that the NHTSA had assured Google, in a document replying to several earlier Google questions, that Google's AV would not need an "occupant seat for the driver" because its self-driving system is the driver (Yadron 2016). Such an approach or rule is not in sync with proposed rules in California where most of the AV research is being done. California "issued draft regulations "that would require a human driver to remain 'in the loop' in a self-driving car" (Markoff 2016, 1). Thus, clearly, and not surprisingly, the regulatory approach and its politics is complex and very much a work in progress.

Other key AV developments in the US are alliances forming between and among traditional automakers and technology companies (Vlasic 2016b). Ford Motor and Google have "joined to lead a coalition of companies that advocate federal approval of driverless cars in the near future" (ibid., 1). Calling itself the Self-Driving Coalition for Safer

Streets, the coalition includes "the Swedish carmaker Volvo and the ride-sharing firms Lyft and Uber" (ibid., 2).

A further recent phase of debate in the US occurred when a self-driving Tesla Model S electric sedan was involved in a crash that killed the driver of the vehicle (Vlasic and Boudette 2016). A tractor-trailer "made a left turn in front of the Tesla and the car failed to apply the brakes" (ibid., 1). The car was being self-driven rather than by its human driver with the latter also not responding, if indeed he could have. Inquiries into the crash followed quickly and have led to immediate advocacy for the need for diverse testing sites, including city or city-like test sites that can offer up more diverse, unpredictable situations for the driverless car "laboratory" (Boudette 2016a, 2016b).

As a result of these intricate and fast-moving, uncertain, multidimensional developments, the US government announced a new set of guidelines on safety assessment which consisted of a fifteen-point safety standard for the design and development of autonomous vehicles (Kang 2016a, 2016b). Using terms such as guidelines and standards, but falling short of being regulations, the announcement constituted a form of significant US "backing for self-driving cars" (Kang 2016a, 1). The issues and challengers covered include "how driverless cars should react if their technology fails, what measures to put in place to preserve passenger privacy, and how occupants will be protected in crashes" (ibid., 2), not to mention several other features such as data sharing between car makers and regulators, digital security to prevent online attacks, and consumer education of complex kinds (Kang 1016b).

In Canada, the development of policy for AVs is much more sluggish at all levels of government (Goodmark et al. 2015; Flemming 2016). There is some awareness of the AV issue in federal and provincial transport departments but not much evidence of even early policy speculation. A 2015 research study by Goodmark et al. looked at social and economic impacts and argued that "no major infrastructure project should be undertaken in Canada without an 'AV impact audit' that governments and the private sector should be conducting (ibid., ii–iii). The authors' five recommended priorities for Canada include calls for augmented, enhanced, or boosted leadership by each level of government (ibid., iv). In a speech to the Association of Canadian Engineering Companies, Brian Flemming (2016), one of the coauthors of the Goodmark et al. study, explained the growing importance of AVs, showed the profound nature of the transformation to society that is likely to result from this transportation shock wave, and urged policy makers everywhere to get on with the job of dealing with it.

There has been a response to this call from both the Ontario Transportation Minister and the Economic Development Minister. Ontario has thus announced that it would be the first province to allow driverless cars to be tested on its roads (Csanady 2015). Ontario has been an active participant in events such as a conference in September 2015 on the future of the car (Kalinowsky 2015).

Without doubt the initial most comprehensive Canadian scenario-developing study is that by David Ticoll (2015). Commissioned by the City of Toronto and linked to related work at the University of Toronto, his analysis traces the global origins and state of AV technology but examines these kinds of technology via a "bottom-up analysis based on Toronto-specific data" (ibid., 4). Ticoli suggests that,

> The result is a conservative estimate that were AVs to be at a 90% adoption rate in Toronto today, the result would be annual savings of $6 billion or 4% of the City's $150 billion gross domestic product. This includes $1.2 billion from reduced collisions, $2.7 billion out of congestion costs, $1.6 billion from insurance, and $0.5 billion from parking fees and fines. AVs will provide other quantifiable social and economic benefits that range from fewer deaths and hospitalizations thanks to lower particle emissions, to productivity gains in many business sectors. (Ibid., 4)

Ticoli also previews other benefits beyond costs savings including those centred on safety, equity and accessibility, environment, lower operating costs, and reductions in congestion (ibid., 4–5). He also notes that Canada has catching up to do relative to some other countries but that this is more than possible. Not surprisingly, he sees multiple types of desirable/possible objectives and complex policy and planning items to address, based on both positive and negative impacts or uncertain ones. The objectives previewed include

- Foster complete streets
- Increase car occupancy rate
- Increase multimodal travel
- Reduce rush-hour congestion
- Seamless multimode transportation GTA and beyond
- Strengthening downtown & other hubs

- Equitable funding and pricing
- Improve freight/goods movement roads & curbside
- Increase road safety for everyone
- Social equity and inclusion
- Foster complete communities
- Increase fewer & shorter trips
- Reduce car dependencies
- Increase transit use
- Increase walking and cycling
- Reduce vehicle travel demand
- Shift travel from peak to off-peak periods. (Ibid., 5)

In policy-related terms, however, even the above kind of multifaceted advocacy and scenario-setting items are incomplete. Thus policies and challenges are also related to the likelihood of major reductions in parking spaces needed, AVs in winter, data provision and analysis, and fiscal impacts (ibid., 6). The analysis also plays with three scenarios "for private vs shared AVs during the 2030s decade," ownership leads, on-demand leads, and split outcome mobility service (ibid., 7).

A second Canadian study offers closer but still broad Canadian policy scenarios on automated vehicles (Zon and Ditta 2016). These include policy implications and challenges regarding safety, accessibility, environment and urban planning, economic growth and labour markets; insurance and liability; government fiscal position, infrastructure, and data and privacy (ibid., 9–17). Its broader strategic advice to governments begins with a call to "stay technology agnostic" in a fast changing set of technologies and choices and then extends to the need to "build avenues for cross sector and intergovernmental cooperation," emphasize "transparency and trust," and "invest in multi-use infrastructure" (ibid., 20–1).

Also on offer is a white paper published by the Canadian Automated Vehicles Centre of Excellence (CAVCOE) (2015) prepared for the government of Canada. This analysis covers some of the same policy and political–economic and technological challenges noted above, but heading the list of its thirty recommendations is that the government appoint "a Minister for AVs that has a voice in the Cabinet who would champion and coordinate this nascent sector across all of the Federal Government. ... The Canadian Minister of Communications role (1969–1996) can be considered a precedent for a Minister to oversee an emerging technology sector" (ibid., 1). Other policy recommendations are grouped in relation to the economy; transportation and traffic; transit; quality of life, health, climate change and mobility equity; auto and technology industries; oil and pipeline industries; national security and policing; and provinces, territories and municipalities (ibid., 7–17).

What few, if any, Canadian or even US policy makers seem to have tackled to date are questions of such far reaching policy significance as whether there should be a moratorium on further investments in road construction (AVs, by travelling more closely together, will let far more traffic flow through the existing road network than human drivers possibly can), whether – as implied in the Ticoli list – there should be a complete overhaul of parking policies in cities (AVs may not need any on-street parking or parking lots in close proximity to shopping or work venues because after dropping off their passengers they can park themselves much farther away), how to change the health-care system and its financing (fewer people will be injured in car crashes and need medical attention, and the elderly will retain their mobility much later in life, stay in their homes and remain active and healthier for longer, and need less medical attention), whether there should be a rethink of housing strategies (the turnover rate of housing stock from older to younger people will slow down), how to revamp the system and the financing of law enforcement and the courts (with AVs there will be fewer traffic violations and fewer accidents), how to rethink and restructure conventional standards of road maintenance (AVs will behave differently than human drivers on snow- and ice-covered roads), and so on. Also on the agenda in potentially major ways is the expanded use of driverless trucks. These were discussed briefly in chapter 3 regarding cabotage policy and Canadian–US trucking (Beilock and Prentice 2007) in the US as an employment and unemployment issue for the 3.5 million US truckers and with regard to safety and security issues concerning digital hacking and interference with such trucking systems (Solon 2016). Some aspects of these overall Canada–US cross-border issues have been discussed via the joint Regulatory Cooperation Council but with practical outcomes not particularly clear or evident.

In short, the advent of AVs is introducing a massive policy and governance workload, but the rate of progress to that end is, not surprisingly, going nowhere nearly as fast. Perhaps the most important insight from the above studies is their use of the conditional tense in so many of the verbs. The public policy issues are described as not much more than possibilities, even though vehicles embodying the technology are not far from entering service in the hands of ordinary people using them on public roads. It looks like an example of policy makers being caught flat-footed but often for good reasons. Given both its US and Canadian dimensions and history to date, there is considerable presence of both the Coglianese "regulatory breakdown" insight and argument and the "unruliness" of policy and regulatory systems identified by Doern, Prince, and Schultz, both previewed briefly in chapter 1.

Without doubt the most ambitious study report and the one with the most expanded scope is that of the Standing Senate Committee on Transport and Communications (2018). Titled *Driving Change*, it seeks to advocate and evaluate technology and the future of the automated vehicle, and it advocates and evaluates "connected vehicles." The study was conducted at the request of the minister of Transport and involved testimony from "over 78 witnesses from across Canada and the United States" as well as written submissions. The operative definition of automated vehicles was consistent with material we have looked at earlier but connected vehicles as defined by the Senate Committee referred to "two types of connected technologies: consumer convenience and infotainment, and vehicle to vehicle and vehicle to infrastructure communications" (ibid., 9).

The report highlights its view that "Canada is ill-prepared for the fast-approaching future of transportation" but its other highlighted points include both strong benefits and serious problems such as an end to the nearly "1,700 road deaths and 117,000 injuries that occurred in 2015," a "nightmare of significant job losses, car hacking and erosion of personal privacy," "automated cars could also provide greater freedom to the elderly or people with mobility issues," hundreds "of thousands of jobs could also be lost" including those related to the "taxi transportation and parking industries" that employ more than 1.1 million people.

The committee recommends that federal departments "create a joint policy unit to coordinate federal efforts to implement a national strategy on automated and connected vehicles" and also that Transport Canada work with provincial and territorial governments on a model provincial policy for the use of these vehicles on public roads" (ibid., 11). So one of these first two ideas is cast as a "strategy" and the second as a "model" policy. The committee also wants Transport Canada to "develop vehicle safety guidelines, including design aspects to be considered when developing, testing and deploying these vehicles on Canadian roads.. The committee recommends that, "Transport Canada, the Communications Security Establishment and Public Safety Canada develop cybersecurity guidance based on best practices and recognized cybersecurity principles." A further recommendation is federal legislation to "empower the Office of the Privacy Commissioner to proactively investigate and enforce industry compliance with privacy legislation." In these latter three realms of recommendation, one enters a world of "guidelines," cybersecurity "guidance" "best practices" and then, surprisingly in many ways, new laws to investigate and enforce privacy protection. When looking ahead at next steps, the committee argues that previous instances of disruptive technology "have shown that confusion results from a lack of planning" (ibid., 12).

UNMANNED AIR VEHICLES (DRONE) TECHNOLOGY AND POLICY AND GOVERNANCE (2005 TO PRESENT)

The third policy and governance history centres on unmanned air vehicles (UAVs) often referred to as drones. This disruptive technology refers especially to both economic and social–recreational drones in an environment where large volumes of new small-scale UAV products have emerged and are operating in variously defined and undefined air spaces.

The US response to the emergence in the last eight years of civilian, private, and commercial unmanned air vehicles (UAVs) and unmanned air systems (UAS) as a fast developing technology has centred on the Federal Aviation Administration (FAA) (Marshall 2016; Elias 2012). As Marshall argues,

> In the void created by the lack of a statutory mandate to include UAS in its regulatory scheme, the FAA embarked on a perilous journey to regulate this rapidly evolving technology by issuing a series of policy statements, orders, and directives culminating in the creation of a Small UAS Aviation Rulemaking Committee (that was) chartered to recommend a comprehensive set of rules that would permit a gradual integration of small unmanned systems into the national airspace under very limited and controlled operating restrictions. The rulemaking process consumed nearly six years. (Ibid., 123–4)

Operating somewhat separately was a process that resulted in the passage of the FAA Modernization & Reform Act of 2012 (FMRA). After the FMRA passage, there were up to four ways to obtain UAV operational authority: 1) public users (federal, state, and local governments) pursuant to the requirements for a Certificate of Authorization or Waiver (COA), 2) civil users through the mechanism of a special airworthiness certificate in the experimental category, 3) petition for exemption, and 4) process from the small UAS rule (not yet finalized as Marshall was completing his article). As of 22 April 2016, the FAA website shows three regulatory processes, one each for public operations (governmental), civil operations (nongovernmental), and model aircraft (hobby or recreation only) (US Federal Aviation Administration 2016). Also highlighted was a news update that urges nonhobbyist, government, and commercial owners to register via a new automated registration system.

The Marshall analysis focuses on the complexity of the US public regulatory review and implementation process as a focal point for examining why the UAS process has taken so long. The slowness is also because of the dynamics and massive growth of the new small UAS socio-economic product market. He notes that although the FAA prefers "compliance over enforcement, it will bring proceedings that may include substantial civil penalties" (ibid., 134). As a result Marshall concludes as well that "there are multiple land mines and blind allies to trap the unwary entrepreneur or business entity to design, acquire, build, deploy, or otherwise exploit the virtually unlimited opportunities for both profitable and humanitarian uses of unmanned aircraft systems" (ibid., 133).

In contrast to the above analysis, which focused on the length and complexity of the response, there are alternative views about the very recent dynamics that led to the very speedy adoption of the FAA's drone registry. Snead and Seibler (2016) argue that,

On 22 October 2015, the FAA published a rule determining that drones are subject to existing aircraft registry requirements. One month later, the agency's special drone registry task force, composed of government and industry representatives, released a report outlining specific recommendations for a "streamlined registration process." Three weeks later, the FAA published its interim final rule establishing the recreational drone-owners' registry. Seven days after its release, the rule went into effect,

and it officially became a federal felony to operate a drone
weighing more than 0.55 pounds without first registering
as a drone owner. (Ibid., 1–2)

Normal regulatory processes were not used in this instance, and the
process took just two months because the FAA acted "owing to the
immediate dangers that the agency has alleged stem from the proliferation of drones in the national airspace" (ibid., 2). The criticism
of this fast process was also based on the fact that the FAA was not
empowered (by Congress) to criminalize the failure to register a
recreational drone. But overall, the reaction to the new liberalized
rules and their speedy adoption has been seen as long overdue
(Lee 2016).

The other dynamic to emphasize in the US context is the social
media and personal drone movement via such groups as DIY Drones,
an online community formed in 2007 by Chris Anderson. His analysis
(Anderson 2012) shows that DIY Drones then had "26,000 members
who fly drones that they either assemble themselves or buy premade
from dozens of companies that serve the amateur market" (ibid., 4).
Anderson stresses that the reason there are around 1,000 new personal
drones taking to the sky every month "is the same as with every other
digital technology: a Moore's-law-style pace where performance regularly doubles while size and price plummet. In fact, Moore's law of
drone technology is currently accelerating, thanks to the smartphone
industry, which relies on the same components – sensors, optics, batteries, and embedded processors – all of them growing smaller and
faster each year" (ibid., 4). The DIY Drones organization mentioned
above also has its own guidance provisions developed by and for its
members regarding privacy issues and values. As of early 2016, the
organization's membership since 2012 has tripled to 77,477 (DIY
Drones 2016).

Other authors have entered the UAS debate in the US in relation
to issues such as privacy, search and seizure, airspace monitoring,
lawful use, and the potential for domestic terrorism. Milojevich (2016)
calls on the White House Office of Science and Technology to design
a "comprehensive framework for drone policy" because "UAS policy
is especially complicated for two reasons: 1) drone technology is
advancing far more rapidly than associated legislation and regulation,
and 2) the issues span across regulatory agencies and levels of enforcement" (ibid., 1).

Policies on drones in the US have also been analyzed and debated in the context of not just regulatory matters *per se*. They involve constitutional issues including efforts to regulate at the state level (Farber 2014) and approaches centred on an ethical analysis of surveillance issues (West and Bowman 2016). Also different contextually and crucially in the US are concerns and influences about US uses of drones in warfare and the way that this dynamic enters national debate in terms of US military power and in related aspects of international humanitarian law (Rosen 2013). Public attitudes about drone usage in domestic policing activities are also being explored in terms of their implications for developing public policy (Sakiyama et al. 2016). Local governments in the US have their own entry points and concerns about when and how to regulate, and hence there are vast amounts of experimentation. One analysis concludes that, "the challenge of this rapidly developing technology is … well ahead of local government efforts to rein in excessive activities" (Swindell et al. 2016, 1). Other very particular drone technology and policy debates are centred on "delivery drones" including Amazon's plans to have Amazon Air break new ground in the use of airspace (Burzichelli 2016) with Amazon's early developmental work being done in Vancouver (Serebrin 2015).

In Canada, UAVs are also stretching traditional air and product boundaries out of shape but with a, claimed, more favourable regulatory system in terms of innovation and one that has been operationalized earlier and faster, in 1996, than the still sluggish and only very recently reformed US system (Serebrin 2015). Thompson and Saulnier (2015) analyzed all UAV Special Flight Operation Certificates (SFOC) issued by Transport Canada between 2007 and 2012 and concluded that "the issuance of SFOCs is used to publicly demonstrate the validity of UAV usage as well as establish Transport Canada as the overseer of regulated UAV flights" (ibid., 1). That means Transport Canada is working to extend its authority over transportation licensing policy into a new arena. UAVs have spawned new types of industries and uses in many fields, and the rise of their use, "combined with the opaque nature of UAV oversight, constitute the formation of a social moment in Canada in which new challenges regarding safety and privacy need to be carefully considered" (ibid., 1). In other words, conventional structures for applying transportation policy are having to be significantly rethought.

Canada's UAV story demonstrates both the current/recent surge and a longer history dating back to the 1950s and the development of its military surveillance purposes via "a partnership between the Canadian government and the Canadair Corporation [which] produced the first UAV to be used exclusively for surveillance purposes in the British Commonwealth" (Bracken-Roche et al. 2014, 10). The Canadian developments saw later shifts in military focus and then some limited live use of UAVs by Canadian Forces and by Canadian police forces domestically (ibid., 12–13). Canadian dynamics then shifted, as the US story also revealed, into a dynamic and growing market in the civilian context including "locating missing persons in search and rescue operations, tracking and monitoring of animal populations and crime scene and highway accident imagery" (ibid., 15) to name only a few. And then, very swiftly, came the growing use of UAVs for recreational purposes and applications (Office of the Privacy Commissioner of Canada 2013, 2015; Cavoukian 2012) where both their popularity and related concerns about privacy and the practicality of regulatory strategies were being examined. Also of interest analytically and practically is the important issue regarding the use of UAVs in Canada–US border surveillance (Szoo 2015).

The UAV's main lobby group, Unmanned Systems Canada (USC) emerged in 2003 and describes itself as a "not-for-profit association representing the interests of the unmanned vehicle systems community which includes industry, academia, government, military, and other interested parties" (Unmanned Systems Canada 2016, 2). Related objectives include promoting and facilitating the growth of the Canadian UAV community "through education, advocacy, and exchange of ideas and technologies" and "to achieve leadership in research, development, application, and operations" (ibid., 2). Interestingly, the organization also indicates that it is "the recognized voice of the UAS community to Transport Canada as the co-chair of the UAS regulatory development working group" (ibid., 3) (see more below), and it also draws attention to its work in promoting "the sharing of peer-reviewed knowledge through the *Journal of Unmanned Systems*" (ibid., 3).

This kind of peer reviewed journal linkage to a lobby group deserves special mention because the journal's website also presents itself as the "official journal of Unmanned Systems Canada" (Journal of Unmanned Systems Canada 2016). There are precious few lobby groups in Canadian policy making that have established and draw attention to the role of a peer reviewed academic journal. The journal was established in 2013, is published by NRC Research Press quarterly and only electronically, and features "editorials, articles, notes, and letters related to developments in the rapidly emerging international field of unmanned vehicle systems" (aerial, terrestrial, and aquatic). The "journal is themed into four main areas of applications of practical and academic interest: civil, environmental, military and engineering technology" (ibid., 1). Interestingly, the journal's inaugural editor comes with a research background in wildlife biology research including via the use of UAVs. The journal also has twenty-eight associate editors (Canadian and international).

Transport Canada's review of the UAV developments and its consultations on the proposed 28 May 2015 regulatory amendments are still being conducted via the Canadian Aviation Regulations Advisory Council (CARAC), an entity mentioned in chapter 4. Transport Canada's Notice of Proposed Amendment: Unmanned Air Vehicles (Transport Canada 2015c) begins with several contextual views and reference points:

- The rising sales and evolving technology of UAVs make them a rapidly growing part of the aviation industry. ... This presents unique challenges in developing regulations to safely integrate UAV's into Canada's airspace.
- Transport Canada has a permissive regulatory framework that accommodates UAV operations by issuing Special Flight Operation Certificates (SFOCS)
- Transport Canada seeks a balanced approach to both safely integrate UAV's into Canadian airspace and encourage innovation within this important new subsector of civil aviation. At the same time it is important to recognize the unique risks UAVs and UAV users of varying degrees of aviation expertise, pose to other airspace users. Transport Canada must develop Canada's future regulatory framework to be risk-based, flexible, and consistent with international partners, where appropriate.
- In 2016 Transport Canada intends to introduce regulatory requirements for UAVs 25kgs or less that are operated within visual line-of-sight. [These] are intended to ensure the safe and reliable operation of UAV's in Canadian airspace and will:

establish classifications including a proposal for the possibility
of having a very small (lower threshold) category of aircraft;
clarify terminology; establish aircraft marking and registration
requirements; address personnel licensing and training; and
create flight rules.
- Transport Canada intends to preserve the SFOC process to
focus on higher risk operations, including UAVs larger than
25kgs and those operated beyond visual line-of-sight.
(Transport Canada 2015c, 1)

Transport Canada also takes note of key US developments underway
on the regulatory front and also, internationally, the fact that "Canada
will adopt minimum civil aviation standards established by the
International Civil Aviation Organization (ICAO)" (ibid., 4). Transport
Canada also noted the core roles and earlier studies involving
Unmanned Systems Canada (500 members) and the Model Aeronautics
Association (13,000 members), the two organizations that represent
the UAV industry and model aircraft community (ibid., 3). Mention
is also made of the growing presence of UAV applications in academic
and industrial fields such as agriculture, meteorology, and oceanog-
raphy. Transport Canada indicates that it "will continue to work with
the Office of the Privacy Commissioner to emphasize the applicability
and role of Canada's privacy laws to the operations of UAVs by public
and private sector organizations" (ibid., 3).

Table 10.1 below shows at a glance the main features of the initial
2015 proposed regulatory framework centred on three types of
unmanned air vehicles: very small UAVs, small UAVs (limited operations), and small UAVs (complex operations), each with three realms
of requirements (aircraft, pilot, and permissions to fly).

The changed contours and requirements were made public in July
2017 with the department's proposed regulations announcement
(Transport Canada 2017b) being interpreted by one commentator
(Willick 2017) as unexpectedly favourable to "recreational drone
users." But this was not the case overall.

Public consultations were announced under the provisions of the
federal government *Canada Gazette* process for reviewing new regulations. Transport Canada said the "new regulations are easy-to-follow,
flexible and balanced, while supporting innovation and safe recreational use" (Transport Canada 2017b, 1). The "very small drone
operations" category involved pilots who must be 14 years or older

Table 10.1
Initial 2015 proposed Transport Canada regulatory framework
for unmanned air vehicles

Requirements	Very small UAVs	Small UAVs (limited operations)	Small UAVs (complex operations)
AIRCRAFT REQUIREMENTS			
Identification	Yes	No	No
Marking and registration	No	Yes	Yes
Design standard	No	Yes	Yes
PILOT REQUIREMENTS			
Age restrictions	No	Yes	Yes
Knowledge test	Yes (basic)	Yes (basic)	Yes (advanced)
Pilot permit	No	No	Yes
Respect for privacy and other laws	Yes	Yes	Yes
PERMISSION TO FLY			
At night	No	No	Yes
In proximity to an Aerodrome	No	No	Yes
Within 9 km of a built-up area	Yes	No	Yes
Over people	No	No	Yes
Liability insurance	No	Yes	Yes
Operator certificate	Yes	Yes	Yes

Source: Adapted from Transport Canada 2015c, Annex A, 32. See full report for details.

who will be required to mark "their device with their name and contact information, pass a basic knowledge test, have liability insurance, and fly at least 5.5 km from airports, 1.85 km from heliports, and 30m from people" (ibid., 1–2).

The "limited operations (rural)" category is said to cover rural aspects such as "agricultural purposes, wildlife surveys, and natural resources" and involves pilots who "must be 16 years or older." Their requirements are identical to those for the very small drone operations except that "fly at least" strictures have an additional provision/limit of "150m from open-air assemblies (i.e. outdoor concert) 75m from people, vehicles, vessels and 1km from buildings and houses (built-up areas)" (ibid., 2).

It is the third category "complex operations (urban)" that is massively different and more specific than the initial 2015 proposals. It is for "users who intend to fly in urban areas, within controlled airspace or close to anywhere that airplanes, helicopters and floatplanes land and take off" (ibid., 3). The pilot (again 16 years or older) will be required to "hold a pilot permit; have liability insurance; register and mark their device with a unique identification Transport Canada will provide; operate a drone that meets Transport Canada's design standards; meet flight rules that are similar to manned aviation; and fly at least: 150m from open-air assemblies of people ... 30 m from people, vehicles, vessels; 1km from buildings and houses (built-up areas)" (ibid., 3). It is of interest to note that regarding the "liability insurance" requirement, Transport Canada advises drone operators that it "is your responsibility, as the operator, to confirm your insurance coverage" (ibid., 4).

Analysis by Gersher (2014) explores why Canada legislated "civilian use of drones as early as 1996, when the term 'non-piloted aircraft' was introduced" (ibid., 22) into Canadian rules and at a time when Canada was beginning to develop a nonmilitary market for drones. She stresses that in technical terms "there are few drone uses that do *not* require equipment that is intrinsically a surveillance technology" (ibid., 22). Indeed, others have argued for some time that globally there exists in the political economy of surveillance a "surveillance-industrial complex" (Ball and Snider 2014). The Gersher analysis then goes on to argue that as Canada's new plans emerged "Transport Canada and aviation bodies elsewhere, are regulating the airplane characteristics of the technology but not addressing the computing and sending portion of these devices" (ibid., 23). Because of this and other reasons regarding the narrowness of the range of groups involved in past Transport Canada's reviews, Gersher argues for greater formal and direct involvement by privacy and civil liberties representatives, the public and Parliament, and, in addition, that drone regulation should have a "used-based component" given that drones can be used in many circumstances with many different impacts (ibid., 2–3). Finally, she argues that Canada "must attend to privacy, civil liberties and ethical issues before the technology proliferates and is made routine" (ibid., 24).

As noted earlier, privacy regulators in Canada have expressed this need in a basically similar way at the federal level (Office of the Privacy Commissioner of Canada 2013, 2015) and in Ontario (Cavoukian

2012), but it is not clear if they are central players in the above drone regulatory process or players that have to be routinely asked but not necessarily accorded much influence. For example, in the 2015 proposals in table 10.1 above, the proposed piloting provisions use the exhortative language that pilots "should *respect* privacy and other laws." Public opinion analysis of UAVs in Canada (Thompson and Bracken-Roche 2015) also has looked at how opinion varies regarding awareness of the use of UAV technology. The authors conclude that there is "a majority in support of the use of UAVs for safety and emergency-response purposes. However, this support falls away in cases where UAV is used to perform routinized acts of surveillance or identification" (ibid., 156).

On a different analytical front, journalistic commentaries (Omand 2015; Goodyear 2015; Star 2016) have also emerged regarding arguments that Canada's regulatory system on UAVs has for some time been more supportive of innovation than the US system but that these advantages may be disappearing quickly given recent US developments. The case for Canada's system having an innovation economy advantage is examined briefly when Omand (2015) quotes the views of Carleton engineering professor Jeremy Laliberte who says that Canada has long been "ahead of the game" due in part to Canada's decade-long history of regulating drone use compared to the US which is now starting but now "catching up" (Quoted in Omand 2015, 3). The other recent commentaries make similar arguments but then focus on elements such as the fact that anyone can buy a drone but "not everyone is aware of the rules" (Goodyear 2015, 1) and therefore much greater public awareness is needed via reforms to the regulatory system. The general complexity and difficulty of the enforcement process is also cited (Starr 2016). Another feature recently explored (Kennedy 2015) centres on some early progress among Canada's colleges and universities which are "starting to establish programs for early adapters eager to work with unmanned aerial vehicles." These developments include programs at the University of Toronto, University of Victoria, and Carleton University. These developments have emerged partly under funding from the Natural Sciences and Engineering Research Council of Canada (NSERC).

THREE ANALYTICAL ELEMENTS

With the aid of table 10.2 we now look across the three policy and governance histories to see the nature of both change and inertia in this domain via a summary sampling of the three analytical elements featured in the chapter as a whole. We look at each element in turn.

Policy Ideas, Discourses, and Agendas

Not surprisingly, disruptive technology itself features strongly in terms of both policy ideas and related discourse developed by various players but then almost automatically is tied agenda-wise to the core technological benefit or threat on offer or to innovation impacts. Uber ride-sourcing is linked by analysts and advocates to both the growing on-demand economy and society and by some to the sharing economy present especially in cities. Its threats are related to lost or changed jobs in some industries such as the taxi industry and in relation to ideas about lower wage flexible work and jobs. In the fully automated vehicles technological realm, potentially a much larger terrain than ride-sharing, the positive impact claims, though still emerging, relate to safety gains and to a larger revolution in urban connectivity and also potentially major reductions in car ownership and use. The unmanned air vehicles or drone story is literally centred on a much smaller scale product technology with ideas and discourse focusing on socio-economic and recreational use and in research and other uses in different spatial and situational contexts.

In policy and regulatory terms the accompanying goals and advocacy agendas in all three policy and governance histories are centred on varied notions of regulation and innovation, approaches that require flexibility in rule-making, and an appreciation of the inherent complexity, contradictions, and concerns about letting the innovators have the freedom to innovate in order to stay in the game and lead it internationally. In large part, these core ideas are a reflection that each of the technologies are not transportation technologies *per se* but rather involve ideas and technologies centred on digital and smart-phone dynamics and innovation capacities that now are cascading on transportation and the movement of people and goods.

Economic and Social Power

The economic and social power dynamics and structure initially centre on the economic power of the leading technology firms, such as Uber in the ride-sourcing policy history and Google and other auto and vehicle firms in the automated vehicles case. In the case of civilian drone technology there is no obvious single firm as the dominant

Table 10.2
The disruptive technology-enabled transportation domain and the three analytical elements: Highlights

Policy and governance histories	Analytical elements		
	Policy ideas, discourse, and agendas	*Economic and social power*	*Technology and temporal realities and conflicts*
Uber ride-sourcing technology and related taxi and urban transport market governance (2005 to present)	Ride-sourcing as idea and technology	Uber power of initial entry without permission and then varied battles over how and when to regulate	Uber technology rapid entry since 2010 and also multifaceted and continuously experimental
	Taxi industry as regulated oligopoly	Uber versus Lyft competition in US and more integrated policy development and debate but by no means complete	Key complementary tech role of location sensors in smart phones
	UberPool service as kind of instant bus line crafted from collective urban demand	Canadian response much slower but now emerging in Canadian cities and at provincial level regarding ride sourcing versus taxi battles	Rapid emergence in dozens of cities globally including those in China
	On-demand and/or sharing economy ideas and discourse at local urban level	Role of courts in US and threats of court action emerging in Canada	Technology and policy assessment agenda items emerging slowly in Canada including actions regarding safety, driver training and qualifications, accessibility, environment, data sharing, and transit integration
	Light touch proinnovation approach idea versus hard regulatory concepts	Uber-like socioeconomic market niche development in US cities (e.g Uber for children)	
	Flexible working hours ideas, choice and opportunities for workers	Complex dynamics between public and private mobility	Broad policy option strategies being crafted (e.g do nothing, entry with existing taxi category, new separate transport network company category, etc.)
	"Uber economy" and "gig economy"	Canadian federal Competition Bureau policy guidance on innovation and deregulation of taxi industry	Provinces seeming to lean towards transport innovation approach
	Price reduction and increased volumes as causes of transformative transport impacts	Mainly initial public opinion support for Uber in Canadian cities, especially among younger citizens/users	Key city debates in Toronto, Ottawa, Edmonton contentious but leaning to dual system approach
	Reduced car use and congestion overall		
	Reduced transport traffic gas use and emissions		

Autonomous vehicles transport technology and related policy and guidance (2010 to present)			
Ideas/discourse about gradually improving automation versus fully automated driverless vehicles	US origins of disruptive AV technology and key global auto industry involvement	High scale of potential impact of AV and uncertainty as to pathways of AV development as seen by technology companies versus auto firms versus coinvestments by the two	
AV as part of larger revolution in automation and connectivity	Google and other technology companies as lead players	Scenarios published regarding levels of vehicle automation	
Ideas of safety liability shift from drivers to manufacturers	US Department of Transport develops policy guidance for state governments testing AV	US regulators say also that immediate tangible action needed regarding the cyber-security threats to driverless vehicles	
Reform ideas needed to deal with insurance, performance standards, and entrance barriers	Major US $4 billion fund on self-driving car projects and infrastructure	Advocacy in Canada that no major transport infrastructure project should be undertaken without an AV impact audit	
Need for a proactive safety culture with safety innovations not just an enticement for high end customers	Regulatory certification of driverless car	Multidimensional impact and reform agenda being developed but very early days for and in Canada	
High potential for major reductions in car ownership and use	AV policy development much weaker in Canada, no overall initiative at Transport Canada	Projections being proposed about possible scenarios for AV in place in next decade and by the 2030s	
	Some early testing under Ontario departments		
	Ticoli paper for Ontario government projects major benefits from AV in Toronto arising from reduced collisions, congestion, and parking fees/charges and productivity gains in Toronto industries		
	Zon and Ditta study sees need for eight related policies to support and regulate AV and urges need to stay technology agnostic		
	CAVCOE study makes thirty recommendations for federal policy on AVs including appointing a minister of AVs to lead policy		

Table 10.2
The disruptive technology-enabled transportation domain and the three analytical elements: Highlights (*continued*)

Policy and governance histories	Analytical elements		
	Policy ideas, discourse, and agendas	*Economic and social power*	*Technology and temporal realities and conflicts*
Unmanned air vehicles (drone) technology and policy and governance (2005 to present)	Shift from earlier military drones to recreational and economic UAV industry socioeconomic ideas, values, and uses	Canadian awareness of slow moving work of US Small UAS Aviation Rule Making Committee under control of US Federal Air Administration (FAA)	Extensive longer-term military drone usage by US internationally
	Use of UAV versus "drone" discourse pros and cons	Awareness of US policy and regulatory categories and interests under public users (federal, state and local government); civil operators (nongovernmental) and model aircraft and hobby and recreational)	1950s and 1960s early Canadian drone technology for military and policing
	Airspace as idea and realm for expanded and complex regulation and boundaries		Drone flight technology combined with smartphone components, sensors, optics, batteries and embedded processes
	Privacy values and ethical issues regarding surveillance and civil liberties	Canadian system seen as more supportive of innovation because it was less stringent	Moore's law-style pace – performance doubles while size and price plummet
	Reigning in on "excessive activities" in drone usage		US DIY Drone social movement entity membership grows from 26,000 in 2012 to 77,000 in 2015–16
	Safety and privacy as linked values	Amazon Air work in Canada on drone delivery Technology said to have occurred in Vancouver because of Canada's favourable regulatory system	1,000 new personal drones added every month
	Transport Canada's UAV approach governed by a "permissive regulatory framework"	Unmanned System Canada formed in 2003 as Canada's main UAS lobby and socioeconomic entity with recognition of its key role with Transport Canada	Rapid issuance of SFOCs in Canadian system since 2007
	Proinnovation ideas		Canadian faster early UAV regulation in 1996
	UAV usage "within" and beyond users "line of sight"	New peer-reviewed *Journal of Unmanned Systems* established by Unmanned Systems Canada	Six-year process for US small UAS regulation only completed in 2015–16
	Very small UAV classification system		

Unique risks due to widely varying degrees of aviation expertise by users

Seeking a regulatory system that is "risk-based, flexible and consistent with international partners when appropriate"

Federal and Ontario privacy commissioners active in research an advocacy about privacy as key factor in any regulatory system

Transport Canada says it will also support the minimum drone standards as developed by ICAO internationally

General recognition in Canada and US that UAS regulation will deal with issues that span across several regulatory agencies and levels of enforcement

US drone registry finished rapidly in two months including criminalizing failure to register

Debates and concerns about pro-innovation "lead" of the Canadian system versus need now quickly to "catch-up" as US changes its drone regulatory system initial innovator of products. Social power in all three policy and governance histories has been reactive and significant since some of it also advocates and creates new markets and submarkets adapting and becoming social-producers using further versions of the technology.

In this core bilateral economic and social power dynamic, governments have to talk, act, and not act, knowing that disruption and speed and much uncertainty is the new normal or, in this domain, the main normal. The policy and regulatory players are variously and differently at the national, provincial, and city/local levels in Canada. They all function with a watchful eye, and they have some, but always incomplete, knowledge about what is or might be occurring in the US, especially, and globally. Within each level of government, there is always more than one department or agency actually or potentially involved in trying to figure out how to use or adapt its normal policy and regulatory laws, habits, and biases.

Technology and Temporal Realities and Conflicts

Each of the three policy and governance histories shows different disruptive technological, innovation, and temporal dynamics, but each in their different ways have featured speed and demands to respond quickly or with slow caution. The Uber technology has had a rapid emergence since 2010 in the US and rapidly also in hundreds of cities globally. Numerous Canadian cities have had to embark on swift and messy political and policy–regulatory responses with or without systematic underlying research. In the case of automated vehicles, the speed of development has been US-focused and much slower moving compared with the Uber ride-sourcing case. AV technology, however, has been getting considerable media and some initial policy attention largely because of its greater scale in terms of both possible impacts and probabilities. The drone policy history has longer roots in military use, but our focus dealt with its rapid technological emergence in the last several years and with high bursts of new small social–recreational drone products. These were small in scale in products and uses *per se* with fast growing uses in situations beyond line of sight. Thus overall, the responses needed for Uber and for drones were here and now whereas the automated vehicles case was being cast in terms of some short term impacts but most over the next decade or twenty to thirty year periods. In the Canadian case, the other feature of the technology and temporal element was that Canada has been slow on both the Uber and automated vehicles response compared to the US but faster and more innovative and therefore "ahead of the game" regarding drones.

CONCLUSIONS

This chapter has examined the disruptive technology-enabled transport policy domain through three policy and governance histories. It is the last of our seven transportation policy domain analyses. This final domain is different given the presence in it of three disruptive technologies with transportation impacts and challenges and with impacts and challenges beyond the movement of people and goods. Indeed, there are interactive links across these disruptive technologies, particularly, as we have seen, between the Uber developments and automated vehicles. We have argued from the outset that disruptive impacts can also refer to situations when multiple technology disruptions and innovation are occurring simultaneously or over different and overlapping time periods, as is the case in this domain analysis. We have also cautioned regarding assuming forms of technology determinism when policy, governance, and regulatory responses are bound to be complex and varied and thus reduce some immediate pure technology impacts.

It should not be surprising to see the reactive and fast-moving dynamics present with respect to ideas, discourse, and agendas and also as dynamic economic and social power is wielded in the name of both positive benefits and also evident costs and disadvantages for different players and citizens. The three new technologies impacting transportation are catching the policy-making world in Canada and elsewhere off guard. We have also taken note of the fact that several other transport domain technologies and innovations have been examined in chapters 4, 7, and 9. The dynamics traced overall often look like a recipe for prolonged confusion and dysfunction that will mean postponing or forfeiting the benefits of progress, opening the door to misguided uses of technology, wasting society's resources, prolonging the conflict between technology-adopters and resisters, angering citizens, and giving policy makers the appearance and the reality of being shortsighted and ineffectual. The issues and multilevel governance dynamics, globally and in Canada, show that valuable analysis is on offer and with varied experiments and trial runs in place differing in the Canadian case in different cities and provinces and federally, within Transport Canada and in other federal departments and agencies.

11

Conclusions

This book has provided an extensive and in-depth academic account of Canadian multimodal transportation policy and governance. It has been done through an analysis of seven transport policy and governance domains covering a fifty-year period, 1968–2018, across five federal prime ministerial eras – Pierre Trudeau, Brian Mulroney, Jean Chrétien and Paul Martin, Stephen Harper, and Justin Trudeau. This account has emerged through an examination of twenty policy and governance histories and through our analytical framework that also includes an analysis in each domain chapter of three elements designed to help us explain and understand both change and inertia: policy ideas, discourses, and agendas; economic and social power; and technology and temporal realities and conflicts.

We have studied Transport Canada as the lead federal transport policy department, stressing its obvious importance but also that it is not the only federal department that makes federal transport policy or that influences it or governs it structurally. Indeed, to tell the Transport Canada story, the book has had to examine not just the department itself but at least fifteen other federal organizations and linked provincial and interest group entities in the seven transport policy domains we studied (not counting the shared-governance realm involving Canada's dozens of airports) because their work impinges on this complex mix. We also examined the mandate of provincial transport ministries with all their intertwined transportation and infrastructure responsibilities and multistatute duties, including their core policy work connected with highway legislation. We have also included extensive coverage of cities, both middle-sized and larger ones and hence transport policy and governance as a multilevel political and constitutional dynamic.

In chapter 2, we also looked at evidence of transportation policy in federal agenda setting as manifested in speeches from the throne and budget speeches across the five prime ministerial eras and in chapter 3 at international developments and institutions, both in a key Canada–US context including the current Trump administration turbulence in international trade and with regard to major global transportation agencies and their modal and intermodal impacts and struggles.

We now offer our conclusions by referring back to our three key research questions and our seven overall arguments previewed in the book's introduction. We do this in two stages. In the first section below we provide a summary of the transport policy domains examined in chapters 4 to 10. In the second section we present our seven main overall arguments in the context of answering the three principal questions posed in the book's introduction: 1) How and to what extent has Canadian transport policy and its related governance changed in the last fifty years; 2) Where has transport policy resided in federal policy agendas in the last fifty years; and 3) Is Canada developing the needed policies, institutions, and capacities to enable it to have a viable socioeconomic and technologically advanced transportation system that is fit-for-purpose for the challenges of the next twenty-year period and beyond?

THE SEVEN DOMAINS: A FINAL LOOK

We defined the Transport Canada-centred domain in chapter 4 as the transport department *per se*, headed by the minister of Transport as its cabinet minister and as an elected politician appointed to the portfolio. Its core mandate and its large staff and transport expertise place it at the centre of the federal transport policy and governance system, yet it has nothing like a monopoly because of the many other departments and agencies involved in the mix. Some have subject matter authority by virtue of statutes that draw them directly into transportation policy fields, like regulation making, while others have more cabinet clout than Transport Canada by virtue of their power over things like finance and the machinery of government that affect and sometimes sideswipe transportation directly and indirectly.

Our survey of Transport Canada's statutory base shows it plays a role in sixty statutes and dozens of sets of regulations and regulatory plans, many of which are new or being changed and queuing in line for approval in higher volumes. And while the department has a record of explicit economic deregulation agendas and accomplishments, its regulatory purview is expanding. It has faced a remarkably dynamic policy environment, for example with the advent of supply chains, logistics, national and global digitalized imperatives, and "lean production" ideas and practices that transformed the whole freight transportation space, often in unplanned ways.

The four policy and governance histories in chapter 4 show Transport Canada's central role and the array of complex policy challenges it faces. The larger 1968–2018 fifty year story of federal and national transportation policy is our starting point but not the end point because these and other developments embroil not just Transport Canada and the federal government but, ever more so, the provinces and cities as well. Finally, it is not just the overt aspects of "transportation" with which Transport Canada and its ministers have to deal, but also, we stress, all kinds of complexities and conflicts involved in the dynamics of central versus arm's length governance of the transportation sector and everything it touches. We have tried to bring these aspects to light further in chapters 5 to 10. That means chapter 4 alone cannot give an unambiguous verdict about the successes and failures of Transport Canada and its ministers.

The "Grains and Trains Transport Policy Domain" (chapter 5) is explicitly and crucially about railways and a single (historic) industry: the grain industry in Western Canada. Ultimately the account is conjoined with a deep, long-term history about Canada in general and Western Canada in particular during the twentieth century and even before that. It is set against a backdrop of what amounts to early stages of globalization – the rise of surpluses and exports by other grain-growing countries – and by the monumental human enterprise of settling the Canadian Prairies the opening up of which was made possible by rail transport technology and development. Hence our first policy and governance history in this domain is at times a hundred-year-plus set of massive impacts propelled by railway development that created the grain industry in Western Canada. But the grain industry was eventually caught in a Nash Equilibrium of trading nations suffering an over supply of exportable grain relative to market demand. Our analysis showed the complex downstream effects of policy makers and businesses, nationally and particularly in Western Canada, having used transportation as an instrument for (and having subordinated it to) other socioeconomic ideas, pressures, and causes. The second policy and governance history in the chapter showed how deregulating the grain industry, and the rail transport industry along with it, resulted in new arrangements of considerable import – but only after struggling through a long, sluggish, slow, and inertia-laden process that still is not completed.

The thesis of this grains and trains chapter is that transportation policy with respect to grain has been bent to serve the income problem of Western Canadian farmers and varied Prairie populist pressures. It also draws attention to whether or not the logical basis for the use of transportation as an instrument of agricultural policy still remains. Certainly, all countries defend their agricultural sectors and, notwithstanding the advances made through the World Trade Organization and other treaties, protectionism and subsidization have not gone away. What has changed, however, is the supply–demand balance of the world market.

For much of the twentieth century, the incomes of western Canadian farmers were subject to major shocks because of the dependence on one crop, wheat, which accounted for more than 90 per cent of total exports. This began to change with the expansion of canola acreage and the popularity of pulses and special crops. That shift has also been favoured by changes in world import demand for these crops. The agricultural base is more diversified and stable as a result. It can also be observed in the larger picture of the economies of Western Canada. Agriculture is still important, but resources, manufacturing, and food processing are being integrated with a large service economy that can weather commodity cycles much better. When the Crow Rate was being formed, the railways were the only viable means of surface transportation. Farmers were truly captive shippers. Such terms are much less valid in the twenty-first century.

The "Rail Freight and Competition-Market Dispute Domain" (chapter 6) delved into the structure and dynamics of the rail freight transport system from the mid-1960s to the present and the way in which federal regulatory policy and railway operating strategies responded to each other in a *pas de deux* over time. The first three deregulation steps examined gave railways an opportunity to regain financial health, which they used to good effect. Things accelerated in the early twenty-first century when the core optimization strategy of the main railways, first CN and later CP, underwent a profound transformation to "lean production," which had widely unrecognized implications. Competition disputes between railways and shippers were examined in the chapter, including in relation to whether or not normal framework competition law and policy ought to play a bigger role in preference to sector-specific economic regulation, which has been a feature of rail transportation since the late 1800s.

We show that setting and vigorously espousing a primary goal in the rail freight market is a pivotal issue, now that railways and many of their customers have gone lean. But there has not been a primary goal for rail transportation in general, and substantial economic regulatory dysfunction has grown from no one knowing whether railways are expected to satisfy the greatest number of shippers individually or to get the greatest amount of economic value through supply chains that depend on rail. The two are not the same. Optimization theory makes it clear that railways cannot do both. The absence of a primary goal also leaves everyone without guidance when it comes to determining what constitutes "fair" rail service – and fair to whom. And without a clear understanding of that, regulatory policy suffers from a shortfall of legitimacy. Moreover, the absence of a primary goal exacerbates the tricky question of whether the regulator should adjudicate complaints on the basis of a railway's service (and if so, in private), as is the case now or on the basis of whether a railway abused its market power or behaved in some other anticompetitive manner, as judged under a more public marketplace framework based on competition policy and public adjudication. There is a lot to recommend the latter.

In chapter 7, "The Air Transport Policy and Shared-Governance Domain", we contrasted national versus regional values, especially in the context of the 1960s' and 1970s' Liberal-era "managed air transport competition" concept. We also looked at the continuous and understandable presence of concerns over safety and security, and how to deal with them in an age of real or anticipated terrorist acts, especially in light of changes in Canada–US relations that became a more important governance feature in this domain after 9/11. But notwithstanding all that, the most prominent governance feature for Canada is almost certainly the emergence in the early 1990s of shared-governance authority at each of Canada's airports. That was most noticeable at major hubs, and it affected major nonhub cities and even smaller southern-Canadian ones. And the financial arrangement with which these authorities were endowed has had them paying hefty rents arguably in perpetuity to the federal government and losing passengers to nearby subsidized US airports as a result. Global air travel seems virtually certain to continue growing, and Canada needs to continue searching for ways to ensure its competitiveness in attracting that traffic and enabling the competitiveness of the many Canadian industries that depend on it. The cardinal challenge in every mode of commercial transportation, including air transport, is to protect the scale of operations because that is the primary determinant of cost.

The primary feature in the two policy and governance histories in "Transportation in Cities and Federal Infrastructure Policy Domain" (chapter 8) is a double dose of serious inertia for transportation in cities and for federal infrastructure funding and transportation and its impact on transportation. Our analysis shows that transport policy and governance in cities is caught in a seven-way trap that has been growing for decades and from which, despite recent signs of movement on the political front, most large cities in Canada seem unlikely to escape – hence the "elusive" quality we ascribe to the quest for urban mobility. These traps range from the dynamics of NIMBYism and the "free rider problem" to the unwillingness of city governments to put a price on the usage of roads and to the fact that apart from property taxes, municipalities have no way of raising revenues for sustained investment in transport and related infrastructure. As to federal policy and governance for infrastructure financing, the most important factor in the past twenty-five years in federal funding of urban transportation infrastructure has been the profound politicization of decisions about selecting and financing the semiinfinite array of projects using a cornucopia of funding programs, nearly all of which are flexible enough to be spent on almost anything. Not much gets done without distributive retail politics dominating all other considerations, including sound public policy. It invites (and even compels) short-term planning and thinking. Despite the promise of a federal infrastructure removing much of the politics from the funding process, the bank recently announced by the Trudeau Liberals seems likely to help perpetuate the problem rather than alleviate it. It makes building shiny new assets more attractive than looking after deteriorating existing ones, which in turn traps cities in a vicious circle of trying and failing to maintain their decaying transportation infrastructure. Unfortunately, too, in this domain there is not much evidence of any level of government having solid competence in optimization strategies or the expertise needed for determining precisely where to make infrastructure investments that improve urban transportation in a way that gets to the heart of seriously enhancing mobility. The analysis also drew brief attention to the imperative of city planning and land development policy in overall mobility progress,

Our coverage of the transportation, dangerous goods, and environmental policy domain (chapter 9) showed the policy field to be anchored in key ways in Transport Canada, but even here the statutory and policy governance necessarily extends significantly to an array of other federal entities interacting with the federal government. These dangerous goods laws and regulation practices involve the provinces and various users of dangerous goods. We showed as well how the domain dynamics function in complex spatial realms and transport modes as dangerous goods are moved and also when they are stationary and being stored in numerous locations. The story of dangerous goods policy and the recent growth in the transport of oil via pipelines versus rail has some similar features, but the analysis has shown how the array of core institutions broadens to embrace the National Energy Board and links with environmental policy institutions such as the Canadian Environmental Assessment Agency, the Treasury Board, and the Commissioner on the Environment and Sustainable Development. While the interactions among these bodies and the policy values at stake are understandable in some ways, in other senses they are very tentative because of the ways in which the twin dynamics of shale oil versus oil sands transport by rail versus pipeline are increasingly uncertain in their underlying logistics, economics, and political support. Environmental policy values and issues are present overall in this domain but, alas, with an array of ideas that struggle for precedence and clarity. These include older ones such as environmental assessment, sustainable development, or the "triple bottom line" encompassing social, economic, and environmental as balanced considerations and, last and usually least, climate change and greenhouse gas emission reductions.

In "Disruptive Technology-Enabled Transportation Domain" (chapter 10) we mainly examined three disruptive technologies whose impacts and challenges are being and will be felt not just in the movement of people and goods but also in the farthest reaches of society and fields of human endeavour well beyond transportation. But we also stressed that such disruptive and otherwise complex technologies were a part of the story in several of our other domain chapters. The chapter 10 policy and governance histories focused on Uber-like ride-hailing developments, automated vehicles and driverless cars, and drones. We stressed that each such technology has different time frames to date for their emergence and each produces impacts that are likely to be interconnected as they work their way through different mixes of policy and government institutions. The analysis also cautions against assuming that technological determinism is automatic when in fact the most prominent forms of regulation and debate occur through political processes. It is also not uncommon for new technologies, including disruptive ones, to share the role of bringing about transformations in commerce and society with other technologies that emerge around the same time. That is partly because every technology represents a "platform" – a fusion of existing technologies – and so, as soon as a new technology is available, others can and almost certainly will start being built on top of it or in relation to it or in competition with it. When one disruptive technology arrives in the marketplace not long before or after another disruptive one, the result is often extremely fast moving dynamics in all kinds of ways including new ideas, new types of discourse and agendas, new forms and sources of economic and social power, and new types of costs and benefits for individual groups of players and citizens. The transformational changes now coming quickly into view in transportation and in the related so-called "sharing economy" are catching the policy-making world in Canada and nearly everywhere else off guard. Unfortunately, the trio of policy and governance dynamics traced in chapter 10 can look to some like a recipe for prolonged confusion and dysfunction, which might mean postponing or forfeiting the benefits of progress, opening the door to misguided uses of technology, wasting society's resources, prolonging the conflict between technology-adopters and -resisters, angering citizens, and giving policy-makers the appearance (and often the reality) of being short-sighted and ineffectual. But more varied and complex policy and governance responses and outcomes are also present and likely, all the more so because international, Canada–US, and multilevel experimentation within Canada is already evident in both studies and early debate.

OUR SEVEN MAIN ARGUMENTS IN THE CONTEXT OF ANSWERING THE THREE RESEARCH QUESTIONS

Our first research question is, "How, why, and to what extent, has Canadian transport policy and its related governance changed in the last fifty years?" We answer this question in relation to three of our arguments.

1 Transportation policy in Canada is, to an ever-increasing
   extent, provincial–urban policy and governance-centered,
   with ongoing, more traditional federal-led nation building
   becoming less present and noticeable.

This argument results from the simple fact that 65 to 70 per cent
of Canadians live in cities – indeed in a handful of very large cities
– and so most of the transport positives and negatives they experience
come from provincial and city-led policies impacting the challenges
of getting to and from work and dealing with their families' everyday
needs like getting their children to school. Urban congestion is a huge,
unpleasant daily reality even though some people walk, cycle, and
take urban transit. But despite the money and heavy lifting invested
by city governments in planning, coordinating, and approving transit
systems and dealing with NIMBYism and all manner of other impediments, transit ridership seldom grows as fast as city populations, and
so the automobile remains the primary choice for most people and
congested roads are the inevitable result. It does not help that cities,
as we have seen in chapter 8, are politically and financially weak when
it comes to improving mobility and transportation infrastructure and
that provincial and federal governments are a main contributor to
these problems rather than a source of solutions.

How this relates to nation building and the latter's earlier seeming
coherence is not a matter of straight-line logic or evidence. Nation
building and the unification of Canada by constructing railways,
for example, is evident and real historically as seen in several domain
chapters. But a lot of that nation building was *ad hoc*, artificial, and
propped up by dysfunctional policy measures that held Canada
back economically, such as the long residues of federal-led rail subsidies and the forced maintenance of unneeded and inefficient branch
lines and under-used rail services. Some of these subsidies are still in
effect today.

2 Transportation policy has shifted across regulatory eras,
   deregulatory phases, and coregulation and regulatory
   capitalism phases, but all forms of regulation are still
   in place and are still contested.

This argument, too, is central to answering our first question.
Economic deregulation is an important part of the story as discussed

in several chapters, particularly those describing the importance of the federal Freedom to Move transportation framework adopted in the mid-1980s. It ushered in not just rail-transport reform but changes to the way in which new developments in international air travel affected Canada, especially the cross-border effects of airline deregulation in the US. Meanwhile, social regulation relating to safety, for example by way of the government compelling carriers to introduce risk-management systems, and later with the security dimension added, especially after 9/11, increased in major ways. Their most notable effects have been on air travel (security) and on the transportation of dangerous goods (safety and security together).

Our discussion of co-regulation, regulatory capitalism, and regulatory unruliness also shows that regulatory institutions in general, and transportation in particular, can no longer be cast as just a simple pairing of economic deregulation and increased social regulation in a two-category world. Our analysis of the cities transit and infrastructure domain shows that much of urban transportation and congestion will need less regulation in some areas but more in others, for example in managing access to transportation arteries in order to improve mobility for everyone who uses them. That constitutes economic regulation at least as much as it does social regulation, because most other solutions involve pouring money into infrastructure. But the potential for changing the regulatory regime, like the spending of money, has high degrees of difficulty given the numerous modes of transport, local jurisdictional constraints, and the often contrary and even contradictory views of urban transport users, residents, and voters.

3 Transportation policy encompasses a world of increasingly complex supply chains, but it interacts with governance networks that often do not have the same institutional boundaries as supply chains.

When supply chains emerged as a concept and operational reality – the idea of "supply chain management" did not appear until the early 1980s – they started to become key features of transportation policy and governance in an overall sense. That was not by accident. We have described its links to domestic, Canada–US, and international transport and logistics developments that were driven by the widespread adoption of just-in-time production and tightly managed distribution systems connected to global markets and sources of supply, much of it made possible by the rise of containerized shipping. Supply chains are extremely complex market supply and logistical systems that also manifest themselves as market "demand" systems. Their operation is, in and of itself, a private–governance managerial and quasi-regulatory system that is so powerful it drives the performance and behaviour of all manner of firms and virtually compels transportation policy to respond accordingly. For example, the successful Asia–Pacific Gateways and Corridors Initiative led by the feds in the mid-2000s was, first and foremost, based on supply-chain policy for containerized freight transportation into and through Canada. Supply chains function across all transport modes – rail, ships, aircraft, trucks, ports, gateways, and border crossing points.

Our analysis shows how these chains and logistics and increasingly digitalized functions do not have the same parameters and limits of influence as statutory transportation policy and governance institutions do. The freight rail domain analysis showed this starkly because, for example, operating disruptions on railways often originate with hiccups in ocean transportation and the timing of ships' arrival in Canadian ports, which is beyond the reach of Canadian policy. So, too, did our account of the St Lawrence Seaway governance in chapter 3 and also systems for regulating dangerous goods, many of which criss-cross multiple supply chains. In short, not much gets done by way of freight transportation policy and multimodal policy without serious consideration of the effects on supply chains and the latter are often not necessarily coterminous with formal statutory transport-related regulatory bodies and laws.

The second research question we posed is "where has transport policy resided in federal policy agendas in the last fifty years?" Our fourth and fifth central arguments are important in addressing this agenda-setting question.

4   Transportation policy has, overall, not been a high priority federal policy sphere compared to others in the agenda of Canada's federal prime ministerial eras in the last fifty years, as revealed in speeches from the throne and budgets as key agenda-setting occasions and processes. The same is true, as we have seen, in measured public opinion.

Chapter 2's account provides the main evidence behind this argument. The data on SFTS and budget speeches showed that transportation issues, when mentioned at all, were rarely expressed as leadoff priorities. And even when they were expressed, it was at middle and lower levels of emphasis and usually paired with other issues. For example, in recent years transportation announcements were often paired with budget cuts and with infrastructure policy, the latter often driven by a priority to stimulate the economy with ramped up spending on infrastructure. In short, transportation policy is often the subordinate. This was reflected also in the high turnover of transport ministers. But still, in a government of some thirty ministers, and formerly about forty on average, the federal departments and policy fields are all caught in the raw political mathematics of lower agenda-setting presence and power. In the final analysis, prime ministers and ministers of Finance are central in determining what ultimately gets expressed, ranked, and ignored or left out in such agenda-setting dynamics. And transportation seldom stacks up all that strongly against the other issues that preoccupy those two people as many other ministers are lobbying them inside the cabinet on a daily, weekly, monthly, or yearly basis. In addition, we also saw in chapter 2 that key agenda dynamics are also located in pivotal crises or conditions that impact on an entire prime ministerial era such as the global fiscal and banking crisis in the 2008–14 period or the decade of deficits in the Mulroney era, and the hyperinflation and energy crisis in the Pierre Trudeau era.

5 Transportation policy is, has been, and will increasingly be a policy challenge of linked and overlapping policy fields including economic deregulation, regulatory safety and security, infrastructure, borders, bridges, oil and gas pipelines, environment, dangerous goods, trade, northern, regional–urban–rural, and transport science, technology, and innovation policy.

All of this is borne out in the fullness of our seven domain analysis chapters, among whose primary messages is the inherent socioeconomic complexity of this policy space and the intertwined effects of nearly everything on nearly everything else. This has something to do with the current structure of government. But even if the federal government had half the number of ministers and departments it does now, these overlaps and boundary imperatives would still be present if not across departments then *inside* them in a smaller cabinet. And of course the situation inside provincial, territorial, and municipal governments would still have some similar dynamics, impacting transportation's many hyphenated imperatives and discourse. At each of these levels the intertwining can be seen in regulations queuing up for adoption in formal plans and in all kinds of other ways too.

Our third question posed, "Is Canada developing the needed policies, institutions, and capacities to enable it to have a viable socio-economic and technologically advanced transportation system that is fit-for-purpose for the challenges of the next twenty-year and longer-term period?" The sixth and seventh arguments we offer support our answer to this third question.

6 Transport policy needs major reforms to deal with transport
   infrastructure as a socio-economic capital asset subjected
   to funding and budgeting limitations and concepts, and the
   growing presence of retail politics in infrastructure policy
   overall. Such infrastructure, and the questions of who shares
   in paying for it, and benefiting from it, includes shippers and
   customers within and across modes, and taxpayers within
   and across political jurisdictions in Canada.

Early in this analysis in chapter 1 we drew attention to the fact that almost all of the provincial transport ministries and departments had become Transport *and Infrastructure* organizations. That means transportation is being associated more and more closely with capital and physical assets rather than with transportation *performance* – which is the growing central issue. On the other hand it means that such ministries were given primary roles and responsibilities for infrastructure leadership and funding among all the other main provincial departments, including over new infrastructure spending and investment for things like highways, bridges, and transportation corridors. That probably would be a good thing for transportation, if only the departments' remits included strengthening rather than displacing "transportation" with infrastructure. Unfortunately that is seldom the case. Federally, Transport Canada has never been renamed "Transport and Infrastructure Canada" although in many ways it has been seen in a bifurcated light. We saw this clearly in the links, especially in the last twenty years, to transportation and infrastructure being combined as priorities and new initiatives expressed in speeches from the throne and in budget speeches.

The apparent subordination of transport programming to infrastructure projects and budgeting has shown up in economic stimulus funding in both the Chrétien–Martin and Harper eras, and now in the Justin Trudeau Liberal era, too. The distributive retail politics of this spending has focused mainly on capital assets, hence the federal claim that it was an "investment" – ostensibly an investment in transportation and mobility benefits. But it was often only through luck and happenstance that transportation benefits and performance and, crucially, mobility in any sense of the word, arose by way of impacts and benefits that were convincingly shown and trackable. That is a pity. The current Trudeau government's effort with city transit infrastructure may yield infrastructure outcomes that are better than the stew into which previous governments fell, but this remains to be seen. Many programs and projects can be understood and assessed only over long asset life-cycles, hence the expressed recent federal proposal to establish an infrastructure bank, which most observers thought would stand a decent chance of being positive but alas still not the full answer. Now, with federal participation in the proposed new bank's financing and governance this looks unlikely to break away from the dysfunctional politicization of so many initiatives in the past. We have shown that the absence of system optimization and logistics analytical expertise, needed for proper infrastructure development, may yet negate the most recent promising initiatives unless it is remedied. These gaps in expertise were shown in chapter 6 on rail freight and chapter 8 on cities and infrastructure and overall in recent reports and studies of transport policy reform in Canada.

7 Transportation policy, as it has evolved over the past five decades, has an uneven record of keeping Canada competitive with the world in this vital realm, and, despite periodic bursts of progress, by and large the country too often has been resting on its laurels.

This final argument has considerable validity in our view, both with regard to the third question we have posed in particular and indeed our findings in general. We acknowledge that, as an argument, it contains some degrees of difficulty and complexity at least in part over what "uneven" and "competitive with the world" actually mean and how they are determined and measured. A benign way of interpreting "uneven" might be that whatever "laurels" Canadian transport policy are too often resting on, are unduly weighted in social terms as opposed to being focused on the nation's underlying economics, efficiency, and performance. The record of federal infrastructure spending, as chapter 8 shows, leaves gaping holes in *any* sort of performance record except perhaps helping politicians maintain their reelectability. Unfortunately that is a benefit for them and not necessarily for anyone else. And "competitive with the world" is a standard that evokes economic market competition, and it could mean competitive not just in terms of significant reduction of congestion in cities but in terms of safety and security, the environment, and the deployment of infrastructure that is fit-for-purpose (or indeed multiple purposes) and that is properly funded. On those dimensions Canada could and should do better. Another possible salve for sensitive Canadian egos might come from deeming the "world" to mean being competitive only with the United States or at least reasonably compatible with changing US transport practices and reforms. But that is short sighted because other countries like China, Singapore, and the Netherlands are setting new benchmarks for transport efficiency and connectivity that eclipse anything being done in North America.

From the outset we have stressed that multimodal transportation is about the movement of people and goods supported by services and information. But the "here to there" movement is complex and fast changing in some modes and slower in others. For a vast continental country, Canada's transport policy and governance has forward motion, to be sure, but metaphorically speaking it has no shortage of stops and congestion points along the way in terms of policy, governance, and politics in a complex federalist system. In other words, transportation amounts to multimodal "motion with conditions" as social and economic values, including safety and security and multiple modal impacts, are asserted, thought-through, or delayed until the next opportunities are presented or forced upon transport policy makers at all three levels of government in Canada.

References

Abel, Zachary T. 2011. "Getting Hazmat Transportation Back on Track: The Need for Hazmat Liability Reform for Rail Carriers." *William and Mary Environmental Law and Policy Review* 35: 973–1012.

Abril, M., F. Barber, L. Ingolotti, M.A. Salido, P. Tormos, and A. Lova. 2007. "An Assessment of Railway Capacity." *ScienceDirect, Transportation Research Part E: Logistics and Transportation Review* 44 (5): 774–806.

Advisory Council on Economic Growth. 2016. "Unleashing Productivity through Infrastructure." Ottawa: Advisory Council on Economic Growth.

Agranoff, Robert. 2007. *Managing within Networks: Adding Value to Public Organizations.* Washington: Georgetown University Press.

Air Canada. 2015. "The Aviation Industry as an Economic Enabler." Submission to the Review of the Canada Transportation Act. Air Canada.

Alexander, J. 2009. *Pandora's Locks: The Opening of the Great Lakes–St. Lawrence Seaway.* East Lansing: Michigan State University Press.

Anderson, Bill. 2011. "The Border and the Ontario Economy." Cross-Border Transportation Centre, University of Windsor.

Anderson, Chris. 2012. "How I Accidentally Kickstarted the Domestic Drone Boom." *Wired*, 22 June 2012. http://www.wired.com/2012/06/ff_drones/.

Andrew, Caroline, and Jeff Morrison. 2001. "Infrastructure." In *Urban Policy Issues: Canadian Perspectives*, edited by David Siegel and Edmund P. Fowler, 237–52. Toronto: Oxford University Press.

Annema, Jan Anne. 2013. "Transport Resistance Factors: Time, Money and Effort." In *The Transport System and Transport Policy: An Introduction*, edited by Bert Van Wee, Jan Anne Annema, and David Banister, 101–24. Cheltenham, UK: Edward Elgar.

Association of American Railroads. 2015. "Overview of America's Freight Railroads." Association of American Railroads.

Atkins, Eric. 2015. "Canadian Railway Seeks Permission to Refuse Dangerous Shipments." *Globe and Mail*, 8 March 2015.

Atkins, Eric, and Verity Stevenson. 2015. "Six Former Railway Employees Charged in Lac-Megantic Disaster." *Globe and Mail*, 22 June 2015.

Atkinson, M., D. Beland, G. Marchildon, K. McNutt, P. Phillips, and K. Rasmussen. 2013. *Governance and Public Policy in Canada: A View from the Provinces*. Toronto: University of Toronto Press.

Aucoin, Peter. 1997. *The New Public Management: Canada in Comparative Perspective*. Montreal & Kingston: McGill-Queen's University Press.

– 2008. "New Public Management and New Public Governance: Finding the Balance." In *Professionalism and Public Service: Essays in Honour of Kenneth Kernaghan*, edited by David Siegel and Ken Rasmussen, 16–33. Toronto: University of Toronto Press.

Auditor General of Canada. 2000. "Transport Canada–Airport Transfers: National Airports System" In *2000 Report of the Auditor General of Canada*, chapter 10. Office of the Auditor General.

– 2011. *2011 Spring Report of the Auditor General of Canada*. Office of the Auditor General, 5 April 2011.

– 2013. "Oversight of Rail Safety–Transport Canada." In *Report of the Auditor General. Fall 2013*, Chapter 7. Office of the Auditor General.

Auld, Douglas. 1985. *Budget Reform: Should There Be a Capital Budget for the Public Sector?* Toronto: C.D. Howe Institute.

Bailey, Ian. 2016. "Ride-Sharing Services 'Inevitable' in B.C., Transportation Minister Says." *Globe and Mail*, 20 January 2016.

– 2017. "B.C. Parties Forge Election Battle Lines over Bridge Tolls in Surrey." *The Globe and Mail*, 9 April 2017. Accessed 18 February 2018. https://www.theglobeandmail.com/news/british-columbia/bc-parties-forge-election-battle-lines-over-bridge-tolls-in-surrey/article34649520/.

Baldwin, J.R. 1977. "The Evolution of Transportation Policy in Canada." *Canadian Public Administration* (Winter): 600–31.

Baldwin, Richard E. 2012. *Global Supply Chains: Why They Emerged, Why They Matter, and Where They Are Going*. Centre for Policy Research, National Bureau of Economic Research. Paper No. DP9103.

Ball, Kirstie, and Laureen Snider, eds. 2014. *The Surveillance-Industrial Complex: A Political Economy of Surveillance*. London: Routledge.

Bauer, Martin W. 2015. *Atoms, Bytes and Genes*. London: Routledge.

Baylis, John, Steve Smith, Patrica Owens, eds. 2014. *The Globalization of World Politics: An Introduction to International Relations*. 6th ed. Oxford: Oxford University Press.

BBC. 2015. "Who Is Responsible for a Driverless Car Accident." BBC News, *Technology*, 8 October 2015.

Beeby, Dean. 2017. "Ottawa Hires Consultants to Advise on Airport Sell-Offs." CBC News, 19 July 2017. https://www.cbc.ca/news/politics/airports-pwc-credit-suisse-morneau-sale-equity-lease-c-d-howe-cdev-finance-canada-1.4210703.

Beilock, Richard, and Barry E. Prentice. 2007. "A Single North American Trucking Market Experiment: The Open Prairies Proposal." Working paper. North American Center for Transborder Studies, Arizona State University, September.

Bell, S., and Andrew Hindmoor. 2009. *Rethinking Governance: The Centrality of the State in Modern Society*. Cambridge, UK: Cambridge University Press.

Bice, Sara. 2014. "What Gives You a Social Licence? An Exploration of the Social Licence to Operate in the Australian Mining Industry." *Resources* (3): 62–80.

Bird, Richard, and Enid Slack. 1993. *Urban Public Finance in Canada*. 2nd ed. Hoboken, NJ: John Wiley and Sons.

Bird, Richard, Enid Slack, and Almos Tasronyi. 2012. *A Tale of Two Taxes: Property Tax Reform in Ontario*. Massachusetts: Lincoln Institute of Land Policy.

Bishop, Grant. 2013. "After Lac-Mégantic, How Should We Regulate Risk?" *Globe and Mail*, 16 July 2013.

Black, Leeora, and Sara Bice. 2015. "Defining the Elusive and Essential Social Licence to Operate." http://www.csrconnected.com.au.

Blank, Stephen, and Barry E. Prentice. 2012. "Widening Competition in North American Freight Transport: The Impact of Cabotage." Commentary. The Macdonald-Laurier Institute, April.

Boardman, Anthony E., Claude Laurin, Mark A. Moore, and Aidan R. Vining. 2013. "Efficiency, Profitability, and Welfare Gains from the Canadian National Railway Privatization." *Research in Transportation Business and Management* 6 (April): 19–30.

Boisvert, Yves. 2016. "Uber in Quebec: Innovation Is Not an Excuse to Escape the Law." *Globe and Mail*, 20 May 2016. https://www.theglobeandmail.com/opinion/uber-in-quebec-innovation-is-no-excuse-to-escape-the-law/article30099161/.

Bombardier Recreational Products. 2016. "Profile." http://www.brp.com/en-ca/company/about-brp/profile.

Bondy, K., J. Moon, and D. Matten. 2012. "An Institution of Corporate Social Responsibility (CSR) in Multi-National Corporations: Form and Implications." *Journal of Business Ethics* 111: 281–99.

Bordeleau, Christian. 2012. "Public-Private Partnerships Canada and the P3 Fund: Shedding Light on a New Meso Institutional Arrangement." In *How Ottawa Spends 2012–2013: The Harper Majority, Budget Cuts and the New Opposition*, edited by G. Bruce Doern and Christopher Stoney, 145–60. Montreal & Kingston: McGill-Queen's University Press.

Borins, Sandford. 1983. *The Language of the Skies: The Bilingual Air Traffic Control Conflict in Canada*. Montreal & Kingston: McGill-Queen's University Press.

Borins, Sandford, and David Brown. 2008. "E-consultation: Technology at the Interface between Civil Society and Government." In *Professionalism and Public Service: Essays in Honour of Kenneth Kernaghan*, edited by David Siegel and Ken Rasmussen, 178–206. Toronto: University of Toronto Press.

Bothwell, Robert. 1984. *Eldorado: Canada's National Uranium Company*. Toronto: University of Toronto Press.

Botts, Lee, and Paul Muldoon. 2005. *Evolution of the Great Lakes Water Quality Agreement*. East Lansing, MI: Michigan State University Press.

Boudette, Neil E. 2016a. "For Driverless Cars, Citylike Test Sites Offer the Unpredictable." *New York Times*, 4 June 2016. https://www.nytimes.com/2016/06/06/business/for-driverless-cars-citylike-test-sites-offer-the-unpredictable.html.

– 2016b. "Testing Sites for Self-Driving Cars Become a Priority." *New York Times*, 22 July 2016. https://www.nytimes.com/2016/07/23/business/testing-sites-for-self-driving-cars-become-a-priority.html.

Bracken-Roche, Clara, David Lyon, Mark J. Mansour, Adam Molnar, Alana Saulnier and Scott Thompson. 2014. "Surveillance Drones: Policy Implications of the Spread of Unmanned Aerial Vehicles (UAVs) in Canada." A Report to the Office of the Privacy Commissioner of Canada. Surveillance Studies Centre, Queen's University, 30 April.

Bradbury, Susan L. 2010. "An Assessment of the Free and Secure Trade (FAST) Program Along the Canada–US Border." *Transport Policy* 17 (6): 367–80.

Bradford, Neil, and Allison Bramwell. 2014. *Governing Urban Economies: Innovation and Inclusion in Canadian-City Regions*. Toronto: University of Toronto Press.

Braithwaite, John. 2008. *Regulatory Capitalism*. Cheltenham, UK: Edward Elgar.

Braithwaite, John, and Peter Drahos. 2000. *Global Business Regulation*. Cambridge: Cambridge University Press.

Brooks, Mary. 2008. *North American Freight Transport: The Road to Security and Prosperity*. Cheltenham, UK: Edward Elgar.

Budget speech. 1974. http://www.lop.parl.gc.ca/Parlinfo/Documents/Budgets/English/1974-11-18.pdf.

– 1975. http://www.lop.parl.gc.ca/Parlinfo/Documents/Budgets/English/1975-06-23.pdf.

– 1976. http://www.lop.parl.gc.ca/Parlinfo/Documents/Budgets/English/1976-05-25.pdf.

– 1978. http://www.lop.parl.gc.ca/Parlinfo/Documents/Budgets/English/1978-04-10.pdf.

– 1980. http://www.lop.parl.gc.ca/Parlinfo/Documents/Budgets/English/1980-10-28.pdf.

– 1983. http://www.lop.parl.gc.ca/Parlinfo/Documents/Budgets/English/1983-04-19.pdf.

– 1985. http://www.lop.parl.gc.ca/Parlinfo/Documents/Budgets/English/1985-05-23.pdf.

– 1986. http://www.lop.parl.gc.ca/Parlinfo/Documents/Budgets/English/1986-02-26.pdf.

– 1987. http://www.lop.parl.gc.ca/Parlinfo/Documents/Budgets/English/1987-02-18.pdf.

– 1988. http://www.lop.parl.gc.ca/Parlinfo/Documents/Budgets/English/1988-02-10.pdf.

– 1989. http://www.lop.parl.gc.ca/Parlinfo/Documents/Budgets/English/1989-04-27.pdf.

– 1992. http://www.lop.parl.gc.ca/Parlinfo/Documents/Budgets/English/1992-02-25.pdf.

– 1995. http://www.lop.parl.gc.ca/Parlinfo/Documents/Budgets/English/1995-02-27.pdf.

– 2001. http://www.lop.parl.gc.ca/Parlinfo/Documents/Budgets/English/2001-12-10.pdf.

– 2004. http://www.lop.parl.gc.ca/Parlinfo/Documents/Budgets/English/2004-03-23.pdf.

– 2005. http://www.lop.parl.gc.ca/Parlinfo/Documents/Budgets/English/2005-02-23.pdf.

– 2006. http://www.lop.parl.gc.ca/Parlinfo/Documents/Budgets/English/2006-05-02.pdf.

– 2007. http://www.lop.parl.gc.ca/Parlinfo/Documents/Budgets/English/2007-03-19.pdf.

– 2008. http://www.lop.parl.gc.ca/Parlinfo/Documents/Budgets/English/2008-02-26.pdf.

- 2009. http://www.lop.parl.gc.ca/Parlinfo/Documents/Budgets/English/
  2009-01-27.pdf.
- 2010. http://www.lop.parl.gc.ca/Parlinfo/Documents/Budgets/English/
  2010-03-04.pdf.
- 2011. http://www.lop.parl.gc.ca/Parlinfo/Documents/Budgets/English/
  2011-03-22.pdf.
- 2013. http://www.lop.parl.gc.ca/Parlinfo/Documents/Budgets/English/
  2013-02-21.pdf.
- 2014. http://www.lop.parl.gc.ca/Parlinfo/Documents/Budgets/English/
  2014-02-11.pdf.
- 2015. http://www.lop.parl.gc.ca/Parlinfo/Documents/Budgets/English/
  2015-04-21.pdf.
- 2016. http://www.lop.parl.gc.ca/Parlinfo/Documents/Budgets/English/
  2016-03-22.pdf.

Budget plan. 2016. *https://www.budget.gc.ca/2016/home-accueil-en.html*.
- 2017. *https://www.budget.gc.ca/2017/docs/plan/budget-2017-en.pdf*.
- 2018. https://www.budget.gc.ca/2018/docs/plan/toc-tdm-en.html.

Bureau of Transportation Statistics, United States Department of
  Transportation. 2011. "Border Crossing/Entry Data: Quick Search
  by Rankings." Accessed 5 December 2016. https://transborder.bts.gov/
  programs/international/transborder/TBDR_BC/TBDR_BC_QuickSearch.
  html.

Bursey, David. 2015. "Rethinking Social Licence to Operate: A Concept in
  Search of Definition and Boundaries." *Environment and Energy Bulletin*.
  Business Council of British Columbia.

Burzichelli, Corinne Dowling. 2016. "Delivery Drones: Will Amazon Air
  See the National Airspace?" *Rutgers Computer and Technology Law
  Journal* (42): 162–75.

Butler, Sarah, and Gwyn Topham. 2017. "Uber Stripped of London
  Licence Due to Lack of Corporate Responsibility." *The Guardian*,
  23 September 2017. https://www.theguardian.com/technology/2017/
  sep/22/uber-licence-transport-for-london-tfl.

Cairns, Malcolm. 2013a. "Crude Oil By Rail: Parts I and II: Potential for
  the Movement Of Alberta Oil Sands Crude Oil and Related Products
  by Canadian Railways." Canadian Transportation Research Forum,
  11 June,
- 2013b. "Rail Safety in Transporting Dangerous Goods in Canada."
  Canadian Transportation Research Forum, 4 November.

Calder, Simon. 2015. "Government Wants Airport Drop-off Charges
  to Spread." *The Independent*, 24 November 2015.

Cameron, David. M. 1974. "Urban Policy." In *Issues in Canadian Public Policy*, edited by G. Bruce Doern and V. Seymour Wilson, 228–52. Toronto: Macmillan of Canada.

Cameron, Duncan, ed. 1988. *The Free Trade Deal*. Toronto: James Lorimer and Company.

Cameron, Maxwell A., and Brian W. Tomlin. 2000. *The Making of NAFTA: How the Deal Was Done*. Ithaca: Cornell University Press.

Campion-Smith, Bruce. 2016. "Ottawa Eyes Airport Sell-off to Raise Infrastructure Cash." *Toronto Star*, 13 July 2016. https://www.thestar.com/news/canada/2016/07/03/ottawa-eyes-airport-sell-off-to-raise-infrastructure-cash.html.

Canada, Government of. 1985. "Freedom to Move: A Framework for Transportation Reform." Minister of Transport.

– 2001. "Vision and Balance: Report of the Canada Transportation Act Review Panel." Minister of Public Works and Government Services, June.

– 2010. "National Policy Framework for Strategic Gateways and Trade Corridors." Transport Canada. http://www.canada'sgateways.gc.ca.

– 2011a. "Rail Freight Service Review: Final Report." Transport Canada.

– 2011b. "Canada's Economic Action Plan: Terms of Reference for the United States–Canada Regulatory Cooperation Council." 3 June 2011. http:/www.actionplan.gc.ca/ page/rcc-cer/terms-reference.

– 2013. Standing Committee on Transportation, Infrastructure, and Communities. Number 061, First Session, Forty-first Parliament. Evidence. 28 February 2013.

– 2014. Asia–Pacific Gateway and Corridor Initiative website. Government of Canada, 10 March 2014.

– 2015. "Regulations Amending the Transportation of Dangerous Goods Regulations (TC 117 Tank Cars)." *Canada Gazette*, archived, 20 May.

– 2017a. "Picking up Steam: Growing Canada's Economy with Modernized Rail Transportation." (The Transportation Modernization Act). Bill C-49. Backgrounder from Transport Canada. https://www.canada.ca/en/transport-canada/news/2017/05/picking_up_steamgrowingcanadaseconomywithmodernizedrailtransport.html.

– 2017b. "Traveller Initiatives: Air Passenger Rights." https://www.canada.ca/en/transport-canada/news/2017/05/travellers_initiatives.html.

Canada Grains Council. 1973. *State of the Industry*. Winnipeg, MB: Canada Grains Council.

Canada Minister of Infrastructure. 1997. "Canada Infrastructure Works." *Bulletin* 1 (8).

Canada Transportation Act Review Panel. 2001. "Vision and Balance." Report of the Canada Transportation Act Review Panel.

Canada Transport Act Review. 2014. "Discussion Paper: Canada Transportation Act Review."

– 2015. "Pathways: Connecting Canada's Transportation System to the World." Government of Canada.

Canadian Air Transport Security Authority. 2016. CATSA *Review*. https://www.tc.ca/eng/aviationsecurity/page-168.htm.

– 2015a. "2014/15–2018/19 Corporate Plan." CATSA.

– 2015b. CATSA *2015 Annual Report*. Ottawa: CATSA.

Canadian Automated Vehicles Centre of Excellence. 2015. "Preparing for Autonomous Vehicles in Canada: A White Paper Prepared for the Government of Canada." CAVCOE, 16 December.

Canadian Centre for Policy Alternatives. 2015. *Making Sense of the* CETA: *An Analysis of the Final Text of the Canada–European Union Comprehensive Economic and Trade Agreement*. Ottawa: CCPA.

Canadian Chamber of Commerce. 2013. "The Foundations of a Competitive Canada: The Need for Strategic Infrastructure Investment." Canadian Chamber of Commerce, 18 December.

Canadian Environmental Assessment Agency. 2013. "2013–14 Report on Plans and Priorities." Canadian Environmental Assessment Agency.

Canadian Federation of Municipalities. 2016. "Our Members." http://www.fcm.ca/home/about-us/membership/our-members; http://www.fcm.ca/home/about-us/big-city-mayors-caucus.htm.

Canadian Pacific Consulting Services. 2014. "Evolution of Canadian Railway Economic Regulation and Industry Performance Under Commercial Freedom." The Railway Association of Canada, November.

Canadian Recreational Vehicle Association. 2016. "CRVA Certification and Standards." http://www.crva.ca/rvstandards/.

Canadian Transportation Agency. 2001. "Canadian Transportation Agency Issues Decision on a Complaint Filed by Naber Seed and Grain Company against the Canadian National Railway Company." Canadian Transportation Agency, 29 May.

– 2002. "In the Matter of complaints filed by Naber Seed & Grain Co. Ltd., pursuant to section 116 of the Canada Transportation Act, S.C., 1996, c. 10 … " Decision No. 323-R-2002. 11 June.

– 2014. Letter Decision No. 2014-10-03. "Application by Louis Dreyfus Commodities Canada Ltd. against the Canadian National Railway

Company, pursuant to section 116 of the Canada Transportation Act, S.C., 1996, c. 10, as amended." 3 October.

– 2015. *Annual Report 2014–2015.* Gatineau: Canadian Transportation Agency.

– 2016a. "Mission, Mandate, Vision and Values," 1. https://www.otc-cta.gc.ca/eng/mission-mandate.

– 2016b. "Code of Conduct for Members of the Agency," 2. https://www.otc-cta.gc.ca/eng/code-conduct-members-agency.

– 2016c. "Regulating the Industry," 1. https://www.otc-cta.gc.ca/eng/regulating-industry.

– 2016d. "100 Years at the Heart of Transportation – An Historical Perspective." Catalogue No. TT4-2/2015E https://www.otc-cta.gc.ca/eng/publication/100-years-heart-transportation-historical-perspective.

Carleton University. 2014. "A Critical Conversation on Railway-Shipper Relations: Report on Proceedings." Carleton University, 16 October.

Cavoukian, Ann. 2012. "Privacy and Drones: Unmanned Aerial Vehicles." Information and Privacy Commissioner Ontario, Canada, August.

CBC News. 2004. "Air Canada, WestJet Trade Accusations." CBC News, 9 July 2004. https://www.cbc.ca/news/canada/air-canada-westjet-trade-accusations-1.494825.

– 2006. "Air Canada, WestJet Settle Spying Lawsuit." CBC News, 30 May 2006. https://www.cbc.ca/news/business/air-canada-westjet-settle-spying-lawsuit-1.589059.

– 2013. "Lac-Megantic Disaster Railway Gets Bankruptcy Protection." CBC News, 8 August 2013. https://www.cbc.ca/news/canada/montreal/lac-m%C3%A9gantic-disaster-railway-gets-bankruptcy-protection-1.1341715.

– 2016. "WestJet Ends 2015 with Weak Q4 Profit, Revenue; Plans Increased Share Buyback." CBC News, 2 February 2016. https://www.cbc.ca/news/canada/calgary/westjet-2015-weak-q4-profit-1.3429872.

– 2017. "Uber Threatens to Leave If Quebec Insists on Stricter Rules." CBC News, 26 September 2017. http://www.cbc.ca/news/canada.montreal/uber-quebec-leave-1.4307065.

– 2018a. "Lac-Megantic Residents Grapple with Verdict While Looking to Future." CBC News, 22 January 2018. https://www.cbc.ca/news/canada/montreal/lac-megantic-concerns-after-verdict-1.4497742.

– 2018b. "Railway to Churchill, Man., Sold – Repairs to Begin 'Immediately.'" CBC News, 31 August 2018. https://www.cbc.ca/news/canada/manitoba/churchill-raiway-sale-omnitrax-1.4807450.

Cervero, Robert, Erock Guerra, and Stefan Al. 2017. *Beyond Mobility: Planning Cities for People and Places*. Washington, DC: Island Press.

Champagne, Eric. 2014. "Tracking the Growth of the Federal Municipal Infrastructure Program under Different Political Regimes." In *Canada in Cities: The Politics and Policy of Federal-Local Governance*, edited by Katherine Graham and Caroline Andrew, 164–92. Montreal & Kingston: McGill-Queen's University Press.

Chatfield, Dean C., Jeon G. Kim, Terry P. Harrison, and Jack C. Hayya. 2004. "The Bullwhip Effect – Impact of Stochastic Lead Time, Information Quality, and Information Sharing: A Simulation Study." *Production and Operations Management* 13 (4): 340–53.

Christensen, Clayton M., Michael Raynor, and Rory McDonald. 2015. "What Is Disruptive Innovation?" *Harvard Business Review* (December): 3–11.

Christopher, Martin. 2016. *Logistics and Supply Change Management*. 5th ed. London: FT Publishing International.

City of Winnipeg. 2011. "Winnipeg Transportation Master Plan: Executive Summary." City of Winnipeg.

– 2016. "Departments." http://winnipeg.ca/interhom/toc/departments.asp.

Clamen, M. 2013. "The IJC and Transboundary Water Disputes: Past, Present, Future." In *Water without Borders: Canada, the United States and Shared Waters*, edited by E.S. Norman, E.S. Cohen, and K. Bakker, 70–87. Toronto: University of Toronto Press.

Cleland, Michael, Nora Nourallah, and Stewart Fast. 2016. "Fair Enough: Assessing Community Confidence in Energy Authorities." Calgary: Canada West Foundation, 11 April.

Coalition of Rail Shippers. 2010. "Submission to the Rail Freight Service Review Panel." Coalition of Rail Shippers.

Coglianese, Cary, ed. 2012. *Regulatory Breakdown: The Crisis of Confidence in U.S. Regulation*. Philadelphia: University of Pennsylvania Press.

Coglianese, Cary, and Thomas R. Menzies. 2017. "Designing Safety Regulations for High-Hazard Industries." *The Regulatory Review*. 4 October. https://www.theregreview.org/2017/10/04/coglianese-menzies-safety-regulations-hazard-industries/.

Cohn, Martin Regg. 2015. "Collision of Ideologies, Technologies over Uber." *Toronto Star*, 10 November 2015.

Coleman, John. 2015a. "Linking Railway Capacity and Transportation Policy: Understanding the Former, Contributing to the Latter." Paper for Transport Canada. 30 March.

– 2015. "Understanding Interrelationships among Capacity, Congestion, System Optimization, and Levels of Service in Canadian Freight Rail Transportation." TPaper for the Canada Transportation Act Review Panel. July.

Coleman, John and G. Bruce Doern. 2014. "Railway-Shipper Relations in a Networked Governance Model." Ottawa: School of Public Policy and Administration, Carleton University.

– 2015. "Submission to Canada Transportation Act Review Panel with a Focus on Canadian Transportation Policy, Governance, and Regulation." Ottawa: School of Public Policy and Administration, Carleton University, 20 January.

Coleman, Stephen, and Jay G. Blumler. 2009. *The Internet and Democratic Citizenship*. New York: Cambridge University Press.

Commissioner of Competition. 2013. *Annual Report of the Commissioner of Competition for the Year Ending March 31st, 2013*. Ottawa: Competition Bureau.

Commissioner of the Environment and Sustainable Development. 2011. "Transportation of Dangerous Goods." Office of the Auditor General of Canada.

– 2015. "Oversight of Federally Regulated Pipelines." Office of the Auditor General of Canada.

Competition Bureau. 2014. "Competition Bureau Submission to the OECD: Competition Roundtable on Airline Competition." http:www.competitionbureau.gc.ca/eic/cb-bc.nsf/eng/h_03746.html.

– 2015a. "Competition." Competition Bureau. http:www.competitionbureau.gc.ca/eic/cb-bc.nsf/eng/h_00125.html.

– 2015b. "Modernizing Regulation in the Canadian Taxi Industry." Competition Bureau.

Conference Board of Canada. 2015. "Transportation and Infrastructure Policy in Canada." Centre for Transportation Infrastructure.

Corbett, D.C. 1965. *Politics and the Airlines*. Toronto: University of Toronto Press.

Council on Foreign Relations. 2018. "What Is the Trans-Pacific Partnership TPP?" 15 May. https://www.cfr.org/backgrounder/what-trans-pacific-partnership-tpp.

Coyne, Andrew. 2016. "Toronto Plan Hardly Takes Toll on Drivers." *National Post*, 26 November 2016.

Cramer, Barton E. 2007. "North American Freight Rail: Regulatory Evolution, Strategic Rejuvenation and the Revival of an Ailing Industry." Doctoral dissertation, Department of Geography, University of Iowa.

Cramer, Judd, and Alan B. Krueger. 2016. "Disruptive Change in the Taxi Business: The Case of Uber." National Bureau of Economic Research. NBER Working Paper No. 22083. http://www.nber.org/papers/w22083. pdf.

Crawford, Susan P. 2010. "Transporting Communications." *Boston University Law Review* 89: 871–925.

Creighton, D.G. 1932. *The Commercial Empire of the St. Lawrence 1760–1850*. Toronto: Ryerson Press.

– 1956. *The Empire of the St. Lawrence: A Study of Commerce and Politics*. Toronto: Macmillan of Canada.

Cruikshank, Ken. 1991. *Close Ties: Railways, Government and the Board of Railway Commissioners*. Montreal & Kingston: McGill-Queen's University Press.

Csanady, Ashley. 2016. "If the Uber Debate Is Really about Safety, Why Are Women's Voices Being Sidelined?" *National Post*, 26 April 2016.

– 2015. "Ontario Set to Become First Province to Allow Driverless Cars to Be Tested on Its Roads." *National Post*, 13 October 2015.

Currie, A.W. 1967. *Canadian Transportation Economics*. Toronto: University of Toronto Press.

Dahlgren, Peter. 2013. *The Political Web: Media, Participation and Alternative Democracy*. Basingstoke, UK: Palgrave MacMillan.

Darling, Howard. 1980. *The Politics of Freight Rates*. Toronto: McClelland & Stewart.

Demers, Fanny, and Michel Demers. 2016. "Infrastructure Policy and Spending: An Initial Look at the Trudeau Liberal Plan." In *How Ottawa Spends 2016–2017: The Trudeau Liberals in Power*, edited by G. Bruce Doern and Christopher Stoney, 30–84. Ottawa: School of Public Policy and Administration, Carleton University.

Department of Agriculture (USA). 2013. "Petition for Rulemaking to Adopt Revised Competitive Switching Rules." Submitted to US Surface Transportation Board. STB *Ex Parte* No. 711. 30 May 2013.

Department of Finance Canada. 2008. "The Budget Plan 2008: Responsible Leadership." 26 February 2008.

Devine-Wright, Patrick. 2009. "Rethinking NIMBYism: The Role of Place Attachment and Place Identity in Explaining Place-Protective Action." *Journal of Community and Applied Social Psychology* 19 (6): 426–41.

Diebel, Linda. 2016. "Olive Branch Could End Detroit–Windsor Bridge Wars." *Toronto Star*, 13 February 2016. https://www.thestar.com/news/

canada/2016/02/13/olive-branch-could-end-detroit-windsor-bridge-wars.html.

Dingler, Mark. 2010. "The Impact of Operational Strategies and New Technologies on Railroad Capacity." Master's thesis, Science in Civil Engineering. University of Illinois at Urbana–Champaign.

Dinning, Jim. 2012. "Facilitator's Final Report: Service Agreement Template and Commercial Dispute Resolution Process." Report to Transport Canada, 12 May.

Dirnberger, Jeremiah. 2006. "Development and Application of Lean Railroading to Improve Classification Terminal Performance." Master's thesis, Science in Civil Engineering. University of Illinois at Urbana–Champaign.

DIY Drones. 2016. "Members." http://diydrones.com/.

Doan, Darcie, Brian Paddock, and Jan Dyer. 2003. "Grain Transportation Policy and Transformation in Western Canadian Agriculture." https://www.researchgate.net/publication/23511996_Grain_Transportation_Policy_and_Transformation_in_Western_Canadian_Agriculture.

Dodge, David. 2016. "Don't Just Focus on 'Shovel-Readiness', says David Dodge." Interview with Chris Hall. CBC Radio, *The House*, 23 January 2016.

Doern, G. Bruce. ed. 1982. *How Ottawa Spends 1982: National Policy and Economic Development*. Toronto: James Lorimer and Company Ltd.

– ed. 2002. *How Ottawa Spends 2002–2003: The Security Aftermath and National Priorities*. Toronto: Oxford University Press Canada.

– 2006. "The Adequacy of Consumer Input in Federal Policy Processes." Office of Consumer Affairs, Industry Canada.

– 2007. "Red-Tape, Red Flags: Regulation for the Innovation Age." Conference Board of Canada.

– 2009. "Evolving Budgetary Policies and Experiments: 1980 to 2009–2010." In *How Ottawa Spends 2009–2010: Economic Upheaval and Political Dysfunction*, edited by Allan Maslove, 14–46. Montreal & Kingston: McGill-Queen's University Press.

– 2010. "The Relationships Between Regulation and Innovation in The Transport Canada Context." Transport Canada.

– 2015. "The Relevance of Common Carrier Provision in the Context of 'Social Licence' and Social Regulation Concepts: Key Priorities, Complexity and Legitimacy in Long Term Canadian National Transportation Policy and Governance." Canada Transportation Act Review Secretariat, 15 July.

Doern, G. Bruce, Graeme Auld, and Christopher Stoney. 2015. *Green-lite: Complexity in Fifty Years of Canadian Environmental Policy, Governance and Democracy*. Montreal & Kingston: McGill-Queen's University Press.

Doern, G. Bruce, David Castle, and Peter Phillips. 2016. *Canadian Science, Technology and Innovation Policy: The Innovation Economy and Society Nexus*. Montreal & Kingston: McGill-Queen's University Press.

Doern, G. Bruce, and Tom Conway. 1994. *The Greening of Canada*. Toronto: University of Toronto Press.

Doern, G. Bruce, and Monica Gattinger. 2003. *Power Switch: Energy Regulatory Governance in the Twenty-First Century*. Toronto: University of Toronto Press.

Doern, G. Bruce, and Robert Johnson, eds. 2006. *Rules, Rules, Rules, Rules: Multilevel Regulatory Governance*. Toronto: University of Toronto Press.

Doern, G. Bruce, and Jeffrey Kinder. 2007. *Strategic Science in the Public Interest: Canada's Government Laboratories and Science-based Agencies*. Toronto: University of Toronto Press.

Doern, G. Bruce, and Mark MacDonald. 1999. *Free-Trade Federalism: Negotiating the Canadian Agreement on Internal Trade*. Toronto: University of Toronto Press.

Doern, G. Bruce, Allan Maslove, and Michael J. Prince. 2013. *Canadian Public Budgeting in the Age of Crises: Shifting Budgetary Domains and Temporal Budgeting*. Montreal & Kingston: McGill-Queen's University Press.

Doern, G. Bruce, and Richard Phidd. 1983. *Canadian Public Policy: Ideas, Structure, Process*. Toronto: Methuen.

– 1992. *Canadian Public Policy: Ideas, Structure, Process*. 2nd ed. Toronto: Nelson Canada.

Doern, G. Bruce, and Michael J. Prince. 2012. *Three Bio-Realms: Biotechnology and the Governance of Food, Health and Life in Canada*. Toronto: University of Toronto Press.

Doern, G. Bruce, Michael J. Prince, and Richard J. Schultz. 2014. *Rules and Unruliness: Canadian Regulatory Democracy, Governance, Capitalism and Welfarism*. Montreal & Kingston: McGill-Queen's University Press.

Doern, G. Bruce, and Glen Toner. 1985. *The Politics of Energy*. Toronto: Methuen.

Doern, G. Bruce, and Stephen Wilks, eds. 1996. *Comparative Competition Policy: National Institutions in a Global Market*. Oxford: Clarendon Press.

Doern, G. Bruce, and Brian W. Tomlin. 1991. *Faith and Fear: The Free Trade Story*. Toronto: Stoddart.

Donnan, Shawn. 2018. "Trump Takes Aim at Canada over Trade Frustrations." *Financial Times*, 25 January 2018. https://www.ft.com/content/7c842d76-11e8-9650-9c0ad7c5b5.

Dourade, Eli. 2016. "Airport Noise NIMBYism: An Emperical Investigation." Technology Policy, Mercatus on Policy Series, 17 October 2016. https://www.mercatus.org/publications/airport-noise-nimbyism.

Dupuis, Jean. 2015. *Via Rail Inc. and the Future of Passenger Rail in Canada*. Library of Parliament. Publication No. 2015-55-E, 31 August 2015.

Earl, Paul D. 2009. "Public Sector, Private Sector: Jane Jacobs' Non-Ideological Views on What Belongs Where." Paper and presentation at Canadian Transportation Research Forum 44th Annual Conference.

– 2011. "'The Holy Crow': A Lesson in the Perverse Nature of Good Intentions." Proceedings of the Administrative Sciences Association of Canada (ASAC). Annual Conference 2011, Montreal, Quebec.

Earl, Paul D., and Barry E. Prentice. 2016. "Western Grain Exceptionalism: Transportation Policy Change since 1968." Canadian Transportation Research Forum, proceedings issue, 51st annual meeting, 472–9.

Eby, Clifford. 2008. "Common Carrier Obligation of Railroads: Transportation of Hazardous Materials." Statement of the United States Department of Transportation, 22 July 2008.

Economist. 2014a. "Everybody Wants to Rule The World." *The Economist*, 29 November 2014, 19–21.

– 2016a. "Schumpeter: McJobs and UberJobs." *The Economist*, 4 July 2016, 58.

– 2016b. "Uberworld." *The Economist*, 3 September 2016, 9.

– 2016c. "Briefing Uber: From Zero to Seventy (Billion)." *The Economist*, 3 September 2016, 17–19.

– 2017. "Maple Grief: The Lessons from Canada's Attempts to Curb its House-price Boom." *The Economist*, 17 June 2017, 16–17.

– 2018a. "NAFTA Rule Brakers." *The Economist*, 3 February 2018, 68.

– 2018b. "Briefing Global Logistics: Thinking Outside the Box." *The Economist* 2018, 28 April, 18–20.

Egan, Kelly. 2016. "'Complete Streets' or Total Fiasco? Project Scorned." *Ottawa Citizen*, 30 November 2016.

Eisler, Dale. 2014. "Licence to Act" *Policy Options*, January. http://policyoptions.irpp.org/issues/technology/eisler/.

Eissler, Rebecca, Annelise Russell, and Bryan D. Jones. 2014. "New Avenues for the Study of Agenda Setting." *Policy Studies Journal* 42, issue supplement: S71–S86.

Elias, Bartholomew. 2009. *Airport and Aviation Security: U.S. Policy and Strategy in the Age of Global Terrorism*. London: CRC Press.

Elias, Bart. 2012. "Pilotless Drones: Background and Considerations for Congress Regarding Unmanned Aircraft Operations in the National Airspace System." Washington, DC: Congressional Research Service, 10 September.

Enns, Andrew, and Nadia Papineau-Couture. 2009. "Survey of Shippers/ Report Prepared for the Rail Freight Service Review." eNRG Research Group in collaboration with University of Manitoba Transportation Institute, November.

Environmental Assessment Agency. 2013. "Mandate."

Esty, William Z. 1998. "Grain Handling and Transportation Review." Transport Canada.

Etzioni, Amitai. 2013. "The Privacy Merchants: What Is to Be Done?" *University of Pennsylvania Journal of Constitutional Law* 14 (4): 929–51.

European Commission. 2016. "Transport: Road Cabotage." http:// ec.europa.eu/transport/modes/road/haulage/cabotage_en.html.

Fagnant, Daniel J., and Kara Kockelman. 2014. "Preparing a Nation for Autonomous Vehicles: Opportunities, Barriers and Policy Recommen- dations for Capitalizing on Self-Driven Vehicles." Presentation at the 93rd Annual Meeting of the Transportation Research Board. Washington, January.

Farber, Hillary B. 2013. "Eyes in the Sky: Constitutional and Regulatory Approaches to Domestic Drone Deployment." *Syracuse Law Review* 64 (1): 1–48.

Fast, Stewart. 2014. "NIMBYs Are Not the Problem." *Policy Options*, 2 September 2014.

Feinman. Joshua N. 2016. "Backlash against globalization: Déjà vu?" *Deutsche Asset Management*, December.

Federal Court of Appeal. 2016. "Canadian National Railway Company v. Dreyfus, 2016 FCA 232 (CanLII), Docket A-140-15. 16 September.

Fekete, Jason. 2015. "Minority Using Notion of Social Licence to Try to Block Resource Projects, Joe Oliver Says." *Ottawa Citizen*, 6 March 2015.

– 2016. "Free VIA from Limited Access CN Tracks with Its Own $3B Corridor from Toronto to Montreal: Report." https://nationalpost. com/news/canada/

free-via-from-limited-access-cn-tracks-with-its-own-3b-corridor-from-toronto-to-montreal-report.

Fentus, Paul. 2012. "Effective Speed: Cycling Because It's Faster." In *City Cycling*, edited by John Pucher and Ralph Buehler, 57–74. Cambridge, MA: MIT Press.

Filion, P., M. Moos, Ryan Walker, and Tara Vinodrai, eds. 2015. *Canadian Cities in Transition*. 5th ed. Toronto: Oxford University Press.

Financial Times. 2015. "Urban Traffic Problems Start to Pile Up for Uber." London edition, 12 October 2015, 10.

Fisher, Ken. 2016. "Uber CEO: History Repeats Itself When We Resist Transportation Innovation." *Cars Technica*, 17 February 2016.

Flemming, Brian. 2012. "A White Paper on Reforming Canada's Transportation Policies for the 21st Century." University of Calgary, School of Public Policy, volume 5, issue 18, June.

– 2014a. "The 2014–2015 Canada Transport Act Review: Once More unto the Breach, Dear Friends." Conference Board of Canada, 25 November.

– 2014b. "Catching Up: The Case for Infrastructure Banks in Canada." The Van Horne Institute, February.

– 2015. "The Political Economy of Canada's Transportation Policies in 2015: The 'What' Is Easy; the 'How' Is Hard." Keynote address to the Atlantic Provinces Transportation Forum 2015, 20 May.

– 2016. "The Automated Vehicle: The Coming of the Next Disruptive Technology." Address to the Association of Canadian Engineering Companies, 28 January.

Flemming, Brian, Philip Bazel, and Peter Wallis. 2013. "Summary Report on Transportation Policy Roundtables: Held in Six Canadian Cities in February 2013." The Van Horne Institute, December.

Freight Management Association of Canada. 2016. "Membership." http://www.fma-agf/membership/member-companies.

Frid, Nina. 2014. "Bill C-52 and Bill C-30: New Rail Provisions." Presentation to the Chartered Institute of Logistics and Transportation in North America, Ottawa chapter, for the Canadian Transportation Agency, 11 September.

Floridi, Luciano. 2014. *The 4th Revolution: How the InfoSphere Is Reshaping Human Reality*. Oxford: Oxford University Press.

Foucault, Michel. 1980. *Power/Knowledge*. Brighton: Harvester.

– 1991. "Governmentality." In *The Foucault Effect: Studies in Governmentality*, edited by G. Burchell, Colin Gordon, and Peter Miller, 87–104. Chicago: University of Chicago Press.

– 2008. *The Birth of Biopolitics: Lectures at the College de France 1978–1979*. London: Palgrave MacMillan.

Fowler, Edmond P., and Jack Layton. 2001. "Transportation Policy in Canadian Cities." In *Urban Policy Issues: Canadian Perspectives*, edited by David Siegel and Edmund P. Fowler, 108–38. Toronto: Oxford University Press.

Fraser, Kaitie. 2018. "Canada's Infrastructure Minister, Mich. Governor Break Ground on Gordie Howe International Bridge." CBC News, 17 July 2018.

Furth, Peter G. 2012. "Bicycling Infrastructure for Mass Cycling." In *City Cycling*, edited by John Pucher and Ralph Buehler, 105–40. Cambridge, MA: MIT Press.

Gandalf Group. 2010. "Railway Service Satisfaction Research Report Evaluation." Memorandum included in submission from Canadian National to Rail Freight Service Review, 30 April.

Gattinger, Monica, and Geoffrey Hale, eds. 2010. *Borders and Bridges: Canada's Policy Relations in North America*. Toronto: Oxford University Press Canada.

Gensher, Shayna. 2013. "Canada's Domestic Regulatory Framework for RPAS: A Call for Public Deliberation." *Journal of Unmanned Vehicle Systems* (December): 1–4.

– 2014. "Regulating Spies in the Skies: Recommendations for Drone Rules in Canada." *IEEE Technology and Society Magazine* (Fall): 22–5.

Georges, Patrick. 2017. *Canada's Trade Policy Options under Donald Trump: NAFTA's Rules of Origin, Canada–U.S. Security Perimeter and Canada's Geographic Trade Diversification Opportunities*. Working Paper 1707E. Department of Economics. Faculty of Social Sciences, University of Ottawa. 2017. https://socialsciences.uottawa.ca/economics/sites/socialscience.uottawa.ca.economics/files/1707e.pdf.

Geyer, Robert, and Samie Rihani. 2010. *Complexity and Public Policy*. Abingdon-on-Thames: Routledge.

Gibbins, Roger, Antonia Maioni, and Janice Gross Stein. 2006. *Canada by Picasso: The Faces of Federalism*. Ottawa: Conference Board of Canada.

Gibson, Brian J., John T. Menzer, and Robert L. Cook. 2005. "Supply Chain Management: The Pursuit of a Consensus Definition." *Journal of Business Logistics* 26 (2): 17–25.

Gidengil, Elisabeth, and Heather Bastedo, eds. 2014. *Canadian Democracy from the Ground Up: Perceptions and Performance*. Vancouver: UBC Press.

Gill, Vijay. 2014. *Defining a New National Transportation Policy.* Ottawa: Conference Board of Canada, 13 March.

Gillen, David. 2011. "The Evolution of Airport Ownership and Governance." *Journal of Air Transport Management* (17): 3–13.

Glazebrook, G.P. de T. 1964. *A History of Transport in Canada.* Vol. 2. Montreal & Kingston: McGill-Queen's University Press.

Globerman, Steven, and Paul Storer. 2006. "The Impacts of 9/11 on Canada–US Trade." Border Policy Research Institute, Western Washington University, Bellingham WA.

Goldratt, Eliyahu. 1984. *The Goal.* Great Barrington, MA: North River Press.

Gollom, Mark. 2017. "Has Ambassador Bridge Owner Matty Moroun 'Outmanoeuvred Everybody?' Liberals Say No." CBC News, 25 September 2017. https://www.cbc.ca/news/business/bridge-gordie-howe-ambassador-moroun-windsor-detroit-1.4294977.

Goldratt, Eliyahu. 1990. *Theory of Constraints.* Great Barrington, MA: North River Press.

Goodmark, Paul, Barrie Kirk, Vijay Gill, and Brian Flemming. 2015. *Automated Vehicles: The Coming of the Next Disruptive Technology.* Ottawa: Conference Board of Canada.

Goodyear, Sheena. 2015. "Drones Get More Popular, and the Rules Are Getting Stricter." CBC News, 9 November 2015. https://www.cbc.ca/news/technology/canada-u-s-drones-rules-1.3280065.

Graham, Katherine, and Caroline Andrew, eds. 2014. *Canada in Cities: The Politics and Policy of Federal-Local Governance.* Montreal & Kingston: McGill-Queen's University Press.

Gratwick, John. 2001. "The Evolution of Canadian Transportation Policy." Canada Transportation Act Review, March.

Gaudreault, Valerie, and Patrick Lemire. 2003. "The Age of Public Infrastructure in Canada." Statistics Canada.

Giuliano, Genevieve, and Susan Hanson, eds. 2017. *The Geography of Urban Transportation.* 4th ed. New York: Guilford Press.

Goetz, Andrew R., and Timothy M. Vowles. 2009. *Journal of Transport Geography* 17 (4): 251–63.

Greater Toronto Airport Authority. 2014. "GTAA Annual Report 2014." Greater Toronto Airport Authority.

Great Lakes St Lawrence Seaway System. 2016. "The Seaway." http://www.greatlakes-seaway.com/en/seaway/history.

Guardian. 2016. "UN Panel Backs Banning Lithium-Ion Battery Shipments on Passenger Planes." https://www.theguardian.com/world/2016/jan/28/

un-panel-backs-banning-lithium-ion-battery-shipments-on-passenger-planes.

Gunningham, Neil, Robert A. Kagan, and Dorothy Thornton. 2004. "Social Licence and Environmental Protection: Why Businesses Go Beyond Compliance." *Law and Social Inquiry* 29 (2): 307–41.

Gwyn, Richard. 2011. *Nation Maker: Sir John A. Macdonald: His Life, Our Times.* Toronto: Random House Canada.

Haavardsrud, Paul. 2016. "Uber Playbook: Why the Ride-Hailing App Will Be Coming to a City Near You." CBC News, 22 January 2016. http// www.cbc.ca/news/business/uber-playbook-taxis-Canada-1.3411401.

Haldane, Andrew G. 2013. "Why Institutions Matter (More than Ever)." Speech presented to the Centre for Research on Socio-Cultural Change Annual Conference, School of Oriental and African Studies, London.

Hale, Geoffrey E. 2012. "Toward a Perimeter: Incremental Adaptation or a New Paradigm for Canada–US Security and Trade Relations?" In *How Ottawa Spends 2012–2013: The Harper Majority, Budget Cuts and the New Opposition*, edited by G. Bruce Doern and Christopher Stoney, 106–26. Montreal & Kingston: McGill-Queen's University Press.

Halifax Municipal Government. 2014. "Making Connections: 2014–19 Halifax Active Transportation Priorities Plan." Halifax Municipal Government.

– 2016. "Government." http://www.halifax.ca/government/.

Hall, Randolf, ed. 1999. *Handbook of Transportation Science*. New York: Springer Science and Business.

Hall Commission. 1977. *Grain and Rail in Western Canada. The Report of the Grain Handling and Transportation Commission*. Vol. 1. Ottawa: Grain Handling and Transportation Commission.

Hara Associated. 2015. "Taxi Economics – Old and New." City of Ottawa Taxi and Limousine Regulations and Service Review.

Hardy, Quentin. 2016. "UberPool and the Marvels of Measurement." *New York Times*. https://www.nytimes.com/2016/03/31/technology/ uberpool-and-the-marvels-of-measurement.html.

Harris, Ralph. 1978. "The Regulation of Air Transportation." In *The Regulatory Process in Canada*, edited by G. Bruce Doern, 212–36. Toronto: Macmillan of Canada.

Hart, Michael, and Brian Tomlin. 2002. "Inside the Perimeter: The US Policy Agenda and Its Implications for Canada." In *How Ottawa Spends Canada 2002–2003: The Security Aftermath and National Priorities*, edited by G. Bruce Doern, 48–68. Toronto: Oxford University Press Canada.

Heaver, Trevor D. 2009. "Canadian Railway Service Issues in 2009." Presentation to Canada Transportation Research Forum Conference, 24–7 May.

– 2013. "Submission to the Standing Committee on Transport, Infrastructure and Communities." Parliament of Canada, 15 February.

– 2014. "Research and Innovation for Transport." Submission to the Canadian Transportation Act Review Committee, 29 December.

Hern, Alex. 2016. "Uber Reverses Out of China with $7bn Sale to Didi Chuxing." *The Guardian*, 1 August 2016. https://www.theguardian.com/technology/2016/aug/01/uber-china-didi-chuxing.

Heydon, Kenneth, ed. 2012. *International Trade Policy*. London: Ashgate.

Hill, Margaret M. 1988. "Freedom to Move: Explaining the Decision to Deregulate Canadian Air and Rail Transportation." Unpublished research paper. School of Public Administration, Carleton University.

– 1999. "Recasting the Federal Transport Regulator: The Thirty Year's War." In *Changing the Rules: Canadian Regulatory Regimes and Institutions*, edited by Bruce Doern, Margaret Hill, Michael J. Prince, and Richard J. Schultz, 57–81. Toronto: University of Toronto Press.

Hill, Steven. 2015. *Raw Deal: How the "Uber Economy" and Runaway Capitalism Are Screwing American Workers*. New York: St Martin's Press.

Hodgson, J.R.F., and Mary R. Brooks. 2012. "Canada's Maritime Cabotage Policy." Marine Affairs Program, Dalhousie University.

– 2007. "Towards a North American Cabotage Regime: A Canadian Perspective." *Canadian Journal of Transportation* 1 (1): 19–35.

Horack, Martin, and Robert Young, eds. 2012. *Sites of Governance: Multilevel Governance and Policy Making in Canada's Big Cities*. Montreal & Kingston: McGill-Queen's University Press.

House of Commons of Canada, 2017. "Bill C-49. An Act to amend the Canada Transportation Act and other Acts respecting transportation and to make related consequential amendments to other acts." First session, forty-second Parliament.

Howlett, Michael. 2011. *Designing Public Policies: Principles and Instruments*. London: Routledge.

Howlett, Michael, and Jeremy Rayner. 2013. "Patching vs. Packaging in Policy Formulation: Assessing Portfolio Design." *Politics and Governance* 1 (2): 170–82.

Hui, Ann. 2015. "Face of Uber Canada Pushes for a 'Nicer' Approach." *Globe and Mail*, 6 November 2015.

Hutton, Will. 2016. "The Gig Economy Is Here to Stay. So Making It Fairer Must Be a Priority." *The Guardian*, 3 September 2016. https://www.

theguardian.com/commentisfree/2016/sep/03/gig-economy-zero-hours-
    contracts-ethics.
Iacobucci, E., Michael Trebilcock, and Ralph Winter. 2006. "The Political
    Economy of Deregulation in Canada." Phelps Centre for the Study
    of Government and Business, Sauder School of Business, University
    of British Columbia, 2006–05.
Industry Canada. 2014. "Seizing the Moment: Moving Forward in Science,
    Technology and Innovation." Industry Canada.
– 2015a. "SME Profile: Tourism Industries in Canada." Industry Canada.
– 2015b. "Logistics and Supply Chain Management." Industry Canada.
Infrastructure Canada. 2011. "Border Infrastructure Fund Projects."
    26 October. Accessed 7 February 2016. http://www.infrastructure.gc.ca/
    prog/bif-fif-eng.html.
– 2014a. "The Federal Gas Tax Fund." 31 March. Accessed 5 December
    2016. http://www.infrastructure.gc.ca/alt-format/pdf/GTF-FTE-
    20140905-eng.pdf.
– 2014b. "Final Report: Evaluation of the Gas Tax Fund." 14 August.
– 2015a. "Reports on Plans and Priorities 2015–16." 31 March. Accessed
    7 February 2016. http://www.infrastructure.gc.ca/pub/rpp/2015-16/
    2015-supp-hi-ih-eng.html.
– 2015b. "Other Programs." Accessed 7 February 2015.
– 2016a. "Gas Tax Fund: National GTF Investments." 31 May. Accessed
    5 December 2016. http://www.infrastructure.gc.ca/plan/gtf-fte/gtf-fte-
    04-eng.html#cb.
– 2016b. "The 2014 New Building Canada Fund." 17 May. Accessed
    5 December 2016. http://www.infrastructure.gc.ca/plan/nbcf-nfcc-eng.
    html.
– 2016c. "Public Transit Infrastructure Fund: Program Overview." 16 May.
    Accessed 7 December 2016. http://www.infrastructure.gc.ca/plan/ptif-
    fitc/ptif-program-programme-eng.html.
– 2016d. "Building Strong Cities Through Investments in Public Transit."
    22 November. Accessed 7 December 2016. http://www.infrastructure.
    gc.ca/plan/ptif-fitc-eng.php.
– 2016e. "New Building Canada Fund: National Infrastructure Component.
    Project Business Case Guide." Accessed 5 March 2016. http://www.
    infrastructure.gc.ca/plan/nic-vin/bc-ar03-eng.html.
– 2017. "Canada Infrastructure Bank." http://www.infrastructure.gc.ca/
    CIB-BIC/index-eng.html.
Institute for Governance of Private and Public Organizations. 2014.
    The Governance of Canadian Airports: Issues and Recommendations.
    Montreal: Institute for Governance of Private and Public Organizations.

Innovative Research Group. 2013. "Trends in Nimbyism and Reaction to Nymbys." Study prepared for the *Globe and Mail*, 23 December 2013.

International Air Transport Association. 2015. "Annual Review 2015." International Air Transport Association.

International Civil Aviation Organization. 2015. "MRTD Report: Building Trust."

– 2016. "About ICAO." http://www.icao.int/about-icao/pages/.

– 2018. "The Regional Offices of ICAO." https://www.icao.int/Pages/contact_us.aspx.

International Maritime Organization. 2014. "Annual Report of the ICAO Council: 2014." http://www.icao.int/annual-report-2014/pages/.

– 2015. *Strategic Plan for the Organization (For the Six-Year Period 2016 to 2021)*. London: International Maritime Organization.

– 2016a. "Introduction to IMO." http://.imo.org/en/About/Pages.

– 2016b. "Brief History of IMO." http://.imo.org/en/About/HistoryOfIMO/pages.

International Transport Forum. 2012a. *Seamless Transport: Making Connections*. Paris: International Transport Forum, November.

– 2012b. *Seamless Transport for Greener Growth*. Paris: International Transport Forum, May.

– 2013. *Seamless Public Transport for All*. Paris: International Transport Forum, March.

– 2014. *Renewed Mandate of the International Transport Forum*. Paris: International Transport Forum.

– 2015a. "Automated and Autonomous Driving: Regulation under Uncertainty." http://www.internationaltransportforum.org/Pub/new.html.

– 2015b. *Carbon Valuation, Risk and Uncertainty*. Paris: International Transport Forum.

– 2015c. *Liberalization of Air Transport*. Paris: International Transport Forum.

– 2016a. "About." http://www.internationaltransportforum.org/about/about.html.

– 2016b. "Publications." http://www.internationaltransportforum.org/Pub/new.html.

– 2016c. "Decarbonizing Transport." http://www.internationaltransportforum.org/Pub/new.html.

Inwood, Gregory J., and Carolyn Johns, eds. 2014. *Commissions of Inquiry and Policy Change: A Comparative Analysis*. Toronto: University of Toronto Press.

Isaac, Mike. 2016. "Uber Settles Suit over Driver Background Checks."
  New York Times, 8 April 2016. https://www.nytimes.com/2016/04/08/
  technology/uber-settles-suit-over-driver-background-checks.html.

Jackson, Andrew, and Bob Baldwin. 2007. "Policy Analysis by the
  Labour Movement in a Hostile Environment." In *Policy Analysis in
  Canada: The State of the Art*, edited by Laurent Dobuzinskis,
  Michael Howlett, and David Laycock, 473–96. Toronto: University
  of Toronto Press.

Jacobs, Emma. 2015. "Knowledge College for Cabbies to Close." *Financial
  Times*, 2 November 2015.

Jacobs, Jane. 1994. *Systems of Survival: A Dialog on the Moral Foundations
  of Commerce and Politics*. New York: Vintage Books.

Janisch, Hudson. 1977. "The Regulatory Process of the Canadian
  Transport Commission." Law Reform Commission of Canada.

– 1999. "Competition Policy Institutions: What Role in the Face of
  Continued Sectoral Regulation?" In *Changing the Rules: Canada's
  Changing Regulatory Regimes and Institutions*, edited by G. Bruce
  Doern, Margaret M. Hill, Michael J. Prince, and Richard J. Schultz,
  101–21. Toronto: University of Toronto Press.

Jenish, D'Arcy. 2009. *The St. Lawrence Seaway: Fifty Years and Counting*.
  Newcastle, ON: Penumbra Press.

Jetoo, S., Adam Thorn, Kathryn Friedman, Sara Gosman, and Gail
  Krantzberg. 2014. "Governance and Geopolitics as Drivers of Change
  in the Great Lakes–St. Lawrence Basin." *Journal of Great Lakes
  Research* (1): 1–11.

Johnson, Tracy. 2017. "After Years of Turbulence, Ultra-Low-Cost-Carriers
  Could Finally Take Flight in Canada." CBC News, 6 August 2017.
  https://www.cbc.ca/news/business/what-s-up-with-canada-s-ultra-low-
  cost-carriers-1.4234226.

Jones, Allison. 2016. "Ontario Uber Drivers Now Automatically Insured."
  Toronto Star, 7 July. https://www.thestar.com/business/2016/07/07/
  ontario-uber-drivers-now-automatically-insured.html.

Jones, Bryan D., and Frank R. Baumgartner. 2005. *The Politics of Attention:
  How Government Prioritizes Problems*. Chicago: University of Chicago
  Press.

– 2012. "From There to Here: Punctuated Equilibrium to the General
  Punctuation Thesis to a Theory of Government Information Processing."
  Policy Studies Journal (40): 1–20.

Jones, Erick C., and Christopher A. Chung. 2007. *RFID in Logistics:
  A Practical Introduction*. Boca Raton: CRC Press.

Jones, David P., and Anne S. de Villars. 2014. *Principles of Administrative Law*. 6th ed. Toronto: Carswell.

Journal of Unmanned Vehicle Systems. 2016. "About the Journal." http://www.nrcresearchpress.com/page/juvs/editors.

Justice Canada. 2013. An Act to Amend the Canada Transportation Act. Assented to. 26 June 2013. Bill C-52.

– 2016a. Aeronautics Act., Regulations Made Under This Act.

– 2016b. Aeronautics Act.

– 2016c. Transportation of Dangerous Goods Act.

Kalinowski, Tess. 2015. "Driverless Cars Shaking up Ontario's Auto Industry, Warns Minister." *Toronto Star*, 17 September 2015. https://www.thestar.com/news/gta/transportation/2015/09/17/driver-less-cars-shaking-up-ontarios-auto-industry-warns-minister.html.

Kang, Celia. 2016a. "U.S. Signals Backing for Self-Driving Cars." *New York Times*, 19 September 2016. https://www.nytimes.com/2016/09/20/technology/self-driving-cars-guidelines.html.

– 2016b. "U.S. Signals Backing for Self-Driving Cars." *New York Times*, 20 September 2016. https://www.nytimes.com/2016/09/21/technology/the-15-point-federal-checklist-for-self-driving-cars.html.

Kaplan, Harold. 1989. *Policy and Rationality: The Regulation of Canadian Trucking*. Toronto: University of Toronto Press.

Keen, Andrew. 2015. *The Internet Is Not the Answer*. London: Atlantic Books.

Keenan, Edward. 2016a. "The Good and Bad of Toronto NIMBYism." *Toronto Star*, 2 January 2016.

– 2016b. "Everywhere Is Someone's Backyard." *Toronto Star*, 3 January 2016.

– 2016c. "Great (and Less Great) Moments in Toronto NIMBYism." *Toronto Star*, 4 January 2016.

Kellogg, Sarah. 2012. "US Transport Policy in a Time of Retrenchment." Price School, University of Southern California. http://priceschool.usc.edu/newsletter/january-2012/transportation.

Kennedy, David. 2015. "Canada's Drone Industry? It's Just Getting Off the Ground." *Maclean's*, 29 December. https://www.macleans.ca/education/canadas-drone-industry-its-just-getting-off-the-ground/.

Kernaghan, Kenneth, Brian Marson, and Sandford F. Borins. 2000. *The New Public Organization*. Toronto: Institute of Public Administration of Canada.

King, Janice, 2014. "How Transportation Technologies Will Change Everything." *Government Technology* (4 November): 1–12.

Kirby, Jason. 2013. "WestJet's Plan to Crush Air Canada." *Maclean's*, 6 October 2013.

Knight, Bruce I. 2008. *Common Carrier Obligation of Railroads*. Comments of the US Department of Agriculture, 24 April.

Knight, Sam. 2016. "How Uber Conquered London." *The Guardian*, 27 April 2016. https://www.theguardian.com/technology/2016/apr/27/how-uber-conquered-london.

Kroeker, Arthur. 1981. "Hard Going: Transportation Development in Lean Times." *Policy Options* (July/August): 13–15.

– 2009. *Retiring the Crow Rate: A Narrative of Political Management*. Calgary: University of Alberta Press.

Krugel, Lauren. 2014. "Canada's Oil-by-Rail Liability Rules Pit Regulators against Energy Players." *Huffington Post*, 24 May 2014.

LaFramboise, Kalina, and Alison Brunette. 2018. "All 3 MMA Rail Workers Acquitted at Lac-Megantic Disaster Trial." CBC News, 19 January 2018. https://www.cbc.ca/news/canada/montreal/lac-megantic-criminal-negligence-verdict-1.4474848.

Langford, John. 1976. *Transport in Transition: The Reorganization of the Federal Transport Portfolio*. Montreal & Kingston: McGill-Queen's University Press.

– 1981. "Air Canada." In *Public Corporations and Public Policy in Canada*, edited by Allan Tupper and G. Bruce Doern, 251–84. Montreal: Institute for Research on Public Policy.

– 1982. "Transport Canada and the Transport Ministry: The Attempt to Retreat to Basics." In *How Ottawa Spends Your Tax Dollars: National Policy and Economic Development 1982*, edited by G. Bruce Doern, 147–72. Toronto: James Lorimer Publishers.

Langford, John, and Ken Huffman. 1988. "Air Canada." In *Privatization, Public Policy and Public Corporations in Canada*, edited by Allan Tupper and G. Bruce Doern, 93–150. Halifax. Institute for Research on Public Policy.

Laucius, Joanne. 2015. "Uber Customer Service Better Than Taxis, Say Ottawa Focus Groups." *Ottawa Citizen*, 29 October 2015.

Laycock, David. 1990. *Populism and Democratic Thought in the Canadian Prairies 1910–45*. Toronto: University of Toronto Press.

Lee, Dave. 2016. "Drone Industry Delight at New US Rules." BBC News, 22 June 2016. http://www.bbc.co.uk/news/technology-36584515.

Legislative Assembly of Saskatchewan. 1975. *Hansard*, 13 March 1975, 774. http://docs.legassembly.sk.ca/legdocs/Legislative%20Assembly/Hansard/17L5S/750313Handsard.pdf.

Leiner, Barry M., Vinton G. Cerf, David D. Clark, Robert E. Kahn, Leonard Kleinrock, Daniel C. Lynch, Jon Postel, Larry G. Roberts, and Stephen Wolff. 2014. "Brief History of the Internet." Internet Society. www.internetsociety.org.

Levinson, David, and Lei Zhang. 2004. "Ramp Meters on Trial: Evidence from the Twin Cities Metering Holiday." *ScienceDirect, Transportation Research Part A* 40 (15 December 2006): 810–28.

Litman, Todd. 2017. *Evaluating Transportation Diversity: Multimodal Planning for Efficient and Equitable Communities.* Victoria, BC: Victoria Transport Policy Institutes.

Loffi, Jon M., and Ryan J. Wallace. 2014. "The Unmitigated Insider Threat to Aviation (Part 1): A Qualitative Analysis of Risks." *Journal of Transportation Security* 7 (4): 289–305.

Logistics Institute. 2016. "History." http://www.loginstitute.ca/about.html.

Lohr, Steve. 2015. "FCC Plans Strong Hand to Regulate the Internet." *New York Times*, 4 February 2015.

Lovink, J.A.A. 2001. "Improving the Governance of Airport Authorities." *Policy Options*, 1 April 2001.

Lund, Susan, and Laura Tyson. 2018. "Globalization Is Not in Retreat: Digital Technology and the Future of Trade." *Foreign Affairs* 97 (3): 130–40.

Lyon, David. 2006. "Airport Screening, Surveillance, and Social Sorting: Canadian Responses to 9/11 in Context." *Canadian Journal of Criminology and Criminal Justice* 46 (4): 423–56.

Macfarlane, D. 2014. *Negotiating a River: Canada and the U.S. and the Creation of the St. Lawrence Seaway.* Vancouver: UBC Press.

Mackenzie, David. 2010. *ICAO: A History of the International Civil Aviation Authority.* Toronto: University Of Toronto Press.

Mackenzie, H. 2013. *Canada's Infrastructure Gap: Where It Came From and Why Will It Cost So Much to Close.* Ottawa: Centre for Policy Alternatives.

Mackrael, Kim. 2013. "Safety Board Warns against Blaming One Person for Lac-Megantic Disaster." *Globe and Mail*, 13 July 2013.

Madar, Daniel. 2000. *Heavy Traffic: Deregulation, Trade, and Transformation in North American Trucking.* Vancouver: UBC Press.

Manjoo, Farhad. 2016. "Car-Pooling Helps Uber Go the Extra Mile." *New York Times*, 30 March 2016. https://www.nytimes.com/2016/03/31/technology/car-pooling-helps-uber-go-the-extra-mile.html.

– 2017. "Uber's C.E.O. Choice Faces a Question of Ambitions." *New York Times*, 28 August 2017. https://www.nytimes.com/2017/08/28/technology/uber-new-ceo.html.

Markoff, John. 2016. "Google Car Exposes Regulatory Divide on Computers as Drivers." *New York Times*, 10 February 2016. https://www.nytimes.com/2016/02/11/technology/nhtsa-blurs-the-line-between-human-and-computer-drivers.html.

Marshall, Douglas. 2015. "'What a Long Strange Trip It's Been': A Journey through the FAA's Drone Policies and Regulation." *DePaul Law Review* 54 (1): 123–34.

Mazzacato, Mariana. 2013. *The Entrepreneurial State*. London: Anthern Press.

McCullough, Michael. 2014. "Interview: WestJet CEO Gregg Saretsky on the Power of Culture." *Canadian Business*, 7 August 2014.

McGrane, David. 2013. "National Unity through Disengagement: The Harper Government's One-Off Federalism." In *How Ottawa Spends 2013–2014: The Harper Government: Mid-Term Blues and Long-Term Plans*, edited by Christopher Stoney and G. Bruce Doern, 114–26. Montreal & Kingston: McGill-Queen's University Press.

McGuire, Cecelia. 2004. *100 Years at the Heart of Transportation: An Historical Perspective*. Ottawa: Canadian Transportation Agency.

Meggs, Geoff. 2017. "Battle over Tolls Erupts as First Major Issue of Provincial Campaign." CBC News, 15 April 2017. Accessed 18 February 2018. http://www.cbc.ca/news/canada/british-columbia/to-toll-or-not-to-toll-1.4071853.

Mendoza, M.R., Patrick Low, and B. Kotschwar, eds. 1999. *Trade Rules in the Making*. Washington: Organization of American States, Brookings Institution Press.

Miller, Jeff. 2012. "Net Neutrality Regulation in Canada: Assessing the CRTC's Statutory Competency to Regulate the Internet." *Appeal Review of Current Law and Law Reform* (17): 47–62.

Milojevich, Allyn. 2006. "Proliferation of Unmanned Aerial Systems and Policy Challenges on the Horizon: A Policy Memorandum to John P. Holdren." *Journal of Science Policy and Governance* 8 (1): 1–5.

Minister of Transport. 2008. "The Government of Canada Delivers on a Rail Freight Service Review: Final Terms of Reference Announced and Request for Proposals Issued." Press release, 12 August.

Molot, Maureen, ed. 2002. *Canada among Nations: A Fading Power*. Toronto: Oxford University Press Canada.

Monbiot, George. 2016. "Our Roads Are Choked. We're on the Verge of Carmageddon." *The Guardian*, 20 September 2016.

Monteeiro, Joseph, and Barry E. Prentice. 2016. "The Tale of Taxi Reforms in Two Cities: The Failure of Closed Entry." Canadian Transportation Research Forum. Proceedings Issue: 51st Annual Meeting, 46–53.

– 2017. *The Tale of Taxi Reforms in Two Cities: The Failure of Closed Entry – Continued.* Canadian Transportation Research Forum. Proceedings Issue: 52nd Annual Meeting, 65–76.

– 2018. *Competition in the Canadian Taxi Industry.* Canadian Transportation Research Forum. Proceedings Issue: 53rd Annual Meeting, 3–6 June, 1–8.

Mooney, Chris. 2005. *The Republican War on Science.* New York: Basic Books.

Moore, Karl. 2016. "Air Canada Boss Speaks about Learning from WestJet and Fighting Porter." *Financial Post*, 17 March 2016.

Morali, Oguz, and Cory Searcy. 2013. "A Review of Sustainable Supply Chain Management Practices in Canada." *Journal of Business Ethics* 117 (3): 635–58.

Morcol, Goktug. 2012. *A Complexity Theory for Public Policy.* London: Routledge.

Morrison, John. 2014. Business and Society: Defining the 'Social Licence.'" *The Guardian*, 29 September 2014.

Mouawad, Jad and Coral Davenport. 2016. "UN Agency Proposes Limits on Airlines' Carbon Emissions." *New York Times*, 8 February 2016. https://www.nytimes.com/2016/02/09/business/energy-environment/un-agency-proposes-limits-on-airlines-carbon-emissions.html.

Murray, Tom. 2011. *Rails across Canada: The History of Canadian Pacific and Canadian National Railways.* Minneapolis: MBI Publishing.

Nagy, Delmer J., Joseph Schuessier, and Alan Dubinsky. 2016. "Defining and Identifying Disruptive Innovations." *Industrial Marketing Management* 57 (August): 119–26.

National Academies of Sciences, Engineering and Medicine. 2017. *Designing Safety Regulations for High-Hazard Industries.* Washington: The National Academies Press. https://doi.org/10.17226/24907.

National Airlines Council of Canada. 2015. "Rules and Regulations." http://www.airline council.ca/en/rules-and-regulations.html.

– 2015a. "Connecting Canada: An Aviation Policy Agenda for Global Competitiveness and Economic Prosperity." Submission to the Canada Transportation Act Review. Canadian Airlines Council, January.

– 2015b. "NAV Canada and the Canadian Airports Council Announce Measures to Ensure Effective Public Engagement on Changes to Flight Paths." Canadian Airports Council.

National Rail. 2015. "Network Rail: Our History." http://www.networkrail.co.uk/aspx.

National Recreational Boating Advisory Council. 2016. "National Recreational Boating Advisory Council." Transport Canada. http://tc/gc.ca/archive/eng/marinesafety/debs-obs-nrbac-menu.

Naughton, John. 2012. *From Gutenberg to Zuckerberg: What You Really Need to Know about the Internet*. London: Quercus.

NAV Canada. 2014. "Annual Report 2014: Pushing Boundaries." Ottawa: NAV Canada.

– 2015a. "The Test of Time. NAV Canada: How NAV Canada Really Works." Ottawa: NAV Canada.

– 2015b. "Annual Report 2015: Connections." Ottawa: NAV Canada.

– 2016a. "Who We Are." http://www.navcanada.ca/en/about-us/Pages. who-we-are.aspx.

– 2016b. "Corporate Governance." http://www.navcanada.ca/en/about-us/Pages/governance.aspx.

– 2016c. "Our Vision, Mission and Objectives." http://www.navcanada.ca/en/about-us/Pages/vision.aspx.

– 2016d. "Investor Relations." http://www.navcanada.ca/en/about-us/Pages/investor-relations.aspx

Nelson, J., and M. Scoble. 2006. "Social Licence to Operate Mines: Issues of Situational Analysis and Process." Department of Mining Engineering, University of British Columbia.

Network Rail. 2015. "Our History." http://www.networkrail.co.uk/about.

Ngo, Victor. 2015. "Transporting Network Companies and the Ridesourcing Industry: A Review of Impacts and Emerging Regulatory Frameworks for Uber." University of British Columbia School of Community and Regional Planning.

Nichols, P. 1987. "Redefining Common Carriage: The FCC's Attempt at Deregulation by Definition." *Duke Law Journal* 3: 501–20.

Noam, Eli M. 1994. *Beyond Liberalization II: The Impending Doom of Common Carriage*. Columbia University, Graduate School of Business. March.

Norberg, Jon, and Graeme S. Cumming, eds. 2012. *Complexity Theory for a Sustainable Future*. New York: Columbia University Press.

Nordman, A. 2004. *Converging Technologies: Shaping the Future of European Societies*. http://www.ntnu.no/2020/pdf/final_report_en.pdf.

Nye, David E. 2006. *Technology Matters: Questions to Live With*. Cambridge, MA: MIT Press.

O'Doherty, Kieran, and Edna Einsiedel, eds. 2013. *Public Engagement and Emerging Technologies*. Vancouver: UBC Press.

Office of the Privacy Commissioner of Canada. 2013. "Drones in Canada: Will the Proliferation of Domestic Drone Use in Canada Raise New Concerns for Privacy?" Ottawa: Office of the Privacy Commissioner of Canada.

– 2015. "OPC Comment to Transport Canada on Unmanned Aerial Vehicles." Ottawa: Office of the Privacy Commissioner of Canada, 27 August.

O'Malley, Pat. 2006. "Risks, Ethics, and Airport Security." *Canadian Journal of Criminology and Criminal Justice* 48 (3): 413–22.

Omand, Geordon. 2015. "Experts Disagree on Whether Canada's Drone Regulations Are Too Permissive." *Ottawa Citizen*, 3 June. http://www.ottawacitizen.com/technology/Experts.

Ostrom, Elinor. 1990. *Governing the Commons: The Evolution of Institutions for Collective Action.* New York: Cambridge University Press.

– 2012. *The Future of the Commons: Beyond Market Failure and Government Regulation.* London: Institute of Economic Affairs.

Ostry, Sylvia. 1997. *The Post-Cold War Trading System: Who's on First?* Chicago: University of Chicago Press.

Oum, Tae Hoon, W.T. Stanbury, and Michael W. Tretheway. 1991. "Airline Deregulation in Canada and its Economic Effects." *Transportation Journal* 30 (4): 4–22.

Pagliaro, Jennifer. 2016. "Toronto Taxi Industry Trying to Block UberX in Court." *Toronto Star*, 14 March 2016. https://www.thestar.com/news/city_hall/2016/03/14/toronto-taxi-industry-trying-to-block-uberx-in-court.html.

Pal, Leslie A. 2011. "Into the Wild: The Politics of Economic Stimulus." In *How Ottawa Spends 2011–2012: Trimming Fat or Slicing Pork*, edited by Christopher Stoney and G. Bruce Doern, 39–59. Montreal & Kingston: McGill-Queen's University Press.

– 2013. *Beyond Policy Analysis: Public Issue Management in Turbulent Times.* 5th ed. Toronto: Nelson.

Pal, Leslie, and Judith Maxwell. 2003. "Assessing the Public Interest in the 21st Century: A Framework." Ottawa: External Advisory Committee on Smart Regulation.

Patenaude, Jean. 2016. "Recent Public Policy Initiatives in Respect of Railway Services." Canadian Transportation Research Forum, 51st Annual Conference, 1–4 May.

Perl, Anthony. 1994. "Public Enterprise as an Expression of Sovereignty: Reconsidering the Origin of Canadian National Railways." *Canadian Journal of Political Science* 27 (1): 23–52.

– 2002. *New Departures: Rethinking Rail Passenger Policy in the Twenty-First Century.* Lexington: University of Kentucky Press.

Phillips, Peter W.B. 2007. *Governing Transformative Technological Innovation: Who's in Charge?* London: Edward Elgar.

Phillips, Peter W.B., and James Nolan. 2007. "Strategic Options in Canadian Transportation Policy: The Interface Between Trade Pressures and Domestic Policy." Presented at International Conference on Transport Gateways.

Picker, Leslie, and Mike Isaac. 2015. "Uber Said to Plan Another $1 Billion in Fund-Raising." New York Times, 23 October 2015.

Pickersgill, J.W. 1969. "Canada's National Transport Policy." Transportation Law Journal 1 (1969). Accessed 15 May 2016. http://www.law.du.edu/documents/transportation-law-journal/past-issues/vo1/canadas-national-transport-policy.pdf.

Pigott, Peter. 2014. Air Canada: The History. Toronto: Dundurn.

Pipeline and Hazardous Materials Safety Administration. 2012. "Strategic Plan." Washington: Pipeline and Hazardous Materials Safety Administration.

– 2015. "PHMSA Notice Regarding Emergency Response Notifications for Shipments of Petroleum Crude Oil by Rail." Washington: Pipeline and Hazardous Materials Safety Administration, 28 May.

– 2016. "DOT Announces Final Rule to Strengthen Safe Transportation of Flammable Liquids by Rail." Washington: Pipeline and Hazardous Materials Safety Administration, 1 May.

Plimmer, Gill. 2015. "Watchdog Questions Network Rail's Ability to Deliver." Financial Times, 12 June 2015, 4.

Pratte, Steve. 2016. "Government Hopper Cars and the Canadian Grain Handling and Transportation System." Canadian Transportation Research Forum. Proceedings Issue: 51st Annual Meeting, 464–71.

Prentice, Barry E. 2015a. "Peak-Load Management and Surge Capacity in Western Grain Transportation." Canadian Transportation Research Forum. Proceedings Issue: 50th Annual Meeting, 382–96.

– 2015b. "Canadian Airport Security: The Privatization of a Public Good." Journal of Air Transport Management (48): 52–9.

Prentice, Barry E., Jake Kosior, and Bob McLeod. 1996. "Agriculture Trucking in Manitoba." University of Manitoba, Transport Institute, Research Bulletin 16.

Pretto, Andre, and Joseph F. Schulman. 2015. "Canada–United States Freight Rail Economic Regulation Comparison." Presented to the Canadian Transport Research Forum, May 2015.

Prince, Michael J. 1999. "Civic Regulation: Regulating Citizenship, Morality, Social Order and the Welfare State." In Changing the Rules: Canadian Regulatory Regimes and Institutions, edited by Bruce Doern,

Margaret Hill, Michael Prince, and Richard Schultz, 201–27. Toronto: University of Toronto Press.

Prime Minister of Canada. 2016. "Minister of Transport Mandate Letter. http://pm.gc.ca/eng/minister-transport-mandate-letter.

Prno, Jason, and D. Scott Slocombe. 2012. "Exploring the Origins of 'Social Licence' in the Mining Sector: Perspectives from Governance and Sustainability Theories." *Resources Policy* 37 (3): 346–57.

Prokop, Darren. 1999. "In 1988 We Freed Trade, Now Let's Free Transport." *Policy Options*: 35–40.

Prud'Homme, Alex. 2014. *Hydrofracking*. Oxford: Oxford University Press.

PPP Canada. 2009a. "Public Private Partnerships: Building Infrastructure." 2008–09 Annual Report.

– 2009b. "Summary Amended Corporate Plan 2008 to 2012, Summary Amended Operating And Capital Budgets 2008."

– 2015–16. "Summary Corporate Plan for the 2015–16 to 2019–20 Planning Period."

– 2016. "Public Private Partnerships: Transforming Infrastructure Delivery." Annual Report 2008–09.

Public Interest Advocacy Centre. 2015. "Consumer Protections for Airline Passengers." PIAC.

Public Policy Forum. 2014. "Canada's Nuclear Energy Sector: Where to From Here?" PPF.

– 2015. "Canada's Airports: Advancing a Prosperity and Trade Agenda." PPF, January.

Quigley, Kevin. 2014. *An Analysis of Transportation Security Risk Regulation Regimes: Canadian Airports, Seaports, Rail, Trucking and Bridges*. Halifax: School of Public Administration, Dalhousie University.

Quorum. 2016. "The Western Canadian GHTS." University of Saskatchewan Workshop on Grain Transportation, 15 December 2016 (slide presentation).

Railway Association of Canada. 2015. "Rail Trends 2015." Ottawa: RAC.

Rainie, Lee, and Barry Wellman. 2012. *Networked: The New Social Operating System*. Cambridge, MA: MIT Press.

Ragan, Chris, Elizabeth Beale, Paul Boothe, Mel Cappe, Bev Dahlby, Don Drummond, Stewart Elgie, Glen Hodgson, Pal Lanoie, Richyard Lipsey, Nancy Olewiler, and France St-Hilaire. 2015. "We Can't Get There from Here: Why Pricing Traffic Congestion Is Critical to Beating It." Montreal: Canada's Ecofiscal Commission, November.

Ranger, Louis. 2010. "In Search of Innovation Policies in the Transport Sector." Presented to the International Transport Forum, Leipzig Germany, 26–28 May.

Ratushnay, Ed. 2009. *The Conduct of Public Inquiries: Law, Policy and Practice*. Toronto: Irwin Law Inc.

Rauch, Daniel E. and David Schleicher. 2015. "Like Uber, but for Local Government Policy: The Future of Local Regulation of the Sharing Economy." *George Mason Law and Economics Research Paper* 15 (01).

Rayle, Lisa, Danielle Dai, Nelson Chan, Robert Cervero, and Susan Shaheen. 2016. "Just a Better Taxi? A Survey-based Comparison of Taxis, Transit, and Ridesourcing Services in San Francisco." *Transport Policy* (45): 168–78.

Reevely, David. 2016. "Ottawa, Toronto Unlikely Champions for Road Tolls." *Ottawa Citizen*, 26 November 2016.

Regulatory Governance Initiative. 2015. "A Critical Conversation on Railway-Shipper Relation: A Report on Proceedings. School of Public Policy and Administration." Carleton University.

Reid, E.P. 1960. "Statutory Grain Rates." Royal Commission on Transportation.

Remiorz, Ryan. 2016. "Montreal Cabbies Target Airport in Uber Protest." *Toronto Star*, 10 February 2016. https://www.thestar.com/news/canada/2016/02/10/montreal-cabbies-target-airport-in-uber-protest.html.

Richer, Jocelyne. 2015. "Couillard Open to Legalizing UberX-Style Modes of Transportation." *Ottawa Citizen*, 15 August 2015. http://www.ottawacitizen.com/business/Couillard-open-legalizing.

Rider, David. 2016a. "Toronto to Propose Separate Rules for Uber, Taxis." *Toronto Star*, 6 April 2016. https://www.thestar.com/news/city_hall/2016/04/06/toronto-to-propose-separate-rules-for-uber-taxis.html.

– 2016b. "Edmonton Legalizes Uber, Paving Way for Toronto." *Toronto Star*, 28 January 2016. https://www.thestar.com/news/city_hall/2016/01/28/edmonton-legalizes-uber-paving-way-for-toronto.html.

– 2016c. "Edmonton's Taxi-Uber Advice for Toronto." *Toronto Star*, 7 February 2016. https://www.thestar.com/news/city_hall/2016/02/07/edmontons-taxi-uber-advice-for-toronto.html.

Rider, David, and Jennifer Pagliaro. 2016. "Toronto Rolls Out Welcome Mat for Uber with New Rules." *Toronto Star*, 3 May 2016. https://www.thestar.com/news/city_hall/2016/05/03/toronto-city-council-debates-uber-rules.html.

Riley, John L. 2014. *The Once and Future Great Lakes Country: An Ecological History*. Montreal & Kingston: McGill-Queens University Press.

Rodrigue, Jean-Paul, Claude Comtois, and Brian Slack. 2016. *The Geography of Transport Systems*. Aldershot: Routledge.

Robertson, Grant. 2016a. "New Info Shows Backup Brake May Have Averted Lac-Megantic Disaster." *Globe and Mail*, 7 March 2016.

– 2016b. "Reining in Runaway Trains Top Priority, Marc Garneau Says." *Globe and Mail*, 5 June 2016.

Robins, Allison, James Knowles, and Len Coad. 2015. *A Long Hard Road: Reducing GHG Emissions in Canada's Road Transportation Sector by 2050*. Ottawa: Conference Board of Canada.

Rose, Nikolas, Pat O'Malley, and Mariana Valverde. 2006. "Governmentality." *Annual Review of Law and Social Science* 2 (December): 83–104.

Rosekind, Mark R. 2015. "Remarks: Symposium on Self-Driving Cars." National Highway Traffic Safety Administration. Washington, 8 October.

Rosen, Frederik. 2013. "Drone Technology and International Law." *Journal of Conflict and Security Law*, 4 November. http://blog.oup.com/2013/11/drone-technology-interational-humanitarian.

Rothstein, Tracey. 1989. "Manitoba History: A History of Western Canadian Grain Rates 1897–1984." *Manitoba History* 18 (Autumn). http://www.mhs.mb.ca/docs/mb_history/18/grainrates.shtml.

Rousseau, Marie-Helene, and Claude Rivest. 2018. "What the Jury in the Lac-Megantic Trial Didn't Hear." CBC News, 11 January 2018. https://www.cbc.ca/news/canada/montreal/lac-m%C3%A9gantic-rail-disaster-1.4481968.

Royal Commission on Transportation (the MacPherson Commission). 1962. *Final Report 1961–1962*. Ottawa: Queen's Printer.

Royal Commission on Canada's Economic Prospects (the Gordon Commission). 1956. *Final Report*. Ottawa: Government of Canada.

Royal Commission on the Economic Union and Development Prospects for Canada (the Macdonald Commission). 1985. *Final Report*. Ottawa: Minister of Supply and Services.

Royal Commission on National Passenger Transportation. 1992. *Directions*. Final Report. Ottawa: Royal Commission on National Passenger Transportation.

Ruiz, Rebecca. 2015. "F.C.C. Sets Net Neutrality Rules." *New York Times*, 12 March 2015, 1.

Ruppenthal, Karl, and W.T. Stanbury, eds. 1976. *Transportation Policy: Regulation, Competition and the Public Interest*. Centre for Transportation Studies, University of British Columbia.

Ryan, Leo. 2015. "CETA and Shortsea Shipping: Canada's Marine Industry
    Draws Battle Lines." *Canadian Shipper*. http://www.canadianshipper.
    com/features/ceta-shortsea-shipping/.

Sakiyama, Mari, Terance D. Miethe, Joel D. Lieberman, Miliaikeala Heen,
    and Olivia Tuttle. 2016. "Big Hover or Big Brother? Public Attitudes
    About Drone Usage in Domestic Policing Activities." *Security Journal*.
    Online publication, 7 March 2016.

Saint Lawrence Seaway Development Corporation. 2014. "Fiscal Year
    2014 Annual Report." Washington.

Salter, Liora. 2007. "The Public of Public Inquiries." In *Policy Analysis
    in Canada: the State of the Art*, edited by Laurent Dobuzinskis, Michael
    Howlett, and David Laycock, 291–314. Toronto: University of Toronto
    Press.

Salter, Mark B. 2007. "SEMS and Sensibility: Security Management Systems
    and the Management of Risk in the Canadian Air Transport Security
    Authority." *Journal of Transport Management* 13 (6): 389–98.

– 2008a. "Political Science Perspectives on Transportation Security."
    Journal of Transportation Security 1 (1): 29–35.

– 2008b. "Securitization and Desecuritization: A Dramaturgical Analysis of
    the Canadian Air Transport Security Authority." *Journal of International
    Relations and Development* 11: 321–49.

Savage, Luiza Ch. 2015. "Land of the Freeloaders: The Battle for a New
    Cross-Border Bridge." *MacLean's*, 21 May 2015. https://www.macleans.
    ca/news/canada/land-of-the-freeloaders-the-battle-for-a-new-cross-
    border-bridge/.

Schaller, Bruce. 2007. "Entry Controls in Taxi Regulation: Implications
    of US and Canadian Experience for Taxi Regulation and Deregulation."
    Transportation Policy 14 (6): 490–506.

Schiller, Preston L., Eric C. Bruun, and Jeffrey R. Kenworthy. 2010.
    *An Introduction to Sustainable Transportation: Policy, Planning and
    Implementation*. London: Earthscan.

Schneirer, Bruce. 2015. *Data and Goliath: The Hidden Battles to Collect
    Your Data and Control Your World*. New York: W.W. Norton.

Schultz, Richard. 1995. "Paradigm Lost: Explaining the Canadian Politics
    of Deregulation." In *Canada's Century: Governance in a Maturing
    Society-Essays in Honour of John Meisel*, edited by C.E.S. Franks,
    110–23. Montreal & Kingston: McGill-Queen's University Press.

– 2000. *The Consumers Association of Canada and the Federal Regulatory
    System*. Vancouver: SFU–UBC Centre for the Study of Government
    and Business.

Schultz, Richard, and Alan Alexandroff. 1985. *Economic Regulation and the Federal System*. Toronto: University of Toronto Press.

Schumpeter, Joseph A. 1934. *The Theory of Economic Development*. Cambridge, MA: Harvard Economic Studies, Harvard University Press.

– 1942. *Capitalism, Socialism and Democracy*. New York: Harper and Brothers.

– 1954. *History of Economic Analysis*. London: Allen and Unwin.

Sell, Susan. 1998. *Power and Ideas: North-South Politics of Intellectual Property and Antitrust*. New York: State University of New York Press.

Serebrin, Jacob. 2015. "Canada's Huge Opportunity to Become 'Drone Valley.'" *Techvibes*, 13 April 2015. https://techvibes.com/2015/04/13/drone-valley-2015-04-13.

Shecter, Barbara, and Drew Hasselback. 2016. "Trudeau's Investment Pitch Wins Praise as Ottawa Courts World's Most Powerful Investors." *Financial Post*, 14 November 2016.

Siegel, David, and Edmund P. Fowler, eds. 2001. *Urban Policy Issues: Canadian Perspectives*. Oxford: Oxford University Press.

Slattery, Brian, Bryan Riley, and Nicolas D. Loris. 2014. "Sink the Jones Act: Restoring America's Competitive Advantage in Maritime-Related Industries." The Heritage Foundation, backgrounder No. 2886, 22 May 2014.

Slee, Tom. 2016. *What's Yours Is Mine: Against the Sharing Economy*. New York: OR Books.

Snead, Jason and John-Michael Seibler. 2016. "The FAA Drone Register: A Two-Month Crash Course in How to Overcriminalize Innovation." Issue brief no. 4525 on Legal Studies. http://www.heritage.org/research/reports/2016/03/the-faa-drone-regis.

Solon, Olivia. 2016. "Self-Driving Trucks: What's the Future for America's 3.5 Million Truckers?" *The Guardian*, 16 June 2016. https://www.theguardian.com/technology/2016/jun/17/self-driving-trucks-impact-on-drivers-jobs-us.

Sorensen, Chris. 2010. "WestJet's Plans to Conquer Air Canada and Then the World." *MacLean's*, 22 May 2010.

Sorkin, Andrew R. 2016. "Why Uber Keeps Raising Billions." *New York Times*, 20 June 2016. https://www.nytimes.com/2016/06/21/business/dealbook/why-uber-keeps-raising-billions.html.

Spaeth, Andreas. 2014. "Best of Airways: Porter Airlines." *Airways Magazine*, July.

Speech from the Throne. 1973. Parliament of Canada, 4 January,
    29th Parliament, 1st Session (1973.01.04–1974.02.26). http://www.parl.
    gc.ca/Parlinfo/Documents/ThroneSpeech/29-01-e.pdf.
– 1974. Parliament of Canada, 27 February, 29th Parliament, 2nd Session
    (1974.02.27–1974.05.09). http://www.parl.gc.ca/Parlinfo/Documents/
    ThroneSpeech/29-02-e.pdf.
– 1978. Parliament of Canada, 11 October, 30th Parliament, 4th Session
    (1978.10.11–1979.03.26). http://www.parl.gc.ca/Parlinfo/Documents/
    Throne Speech/10.11-e.pdf.
– 1980. Parliament of Canada, 14 April, 32nd Parliament, 1st Session
    (1980.04.14– 1983.11.30). http://www.parl.gc.ca/Parlinfo/Documents/
    ThroneSpeech/32-01-e.pdf.
– 1983. Parliament of Canada, 7 December, 32nd Parliament, 2nd Session
    (1983.12.07–1984.07.09). http://www.parl.gc.ca/Parlinfo/Documents/
    ThroneSpeech/32-02-e.pdf.
– 1984. Parliament of Canada, 5 November, 33rd Parliament, 1st Session
    (1984.11.05–1986.08.28). http://www.parl.gc.ca/Parlinfo/Documents/
    ThroneSpeech/33-01-e.pdf.
– 1986. Parliament of Canada, 1 October, 33rd Parliament, 2nd Session
    (1986.09.30– 1988.10.01). http://www.parl.gc.ca/Parlinfo/Documents/
    ThroneSpeech/33-02-e.pdf.
– 1989. Parliament of Canada, 3 April, 34th Parliament, 2nd Session
    (1989.04.03– 1991.05.12). http://www.parl.gc.ca/Parlinfo/Documents/
    ThroneSpeech/34-02-e.pdf.
– 1991. Parliament of Canada, 13 May, 34th Parliament, 3rd Session
    (1991.05.13–1993.09.08). http://www.parl.gc.ca/Parlinfo/Documents/
    ThroneSpeech/34-3-e.html.
– 1994. Parliament of Canada, 18 January, 35th Parliament, 1st Session
    (1994.01.17–1996.02.02). http://www.parl.gc.ca/Parlinfo/Documents/
    ThroneSpeech/35-1-e.html.
– 1996. Parliament of Canada, 27 February, 35th Parliament, 2nd Session
    (1996.02.27–1997.04.27). http://www.parl.gc.ca/Parlinfo/Documents/
    ThroneSpeech/35-2-e.html.
– 1997. Parliament of Canada, 23 September, 36th Parliament, 1st Session
    (1997.09.22– 1999.09.18). http://www.parl.gc.ca/Parlinfo/Documents/
    ThroneSpeech/36-1-e.html.
– 1999. Parliament of Canada, 12 October, 36th Parliament, 2nd Session
    (1999.10.12– 2000.10.22). http://www.parl.gc.ca/Parlinfo/Documents/
    ThroneSpeech/36-2-e.html.

- 2001. Parliament of Canada, 30 Januar, 37th Parliament, 1st Session (2001.01.29–2002.09.16). http://www.parl.gc.ca/Parlinfo/Documents/ThroneSpeech/37-1-e.html.
- 2002. Parliament of Canada, 30 September, 37th Parliament, 2nd Session (2002.09.30–2003.11.12). http://www.parl.gc.ca/Parlinfo/Documents/ThroneSpeech/37-2-e.html.
- 2004. Parliament of Canada, 2 February, 37th Parliament, 3rd Session (2004.02.02– 2004.05.23). http://www.parl.gc.ca/Parlinfo/Documents/ThroneSpeech/37-3-e.html.
- 2004. Parliament of Canada, 5 October, 38th Parliament, 1st Session (2004.10.04– 2005.11.29). http://www.parl.gc.ca/Parlinfo/Documents/ThroneSpeech/37-3-e.html.
- 2007. Parliament of Canada, 16 October, 39th Parliament, 2nd Session (2007.10.16–2008.09.07). http://www.parl.gc.ca/Parlinfo/Documents/ThroneSpeech/39-2-e.html.
- 2008. Parliament of Canada, 18 November, 40th Parliament, 1st Session (2008.11.18–2008.12.04). http://www.parl.gc.ca/Parlinfo/Documents/ThroneSpeech/40-1-e.html.
- 2009. Parliament of Canada, 26 January, 40th Parliament, 2nd Session (2009.01.26–2009.12.30). http://www.parl.gc.ca/Parlinfo/Documents/ThroneSpeech/40-2-e.html.
- 2010. Parliament of Canada, 3 March, 40th Parliament, 3rd Session (2010.03.03–2011.03.26). http://www.parl.gc.ca/Parlinfo/Documents/ThroneSpeech/40-3-e.html.
- 2011. Parliament of Canada, 3 June, 41st Parliament, 1st Session (2011.06.02–2013.09.13. http://www.parl.gc.ca/Parlinfo/Documents/ThroneSpeech/41-1-e.html.
- 2013. Parliament of Canada, 16 October, 41st Parliament, 2nd Session (2013.10.16–2015.08.02). http://www.parl.gc.ca/Parlinfo/Documents/ThroneSpeech/41-2-e.html.
- 2015. Parliament of Canada, 3 December, 42nd Parliament, 1st Session (2015.12.03) http://www.parl.gc.ca/Parlinfo/Documents/ThroneSpeech/42--1--e.html.
Sproule-Jones, M., C. Johns, and B.T. Heinmiller. 2008. *Canadian Water Politics: Conflicts and Institutions*. Montreal & Kingston: McGill-Queen's University Press.
Stabler, Jack C. 1986. "Branch Line Abandonment and Prairie Towns – One More Time." *Canadian Journal of Regional Science* 9 (2): 207–19.

Stanbury, William T. 1980. "Government Regulation: Scope, Growth and Process." Institute for Research on Public Policy.

Standing Senate Committee on Transport and Communications. 2012. "The Future of Canadian Air Travel: Toll Booth or Spark Plug?" Senate of Canada, June.

– 2018a. "Driving Change: Technology and the Future of the Automated Vehicle." Senate of Canada. Ninth Report, January.

– 2018b "Amendments to Bill C-49." Senate of Canada. Tenth Report, March.

Starr, Katherine. 2016. "Drone Regulations Coming, Says Transport Canada." CBC News, 5 January 2016. https://www.cbc.ca/news/politics/drone-regulations-transport-canada-1.3390895.

Statutes of Canada. 2013. "Chapter 31: An Act to Amend the Transportation Act." Ottawa: Parliament of Canada.

– 2014. "Chapter 8: An Act to Amend the Grain Act and the Transportation Act." Ottawa: Parliament of Canada.

Stevenson, Garth. 1981. "Canadian National Railways." In *Public Corporations and Public Policy in Canada*, edited by Allan Tupper and G. Bruce Doern, 319–52. Montreal: Institute for Research on Public Policy.

St Lawrence Seaway Management Corporation. 2015a. "Corporate Social Responsibility." Cornwall: SLSMC.

– 2015b. "Annual Corporate Summary 2014–2015." Cornwall: SLSMC.

Stolte, Elise. 2016. "Edmonton Becomes First City in Canada to Pass Uber-Friendly Bylaw." *Edmonton Journal*, 28 January 2016.

Sundararajan, Arun. 2015. "The 'Gig Economy' Is Coming: What Will It Mean for Work?" *The Guardian*, 26 July 2015.

Sussman, G. 1978. *The St. Lawrence Seaway: History and Analysis of a Joint Water Highway*. Toronto: C.D. Howe Research Institute.

Sparrow, Malcolm. 2008. *The Character of Harms: Operational Challenges in Control*. Cambridge: Cambridge University Press.

Soberman, Richard M. 2010. "Making Transit Work: The Main Ingredients." Canadian Transportation Research Forum 45th Annual Conference, 30 May–2 June.

Songer, Gerri K. 2014. "Background: Canadian National and EJ&E Railroad." Wordpress.com, 1 June.

Soroka, Stuart N. 2002. *Agenda-Setting Dynamics in Canada*. Vancouver: UBC Press.

Standing Committee on Public Accounts. 1998. "Transport Canada: The Commercialization of the Air Navigation System." Fourth Report, House of Commons.

Standing Committee on Transport, Infrastructure and Communities. 2013. "Innovative Transportation Technologies." House of Commons, 41st Parliament, 1st Session, February.

– 2015. "Review of the Canadian Transportation Safety Regime: Transportation of Dangerous Goods and Safety Management Systems." House of Commons, 41st Parliament, 2nd Session, March.

Statistics Canada, CANSIM Tables 029-0033 and 029-0012, supplemented by data from Railway Association of Canada "Rail Trends 2013" and from CN and CP Annual Reports.

Statutes of Canada. 2013. "Chapter 31: An Act to Amend the Transportation Act." Parliament of Canada.

– 2014. "Chapter 8: An Act to Amend the Grain Act and the Transportation Act." Parliament of Canada.

– 2017. "Chapter 20. Section 403. Canada Infrastructure Bank Act." Parliament of Canada.

Stevenson, Garth. 1981. "Canadian National Railways." In *Public Corporations and Public Policy in Canada*, edited by Allan Tupper and G. Bruce Doern, 251–84. Montreal: Institute for Research on Public Policy.

– 1987. *The Politics of Canada's Airlines: From Diefenbaker to Mulroney*. Toronto: University of Toronto Press.

– 1988. "Canadian National Railways and Via Rail." In *Privatization, Public Policy and Public Corporations in Canada*, edited by Allan Tupper and G. Bruce Doern, 45–92. Halifax: Institute for Research on Public Policy.

Stoney, Christopher. 2016. "Challenges for Smart Growth: Governing from the Periphery." Presentation to Joint Meeting of the Chartered Institute of Logistics and Transport in North America and Carleton University School of Public Policy and Administration, 5 October.

Stoney, Christopher, and K. Graham. 2009. "Federal–Municipal Relations in Canada: The Changing Organizational Landscape." *Canadian Public Administration* 52 (3): 371–94.

Stopher, Peter and John Stanley. 2014. *Introduction to Transport Policy: A Public Policy View*. Cheltenham, UK: Edward Elgar.

Swanson, Ana. 2018. "Boeing Denied Bid for Tariffs on Canadian Jets." *New York Times*, 26 January 2018. https://www.nytimes.com/2018/01/26/us/politics/boeing-bombardier-tariffs.html.

Swindell, David, Kevin C. Desouza, and Sabrina P.K. Glimcher. 2015. "Drones and the 'Wild West' of Regulatory Experimentation." Brookings Institution, 17 August. https://www.brookings.edu/blog/techtank/2015/08/17/drones-and-the-wild-west-of-regulatory-experimentation/.

Szoo, Adam. 2015. "The Impacts of the Use of UAVs on the Nature,
    Organization and Regulation of Canada–U.S. Border Surveillance."
    Research thesis, University of Laval.

Thomas, Zoe. 2016. "Ride-Hailing Apps and the War for Drivers." BBC
    News, 13 July 2016. http://www.bbc.co.uk/news/business-36592208.

Thompson, G., J. Frances, R. Levacic, and J. Mitchell, eds. 1991. *Markets,
    Hierarchies and Networks: The Coordination of Social Life.* London:
    Sage Publishers.

Thompson, Scott, and Alana Saulnier. 2015. "The 'Rise' of Unmanned
    Aerial Vehicles (UAVs) in Canada: An Analysis of Special Flight
    Operation Certificates (SFOCs)." *Canadian Public Policy* 41 (3): 207–22.

Thompson, Scott, and Ciara Bracken-Roche. 2015. "Understanding Public
    Opinion of UAVs in Canada: A 2014 Analysis of Survey Data and Its
    Policy Implications." *Journal of Unmanned Vehicle Systems* (3):
    156–75.

Ticoli, David. 2015. *Driving Changes: Automated Vehicles in Toronto.*
    Report for the City of Toronto Transportation Services Division as part
    of a broader project under the University of Toronto Transportation
    Research Institute (UTTRI).

Tomesco, Frederic. 2018. "Senate Changes Rail-Ownership Law to Focus
    on Farmers, Shippers and Airline Passengers." *Toronto Star*, 13 April
    2018. https://www.thestar.com/business/2018/04/13/senate-changes-rail-
    ownership-law-to-focus-on-farmers-shippers-and-airline-passengers.html.

Toner, Glen, and James Meadowcroft. 2009. "The Struggle of the
    Canadian Federal Government to Implement Sustainable Development."
    In *Canadian Environmental Policy and Politics*, edited by Deborah
    VanNijnatten and Robert Boardman, 77–90. Toronto: Oxford
    University Press.

Tourism Industry Association of Canada. 2015. *Gateway to Growth:
    Annual Report on Canadian Tourism.*

Transport Canada. 1982. "New Coasting Trade Policy: A Background
    Paper." Ottawa: Transport Canada.

– 1985. "Freedom to Move: A Framework for Transportation Reform."
    Ottawa: Transport Canada.

– 2000. "Monitoring the Canadian Grain Handling and Transportation
    System." http://data.tc.gc.ca/archive/eng/policy/report-acg-
    grainmonitoringprogram-ghts_executive_summary-1342.htm.

– 2001. "Transport Canada 2001–2002 Report on Plans and Priorities."
    Ottawa: Transport Canada.

– 2003. "Canada Marine Act Review." Ottawa: Transport Canada.

– 2005. "Transport Canada 2005–2006 Report on Plans and Priorities."
Ottawa: Transport Canada.
– 2010. "Transport Canada Regulatory Machinery." Transport Canada
Strategies and Integration, Legislative Affairs, June.
– 2011a. "Transport in Canada 2011: Gateways and Corridors." Ottawa:
Transport Canada.
– 2011b. "International and Intergovernmental Relations." http://www.
tc.gc.ca/eng/policy/acc-accc-menu.htm.
– 2011c. "Updated Feasibility Study of a High Speed Rail Service in
The Quebec City-Windsor Corridor." Ottawa: Transport Canada.
– 2012. Transportation in Canada 2011. Ottawa: Transport Canada.
– 2014. Transportation in Canada 2013. Ottawa: Transport Canada.
– 2015a. "The Transport Canada Portfolio." Ottawa: Transport Canada.
– 2015b. "Report on Plans and Priorities." Ottawa: Transport Canada
– 2015c. "Notice of Proposed Amendment (NPA): Unmanned Air
Vehicles." CARAC Activity Reporting Notice #2015-012, 28 May.
– 2015d. "Transport Canada 2015–2016 Report on Plans and Priorities."
Ottawa: Transport Canada.
– 2016a. "The Transport Canada Portfolio." Ottawa: Transport Canada.
http://www.tc.ca/eng/aboutus-abouttc.html.
– 2016b. "Organization." http://www.tc.ca/eng/aboutus-department-
overview.html.
– 2016c. "What We Do." http://www.tc.ca/eng/aboutus-whatwedo.html.
– 2016d. "Acts and Regulations." http://www.tc.ca/eng/acts-regulations.
html.
– 2016e. "Forward Regulatory Plan: 2015–2017." 1–2. http://www.tc.ca/
eng/acts-regulations.html.
– 2016f. "Air Transportation." http://www.tc.ca/eng/air-menu.html.
– 2016g. "Air Policy." http://www.tc.ca/eng/ace-menu.html.
– 2016h. "Civil Aviation." http://www.tc.ca/eng/civilaviation.html.
– 2016i. "National Aircraft Certification." http://www.tc.ca/eng/
civilaviation/certification/menu.html.
– 2016j. "National Airports Policy." http://www.tc.ca/eng/programs/
airports-policy-nas-1129.html.
– 2016k. "Transportation of Dangerous Goods. Who We Are." http://
www.tc.gc.ca/eng/tdg/who-233.htm.
– 2016l. "Transportation of Dangerous Goods General Policy Advisory
Council." http://www.tc.gc.ca/eng/tdg/consult-advisorycouncil-488.htm.
– 2016m. "Environmental Assessment." https://www.canada.ca/en/
environmental-assessment-agency.html

– 2016n. "Strategic Environmental Assessment." https://www.canada.ca/en/environmental-assessment-agency/programs/strategic-environmental-assessment.html.

– 2016o. "Report on Plans and Priorities 2016–17." Ottawa: Transport Canada.

– 2016p. "New Measures Enhance Transparency on Rail Safety and Dangerous Goods." Ottawa: Transport Canada, 16 April.

– 2016q. "Increasing Safety of Canadians by Investing in Rail Improvements." Ottawa: Transport Canada, 12 October.

– 2016r. "Transportation 2030." Ottawa: Transport Canada, 3 November.

– 2016s. "Let's Talk Transportation of Dangerous Goods." Ottawa: Transport Canada.

– 2016t. "Training in the Transportation of Dangerous Goods: A White Paper." Ottawa: Transport Canada.

– 2017a. "Minister Garneau Announces the $2.1B Trade and Transport Corridors Initiative To Support Canadian Business and Spur Job Creation." https://www.canada.ca/en/transport-canada/news/2017/06/minister_garneauannouncesthe21btradeandtransportationcorridorsino.html.

– 2017b. "Proposed Rules for Drones in Canada." https://www.tc.gc.ca/en/services/aviation/drone-safety/proposed-rules-drones-canada.html.

– 2017c. "Minister Garneau Introduces Legislation to Support Canadian Travellers and Promote Economic Growth." https://www.canada.ca/en/transport-canada/news/2017/05/minister_garneauintroduceslegislationtosupportcanadiantravellers.html.

– 2017d. "Travellers Initiatives." https://www.canada.ca/en/transport-canada/news/2017/05/travellers_initiatives.html.

– 2017e. "Picking Up Steam: Growing Canada's Economy With Modernized Rail Transportation." https://www.canada.ca/en/transport-canada/news/2017/05/picking_up_steamgrowingcanadaseconomywithmodernizedrailtransport.html.

Transport Canada, US Army Corps of Engineers, US Department of Transportation, St Lawrence Seaway Management Corporation, Saint Lawrence Seaway Development Corporation, Environment Canada, and US Fish and Wildlife Service. 2007. "The Great Lakes St. Lawrence Seaway Study." Final Report. Ottawa and Washington.

Transportation Safety Board of Canada. 2014. "Railway Investigation Report R13D0054." Transportation Safety Board of Canada.

– 2015. "Report on Plans and Priorities: 2015–2016." Transportation Safety Board of Canada.

– 2016a. "Investigation Process." https://www.tsb.gc.ca/eng/enquetes-investigations/index.asp.

– 2016b. "History of the TSB." https://www.tsb.gc.ca/eng/spec/25/bst-tsb-25-hist.html.

– 2016c. "Lac-Megantic Runaway Train and Derailment Investigation Summary." https://www.tsb.gc.ca/eng/rapports-reports/rail/.

Transportation for America. 2011. "Transportation 101: An Introduction to Federal Transportation Policy." Washington, Transportation for America.

Transportation Research Board. 2015a. *Between Public and Private Mobility: Examining the Rise of Technology-Enabled Transport Services.* Washington: Transportation Research Board.

– 2015b. *Modernizing Freight Rail Regulation.* Washington: Transportation Research Board.

Trebilcock, Michael J. 2011. *Understanding Trade Law.* London: Edward Elgar.

Trebilcock, Michael J., and Robert House. 1995. *The Regulation of International Trade.* 2nd ed. London: Routledge.

Trebilcock, Michael, Robert House, and Antonia Eliason. 2013. *International Trade.* 4th ed. London: Routledge.

Treasury Board Secretariat. 2013. "Cabinet Directive on Regulatory Management." Ottawa.

– 2015. "Border Infrastructure Fund. Performance Highlights." 30 November. Accessed 7 February 2016. https://www.tbs-sct.gc.ca/hidb-bdih/plan-eng.aspx?Org=0&Hi=54&Pl=614.

Tupper, Allan. 1981. "Pacific Western Airlines." In *Public Corporations and Public Policy in Canada,* edited by Allan Tupper and G. Bruce Doern, 285–318. Montreal: Institute for Research on Public Policy.

Tyrchniewicz, E.W. 1984. "Western Grain Transportation Initiatives: Where Do We Go from Here?" *Canadian Journal of Agricultural Economics* 32 (2): 253–68.

Unmanned Systems Canada. 2016. "About Us." http://unmannedsystems.ca/about-us/.

US Department of Transport. 1999. "International Aviation Developments: Global Deregulation Takes Off." US Department of Transport.

– 2000. "International Aviation Developments: Transatlantic Deregulation, the Alliance Network Effect." US Department of Transport.

– 2013. "National Highway Safety Administration Preliminary Statement of Policy Concerning Automated Vehicles." US Department of Transport, 13 May.

– 2016. "Traffic Volume Trends, Estimated Vehicle Miles Travelled on All Roads." Reported on website of *Advisor Perspectives*. 5 December 2016. Accessed 13 December 2016.

US Federal Aviation Administration. 2016. "Unmanned Aircraft Systems." https://www.faa.gov/uas.

Van Harten, Gus, Geraild Heckman, and David Mullan. 2010. *Administrative Law: Cases, Text and Materials*. 6th ed. Toronto: Edmond Montgomery.

Van Praet, Nicholas. 2016. "Quebec Cabbies to File Court Injunction in Hopes of Getting Uber Off the Roads." *Globe and Mail*, 31 January 2016.

van Wee, Bert, Jan Anne Annema, and David Banister, eds. 2013. *The Transport System and Transport Policy*. Cheltenham UK: Edward Elgar.

VIA Rail Canada. 2018. "VIA Rail's Plan for Dedicated Tracks." https://www.viarail.ca/en/about-via-rail/governance-and-reports/dedicated-tracks.

Vlasic, Bill. 2016a. "US Proposes Spending $4 Billion on Self-Driving Cars." *New York Times*, 14 January 2016. https://www.nytimes.com/2016/01/15/business/us-proposes-spending-4-billion-on-self-driving-cars.html.

– 2016b. "Ford and Google Team Up to Support Driverless Cars." *New York Times*, 27 April 2016. https://www.nytimes.com/2016/04/28/business/ford-and-google-team-up-tosupport-driverless-cars.html.

Vlasic, Bill, and Neal E. Boudette. 2016. "Self-Driving Tesla Was Involved in Fatal Crash, U.S. Says." *New York Times*, 30 June 2016. https://www.nytimes.com/2016/07/01/business/self-driving-tesla-fatal-crash-investigation.html.

Walby, Sylvia. 2007. "Complexity Theory, Systems Theory, and Multiple Intersecting Social Inequalities." *Philosophy of the Social Sciences* 37 (4): 449–70.

West, Jonathan P. and James S. Bowman. 2016. "The Domestic Use of Drones: An Ethical Analysis of Surveillance Issues." *Public Administration Review* 76 (4): 649–59.

Wells, Paul. 2016. "Risks Abound as Trudeau Makes Big Pitch to Giant Investors." *Toronto Star*, 13 November 2016. https://www.thestar.com/news/canada/2016/11/13/trudeau-aims-to-attract-billions-in-private-sector-capital-for-infrastructure-projects.html.

Whitaker, Reg. 2003. "More or Less Than Meets the Eye? The New National Security Agenda." In *How Ottawa Spends 2003-2004: Regime Change and Policy Shift*, edited by G. Bruce Doern, 44–58. Toronto: Oxford University Press.

Whittington, Les. 2015. "Oliver Ups Ante in Conflict With Environmental Movement." *Toronto Star*, 6 March 2015.

Whiteside, Heather. 2016. "How Ottawa Shifts Spending: Private Financing and the Municipal Infrastructure Gap." In *How Ottawa Spends 2015–2016: The Liberal Rise and the Tory Demise*, edited by G. Bruce Doern and Christopher Stoney, 65–78. School of Public Policy and Administration, Carleton University.

Wilks, Stephen. 1996. "The Prolonged Reform of United Kingdom Competition Policy." In *Comparative Competition Policy: National Institutions in a Global Market*, edited by G. Bruce Doern and Stephen Wilks, 139–84. Oxford: Clarendon Press.

Willick, Frances. 2017. "Transport Canada Quietly Loosens Rules on Flying Small Drones." CBC News, 30 July 2017. https://www.cbc.ca/news/canada/nova-scotia/transport-canada-loosens-rules-on-small-drones-1.4228224.

Willing, Jon. 2016. "Watson Has 'No Interest' in Road Tolls." *Ottawa Citizen*, 5 March 2016.

Wilson, C.F. 1978. *A Century of Canadian Grain*. Saskatoon, SK: Western Producer Prairie Books.

Windsor–Detroit Bridge Authority. 2016. "About the WDBA." https://www.wdbridge.com/en.

Windsor–Detroit Bridge History. 2016. https://www.wdbridge.com/en/history.

Winston, Clifford. 2010. *Last Exit: Privatization and Deregulation of the US Transportation System*. Washington: Brookings Institution.

Wolfe, Michelle, Bryan D. Jones, and Frank R. Baumgartner. 2013. "A Failure to Communicate: Agenda Setting in Media and Policy." *Political Communication* 30, 2: 175–92.

Woods, Allan. 2016. "Fish Deformities Spiked after Lac-Megantic Oil Spill, Report Says." *Toronto Star*, 10 February 2016.

Wyatt, Edward. 2014. "F.C.C., in a Shift, Backs Fast Lanes for Web Traffic." *New York Times*, 23 April 2014.

– 2014a. "F.C.C. Backs Opening Net Neutrality Rules for Debate." *New York Times*, 15 May 2014.

Yadron, Danny. 2016. "Google Computers Qualify as Drivers in Automated Cars, US Government Says." *The Guardian*, 3 February 2016. https://www.theguardian.com/technology/2016/feb/09/google-computers-self-driving-cars-human.

Yates, Athol, and Nara Srinivasan. 2014. "How Civil Aviation Threatens National Security." *Journal of Transportation Security* 7 (3): 227–54.

Zaidi, Kamaal. 2008. "Aviation Security in Canada and the United States: Promoting Security and Commerce in a Multi-Layered Regime Within a Federal Regulatory Framework." Unpublished paper. Faculty of Law, University of Calgary.

Zimmerman, Eilene. 2016. "Ride-Hailing Start-Ups Compete in 'Uber for Children' Niche." *New York Times*, 13 April 2016. https://www.nytimes.com/2016/04/14/business/smallbusiness/ride-sharing-start-ups-compete-in-uber-for-children-niche.html.

Zon, Noah, and Sara Ditta. 2016. *Robot, Take the Wheel: Public Policy for Automated Vehicles*. Toronto: University of Toronto, Mowat Centre.

Zussman, David. 2014. "Preparing for the Impact of Disruptive Technologies." *Canadian Government Executive* (November): 30–1.

Index